SCHUMANN'S *DICHTERLIE*
EARLY ROMANTIC PO

This book offers a theory of Romantic song by re-evaluating Schumann's *Dichterliebe* of 1840, one of the most enigmatic works of the repertoire. It investigates the poetics of Early Romanticism in order to understand the mysterious magnetism and singular imaginative energy that imbues Schumann's musical language. The Romantics rejected the ideal of a coherent and organic whole and cherished the suggestive openness of the Romantic fragment, the disconcerting tone of Romantic irony and the endlessness of Romantic reflection – thereby realizing an aesthetic of fragmentation. Close readings of many songs from *Dichterliebe* show the singer's intense involvement with the piano's voice, suggesting a 'split Self' and the presence of the 'Other'. Seeing Schumann as the 'second poet of the poem' – here of Heine's famous *Lyrisches Intermezzo* – this book considers essential issues of musico-poetic intertextuality, introducing into musicology a hermeneutics that seeks to synthesize philosophical, literary-critical, music-analytical and psychoanalytical modes of thought.

BEATE JULIA PERREY is Junior Research Fellow in Music at Christ's College, Cambridge. She writes on music, art and poetry.

CAMBRIDGE STUDIES IN MUSIC THEORY AND ANALYSIS

GENERAL EDITOR IAN BENT

Published titles

SCHUMANN'S *DICHTERLIEBE* AND EARLY ROMANTIC POETICS

FRAGMENTATION OF DESIRE

BEATE JULIA PERREY

CAMBRIDGE
UNIVERSITY PRESS

CAMBRIDGE UNIVERSITY PRESS
Cambridge, New York, Melbourne, Madrid, Cape Town, Singapore, São Paulo

Cambridge University Press
The Edinburgh Building, Cambridge CB2 8RU, UK

Published in the United States of America by Cambridge University Press, New York

www.cambridge.org
Information on this title: www.cambridge.org/9780521814799

First published 2002
This digitally printed version 2007

A catalogue record for this publication is available from the British Library

Library of Congress Cataloguing in Publication data
Perrey, Beate Julia.
Fragments of desire: Schumann's *Dichterliebe* / Beate Julia Perrey.
p.   cm. – (Cambridge studies in music theory and analysis; 17)
Includes bibliographical references (p.) and index.
ISBN 0 521 81479 0 (hb)
1. Schumann, Robert, 1810–1856. Dichterliebe.   2. Romanticism in music.
I. Title.   II. Series.
MT121.S38 P47   2002
782.4′7 – dc21   2002020552

ISBN 978-0-521-81479-9 hardback
ISBN 978-0-521-04245-1 paperback

CONTENTS

ILLUSTRATIONS

FOREWORD BY IAN BENT

Theory and analysis are in one sense reciprocals: if analysis opens up a musical structure or style to inspection, inventorying its components, identifying its connective forces, providing a description adequate to some live experience, then theory generalizes from such data, predicting what the analyst will find in other cases within a given structural or stylistic orbit, devising systems by which other works – as yet unwritten – might be generated. Conversely, if theory intuits how musical systems operate, then analysis furnishes feedback to such imaginative intuitions, rendering them more insightful. In this sense, they are like two hemispheres that fit together to form a globe (or cerebrum!), functioning deductively as investigation and abstraction, inductively as hypothesis and verification, and in practice forming a chain of alternating activities.

Professionally, on the other hand, 'theory' now denotes a whole subdiscipline of the general field of musicology. Analysis often appears to be a subordinate category within the larger activity of theory. After all, there is theory that does not require analysis. Theorists may engage in building systems or formulating strategies for use by composers; and these almost by definition have no use for analysis. Others may conduct experimental research into the sound-materials of music or the cognitive processes of the human mind, to which analysis may be wholly inappropriate. And on the other hand, historians habitually use analysis as a tool for understanding the classes of compositions – repertories, 'outputs', 'periods', works, versions, sketches, and so forth – that they study. Professionally, then, our ideal image of twin hemispheres is replaced by an intersection: an area that exists in common between two subdisciplines. Seen from this viewpoint, analysis reciprocates in two directions: with certain kinds of theoretical enquiry, and with certain kinds of historical enquiry. In the former case, analysis has tended to be used in rather orthodox modes, in the latter in a more eclectic fashion; but that does not mean that analysis in the service of theory is necessarily more exact, more 'scientific', than analysis in the service of history.

The above epistemological excursion is by no means irrelevant to the present series. Cambridge Studies in Music Theory and Analysis is intended to present the work of theorists and of analysts. It has been designed to include 'pure' theory – that is, theoretical formulation with a minimum of analytical exemplification; 'pure' analysis – that is, practical analysis with a minimum of theoretical underpinning; and writings that fall at points along the spectrum between the two extremes. In these capacities, it aims to illuminate music, as work and as process.

However, theory and analysis are not the exclusive preserves of the present day. As subjects in their own right, they are diachronic. The former is coeval with the very study of music itself, and extends far beyond the confines of Western culture; the latter, defined broadly, has several centuries of past practice. Moreover, they have been dynamic, not static fields throughout their histories. Consequently, studying earlier music through the eyes of its own contemporary theory helps us to escape (when we need to, not that we should make a dogma out if it) from the preconceptions of our own age. Studying earlier analyses does this too, and in a particularly sharply focused way; at the same time it gives us the opportunity to re-evaluate past analytical methods for present purposes, such as is happening currently, for example, with the long-despised methods of hermeneutic analysis of the late nineteenth century. The series thus includes editions and translations of major works of past theory, and also studies in the history of theory.

Schumann's great song-cycle *Dichterliebe* of 1840, the individual songs of which have been perennial subjects for musical analysis, has in recent decades been an object of study by music theorists and historians as a totality possessing 'unity' and 'coherence'. But these sought-for qualities have remained elusive, and Beate Perrey offers now a refreshing and altogether new view of the work which suggests that the goal of these quests was illusory. Dr Perrey posits that the cycle belongs not with the full Romantic tide of the first decades of the nineteenth century but rather with the early Romantic movement in the final years of the eighteenth. She thus locates it in the artistic and intellectual world of Friedrich Schlegel and Novalis, and with their contributions to the short-lived but influential journal *Athenaeum*.

A second debate in recent times has cast doubt on the extent to which Schumann understood Heine's poetry, and thus the degree to which his settings truly reflect the subversive nature of that poetic world. Dr Perrey's fascinating discussion of Heine, and her subsequent analyses of several of the songs from the *Dichterliebe* cycle, make powerfully the case that Schumann understood very well what he was dealing with, and that his music engages knowingly with the poetry to form a critique, indeed a hermeneutic reading of it. She interprets the medium of *Dichterliebe* as a dialectic relationship between three agents: word, human voice and instrument. And her discussions of the two main piano postludes – those of songs 12 and 16, particularly the latter – reveal not so much the unified nature of the song cycle as the fragmentary nature of its form.

PREFACE

Dans l'éclatement de l'univers que nous éprouvons, prodige! Les morceaux qui s'abattent sont vivants.

René Char, *La Parole en archipel*

In the explosion of the universe that we experience, a miracle! The crashing particles are alive.

This book offers a close reading of Schumann's *Dichterliebe*, and a poetics. It aims at a hermeneutics as much as it relies on semiotically inspired analysis and theory, and is, in this decidedly eclectic interpretative practice, almost out of place in today's critical climate, one which often insists on clear distinctions between those two methodological traditions. But although this book, as will be obvious to most readers, is of its recent times – in as much as it would have been inconceivable without the Zeitgeist of anti-formalism and interdisciplinary commitment that revitalized the study of music of the 1990s – my objective was from the outset, rather naturally, given my chosen object, to ask questions about words as well as music, and to work continuously along the interfaces of philosophical enquiry, analytical readings of literary and musical texts, the history of ideas and recent psycho-analytical thought. In the spirit of a fertile interplay between differing and, in my view, complementary modes of critical thought, some terms and concepts may give a preliminary insight into the kinds of issues with which this book is concerned.

STRUCTURE AS MOBILE

When I speak of musical *structure* I mean a formed space, like the space outlined by a *mobile*, that decorative kinetic structure made of pieces of solid matter which, be it by a breeze, hot air or touch, is set into motion. As we contemplate a *mobile*, its pieces are suspended within the space it describes through movement, and yet it is we who are setting it in motion, and who decide from which perspective to look.

A BODY OF VOICES

No doubt there are voices and voices too. There is the idealized, 'authentic' voice of any 'centered self'; and there are all those other voices that are essentially deflections from the authentic voice, transforming it to belong to a 'de-centred' self. But no matter whether centred or decentred, the voice always speaks of – apart from whatever else it may be speaking *about* – the body to which it belongs. For the voice is what we wear: it envelops our body, like the words we speak.

THE FIGURATIVE ART OF SONG

This is why listening to the singing voice, particularly in song, is an engrossing experience. For although the singing voice is certainly an *artefact* of the human voice, as much an abstraction as any instrumental 'voice', song nevertheless enlists the human presence literally – through the singer. In this sense, independently of compositional style or historical moment, song will always be a *figurative* art: it focuses on the human figure; its commitment is to making an image of that figure, and to producing a human likeness. Song, then, unlike any other musical genre, uses a real voice to make an artificial image of itself, and so, intriguingly, song is both fact *and* image. Song transforms the literal world into a figurative one while retaining the intensity of both, of life *and* art.

ON THE ABSENCE OF A STORY

Since the singing voice is written for as well as performed in the first-person singular – the utterance of one unique poetic speaker – the thoughts and emotions expressed lie within that 'poetic singer'. Another figure, the beloved for instance, may be *evoked*, but she is not, in fact, hypostatized and so, in the absence of several interacting characters and because of the impossibility of relations forming between a plurality of figures, no plot, story or narrative develops. This is how song succeeds in generating its subject's sensations – and 'subject' in both of its senses – without the need for narrative. It offers us both the image of the subject and the image of the sensation – a *sensational-subjective image*.

IN THE PRESENCE OF THE LYRIC

The German art song and the Romantic or Modern lyric poem are generically one and the same: we, listening to the song, not only, as has always been true for the reading of a lyric poem, *overhear* the poetic speaker, but as Jonathan Culler beautifully explained recently, we 'must combine this claim with the recognition that lyrics, unlike novels, are also spoken by the reader. When we read a lyric, aloud or silently, we utter the words, we temporarily occupy the position of the speaker, so that we too say "I fall upon the thorns of life, I bleed" or "Let me not to the marriage of true minds admit impediments." We are not simply overhearing the speech of another, whom we strive to identify from this speech but are ourselves trying out, trying on this speech.'[1]

---

[1] Jonathan Culler, *The Pursuit of Signs: Semiotics, Literature, Deconstruction*, with a new preface by the author (London and New York 2001), p. xxii.

THE FRAGMENT

The fragment helps to distil the lyrical image and conveys more acutely the sensation of its subject. A series of fragments, as I suggest in this book, is animated by a dynamic similar to that of the 'association of ideas' – each isolated from the next and effectively cutting off the story between them – if ever there had been one. Story-telling in the orthodox sense becomes difficult when the canvas changes from one image to the next, and impossible when there is only one figure, and always the same, in every canvas. It is in this way, when matters are distilled down into one image and one sensation, however ambiguous it may turn out to be, that the senses can be drawn by a different kind of dramatic charge, not one similar to operatic or social drama, but one much more intimate than that, lying within the subject – in terms of theme as well as figure – and shaping its interiority. While 'story' generally means a movement towards fact, image, on the other hand, mood and sensation, mean a letting go of fact as we move towards a different kind of reality, a reality in which sensation is focused into great intensity and feeling is raised to its full grandeur.

SURPLUS OF SONG

When recognizing the symbolic nature of a poem or a song, and the greatly manifold semantic potential either contains, we cannot be satisfied with perceiving mere appearance or, as critics, with stating only the obvious. For, as Jean Starobinski explained long ago, '*regarder* [to look at, to gaze upon] is a movement that aims to recapture. The gaze does not exhaust itself immediately. It involves perseverance, doggedness, as if animated by the hope of adding to its discovery or reconquering what is already about to escape.' Starobinski, when speaking of the kind of 'impatient energy' that inhabits the act of looking, and the desire 'to see something other than what it is given',[2] tells us of a capacity which reminds us of what Adorno often called the work's 'surplus' (the *Mehr*) – all that which is present *latently* in the meaning of a work of art, and which surfaces once we allow some freedom of movement for our natural desire to explore it in its very materiality, and beyond. Song itself does just that: it passes through words into music, to realize a semantic *potential*. In so doing, it engages the senses through eye, ear and touch, to enhance how the word feels, to up its meaning.

THE FRAGMENTATION OF DESIRE

The inner movements involved in the experience of desire and its destabilizing, revitalizing effects are echoed in the composer's transpositional efforts of catching hold of mobiles, momentary forms, transient ideas, feelings, images, and these same movements are, in *Dichterliebe*, re-echoed in Schumann's animation of such mobile

---

[2] Starobinski, *L'Œil vivant*, p. 12. *The Living Eye*, trans. Arthur Goldhammer, Harvard University Press, Cambridge MA 1989, pp. 2–3.

refractions through sound. Composing here uses and fuses natural energies with those of the human imagination, and miraculously begins to equal the experience of desire itself: by way of freeing the fragments of the endlessly changing rhythms and harmonies of thought and feeling, composing is no longer about the *idea* of movement alone, but is movement *itself* – it shapes time.

The fragment, which anyone will recognize in the first song of *Dichterliebe*, as an emblematic, incomplete form expressing desire, also appears in many different forms that require sophisticated hermeneutical interpretation, in the form, for instance, of the diminished-seventh chord, in the form of repetition as also in the form of the song 'Der schwere Abend' and in the many forms of irony. During the spring reverie in which *Dichterliebe* opens, desire unfolds in its most direct way, then, through harmonic ambiguity and structural openness, provoking a forward movement, towards experience, just as with the singer and the pianist themselves, in a series of fleeting sensational-subjective images, to present everything that a 'fragmentation of desire' may mean: longing, affection and exuberance, curiosity and doubt, pain, fear, jealousy and rage, and love.

Yet this song cycle, which is so grandly extrovert in some of its most memorable moments, while being intimidatingly introverted at other times, also offers its own retelling as it moves through the fluctuating moods and movements of the Romantic poet's mind and heart. The *Dichterliebe* experience, as one might want to call it in tribute to the work's intensity, is perhaps above all about how a story that is essentially not a story reflects upon itself through the means of emotion rather than events. For the scenes of *Dichterliebe* will not add up to acted drama and cannot serve the requisites of the theatre or opera stage. They unfold before us as the changing vistas of an *inner* self, where subjectivity, in both the Romantic and the modern sense, means *Erfahrung* rather than *Erlebnis*[3] and where the poet-singer is a dreamer, travelling in mind and body through a fleeting succession of associated ideas, travelling through the mobiles.

LIGHTNESS

Works of art ask questions and answer them. They offer, through the very form and language they use, a knowing account of life's most essential concerns. And they do so with a mental, that is an intellectual and affective, reasoning about the phenomenon they are revealing.[4] Thus our search for what is generally called content, and what I prefer calling substance, is central to our encounter with a work of art. And this is, it may be added, just as central a concern for the work of art itself. Thus as in philosophy, literature or poetry, so in music the question is: '*What* does this work say, about life, about its emotions, its mysteries and miracles?' And *how* does the music ask as well as answer these questions formally, stylistically, aesthetically? No doubt, the

---

[3] Philippe Lacoue-Labarthe (1986).

[4] Martha Nussbaum, *Love's Knowledge: Essays on Philosophy and Literature* (New York and Oxford, 1990), and *Upheavals of Thought: The Intelligence of Emotions* (Cambridge, 2001).

interplay between these elements, substance and form, is of prime importance. We can certainly say so of the music of Schubert and Mahler, for instance – it is not just Schumann. And so, with *Dichterliebe*, Schumann leads the listener towards a poet's love even while he speaks about it, while he shows its vagaries, contradictions and catastrophes, to close through the final postlude the sensational-subjective images of this work with a lightness of tone that speaks of a 'cathartic eternal return', as I call it in my conclusion, and which is none other than that of love's potential return. But Schumann's lightness of tone, his gracefulness in musical fabric and sonority as well as semantic intent in the last postlude echoes a kind of weightlessness that we sense from the cycle's very outset, from the first song, 'Im wunderschönen Monat Mai'. Of course, the mere mention of this song will for many readers now evoke its first few notes, to be transported by a sense of expectation as well as tension, a sense of momentum that is the essence of a dissonant suspension in its technical sense with which this song indeed begins and which sets the cycle in motion. But here again, the formal openness that characterizes this song carries its meaning, namely that of an eternal return, through such remarkable harmonic colouring. From the first two notes of *Dichterliebe*, then, that dissonant suspension of C♯ over D, Schumann announces, by means of substance, the work's main concern – *Dichterliebe* as a poetics of love, as mobiles of desire.

ACKNOWLEDGEMENTS

My thanks go to all those friends, teachers and colleagues who have inspired, advised and encouraged me in writing this book. To Jonathan Dunsby above all, for his exemplary advice, inspiring enthusiasm and intellectual open-mindedness. To Joseph Kerman for his guidance during my stay in Berkeley, California, in 1995. To Andrew Bowie for his excellent advice on philosophical issues, and to Nigel Reeves for thoughtful comments regarding Heine's *Lyrisches Intermezzo*. I am grateful to many others whose comments and ideas were important at various early or late stages of this research: Jacques Brunschwig, Simon Christmas, Daniel Chua, John Deathridge, Bill Fitzgerald, Walter Frisch, Frédéric Graber, Michel Gribinski, Robin Holloway, Thomas Jansen, David Lewin, Marion Schmidt, David Sedley, Henry Sullivan, Ingrid Wassenaar, Paul Wingfield and Heather Woolfe are all to be thanked for their engagement with my work, their help, practical and otherwise, and their encouragement. Special thanks go to Malcolm Bowie, Robert Pascall and Arnold Whittall. Thanks also to Ian Bent, General Editor of the series, and Penny Souster, my editor at Cambridge University Press, and to an anonymous reader for very perceptive comments, as well as to Ann Lewis, Yves Guichard, Grégoire Tosser and Annie Relph for their highly skilled technical help. Thanks to my father, who produced what must be the ultimate photographic reproduction of pages from Schumann's personal copy of Heine's *Buch der Lieder*, and to my mother, for their love and care. I thank Nina for the many indirect and yet essential ways of helping me finish this book.

I would also like to thank the curators, experts and scholars of a number of institutions for their kind assistance: Bernhard Appel of the Robert-Schumann-Forschungsstelle, Düsseldorf, and Gerd Nauhaus, Director of the Robert-Schumann-Haus, Zwickau, for making available important manuscripts and for a fruitful exchange of ideas; Marianne Bockelkamp, for sharing her expertise about Heine's 'art of arrangement' on the basis of several Heine autograph manuscripts held in the Bibliothèque Nationale, Paris. The Heinrich-Heine-Institut in Düsseldorf has been a marvellous environment to work in, and I am especially indebted to the late Inge Hermstrüwer of the Heinrich-Heine- as well as the Robert-Schumann-Archiv, and to Volkmar Hansen of the Düsseldorfer Heine Edition, now Director of the Goethe Museum Düsseldorf, for their enthusiasm, advice and encouragement throughout my research. Many thanks go to Renate Hilmar-Voit for generously sharing her research findings on issues to do with the two versions of *Dichterliebe*. The staff of the libraries of Cambridge University, the Ecole Normale Supérieure and the Bibliothèque Nationale in Paris provided ideal conditions for my work over the years.

I have had opportunities to present my research in places where, invariably, the discussion led to new and enriching insights. Thanks go to King's College London for various teaching experiences, and to the University of Reading for inviting me to lecture, in both cases including *Dichterliebe*. To the students in the Music Department of Cambridge University for their inspiring engagement with and critical aliveness towards the ideas and issues raised in my teaching of *Dichterliebe* and Romantic song in general. To Jean-Pierre Lefèbvre for inviting me to talk about Heine's poetry at the École Normale Supérieure in Paris. To Prof. Nicolas Méeus, Georges Molinié and Danièle Pistone at the Sorbonne University, Paris IV, for inviting me to present my work in their seminar 'Musique & Style', known today as 'Langages Musicaux'. I would like to thank Trinity College, Cambridge, for generously supporting my work through a doctoral Research Studentship, and for awarding me a Rouse Ball Research Fellowship as well as making available various additional grants along the way. I am grateful to the Master and Fellows of Christ's College, Cambridge for having elected me to a Junior Research Fellowship which has allowed me to continue my research in a stimulating academic environment.

ABBREVIATIONS

For Schumann

Briefe einer Liebe	*Robert und Clara Schumann: Briefe einer Liebe*, ed. Hans-Josef Ortheil (Königstein/Ts.: Athenäum Verlag, 1982).
GS I–IV	Robert Schumann, *Gesammelte Schriften über Musik und Musiker*, 4 vols. (Leipzig: Breitkopf & Härtel, 1854; repr. with epilogue by Gerd Nauhaus, 2 vols., Wiesbaden: Breitkopf & Härtel, 1985).
JB	*Jugendbriefe von Robert Schumann*, ed. Clara Schumann (Leipzig: Breitkopf & Härtel, 1885).
Kreisig GS I, II	Robert Schumann, *Gesammelte Schriften über Musik und Musiker*, 5th edn, ed. Martin Kreisig, 2 vols. (Leipzig: Breitkopf & Härtel, 1914). [Used for material not contained in *GS I–IV*].
MS 83.5037	Schumann's personal copy of the first edition of Heinrich Heine's *Buch der Lieder* (Hamburg: Hoffmann und Campe: 1827); Heinrich-Heine-Institut Düsseldorf, Schumann Archive.
NF	*Robert Schumanns Briefe: Neue Folge*, ed. Gustav F. Jansen (Leipzig: Breitkopf & Härtel, 1886; repr. 1904).
NZfM	*Neue Zeitschrift für Musik* (Leipzig: Breitkopf & Härtel, 1834–).
TB I, II	*Robert Schumann: Tagebücher*, ed. Georg Eismann and Gerd Nauhaus, 2 vols. (Leipzig: VEB Deutscher Verlag für Musik, 1971–87), I: 1827–1838, ed. Georg Eismann (1971), II: 1836–1854, ed. Gerd Nauhaus (1987).
Boetticher, *Einführung*	Wolfgang Boetticher, *Robert Schumann: Einführung in Persönlichkeit und Werk* (Berlin: Hahnefeld, 1941).
Eismann, *Biographie*	Georg Eismann, *Robert Schumann: Eine Biographie in Wort und Bild* (Leipzig: Breitkopf & Härtel, 1964).
Eismann I/II	Georg Eismann, *Robert Schumann: Ein Quellenwerk über sein Leben und Schaffen*, 2 vols. (Leipzig: Breitkopf & Härtel, 1956).

Jansen, *Davidsbündler*	Gustav F. Jansen, *Die Davidsbündler: Aus Schumanns Sturm- und Drangperiode* (Leipzig: Breitkopf & Härtel, 1883).
Litzmann	Berthold Litzmann, *Clara Schumann: Ein Künstlerleben: Nach Tagebüchern und Briefen*, 3 vols., 3rd edn (Leipzig: Breitkopf & Härtel, 1902–08; vol. I: 1906; vol. II: 1907; repr. Hildesheim and New York: Breitkopf & Härtel, 1971).
Wasielewski, *Biographie*	Wilhelm Josef von Wasielewski, *Robert Schumann: Eine Biographie*, ed. Waldemar von Wasielewski, 4th edn (Leipzig: Breitkopf & Härtel, 1906).

For Heine

B I–IV	*Heinrich Heine: Sämtliche Schriften*, ed. Klaus Briegleb, 6 vols. (Munich: Hanser, 1968–76).
DHA	*Heinrich Heine: Sämtliche Werke: Düsseldorfer Ausgabe: Historisch-kritische Gesamtausgabe*, ed. Manfred Windfuhr, 16 vols. (Hamburg: Hoffmann und Campe, 1973–), I: *Buch der Lieder*, ed. Pierre Grappin (1975).
Elster I–VII	*Heinrich Heine: Sämtliche Werke*, ed. Ernst Elster, 7 vols. (Leipzig: Bibl. Institut, 1887–90).
HSA	*Heine Säkularausgabe: Werk – Briefe – Lebenszeugnisse*, ed. Nationale Forschungs- und Gedenkstätten der klassischen deutschen Literatur in Weimar and Centre National de la Recherche Scientifique, 20 vols. (Berlin [East]; Paris: Akademie-Verlag and Editions du CNRS, 1972–).

For Philosophy

Athenaeum	*Athenaeum: Eine Zeitschrift von August Wilhelm und Friedrich Schlegel, I* (Berlin: Vieweg, 1798; Frölich, 1799–1800), ed. Curt Grützmacher (Stuttgart: Rowohlt, 1969). Also available as *Philosophical Fragments*, trans. Peter Firchow (Minneapolis: University of Minnesota Press, 1991).
AWS *SW*	August Wilhelm Schlegel, *Sämtliche Werke*, ed. Eduard Böcking, 16 vols. (Leipzig: Weidmann, 1846).
HK	Friedrich Daniel Ernst Schleiermacher, *Hermeneutik,* ed. Heinz Kimmerle (Heidelberg: C. Winter, 1959).
JP	Jean Paul, *Werke*, ed. Norbert Miller, 12 vols. (Munich: Hanser, 1975), IX: *Vorschule der Ästhetik*.
KdU B	Immanuel Kant, *Kritik der Urteilskraft*, Werkausgabe X, ed. Wilhelm Weischedel (Frankfurt am Main: Suhrkamp, 1968). The page numbers refer to the B version of the original edition.

KrV B	Immanuel Kant, *Kritik der reinen Vernunft*, Werkausgabe III, ed. Wilhelm Weischedel (Frankfurt am Main: Suhrkamp, 1968). The page numbers refer to the B version of the original edition.
KFSA	Friedrich Schlegel, *Kritische Friedrich-Schlegel-Ausgabe in 35 Bänden*, ed. Ernst Behler *et al.*, 35 vols. (Paderborn: Schöningh, 1958–).
NO	Novalis, *Schriften: Die Werke Friedrich von Hardenbergs*, ed. Richard Samuel *et al.*, 5 vols. (Stuttgart: Kohlhammer, 1960–88).
SW I	Friedrich Wilhelm Joseph Schelling, *Sämtliche Werke. I. Abteilung*, ed. Karl Friedrich August Schelling, 10 vols. (Stuttgart: Cotta, 1856–61).

INTRODUCTION

Sometimes I feel as if my objective person wants to separate itself entirely from the subjective one, or as if I stood between my appearance and my being, between figure and shadow.[1]

Schumann in 1831

This book offers a theory of Romantic song by re-evaluating Schumann's *Dichterliebe* – hailed as one of the great masterpieces of German Romanticism, and the quintessential song cycle which later composers viewed as the touchstone for their own explorations of the genre. At the same time, Schumann's elaborate setting of Heinrich Heine's sophisticated poems from the *Lyrisches Intermezzo* of 1822–23[2] renders *Dichterliebe* of 1840 one of the structurally and semantically most enigmatic works of the repertoire. One aim of this book has been to propose for music the Early Romantic conception of form, which rejects the cardinal neo-Classical ideal of a coherent whole, and which advances instead an *aesthetic of fragmentation*. A second aim has been to develop a critical apparatus reappraising the issue of musico-poetic intertextuality, an issue which has been inadequately problematized to date. Methodologically, it is an attempt to introduce into musicology a hermeneutic that would synthesize philosophical, literary-critical, music-analytical and psychoanalytical modes of thought and analysis.

The literature on *Dichterliebe* reflects rather accurately the well-known and ultimately incomprehensible methodological division between 'theory/analysis' and 'history', which cuts through the greater discipline of musicology, and the relentless pursuit of exegetic purism on either side of the divide. Most importantly, however, the critical commentaries on *Dichterliebe* demonstrate two fundamental areas of inadequacy, one of which is particularly striking. The first concerns the remarkable neglect of the poetry on which this song cycle is based, and from which, one must assume, meaning arises. This neglect is all the more evident if seen in the light of Schumann's compositional engagement with the poetry. The second concerns the modes of musical analysis employed. Following the exceptional status the study of manuscripts enjoyed in the post-war period,[3] the 1970s and 1980s witnessed

---

[1] *TB* I, p. 339 [Mir ist's manchmal, als wolle sich mein objectiver Mensch vom subjectiven ganz trennen oder als ständ' ich zwischen meiner Erscheinung u. meinem Seyn, zwischen Gestalt und Schatten].

[2] Heine's poetic cycle *Lyrisches Intermezzo* was written in 1822–23 and first published in the *Buch der Lieder* in 1827.

[3] Hallmark's admirable study *The Genesis of Schumann's Dichterliebe* of 1976 belongs to this musicological tradition.

1

an analytical ebullience which could be described as promoting with determination the understanding of masterworks in unifying terms. In accordance with the
gradual emergence and increasing attention paid to the Schenkerian system in Anglo-
American scholarship, *Dichterliebe* has generally been subject to this or related kinds of
musical analysis.[4] As a result of concentrating exclusively on coherence and closure
as the self-justifying law of aesthetic achievement, certain structural moments in
Dichterliebe, which do not easily fit into such a system of stability, have been ignored.
In setting up its own undivided rule, such analysis became authoritarian in that it
strove to discipline and control on the musical level, and simplistic in its ignorance
towards the structural complexity that a work combining poetry and music offers.

In order to account adequately for such intrinsic complexity, two hitherto un-
explored methods occurred to me as being germane to a new analytical approach
to *Dichterliebe*: the first involved the proposal of a theoretical system able to accommodate, and even elucidate, the various formal inconsistencies or contradictions
that characterize *Dichterliebe*. The second step involved a sustained literary–critical
analysis of Heine's poetry that would enable one to recognize the transformation it
underwent in being set to music by Schumann. These methodological aims explain
the division of the book into three main parts: the first exploring Early Romantic
poetics in order to establish a sound conceptual basis; the second exploring Heine's
idiosyncratic poetic style; and the third exploring *Dichterliebe* in the light of these
earlier considerations. In as much as this study could not rely on the security of a
previously tested theoretical system which would account for Early Romantic procedures in music, or on a hermeneutic path that had already been cleared by others,
it was faced with a challenge.

Part I is a systematic introduction to the aesthetics and poetics of Early Romanticism as developed from 1798 onwards into the very early years of 1800. Focusing
on the writings of the so-called Jena-Romantics, and on texts by Friedrich Schlegel
and Novalis in particular, I shall explain, first of all, the three fundamental forms
of Early Romanticism: the fragment, Romantic irony and reflection. Schlegel's and
Novalis' passionate proposal of a radically new manner of what we are today in the
habit of calling 'expression' and 'communication' took its main impetus from a perceived shift of the function of signs within language: that language reaches beyond
its scientifically definable properties, and that it expands its field of signification in a
manner similar to that of poetry. Here, and with the Early Romantics' main thesis
to 'represent the Unrepresentable',[5] poetry and music came to be considered the
highest forms of art. As I suggest, the extensive discourse about these 'two speaking
arts' (Hegel) provides a basis for addressing successfully the profound hermeneutic

---

[4] Notably Komar (1971) and Neumeyer (1982), but also Hallmark (1976), pp. 129–145. Of course, it is useful to
distinguish between Schenker's own method of analysis, which is often presented in highly figurative language, and
displays a large degree of literary sensibility, and the drier, more formalistic brand of 'Schenkerism' cultivated by
some of Schenker's English-speaking disciples. Pousseur's extensive and inspired analytical study (1993), originally
conceived in 1975, privileges the identification of unifying compositional procedures foreshadowing serialism.

[5] Novalis' programmatic dictum epitomizing the Romantics' aims. See NO III, p. 685, no. 671 [Das Undarstellbare
darstellen].

problem of poetry set to music, that is the combination of the rational capacities of language with the ineffable expressivity of music. In practice, this issue can most pertinently be raised with respect to the Romantic art song. Hence, Schumann's *Dichterliebe* may be considered as realizing aesthetically the Early Romantics' new poetics of form, language and interpretation.

Part I concludes with an overview of the concept of song in nineteenth-century music theory and shows Schumann, by a careful reading of his writings, following a new path in setting words to music. Guided by what he called 'poetic consciousness'[6] and influenced by a number of Romantic poet-philosophers, and in particular Jean Paul, Schumann arrived at an Idealist conception of song – the 'higher sphere of art'[7] – contained in his dictum that 'music is the higher potential of poetry'.[8] Rather than seeking to synchronize text and music with regard to either form or content (which would result in mere tautology), Schumann considered song composition as *the* Romantic medium of sublimation *par excellence*, able to transcend both poetry and music. In this sense, I do not consider Schumann's songs to be even interpretative; rather they uncover what is elusively absent from the written word. Moreover, freeing himself from complying with the text in the spirit of becoming the 'extended author of the poem', Schumann can be seen to be firmly grounded within the Early Romantic tradition, his songs epitomizing a quintessential dichotomy: creation/critique.

Part II of the book consists of an extensive interpretation of Heine's poetic cycle *Lyrisches Intermezzo*. With reference to the poet's deeply sceptical attitude towards the earlier as well as later Romantic movement, this part discusses his critical allusions to a number of sources not previously considered, such as, for example, traditional German folk poetry, the Goethean model of love poetry, and the biblical *Song of Songs*. An empirical survey of Heine's stereotypical representation of the beloved shows how the poet projected his conflicting feelings towards Romanticism on to an *imago* of woman. I have deliberately used the term *imago*, which is essentially the earlier Latin version of the more common 'image', because this term, borrowed from psychoanalytical as well as literary-critical discourse, has the advantage of designating a subjective, entirely imaginative picture of the woman in Heine's poems. Since this use of an *imago* relies on the principle of association, the *Lyrisches Intermezzo* is not, as has often been assumed in the musicological literature, guided by narrative strategies. In addition to investigating Heine's obsessive delight in 'breaking the tone' (*Stimmungsbruch*), a more informed understanding of the structure of this poetry is considered to be essential in order to engage with what can loosely be called a 'comparison' of meaning. What has happened in the transition from Heine's pages to the meaning discernible in Schumann's pages? In this regard, it needs to be pointed out that the decidedly post-Romantic poetic procedures characterizing the *Lyrisches Intermezzo* have been thoroughly transformed in *Dichterliebe*.

---

[6] *JB*, p. 282 [poetisches Bewußtsein]. [7] *NZfM* 1 (1834), p. 193 [höhere Kunstsphäre].
[8] *TB* I, p. 96 [Musik ist die höhere Potenz der Poesie].

Part III of the book comprises four analytical essays. It explores in detail Schumann's compositional reading of Heine's poems on the one hand, and the presence of Early Romantic aesthetic procedures on the other. For reasons to do with the very nature of the procedures that this study seeks to show at work, it does not analyse every single one of the songs of *Dichterliebe*. It aims, rather, to demonstrate where the Early Romantic concepts of poetic time and reflection, that of the Romantic fragment and that of Romantic irony, can constructively be considered in describing certain signifying phenomena in *Dichterliebe* which have hitherto been misunderstood or simply not been recognized. But even within an aesthetic of fragmentation, it is worthwhile reminding oneself that no work of art can consist of continuous rupture, be entirely fragmentary, or be ironic at all times; it requires a familiar system of reference first of all, in order then to overturn that system and to introduce moments of disruption, discontinuity or contradiction. The musical text thereby loses the Classical grace of an all-embracing, harmoniously integrated whole. But it is my express aim to make clear in this study that this loss of wholeness and the denial of definite closure does not mean a deficiency; nor does it mean an aesthetic weakness. It means nothing more and nothing less than the formation of constellations opening up a dimension where it is once more possible to think – to imagine the 'Unrepresentable'. As a condition of the modern art work, the cycle *Dichterliebe* is thus still placed under the sign of finiteness, but by refraining from constructing an absolute, in the sense of a conclusive statement, Schumann demonstrates the strength of allowing for irresolution and ambiguity as an experience lying not beneath, but beyond, the law of limit. To quote Novalis:

From a voluntary denial of the Absolute arises the infinitely free activity within us – the only possible Absolute which can be given to us and which we find only through our incapacity to attain and recognize an Absolute. That Absolute, which is given to us, can be recognized only negatively in that we act and find that through action can be attained what we are searching for. This could be called an absolute postulate. All searching for *One Principle* would be like the attempt to square the circle.[9]

What Novalis calls the 'searching for *One Principle*' is indeed the most prominent aspect of the literature on *Dichterliebe*: many critics have championed a strenuously achieved integrated musical totality resulting from a coherent key scheme or other structural connections. In the few cases where Heine's poems have been taken into account, analysis has found itself trapped in a problematic and ultimately inconclusive argument about tonal narrativity and narrative tonality.[10] This book offers instead

---

[9] NO II, p. 269, no. 566 [Durch das freywillige Entsagen des Absoluten entsteht die unendliche freye Thätigkeit in uns – das Einzig mögliche Absolute, was uns gegeben werden kann und was wir nur durch unsre Unvermögenheit ein Absolutes zu erreichen und zu erkennen, finden. Dies uns gegebene Absolute läßt sich nur negativ erkennen, indem wir handeln und finden, daß durch kein Handeln das erreicht wird, was wir suchen. Dies ließe sich ein absolutes Postulat nennen. Alles Suchen nach Einem Princip wäre also wie der Versuch die Quadratur der Zirkels zu finden].

[10] See especially Neumeyer's attempt (1982, p. 97) to demonstrate 'what can be gained from the "equalizing" of text and music, from treating organic structure as a balanced interaction of narrative and tonal progression', as

some aesthetic parameters for a theoretical and hermeneutic model by which one can reconstruct the formal relationship between text and music in Schumann's *Dichterliebe* which renders the cycle's intrinsic semantic ambiguity meaningful in its very negation of unity, completeness, or what is usually understood as a 'logical sequence of events'.

In this endeavour, my concern has also been to let theory interact with analysis, dynamically, rather than to apply it in Procrustean fashion. The degree of abstraction found in Early Romantic literary theory requires one all the more to turn to a specific work and author whose intellectual and temperamental affinity to the Early Romantic way of thinking allows such an enquiry to be effective in the first place. One then needs to lift that theory out of its speculative discourse, to seek images and metaphorical expressions which help to render theoretical concepts more concrete. In explaining the concept of the Romantic fragment and the even more elusive one of Romantic irony, such an approach seemed beneficial. It also reflects the methodological procedure this investigation develops and maintains throughout. For the hermeneutic potential resting in Early Romantic theory as an authentic expression of the aesthetics of the time to unfold its critical force, the core categories have to be clearly determined and reformulated in a way which makes them accessible to musical composition. The aim is thus not to fit the work into a rigid theoretical scheme but rather to give room, with continuous reference to the individuality of the analytical object, for theoretical modification wherever this is in the service of aesthetic insight.

I found that one such modification involved a reassessment of the very nature of Romantic song, and a questioning as to the 'speaking voice' within it. Bearing in mind the Early Romantic concept of subjectivity, and taking into consideration all that we associate with the stereotyped image of the Romantic artist – that sense of an introvert, hypersensitive, but also solitary and thus 'heroic' individual – led me to propose a hermeneutic stance towards the 'phenomenon' of Romantic song that draws out the theoretical consequences as regards this Romantic disposition. If Novalis speaks of an 'inner self-division'[11] and Friedrich Schlegel of a 'divided mind',[12] the question to be asked is how this division affects manners of writing, how it asserts itself within language, and within the language of song in particular. After tracing the Early Romantics' conception of language and subjectivity (Part I, pp. 40–46), there then evolved a more complex idea of the signifying process than is usually assumed. This leads us to recognize the operating of language on those dual planes of experience which Schumann so eloquently describes in one phrase and with which I chose to open my study: 'Sometimes I feel as if my objective person wants to separate itself entirely from the subjective one, or as if I stood between my appearance and my being, between figure and shadow'.[13] What remains to be

well as Sams (1993). Pousseur (1993) offers a more subtle analysis of what is nevertheless the same hermeneutic strategy.

[11] NO II, p. 547, no. 112 [innere Selbstscheidung].   [12] *KFSA* II, p. 149, no. 28 [der dividierte Geist].

[13] *TB* I, p. 339 [Mir ist's manchmal, als wolle sich mein objectiver Mensch vom subjectiven ganz trennen oder als ständ' ich zwischen meiner Erscheinung u. meinem Seyn, zwischen Gestalt und Schatten].

noted, however, is the silence reigning between the objective and the subjective, and the void separating the figure from its shadow – that very space where poetic language constitutes itself in the desire to speak of the 'gap in our existence'.[14] And it is through this desire that a '*second* world',[15] a 'subterranean firmament',[16] in short the realm of the imaginary and unconscious, is summoned. When Schumann then says 'The darkness of the imagination or its unconscious remains its very poetry',[17] my aim has been to extend the epistemological concern to that level where it can address this apparently abstract idea through forms, gestures and signs perceptible in the musical text. By adopting the model of the unconscious introduced by Freud, in particular what is generally known as the split within the subject (*Ichspaltung*), I am proposing the presence of the Other in Schumann's song, that which can be called the Romantic Solitary's phantasmatic Other – to be located in the singing voice. Of course, the 'voice of the piano' becomes an analytical issue closely bound up with this idea of the singing voice. This also raises the question of meaning with respect to the 'piano's voice' in the wordless preludes, interludes and postludes. In *Dichterliebe* certainly, the piano does not merely form a supportive accompaniment to the voice, but rather keeps disrupting and contradicting it, remains silent or speaks to itself once the singing voice has ceased. The piano is thus one side of the Janus-faced structure of Schumann's song.

The principal mode of speaking performed by Schumann in his songs is essentially that of soliloquy or, to remain within the Early Romantic philosophical cast, monologue. In constant self-reflective discourse, the song realizes structurally the Romantic hero's 'operation' to 'identify the low Self with a better Self'.[18] This means an invocation of the Other in terms of an interlocutor who may fill the existential 'gap'. But this gap is also what defines the Romantic Solitary, is the site and source of his hallucinations. Although there is thus always a 'voice that answers', the song, however, never truly fills the gap, but rather widens it. For, as *Dichterliebe* testifies, the Romantic song's theme is always the impossibility of abundance, the absence of the beloved and the poet's solitude. Metaphorically assuming a kind of mirror situation, the singer, elevated through the power of his invocation and amatory idealization of the Other within the image of his own voice – the *imago* of the beloved – moves closer towards this, his own image.

The lied's . . . true listening space is, so to speak, the interior of the head, *my* head: listening to it, I sing the lied with myself, for myself. I address myself, within myself, to an Image: the image of the beloved in which I lose myself and from which my own image, abandoned, comes back to me. The lied supposes a rigorous interlocution, but one that is imaginary, imprisoned in my deepest intimacy.[19]

---

[14] Friedrich Schlegel in *KFSA* XII, p. 192 [Lücke im Dasein].

[15] Jean Paul's description of poetic language in the *Vorschule der Ästhetik*. See JP IX, p. 30.

[16] JP IX, p. 58 [Sternbilder eines unterirdischen Himmels].

[17] *TB* I, p. 350 [Das Dunkel der Fantasie oder Ihr Unbewusstes bleibt ihre Poësie].

[18] Novalis as quoted in Frank (1989), pp. 272–273 [Das niedre Selbst wird mit einem bessern Selbst in dieser Operation identificirt].

[19] See Barthes (1985b), p. 290.

This process, owing its dynamics to the Early Romantic quest of 'the I that seeks to find itself',[20] is inwardly dramatic. In the song, 'dramatic moments' then occur when a true self-encounter is recognized as impossible. At these moments of emotional intensification, one may speak of a falling apart of the Romantic hero, and of fragmentation in the sense of the mirror falling into a thousand pieces. Desire is then, in its constant attempt to fill the Romantics' longing, the force that leads to fragmentation. But this also implies what may be termed, as the title of this book indicates, the dialectics of the *Fragmentation of Desire*: read as a *genitivus subjectivus*, there is Fragmentation *qua* Desire, read as a *genitivus objectivus*, there is Fragmentation *of* Desire, for it represents the widening gap itself.

As is already apparent from the above, readers will notice that there is occasional recourse to more recent critical thought in addition to what is offered by Early Romantic theory and philosophy. This is not just a matter of intellectual fashion. Rather, it is to emphasize the real indebtedness to Early Romantic thought coming through in the works of a number of today's leading thinkers. The almost direct line of descent leading from the Romantics' concept of the human subject to that developed by Freud may be self-evident. As regards more generally the above-mentioned functional shift within the system of language at the threshold of the nineteenth century, Foucault's trailblazing *The Order of Things*, for example, can hardly be ignored.[21] From a more rigorously philosophical point of view, Walter Benjamin and Hans-Georg Gadamer, as well as Theodor Adorno and Maurice Blanchot, Jean-Luc Nancy and Philippe Lacoue-Labarthe, have contributed greatly to our understanding of the significance of Early Romanticism for contemporary thought. Roland Barthes' late essays on Schumann, neither journalistic play nor examples of 'hedonocentric' self-indulgence, contain, despite their overtones of French post-structuralism and Barthes' indebtedness to Julia Kristeva's *Sémanalyse*,[22] some of the sharpest insights to be had on the subject. If he indeed preferred a more personal style as opposed to the restrained and monotonous tones prevalent in most dissertational discourse, then this was perhaps to dispel the ominous illusion that truth itself was holding the pen. Sometimes extensively, sometimes only in the form of quoting a pivotal phrase or two from this body of twentieth-century thought, I chose to draw attention to what binds together, in the nineteenth century and beyond, lyricism and knowledge – the quest for 'a language that unfolds endlessly in the void left by the gods?'[23]

As I proceed to address the structure of certain selected songs in Schumann's *Dichterliebe*, and especially the issue of how words and music relate or do not relate to each other, I also came to explore, aside from what one might term Schumann's discourse as a split Romantic, Schumann's discourse with Heine. In the first instance, such a comparative approach requires us to ask of both poem and song separately the question of finality: what solution has been found? This question is invariably orientated towards the nature of 'closure': with what and how have we been left?

---

[20] *KFSA* XIX, p. 22, no. 197 [Das Ich, das sich selbst sucht].
[21] Foucault (1970). [22] Kristeva (1969). [23] Foucault (1963), p. 200.

In the case of Heine, we are left with disillusion as to subject matter (love), with self-dispossession as to the means of his art (poetic language), and with devaluation as to artistic expression *per se* (a poem, a poetic cycle). Since there is thus a real sense of nothingness in Heine's deliberately negative poetic aesthetic, it is intriguing to watch how Schumann responded to this. After all, it is undoubtedly always 'easier' to destroy values, as Heine had skilfully done, than to construct, as Schumann did with Heine, out of what seems to offer little hope. Here again, in listening carefully to Schumann's discourse with Heine, we can experience the Early Romantic principle of creation/critique as an ultimately Idealistic, yet highly effective, means of uncovering meaning lying beneath the superficial structural level. In recognizing with empathy Heine's real 'face of pain' behind the great satirist's defensive façade, Schumann succeeded with *Dichterliebe* to lower what he called 'Heine's mask of irony'.[24]

Although it is eventually only through a musico-poetic analysis that we can account for such a fascinating as well as moving achievement on Schumann's part, there is nevertheless additional information that greatly encourages us to recognize a complete absence of a naive or uninformed compositional approach towards Heine's poetry by Schumann. Largely based on sources either not known to Schumann scholarship so far, or not considered in their entirety, Part III includes a discussion of Schumann's sensitivity towards Heine's poetry. First, it seems important to relate the composer's reception of Heine and the *Lyrisches Intermezzo*. For due to insufficient knowledge of the sources, it has frequently been stated somewhat offhandedly that Schumann's choice of poems from the *Lyrisches Intermezzo* was indiscriminate.[25] However, an examination of Schumann's personal copy of the first edition of Heine's poems, which has not previously been consulted, clearly demonstrates a careful reading prior to the compositional stage since it contains indicative markings in Schumann's own hand. Some pages from this manuscript are of great interest and have been reproduced. I shall return to this manuscript once more in two of the four analytical essays where some striking markings reflect interestingly upon Schumann's compositional choices.

Second, despite this song cycle's very great fame, a frequent criticism has also been that Schumann did not offer 'any equivalent for Heine's irony or innuendo', which has been seen as a sign of Schumann failing to understand fully Heine's poetry.[26] While I believe the first objection to be the result of the misguided expectation that a composer's aim would or should be to repeat in musical terms what has already been said poetically – a conception which also overlooks the logically necessary transformation of a text's phonetic and semantic properties once it is sung rather than read or recited – the second assumption about Schumann's failing to understand

---

[24] See Schumann's illuminating statement made five years before setting Heine's poetry to music in *GS* I, p. 145: 'Byron, Heine, Victor Hugo und ähnliche...Die Poesie hat sich, auf einige Augenblicke der Ewigkeit, die Maske der Ironie vorgebunden, um ihr Schmerzensgesicht nicht sehen zu lassen; vielleicht, daß die freundliche Hand eines Genius sie einmal abbinden wird' [...Byron, Heine, Victor Hugo and others...Poetry has, on occasions in eternity, put on the mask of irony so as not to show its face of pain; perhaps the kind hand of a genius will take it off someday].

[25] Sams (1993), p. 3.   [26] Sams (1993), p. 3.

Heine can be dismissed on the basis of previously unconsulted evidence: in various letters and in his diaries Schumann speaks with great critical acumen of Heine's 'burning sarcasm', 'cynicism', 'bitter satire' and the 'bizarre things which are going on in Heine's poems'.

In Part III I also address the vexed question of why four songs were deleted prior to the first publication of *Dichterliebe*, thus creating a group of sixteen instead of twenty songs. The manuscript of *Dichterliebe* shows that Schumann did not try to assure continuity by interpolating new endings or beginnings for adjacent songs in the new arrangement.[27] A number of letters, so far not accounted for in the literature concerned with the publication history of *Dichterliebe*, clearly indicate Schumann's unwavering aim to see the cycle published in its original conception of twenty songs. In either case, however, whether twenty songs or sixteen, no simple narrative unfolds. On the contrary, I shall argue, the intricate metaphorical web of emotions and images around the idea of love dispels the need to read a 'love-story' into either Heine's or Schumann's text. Thus, *Dichterliebe* – in its original (1840) and later (1844) arrangement – forms a paradoxical *magnum opus* that does not need to be analysed or reorganized in the name of hypothetical completeness. This points towards a compositional conception which not only tolerates but which even elevates the notion of the fragmentary to the degree that a work's 'integrity' is not at risk, even if parts of its text are missing or dismissed. Although it has not been one of my primary aims to argue, by way of a musico-poetic analysis of all twenty songs, either for or against the inclusion of the four deleted songs, it is nonetheless for reasons suggested in the last two analytical essays that *Dichterliebe* in its original form could be considered a very viable possibility indeed.

When paying close attention to poem and music separately, the individuality of both Heine and Schumann comes to light with increasing clarity. This is certainly one of the advantageous results of what we could call a comparative approach. However, Heine's and Schumann's temperamental differences are also apparent in sources such as articles, letters and diaries. In the case of Schumann's extensive writings, little notice has been taken of his manner of self-expression or indeed the aesthetic ideas this manner reveals as much as it repeatedly names. Hence, my discussion of Schumann, both historical as well as analytical, includes a critical reading of his own words. By transposing the possible overflow of a foreign Romantic idiom into a post-Freudian diction, one avoids the fallacy of believing that mere repetition would necessarily induce an understanding of a way of thinking that is, after all, far removed from today's technological rationality. Since I consider the idiosyncratic tone and subtle inflection in the language of Heine, Schumann and the Early Romantics to be an essential indicator for their respective styles and ideas, original German, occasionally also French, quotations have been provided almost without exception throughout the book.

Ultimately, then, this study is about language, poetic language as Heine and Schumann had discovered it for themselves under the demanding aegis of the Early

---

[27] Hallmark (1979).

Romantics with their radical repudiation of a language of pure reason, and their sovereign intent to open up and imbue language with subjectivity, a subjectivity both aware and unaware of the source of alienation located within it. In *Dichterliebe*, the desire for such a language makes itself felt, with its two heterogeneous levels of speech, and the kind of isomorphism existing between poetry and music: *Der Dichter spricht*.

PART I

EARLY ROMANTIC FORMS OF DIFFERENCE

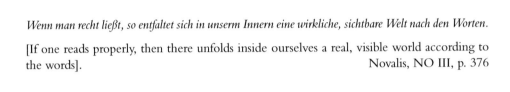

Wenn man recht ließt, so entfaltet sich in unserm Innern eine wirkliche, sichtbare Welt nach den Worten.

[If one reads properly, then there unfolds inside ourselves a real, visible world according to the words].   Novalis, NO III, p. 376

1

INTRODUCTION

So, what is *Poetology*, as the aesthetic and literary theory of early German Romanticism was originally called? Developed in a decidedly analytical, if speculative, mode of thinking, this theory introduced new definitions of literary genres and advanced new forms of expression in a radical move away from the older model of representation and mimesis towards that of creation and imagination. *Poetology* also involves a powerful advocacy of the inseparability of art and life, morality and religion, and as such lies at the heart of the overarching Romantic conception of *Symphilosophy*.[1] Here, all aspects of life, in particular its contradictions, are raised on to a higher aesthetic plane. This process crystallizes in the *Poetic*. The qualifier 'poetic' thus takes on a newer and wider meaning than usually assumed when considered the property of a specific literary genre. The return to its original meaning, to *poiesis* as in 'making' and 'creating', is of paramount importance within the Romantics' new philosophy of life – the *progressive universal poetry* – and receives here its social momentum:

It tries to and should mix and fuse poetry and prose, inspiration and criticism, the poetry of art and the poetry of nature; and make poetry lively and sociable, life and society poetical; poeticize wit and fill and saturate the forms of art with every kind of good, solid matter for instruction, and animate them with the pulsation of humour. It embraces everything that is purely poetic, from the greatest systems of art, containing within themselves still further systems, to the sigh, the kiss that the child who composes breathes forth in artless song.[2]

In this introduction to some central topoi of Early Romantic thought, to the formative concepts of a highly refined kind of Idealism, I shall introduce and define the terms in which the subsequent discussion of Heinrich Heine and Robert Schumann will take place. Although different in their responses, both artists remained faithful

---

[1] Lacoue-Labarthe and Nancy (1987).

[2] Friedrich Schlegel's definition of Romantic poetry in the famous fragment no. 116 of the *Athenaeum* [Sie will und soll auch Poesie und Prosa, Genialität und Kritik, Kunstpoesie und Naturpoesie bald mischen, bald verschmelzen, die Poesie lebendig und gesellig und das Leben und die Gesellschaft poetisch machen, den Witz poetisieren und die Formen der Kunst mit gediegenem Bildungsstoff jeder Art anfüllen und sättigen und durch die Schwingungen des Humors beseelen. Sie umfaßt alles, was nur poetisch ist, vom größten wieder mehre Systeme in sich enthaltende Systeme der Kunst bis zum Seufzer, dem Kuß, den das dichtende Kind aushaucht in kunstlosem Gesang]. *Athenaeum*, p. 119. Unless otherwise indicated, all translations are my own. The original spelling of these texts from nineteenth-century German sources has been left unchanged.

13

to the ideas and poetic practices the Early Romantics developed – an interesting aspect, for Heine and Schumann are latecomers in a movement that made its meteoric rise at the end of the eighteenth century, years before either of them had begun an artistic career.

With the city of Jena as the centre of their congenial intellectual exchange, the Early Romantics developed their theory in a short period of time, effectively between 1798 and 1801, the period in which the journal *Das Athenaeum* appeared. Founded by the brothers Friedrich and August Wilhelm von Schlegel as the organ for their literary-critical and aesthetic re-evaluation, it contains the essence of Early Romantic theoretical thought. Associated with the Jena group are the philosophers Johann Gottlieb Fichte and Friedrich Schelling, the Protestant theologian Friedrich Schleiermacher, and the poets Ludwig Tieck and Wilhelm Wackenroder. The figure of Novalis epitomizes the Early Romantics' aspirations. As the inventor of the Romantic symbol of the Blue Flower,[3] he promoted the Romantic Ideal to its fullest extent. His collection of 114 philosophical-psychological fragments called *Blütenstaub* (Pollen) of 1798, and the late *Hymnen an die Nacht* (Hymns to the Night) of 1799, both published in the *Athenaeum*, show him as advancing his vision intellectually and transcending it poetically on the side of religion, art and life. In the *Hymnen* in particular, the wholeness of mind and body, achieved in the need for an unshakeable God, was first announced and formally suggested through poetry's inherently ascendant powers. Novalis could then meet the afterglow shadowing his art of darkness, for following the beloved, the Mother, the Spirit, meant bringing to life what the power of imagination had already prescribed. Befriending death for real after foretelling it in poetico-theoretical terms adds a further level of complexity to Novalis' work and renders his poetry as one of the most difficult the Romantic spirit engendered.

Just as the sheer intensity of the Early Romantic Idea was force enough to leave behind the 'Age of Reason', the atmospheric orbit of such an idealistic orientation was to hold its sway over future generations long after it was first articulated. Its high intellectual and spiritual values reach into the present, although unrecognized or unacknowledged at times, as they inform the best, or are merely perpetuated in the worst, forms of contemporary critical and philosophical pursuit.[4]

As this enquiry is concerned with the intellectual and aesthetic issues of Early Romanticism, its innovative concepts of artistic structure and representation, the distinction from later forms of Romanticism must be emphasized. If, as is stereotypically suggested, the ideological content of Romanticism rested on a formidable

---

[3] See Novalis' novel *Heinrich von Ofterdingen* of 1802. See Part II for my discussion about Heine's critical preoccupation with the Blue Flower, and my discussion about the Early Romantic concept of the 'language of flowers' as adopted by Schumann in Part III, pp. 87–90.

[4] In philosophy, this has been demonstrated most consistently in the extensive work of Manfred Frank. See also Behler and Hörisch (1987), as well as Bowie (1990). Jerome McGann (1985, p. 12) uncovers and refutes as reactionary the uncritical adoption of Romantic ideology often present in scholarly work dealing with the period – the 'absorption in Romanticism's own self-representation'.

transference in which the Romantics' intense adversity towards their socio-political setting finds itself relocated in poeticized and idealized ways of retreat, then two things need to be borne in mind: first, the term 'Romantic' is, of course, known to be problematic, especially if applied without specific references regarding time, place and person. Quite understandably, then, little consensus exists in the critical literature, for 'Romanticism' cannot be seen as a unified phenomenon, whether historically, culturally or ideologically. The differences to be observed between early and later German Romantic thought are indeed as great as, say, between English and French Romantic poetry, and one must therefore doubt the possibility of some universal 'Romantic ideology' and sentiment. Only with the second generation of the Romantics are nationalism and Catholicism, to mention just two aspects, to be found dispersed among Romantic texts and popular opinion. Since this study focuses on the first generation, the whole notion of 'retreat', for example, turns out to be premature; it simply did not surface until some time later and has no place in either the theory or the mentality of the Early Romantics. Further, in view of the tenaciously repeated assessment that the German Romantic movement in general – of which the Early Romantics laid the foundation – amounted to a proto-Fascist, reactionary force leading directly or indirectly to private and public catastrophe, it is essential to remember that the notion of *Volk*, cultivated in the interests of political restoration or religious orthodoxy, is a distinction with which only later Romanticism was to be burdened. Reactionary conservatism may be seen as a trend emerging after the French Revolution and, in particular, after the abortive 1848 uprising. This is a cultural-political issue that studies of the later nineteenth and early twentieth centuries do, indeed, have to engage with in greater depth. Though no particular effort is made in the present study to discuss the ideological side of Early Romanticism,[5] it may nonetheless be worth mentioning somewhat categorically that its leading figures were decidedly cosmopolitan, progressive and 'modern' in attitude. They were supporters of the French Revolution. Directly opposed to an institutionalized belief in the Saviour or even in the Resurrection, the Early Romantics' promotion of Pantheism grew out of convictions more humanitarian than later generations were able to accommodate.

CRITIQUE AND META-CRITIQUE

Second, in as much as any evaluation of works of the past in general and Romanticism in particular needs to articulate what the relevance of its subject matter can possibly be for the actual present from which we critics operate, one soon discovers that the import of Early Romantic theory and art is topical rather than historical. The major questions with which Postmodernism has concerned itself – the critique of work, author and communication – had been asked and indeed answered in the Early Romantic discourse. Since then, neither its questions nor its answers have lost

---

[5] Frank (1997b).

their impact. Consciously reflecting upon their own position towards modernity and its very condition, the Early Romantics developed a conception of the work of art which carries the ethical question within itself by seizing it as an aesthetic one. The work created is so conditioned, structurally, that from its form arises its message; a message, however, that is never fully stated. It is withheld in order to emphasize the notion of possibility rather than the notion of completion: 'Romantic poetry is still in a state of becoming', Friedrich Schlegel says. 'Indeed, the real essence [of poetry] is that it should forever be becoming and never be perfected.'[6] Contrary to later Romantic poetry which sustains the sense of illusion throughout, Early Romantic poetry thematizes and reflects critically upon the illusions it creates. In the light of the generalizing assumption that Romantic art as a whole aimed at the illusionary, the first point to be made is that the Early Romantics were consciously aware of the unattainability of the Absolute. The Early Romantic notions of imperfectibility, estrangement, loss of communication and consensus are thus aspects that contemporary continental criticism (Gadamer, Adorno and Habermas, as well as Derrida, Foucault, Lyotard, Lacoue-Labarthe and Nancy) has recognized as the beginning and basis of the aesthetic and philosophical discourse on modernity.[7] The modern air that surrounds and breathes through the works of the Early Romantics is precisely then the notion of *critique*. Hence, the Early Romantics did not opt out of their environment; rather, Romantic theory and poetry announces in the most uncompromising terms its critical position towards its own *Poetology*, for the theory itself is defined by what can be called an ever-present paradox. Such self-conscious meta-critique can be observed in the theoretical conceptions that this first Part seeks to introduce.

[6] *Athenaeum*, p. 19 [Die romantische Dichtart ist noch im Werden; ja das ist ihr eigentliches Wesen, daß sie ewig nur werden, nie vollendet sein kann].

[7] Derrida (1967 and 1972), Foucault (1970), Lyotard (1984), Gadamer (1990), Adorno (1993), Habermas (1987). See the collected essays in Lacoue-Labarthe and Nancy (1987) as well as Behler and Hörisch (1987). Whilst one observes in French circles the attempt and ability to fuse philosophical and literary discourse (first developed by Novalis and Friedrich Schlegel – 'Wem gefiele nicht eine Philosophie, deren Keim ein erster Kuß ist?' [Who wouldn't like a philosophy whose kernel was a first kiss?] – [NO II, p. 541, no. 74]), Habermas insists on the traditional demarcation as he reproaches Derrida for the '*aesthetisizing of language, which is purchased with the two-fold denial of the proper senses of normal and poetic discourse*' by asserting that 'art and literature on the one side, and science, morality, and law on the other, are specialized for experiences and modes of knowledge that can be shaped and worked out within the compass of *one* linguistic function and *one* dimension of validity at a time. Derrida holistically levels these complicated relationships in order to equate philosophy with literature and criticism.' See 'Excursus on Levelling the Genre Distinction between Philosophy and Literature' in Habermas (1987), pp. 185–210 (here pp. 205 and 207; emphasis original). Cf. Frank (1989), p. 221: 'Only the early-Romantic authors of the Jena circle inserted aesthetic meaning [ästhetischer Sinn] *into* philosophical production itself' (emphasis original). The reason why works pertaining to the Early Romantic concept of a *Symphilosophy* and *Universal Poetry* – characterized chiefly by the preferred use of the fragment as an expository form (in our case Schumann's *Dichterliebe*) – must be discussed in the light of its philosophical implications lies in the very fact that both the genesis and the meaning of the aesthetic concept of the fragment are inseparable from the philosophical vision it seeks to convey. Hence the Early Romantics' self-designation 'poet-philosophers' whose aim is to merge poetry and philosophy, philosophy and life, morality and religion, and so forth. The generic term for this all-encompassing enterprise is 'Poetry', and the person performing it is a 'poet' – the name Schumann assigned to himself in the spirit of Early Romanticism.

HEINE'S EXPERIENCE OF ROMANTICISM

Heine's critique of Romanticism in his influential book *The Romantic School* (1833) was perhaps the first to address the issue of Romanticism and its ideology construc- tively by way of providing it with what some have described as 'living quarters in a non-Romantic age and consciousness',[8] that is, by admitting his sympathy without losing his integrity. Yet, allowing for a less triumphal trait in Heine's response to his predecessors, his poetry also manifests the anguish of losing the Romantic ideal in Heine's attempt to assert a self, certainly if that self can be located in what Adorno famously called 'the wound'.[9] The estrangement experienced by Heine invaded his poetic language, where an obsession with breaking the tone (*Stimmungsbruch*) means breaking with the universal, clearly Romantic model of poetic expressivity. Heine's tone, artfully unnatural and never melodious, does not derive from a voice in tune with the words it speaks. Speechless in the face of his inner alienation from Romantic Germany, Heine moves like a stranger within his mother tongue, for his uncanny linguistic ability is that of a well-adapted foreigner. Grating irony creeps into his lines like an indefinable accent or the habitual grammatical mistake. It is irritating first of all, and fascinating only insofar as the typical onlooker takes reassuring delight in a fortunate unfamiliarity with the utter negativity Heine's irony affords.

Here, Heine's strikingly limited vocabulary in his early poetry, the constant reap- pearance of certain words and images, merits scrutiny. Although this may well be characteristic of a language not actually lived, but learned by a 'person who uses language like a book that is out of print',[10] the desire invested here is nevertheless very real. For such insistence on a few motifs turns poetry into monotonous speech, as if trying, in an incessant stream of unsuccessful attempts, to bring home to the native speaker what cannot be accomplished – immediacy and real communication through idiomatic speech. This is the sense of 'variations on the same little theme',[11] as Heine himself described the *Lyrisches Intermezzo*, because any one poem is as ap- proximate a formulation as any other. In this sense, Heine's poetry is not expressive; rather, it is ostentatiously impressive. Bedazzled by his perfection of form (folk-song), arrangement and chiselled poetic rhetoric, amused by witty turns of phrase or

---

[8] McGann (1985), p. 11. McGann explores and eventually adopts Heine's critical procedures with great skill in his attempt to 'arrest that process of reification' of the Romantic ideology permeating much of the critical literature.

[9] Adorno's brilliant talk on 'Heine the Wound' (1968/91a) given on the centenary of Heine's death in 1956 contains central insights into Heine's disposition towards nineteenth-century Germany. Emphasizing the political relevance of the case of Heine, Adorno speaks of a 'wound' and 'injury' inflicted upon Heine with indirect reference to the Holocaust: Heine's 'homelessness' as a Jew in an anti-Semitic climate is related to the poet's conciliatory gesture of using 'assimilatory language' as a sign of his desperate yet 'unsuccessful identification'. Marxist in orientation, Adorno asserts that Heine 'took a poetic technique of reproduction . . . that corresponds to the industrial age'. This, however, is debatable in its relative reductionism, for the stylistic complexity of Heine's poetic language rests on a great number of factors whose various effects can only with difficulty be whittled down to be seen as relevant only on a socio-economic level. Nonetheless, Adorno's centenary talk on Heine remains one of the most important statements made about the poet.

[10] Adorno (1968), p. 150. Trans. (1991a), p. 83.

[11] Heine's own description of the poetic cycle. See *HSA* XX, p. 250.

strategically well-placed words out of phase, Heine's reader enjoys the sparkle, but keeps and is always kept well outside. Heine thus belies the Early Romantic thesis of 'reading as becoming the poet of the poem' and instead passes on his linguistic ordeal: 'Blaring trumpets cutting through' this poetry of 'angels sobbing and groaning'[12] make a readerly 'drowning' rather impossible. In Heine, the heightened Romantic sentimentality first invoked functions in inverse proportion to the fall the reader experiences at the moment of Heine's cuts. Yet these same cuts possess an exceptional effectiveness by pointing the way back to the sentimentality originally evoked and remembered as having touched such heights in the first place. Either way, then, the Heinean cut ensures a zero degree of illusion. As images of abysmal maliciousness or intense kitsch come crashing down on us, Heine shows reality naked – the opposite of the Romantics' 'Kingdom Come'. Eventually one realizes that Heine was not blessed with the kind of faith we witness in the Romantics' pursuit of Elysium – indeed there was no other faith that could have filled the void in Heine's fractionally hearted, dissociated self. 'Where no Gods reign, there ghosts reign' (*Wo keine Götter walten, da walten Gespenster*), Novalis knew, and Heine's *imago* of a woman wandering through his poems may be seen as such a ghost, an outgrowth of Heine's deep-seated suspicion and rejection of the Early Romantic spirit.[13]

The abrasiveness of Heine's tone, together with his disturbing passion to leave no aspect of an inherited Romantic imagery innocent, is however a sign of defence. It reveals his ostracism, and makes one pause to reconsider the possible extent of Heine's tolerance towards the Romantic cause that even in his prose would be difficult to recover. Heine's poetry bespeaks a reaction to the Romantic movement that may indeed disturb the modern ideal of conciliation, for this language is as irreconciliatory as language can be. It also, however, bespeaks a kind of preoccupation with that movement's values that derives its tension from welding together two extremes: the horror of an inescapable dependency on, and the solace sought but not to be found in, these very values. Thus, indebtedness is a burden and insecurity is laid bare.

Wunderglaube! Blaue Blume,	Belief in miracles! Blue Flower,
Die verschollen jetzt, wie prachtvoll	Which is now missing, how magnificently
Blühte sie im Menschenherzen	It blossomed in man's heart
Zu der Zeit, von der wir singen!	In those times of which we are singing!
...und die verstorbnen	...and the deceased
Jugendträume, sie erwachen.	Dreams of one's youth awake.
Auf den Häuptern welke Kränze,	On the heads withered wreaths,
Schauen sie mich an wehmütiglich;	Look at me nostalgically;
Tote Nachtigallen flöten,	Dead nightingales are singing,
Schluchzen zärtlich, wie verblutend.[14]	Are sobbing gently, as if bleeding to death.

---

[12] *Lyrisches Intermezzo*, XX [... Trompeten schmettern drein; ... / ... Dazwischen schluchzen und stöhnen / Die guten Engelein].

[13] See Part II, pp. 91–103.

[14] From the Prologue of Heine's late poem *Bimini*, first published posthumously in 1869. B VI/1, pp. 243–249.

SCHUMANN'S EXPERIENCE OF ROMANTICISM

Schumann had a greater feeling of belonging to the Romantic tradition. Ironically, at the same time as Heine's critical *Romantic School* had appeared, Schumann took the momentous step of advocating publicly the beginning of a 'new poetic time' in founding the music-critical journal *Neue Zeitschrift für Musik*. Highly influenced by Romantic poetry and literature, in particular by the fantastical writings of Jean Paul, who told his stories 'through ten thousand reflections and conceits',[15] Schumann's music was the joint work of those characters that had invaded his wandering mind. Calling himself the 'musical fantast'[16] of the secret community of the *Davidsbündler*, Schumann's compositions until 1840 form a complex dialectic of invention, idealization, transformation and denial of self and other personae. His compositional celebration of 'rare' and 'secret states of the soul'[17] means, on perhaps a more abstract level, a similar procedure of casting into sound his mobile, self-reflective imagination. Schumann's constant attention to those moments and events in life which forced him to react and act out musically with the hyper-sensitivity of the affected shows again the same dynamics – the Romantic artist's journey of searching both self and soul to find an authentic space within. Indeed, if Schumann was one of the least cosmopolitan of Romantic composers, it was because he was arrested within his own, Romantic cosmos, and only there did he see 'constellations of a subterranean firmament'.[18] In exploring the unintelligible, he thus left the tranquillity of Reason for the sake of more rarefied atmospheres, capturing forces instead of matter, himself instead of the outside. In this, he cuts the sorry, yet sympathetic figure, not of the one who was deserted, but of the Romantic Solitary, the 'One–Alone' and 'One–All'[19] of German Romanticism: a Romantic hero after all, then, who could render audible the waves of voices which swept across his mind, who could perceive and sublimate the haunting images of an inner truth. Thus in discourse with none but himself, Schumann the composer is self-indulgent and self-absorbed. In this, Schumann took the risk of entering a nocturnal space by giving himself over to the power of his desire. This is also why, in fact, one cannot speak of 'style' in Schumann's music as one can in the case of Heine's words. Whilst the stylist's motivation is to write poems as good as the poetic models he seeks to out-match, and with a judging audience in the forefront of his mind, Schumann's aim was centred within and directed towards himself as he explored his multiple Romantic characters by giving them a voice. Thus, his music is concerned with nothing other than itself, keeps turning back on itself, reflects and contradicts itself in the manner of what one calls *pure poetry* in Early Romanticism. Such intuitive creative processes leave little room for the kind of overtly conscious stylistic finesse we find in Heine, but all the more for direct, unprotected speech. In this sense, Schumann's music is indeed, as Roland Barthes

---

[15] Jean Paul's own description as quoted in Casey (1992), p. 43.
[16] Schumann about himself in *GS* I, p. 54 [musikalischer Phantast].
[17] Kreisig *GS* I, p. 343 [seltene … geheime Seelenzustände].
[18] *JP* IX, p. 58 [Sternbilder eines unterirdischen Himmels].
[19] Deleuze (1988), p. 340.

suggests, of a kind that keeps saying nothing other than '*c'est moi*', and which makes it thus 'an egoistic music'.[20] But Schumann's songs are even more self-involved than this. The space is opened up for yet another voice which makes the Romantic invocation of the Other complete and structurally real. *Dichterliebe* exemplifies this Romantic drama, in which the voice is personified desire, and to which the piano yields and which it opposes. While the dialogical nature of the short piano pieces is still at work, it is the human voice that brings into Schumann's monologue the fictitious solace of the Other. At the core of these songs there is always the 'split Self' of Schumann's Romantic subjectivity,[21] who vacillates between giving in to the voices of desire and making distancing moves so as to preserve his sense of the solitary Romantic artist. For the piano in Schumann's songs, certainly, does not continuously act as supporting accompaniment; rather it keeps disrupting the voice and contradicting it, keeps silent or speaks to itself once the singing voice has ceased. Interestingly, it is also in view of the greater structural scale of *Dichterliebe* that Schumann remains within the desiring mode of a wandering Romantic visionary:

The thread of thought moves imperceptibly forward in constant interconnection until the surprised spectator, after the thread abruptly breaks off or dissolves in itself, suddenly finds himself confronted with a goal he had not at all expected: before him an unlimited, wide view, but upon looking back at the path he has traversed and the spiral of conversation distinctly before him, he realizes that this was only a fragment of an infinite cycle.[22]

SHARED NOTIONS OF CRITIQUE

My own point of view is consciously sited in the hermeneutic tradition as developed by Schleiermacher, whose proposed approach to works of art implies the recognition of an insurmountable distance between artist, work and critic. I do not, therefore, even so much as raise the question of artistic intentionality, not only because it may be a problematic issue but more crucially because it could be considered irrelevant; this stance originated in the Romantics' awareness that the critic is always situated somewhere other than the origin of the work. The Romantic thesis of *différence* is, however, based on more than the usual emphasis on historical and cultural determination. It is carried further in the Romantics' assertion that artistic language does not possess the 'objectivity of gold'[23] and that the work always 'knows more than it says, and intends more than it knows'.[24] The critic, therefore, will be able to bring out a higher level of signification by becoming the 'extended creator' of the work.[25] Thus, to speak with Walter Benjamin, for whose own critical stance the hermeneutic

---

[20] Barthes (1985c), p. 295.

[21] See the discussion on the Early Romantics' awareness of a fragmentary Self on pp. 5–8.

[22] One of Friedrich Schlegel's description of poetry. See *KFSA* III, p. 50. Trans. Behler (1993), p. 141.

[23] Friedrich Schlegel uses the metaphor ironically in his important essay 'On Incomprehensibility' in the last volume of the *Athenaeum*, *KFSA* II, p. 365. See further discussion in Part III, p. 133.

[24] *KFSA* XVIII, p. 318 [Das Werk das mehr weiß als es sagt, und mehr will als es weiß].

[25] Cf. Frank (1985), pp. 358–364 or Behler (1987), pp. 141–160 and (1992), pp. 271–277.

tradition of Early Romanticism turned out to be formative, 'the proper approach
to [the object and its 'truth-content'] is not . . . one of intention and knowledge, but
rather a total immersion and absorption in it'.[26]

At the heart of this hermeneutic procedure, 'the great Romantic shift' as Gadamer
called it,[27] there always lies the autonomy of the art work itself. Although this is
perceptible throughout *Truth and Method*, Gadamer acknowledges his affinity to
Friedrich Schlegel's conception of the 'work' openly when speaking up for the
hermeneutic meaning of the work-concept, which has more recently come under
attack. In obvious opposition to the doubts expressed by Derrida, De Man and
Levinas – the 'Zeitgeist' as Gadamer summarizes it – whose idea of *différence* includes
questioning the very possibility of an 'understanding' that would not at the same
time undermine the presence of the work's constant otherness, Gadamer raises our
sensitivity to the word's root: ' "Work" means nothing else than "ergon" and is,
exactly like the other "ergon", characterized by the fact that it is separated from
producer and its production.' Form and the understanding thereof does not depend
on who produced it, but on who uses it. The 'intentio auctoris' is therefore engrained
in the work which purely biographical or genesis-orientated research might fail to
discover. 'Works of art are detached from their genesis [*Entstehung*] and only for this
reason begin to speak, perhaps even to the surprise of its creator.'[28] Gadamer elicits
the concept of *différence* that distinguishes him from Derrida by way of etymologically
elucidating the German word *Verstehen*:

Its place within the German human sciences does not, of course, so easily find an equivalent in
other languages. What does Verstehen actually mean? Verstehen is 'to stand in for somebody'
[*für jemanden stehen*]. In its original sense, the word applies to someone who is an intercessor
in court, an advocate. He is that person who understands his party, as we in today's usage say
'represents him' [*vertreten*]. He represents his client, he stands in for him, he certainly does
not repeat what he has been told or what has been dictated to him, but he speaks for him.
But that means that he speaks from his point of view, as somebody else, and he addresses
others. *Différence* is obviously implied here. . . . That is not the art of hermeneutics, which
is to nail somebody down on what he has said. It is the art of perceiving what he actually
wanted to say.[29]

One of Gadamer's most compelling images is 'that in all acts of understanding the
horizon of one person merges with the horizon of the other; this certainly does not
mean a lasting and identifiable One, but takes place as a continuing conversation

---

[26] Benjamin (1977), p. 36.   [27] See Gadamer (1990), pp. 188–201.

[28] Gadamer (1987), pp. 258–259.

[29] Gadamer (1987), p. 254 [Sein Ort in der deutschen Geistesgeschichte findet freilich in anderen Sprachen nicht
so leicht eine Entsprechung. Was heißt eigentlich Verstehen? Verstehen ist 'für jemanden stehen'. Das Wort wird
dem ursprünglichen Sinn nach von dem gesagt, der Fürsprecher vor Gericht ist, der Advokat. Er ist der, der
seine Partei versteht, so wie wir im heutigen Sprachgebrauch dafür 'vertreten' sagen. Er vertritt seinen Klienten,
er steht für ihn, er wiederholt nicht etwa, was er ihm vorgesagt oder diktiert hat, sondern er spricht für ihn. Das
heißt aber, er redet von sich aus, als ein anderer, und wendet sich an andere. Différence ist hier selbstverständlich
impliziert . . . Das ist nicht die Kunst der Hermeneutik, jemanden auf etwas festzunageln, was er gesagt hat. Sie
ist die Kunst, das, was er hat eigentlich sagen wollen, aufzunehmen].

[*Gespräch*]'.[30] Here resonates Jaspers's idea of a 'Gespräch der Geister' (conversation of minds) into which one enters with an open mind.

The significance of Romanticism as a literary-philosophical phenomenon lies in its conviction that art, more than philosophy itself, is the ultimate source of human cognition. The Romantics arrived at this position after their revisionist engagement with Kantian subjectivity on the one hand, and their own development of a theory of language on the other. Their speculative exploration of the potential of language in general and the languages of art in particular arguably bears similarities to Foucault's proposition that 'language may sometimes arise for its own sake in an act of writing that designates nothing other than itself'.[31] Within this contemporaneously modernist definition of language, poetry became the paradigmatic art form of Early Romanticism. It stood at the centre of all poetological reflections. Although an Early Romantic theory of music has yet to be reconstructed, the references to music are frequent. In closest proximity to the Romantics' concept of poetry, music was seen to be able to transcend articulate speech so as to 'represent the Unrepresentable'.[32] Given the preference at the time for so-called 'absolute' music, the emergence of the Romantic art song at the beginning of the nineteenth century is a particularly intriguing phenomenon. For in song, two 'most expressive' art forms, poetry and music, were brought together as if to experiment with their differing expressive means. Indeed, the concept of poetry set to music, that is, the combination of the ineffable expressivity of music with the conceptual capacities of language, epitomizes the Early Romantics' theoretical speculations about the two 'speaking arts' (Hegel in the *Vorlesungen über die Aesthetic*). Schumann, the most poetically minded among the Romantic composers, proposed in his writings a concept of the Lied that departs from earlier models of Lied composition in its distinctly Idealist orientation. Rather than seeking to synchronize text and music with regard to either form or content, he conceived of the Lied as a separate independent art form, a 'higher sphere of art'.[33] After having realized the poetic ideal in short piano works, he regarded the Lied as *the* Romantic medium of poetic sublimation able to transcend both the musical and poetical to the highest level of expression. In the Romantic sense, however, Schumann's Lieder are not exclusively interpretative; rather, Schumann was preoccupied with what was elusively absent from the written word. Freeing himself from

---

[30] Gadamer (1987), p. 255 [in allem Verstehen verschmilzt sich der Horizont des einen mit dem Horizont des anderen . . . dies meint wahrlich kein bleibendes und identifizierbares Eines, sondern geschieht in dem weitergehenden Gespräch].

[31] Foucault (1970), p. 304. Beginning with the 'Romantic revolt against a discourse frozen in its own ritual pomp', Foucault speaks here of the new notion of 'literature' in which 'language . . . – in opposition to all other forms of discourse – . . . curve[s] back in a perpetual return upon itself, as if its discourse could have no other content than the expression of its own form.' The idea of language as introduced by the Romantics was the foundation of, so Foucault argues, its use by Mallarmé, for example, where the word 'has nothing to say but itself, nothing to do but shine in the brightness of its being'. See Foucault (1970), p. 300. In the light of this radically modern notion of language, the Romantics came to see musical notation in a similar way.

[32] Novalis' programmatic dictum epitomizing the Romantics' aims. See NO III, p. 685, no. 671 [Das Undarstellbare darstellen].

[33] *NZfM* 1 (1834), p. 193 [höhere Kunstsphäre].

complying with the text in the spirit of becoming the 'second author of the poem' and with the awareness of a 'better understanding', Schumann is firmly grounded within the hermeneutic tradition first proposed by Schleiermacher.[34] With this vision of a 'higher sphere of art', Schumann's Lieder thus epitomize the quintessential Romantic paradox: creation/critique. This brought into song composition a degree of unrestrained creativity which led to the kind of intensity that we instantly recognize to be at work in Schumann's songs. Thus, listening to Schumann's *Dichterliebe* means an involvement with the 'incandescent core of the romantic song',[35] and the hermeneutic approach that I have taken intends to account for the theoretical and intellectual context out of which it originally arose.

One aim of Part I, then, is to bring a measure of exposition to the theoretical ideas of these Early Romantic poet-philosophers, and to convey the historical and intellectual context in which Heine and Schumann must be seen. At the same time, one will also need to measure their different distances from that context, thereby realizing the extent to which Heine distanced himself from the Romantic ideal to which Schumann, in contrast, truly aspired. Here, by way of reference to the sources of this theory, the focus will be on the more hermetic members of the Romantic school, and on Friedrich Schlegel and Novalis in particular. Both realized more than any other exponents of the movement the sublimation of theory into art. And nowhere is the idea of the aesthetic more resonant than in the philosophy of the *Athenaeum*, with their major contributions.[36] In short texts and fragments the central Early Romantic thesis is expounded that the paradigmatic medium of reflection is art, and not, as Fichte had proposed earlier, the 'I'.

FORMS OF DESIRE

My discussion of the Early Romantics' very diverse body of thought is restricted to aspects of language and art, poetry and music, and, above all, their aesthetic of form and expression. Here, I shall focus on three forms: the Romantic fragment, Romantic irony and reflection.[37] Developed as a means to 'represent the Unrepresentable',[38] these concepts are devoted to the visionary *per se*: the Romantic *Sehnen* or 'longing' and the more modern *Verlangen*, 'desire'. Projective in nature compared with their

---

[34] Schleiermacher's famous dictum 'to understand speech [*Rede*] first just as well and then better than its author'. See *HK*, p. 87 [die Rede zuerst eben so gut und dann besser zu verstehen als ihr Autor]. This idea was already suggested, of course, by Kant in the *KrV* B, p. 371.

[35] Barthes (1985b), p. 289.

[36] The important place the *Athenaeum* takes in the development of an Early Romantic aesthetic was first demonstrated by Benjamin (1973) in his masterly dissertation 'Der Begriff der Kunstkritik in der deutschen Romantik' of 1919 to which, among others, Blanchot (1969) has added his own brilliant critiques.

[37] Whilst the two concepts of 'Romantic fragment' and 'irony' will be treated separately (pp. 26–39), a systematic description of the Early Romantics' idea of 'reflection' is provided in connection with the Romantic concept of language and music (pp. 40–46).

[38] NO III, p. 685, no. 671 [Das Undarstellbare darstellen]. Novalis' dictum and thesis of Early Romanticism about the incommensurability of poetic works which can no longer be conceptually grasped; instead the Sublime or Absolute may be divined or anticipated (*geahndet*).

earlier and darker precursor melancholy, or their later, more retrograde nostalgia, *Sehnen* or *Sehnsucht* was, despite its exhausting force, the *movens* which retained its grace under the pressure resulting from the unattainability of the Romantics' aspirations. Although *Sehnsucht* often degenerates into a vague commonplace in those studies of Romanticism where it is simply taken for granted, my attempt is to demonstrate its presence and continuing strength in structural terms. The Romantic fragment is one important means of doing so, for it bears the dynamics of *Sehnsucht* within itself and, together with the subtly disintegrating forces of Romantic irony, is the primary agency able to bring out the forward-thriving movement and projective energy contained within Romantic *Sehnsucht*. In its very inability to attain the desired, to come to fulfilment, the Romantic fragment invokes and evokes endlessly. Hence, in contrast to the concept of a 'work', the fragment contains no fixed or final statement; rather it alludes to and points towards the distant horizon of our desire, and is, no more and no less, an inscription of our 'Sehnsucht nach dem Unendlichen'.[39] But let us say that such inscription of *Sehnsucht* in Heine's and Schumann's work is mediated, for it involves the affective side of a creative process which channels rather than describes or elaborates upon its primary origin. It is esoteric: the stream of an inner truth floating beneath the surface of these poetic texts, as omnipresent as it is elusive.

Another aim of this introduction to Early Romantic poetics is to bring out the uses of fragmentation, which lies at the heart of the Early Romantics' idea of form. Within the mobile dialectical movement of a Romantic play of thoughts and associations, ideas always live in contradiction. What I earlier called the 'paradox' in the Romantic position is indeed the fundamental mechanism behind the concepts of reflection, fragment and irony. Here, the central paradox behind these concepts is that the totality that is posited is also precisely what causes the moment of disintegration. The Romantic fragment represents the middle term around which the other two, reflection and irony, continuously revolve; defined by Frank as an expression of the 'negative dialectic of Early Romanticism',[40] the Romantic fragment will here be discussed in relation to its detotalizing function. Devised to destroy the appearance of finitude and unity, it signifies *ex negativo* a new kind of synthesis: the absence of the Absolute. The contradiction inherent in the fragment's ultimate failure to represent the Absolute explains the presence of some other typically Romantic notions: evocation and ambiguity, instability, contradiction, and endlessness. If *Dichterliebe* has long been examined with the expectation of functions bearing the norms of an organic whole, burdened with rules typically applied to coherent systems, the resistance of a work like *Dichterliebe* to complying with such a system encourages us to explore the expressive possibilities of fragmentary forms. As heard in *Dichterliebe* itself, the atmosphere created by the Romantic fragment is that of anticipation, when

---

[39] *KFSA* XVIII, p. 418, no. 1168. The famous Romantic statement in Friedrich Schlegel's words.
[40] Frank (1989), pp. 300–301.

love remains in suspense, and when the poet will not submit to confessions: 'Is desire not that what remains always *unthought* at the heart of thought?'[41]

The material of Early Romantic aesthetics is both large and complex, not least because it is a part of *Symphilosophie* and progressive *Universalpoesie* – cosmic conceptual constructs. There is always then, as most scholars recognize, the inclination to try to disentangle the colourful web of ideas and eventually reduce them to doctrines and single threads of thought. This misses, however, the character of the body of thought in question. On the one hand, philosophy and poetry, art and life coalesce here on every level – it was the Romantics' achievement to overcome these traditional antitheses. On the other hand, the Romantics' preferred mode of thinking-as-double-reflection is pervasive in all these primary texts-as-fragments. With 'theory often being highly poetical and poetry sometimes deeply theoretical', these texts, as Behler admits, escape from fixed interpretation and draw the reader into their enigmatic logic, thus contributing to their decidedly modern character.[42] As Lacoue-Labarthe and Nancy propose: 'Romanticism is neither mere "literature" (they invented the concept) nor simply a "theory of literature" (ancient and modern). Rather, it is theory itself as literature or, in other words, literature producing itself as it produces its own theory.'[43] Following Novalis, these texts are also only 'the beginning of interesting successions of thought – texts for thinking'.[44] The theory itself was envisioned as a process 'eternally evolving, never to be completed'.[45] In this sense, the following discussion of a number of texts by the Early Romantics is intended as the starting-point and theoretical basis to reflect upon Heine's post-Romantic poetic procedure characterizing the *Lyrisches Intermezzo* and its transformation into Schumann's *Dichterliebe*, a transposition into sound of theoretical speculations that found their highest expression with Friedrich Schlegel and Novalis.

---

[41] Foucault (1970), p. 375. Emphasis original.   [42] Behler (1992), pp. 28–29. Emphasis original.
[43] Lacoue-Labarthe and Nancy (1987), p. 12.
[44] NO III, p. 276 [Anfänge interessanter Gedankenfolgen – Texte zum Denken].
[45] *KFSA* II, p. 183 [ewig nur werden, nie vollendet].

2

THE ROMANTIC FRAGMENT

The form of the Romantic fragment is precisely what its name suggests: a piece which is broken off from a greater whole, say the Hegelian Absolute which itself, however, was thought no longer to exist. As such 'it is not a work', as Friedrich Schlegel asserts, 'but instead just a broken piece . . . , mass, arrangement'.[1] Historically, the emergence of the Romantic fragment as an aesthetic concept coincides with the loss of belief in the doctrine of salvation characteristic of the post-Enlightenment. The future thereby came to be understood as open, and more importantly still, as contingent. As a result, scepticism and a refined sense of insecurity can be said to characterize the Early Romantics' thinking. Since they could no longer maintain a holistic view of the world, instead they developed a philosophy in which the fragmentary was acknowledged as the basic condition of existence. The fragment as one of the central categories of Early Romantic thought was thus 'the form of *fragmentary consciousness*'.[2] It reflects the 'dismembered' and 'incomplete I',[3] as Friedrich Schlegel emphasizes throughout his writings. He asserts: 'Man *does not exist as a whole*, but only in parts. Man can never be present as a whole.'[4] In the same spirit, Novalis writes:

[This situation of] incompleteness seems most bearable in the form of the fragment; as a form of communication, it can also be recommended to that person who is altogether not yet finished, but who has nevertheless single individual and interesting viewpoints to offer.[5]

Novalis here describes the Early Romantics' mode of writing: since an overall co-herent perception and understanding cannot be achieved, the Romantic artist and philosopher concentrates instead on individual ideas. Narrations (*Erzählungen*) written under these conditions are thus 'without coherence, but with association, like

---

[1] *KFSA* XVIII, p. 159, no. 103 [Das Fragment ist kein Werk, sondern nur Bruchstück . . . , Masse, Anlage].

[2] *KFSA* XII, p. 393 [Form des . . . *fragmentarischen Bewußtseins*]. Emphasis original.

[3] *KFSA* XII, pp. 373, 348, 352, and *KFSA* XIII, p. 506, no. 6, and p. 512, no. 73 [Das zerstückelte, unvollständige Ich].

[4] *KFSA* XVIII, p. 506, no. 9 [Der Mensch [ist] *nicht ganz* sondern nur Stückweise da. Der Mensch kann nie da seyn]. Emphasis original.

[5] Novalis as quoted in Frank (1989), p. 276 [Als Fragment erscheint das Unvollkommene noch am Erträglichsten – und also ist diese Form der Mittheilung dem zu empfehlen, der noch nicht im Ganzen fertig ist – und doch einzelne Merckwürdige Ansichten zu geben hat]. Frank's solid introduction to Early Romantic aesthetic thought includes a helpful collection of those Novalis fragments which are not easily accessible to the non-specialist. Whenever this is the case, I shall refer the reader to Frank's introduction (1989, pp. 272–286) for greater convenience.

dreams.[6] Such dreams, however, contain the seed and unspoken implication of a greater whole, the Absolute. This greater whole cannot be represented, but the Romantic writer, endowed with a sense of the poetic, can 'feel' it:

A sense for poetry has much in common with mysticism. It is the sense for the peculiar, the personal, the unknown, the mysterious, *that which is to be revealed*, the necessarily coincidental. It represents the Unrepresentable; sees the Invisible; feels the Impalpable, etc.[7]

The term 'poetry' is here, as in the whole of Early Romantic thought, used in a general sense. It meant a heightened perception of, and reflection on, everything which 'represents the Unrepresentable'. 'The principle', Novalis says, 'lies in every small detail of ordinary life – it is visible *in everything*'.[8] Thus, the Romantic artist is able to maintain a sense of the Absolute by dint of an awareness that the Absolute will never reveal itself in any other form than an incomplete ensemble of particulars. Hence, the Early Romantic text, consisting of fragments, is not characterized by a logical narrative where each incident connects with and leads to all following incidents, thus contributing to a logically satisfying end. The Jena Romantics often compared the wondrous events of a fairy-tale with those fragmentary images making up their own texts. Here, they conceived each fragment to be an unmediated expression of the unconscious. Novalis said: 'A fairy tale is truly like a dream image – without coherence – an *ensemble* of wondrous things and incidents – e.g. a *musical fantasy*'.[9] Thus drawing on an 'inner world'[10] as well as on 'ideas at pleasure', the Romantic artist uses both as 'tools for the sake of arbitrary modifications of the real world'.[11] The Romantic artist's attention is fixed on small incidents and matters because they carry – as individual moments, and like the images occurring in a dream – the potential of a greater meaning. The specific term for this activity was 'to romanticize' or 'to poeticize'. The crucial statements in the literature can again be found among Novalis' fragments:

Everything that surrounds us, all everyday incidents, the ordinary conditions, the habits in our way of life [must be related to] the concept of the Infinite as its original essence. . . . The world must be romanticized. This way one rediscovers the original meaning. To romanticize means nothing other than qualitatively to potentialize. In this operation, the lower Self is being identified with a better Self. This operation is still totally unknown. By way of assigning an elevated meaning to what is common, by way of giving the ordinary a mysterious appearance,

---

[6] Novalis as quoted in Frank (1989), p. 283 [Erzählungen, ohne Zusammenhang, jedoch mit Association, wie *Träume*]. Emphasis original.

[7] Novalis as quoted in Frank (1989), p. 278 [Der Sinn für Poesie hat viel mit Mystizismus gemein. Er ist der Sinn für das Eigenthümliche, Personelle, Unbekannte, Geheimnißvolle, zu *Offenbarende*, das Nothwendigzufällige. Er stellt das Undarstellbare dar. Er sieht das Unsichtbare, fühlt das Unfühlbare etc.]. Emphasis original.

[8] Novalis as quoted in Frank (1989), p. 272 [Das Princip ist in jeder Kleinigkeit des Alltagslebens – *in allem* sichtbar]. Emphasis original.

[9] NO III, p. 454 [Ein Märchen ist eigentlich wie ein Traumbild – ohne Zusammenhang – Ein *Ensemble* wunderbarer Dinge und Begebenheiten – z. B. eine *musikalische Phantasie*]. Emphasis original.

[10] NO III, p. 650 [innere Welt].

[11] NO II, p. 574 [Ideen nach Belieben – . . . als Werkzeuge, zu beliebigen Modifikationen der wirklichen Welt zu gebrauchen].

by raising the well-known to the unknown, and by adding an infinite appearance to the Finite, I thus romanticize.[12]

One of the main representatives of the Early Romantic mode of writing was Wackenroder (1773–98), whose views on perception and creation clearly demonstrate an anti-rationalistic attitude and the belief in a yet-to-be-revealed truth of the unconscious:

Such phantasies that enter our mind often diffuse in a wonderful way a brighter light over an object than the closing speeches of reason; and there lies next to the so-called higher capacities of cognition a magic mirror in our soul, which sometimes perhaps shows us everything at its strongest.[13]

A heightened apperception of the ordinary, as Novalis described it, led first of all to what he called 'classification of the individual moment'[14] and artistically to the expression of 'an inner state and its inner transformations'.[15] This procedure involved an awareness of time as encompassing 'past, present and future'.[16] As Frank explains in detail, these entities relate to three 'modes of consciousness': reminiscence, contemplation and presentiment.[17]

An obvious visual analogy for Romantic fragments and their structural workings are pieces broken off from an ancient vase. The viewer, in meditating their imperfect and non-matching shape, tries to reconstruct and envision the original form and beauty of the whole vase, say the Absolute. There then appears only a vague idea of the original vase, since what is given is materially insufficient to bring about a precise image. In addition, one fragment means only one way of looking at the potential, still only imagined, vase, which will forever remain invisible; and another fragment means another way of looking at it. Both or any number of these broken pieces do not interlock and all fragments taken together amount to what Novalis called an ensemble. For the onlooker, there is thus generated between all fragments a sense of an 'eternal agility' and of 'an infinitely abundant chaos'.[18] What remains missing in such an ensemble of fragments is, first, coherence, and second, a final fragment that would complete the picture; in other words, a fragment that would bring closure to

---

[12] Novalis as quoted in Frank (1989), pp. 272–273 [Alles, was uns umgiebt, die täglichen Vorfälle, die gewöhnlichen Verhältnisse, die Gewohnheiten unserer Lebensart [sind auf den] Begriff des Unendlichen [zu beziehen als auf ihren] ursprünglichen Sinn. Die Welt muß romantisiert werden. So findet man den ursprünglichen Sinn wieder. Romantisieren ist nichts, als eine qualitative Potenzierung. Das niedre Selbst wird mit einem bessern Selbst in dieser Operation identificirt. . . . Diese Operation ist noch ganz unbekannt. Indem ich dem Gemeinen einen hohen Sinn, dem Gewöhnlichen ein geheimnisvolles Ansehn, dem Bekannten die Würde des Unbekannten, dem Endlichen einen unendlichen Schein gebe so romantisire ich es].

[13] Wackenroder (1938), p. 81 [Dergleichen Phantasien, die uns in den Sinn kommen, verbreiten oftmals auf wunderbare Weise ein helleres Licht über einen Gegenstand, als die Schlußreden der Vernunft; und es liegt neben den sogenannten höheren Erkenntniskräften ein Zauberspiegel in unsrer Seele, der uns die Dinge manchmal vielleicht am kräftigsten dargestellt zeigt].

[14] Novalis as quoted in Frank (1989), p. 273 [Classification des individuellen Moments]. Emphasis original.

[15] Novalis as quoted in Frank (1989), p. 279 [eine Äußerung des innern Zustandes, der innern Veränderungen].

[16] Novalis as quoted in Frank (1989), p. 283 [Sie begreift Vorzeit, Gegenwart und Zukunft].

[17] See Frank (1989), p. 288.   [18] KFSA II, p. 263 as quoted in Behler (1993), p. 151.

the situation. The fragment system, or ensemble, thus differs from say a puzzle or a mosaic in that its parts and pieces do not complement one another or neatly fit together, and, most important of all, in that the last stone to complete the picture is always missing. Hegel's doctrine: 'The truth is the whole' is thus fundamentally challenged. It means a mode of writing that, through its very mobility of thought and contradictoriness of presentation, remains open-ended and inconclusive, devoted to an unrealizable and inconceivable higher synthesis.[19]

We must hence clearly differentiate between two forms of Idealism in early nineteenth-century Germany: on the one hand the positive dialectic principle epitomized in Hegelian Idealism, and on the other the negative dialectic principle characterizing Early Romantic Idealism. Hegelians conceive of opposites and contradictions as belonging to a single whole, the Absolute: if one proposition (thesis) opposes another proposition (antithesis), the resulting logical contradiction is resolved on a higher plane of truth (synthesis). The Early Romantics, however, recognized the coexistence of contradictory forces as an 'infinite multitude' whose 'totality can never be completed'.[20] This multitude of irreconcilable positions reflects Novalis' dictum that '*pluralism* is our innermost nature'.[21] Hence, 'a truly synthetic person is a person who is several persons at once'.[22] This generates a 'tendency into all directions' since all contradictory positions remain unresolved and relate to each other only in the sense of a constant state of agility. Thus, also, the fragment system 'is not a work', as Friedrich Schlegel asserted, 'but instead just mass' and 'arrangement'.[23] It amounts to an inherently antithetical ensemble rather than to an organic whole.

The point to be made here, as has been briefly mentioned above, is that the notion of an elusive, fragmentary knowledge relates to the Romantics' idea of the 'I that seeks itself' (*Das Ich, das sich selbst sucht*): 'the actual contradiction within our I is that we perceive ourselves as at once finite and infinite'.[24] Instead of having a sense of being a harmonious whole, the Early Romantics perceived the Self to be fragmentary. This involves, as Schlegel writes, the realization that the I can never define and grasp itself 'in one single glance'.[25] The I, limited in its Self-discovery, then 'finds itself split and divided, full of contradictions and incomprehensibilities, in short a patch-work, essentially opposed to *unity*'.[26] This absence of self-knowledge is the 'gap in our existence'[27] from which there arises the longing to see and understand nonetheless – a

---

[19] See Behler (1993), p. 153.

[20] *KFSA* XII, pp. 166 and 328 [unendliche Fülle ... Totalität nie vollendet werden kann].

[21] NO III, p. 571, no. 107 [*Pluralism* [sic] ist unser innerstes Wesen]. Emphasis original.

[22] NO III, p. 250, no. 63 [Eine ächt synthetische Person ist eine Person, die mehrere Personen zugleich ist].

[23] *KFSA* XVIII, p. 159, no. 103 [Das Fragment ist kein Werk, sondern nur Bruchstück ..., Masse, Anlage].

[24] *KFSA* XII, p. 335 [Das eigentlich Widersprechende in unserm Ich ist, daß wir uns zugleich endlich und unendlich fühlen].

[25] *KFSA* XII, p. 381 [mit einem einzigen Blick].

[26] *KFSA* XII, p. 381 [Das endliche Ich findet sich selbst gespalten und getrennt, voller Widersprüche und Unbegreiflichkeiten, kurz als Stückwerk, der *Einheit* vielmehr entgegengesetzt]. Emphasis original.

[27] *KFSA* XII, p. 192 [Lücke im Dasein].

philosophical question which leads within the artistic realm to fragmentary art forms. Diametrically opposed to the aphorism, which provides full knowledge in compressed form, or the maxim, which, often moral in nature, is a concise axiomatic statement, the fragment rather identifies with the above-mentioned 'gap in our existence', as it can only point towards the Absolute, but never represent it. In its individuality, the fragment posits itself against other fragments, which are equally singular in their individuality. In combination with other fragments, each fragment stands on its own, unconnected with the surrounding fragments and opposed to the idea of contributing to a greater unity. Instead, there is a sense of contradiction and overall incoherence which Friedrich Schlegel poignantly expressed by saying: '*Everything contradicts itself* '.[28] But, as Frank explains, an ensemble of fragments does not merely result in a 'boundless multitude of forms', a random assemblage, since that would not enable all fragments to realize a 'true contradiction amongst each other', for 'contradiction can only exist if logically irreconcilable opinions are orientated towards the same position' – namely the Absolute.[29] However, as part of a system whose main principle it is 'to destroy the illusion of finitude'[30] with a 'polemic against consistency',[31] each fragment posits itself against all others in order to assert its difference from these other fragments, and, as a result, posits itself against unity and harmony. Thus, although the fragment is part of a system, this system does not constitute an organic whole; rather, an Early Romantic ensemble or constellation of fragments is devoted to demonstrating that wholeness and unity can never be achieved. Conceptually, we arrive at what Friedrich Schlegel called an 'antithetical synthesis'.[32] Blanchot describes the absence of a core or centre within fragmentary writing as:

the sheer suspense which without restraint breaks the seal of unity by, precisely, not breaking it, but by leaving it aside without this abandon's ever being able to be known. It is thus, inasmuch as it separates itself from the manifest, that fragmentary writing does not belong to the One. And thus, again, it denounces thought as experience (in whatever way this word be taken), no less than thought as the realization of the whole.[33]

Adorno, writing in the same theoretical vein a century after the Early Romantics, considered the fragment as the quintessential artistic form of modernity, and explains in his *Aesthetic Theory* that 'the fragment is that part of a work's totality which opposes it'.[34] What Adorno calls here 'totality' corresponds with what Friedrich Schlegel called 'universality', the fragmentary parts of which do not amount to a synthesis, but which rather contribute to what Schelling called 'asystasy', 'non-consistency' and 'non-unity'.[35] Likewise, Tieck said: 'One of the most unpleasant thoughts is for me

---

[28] *KFSA* XVIII, p. 86, no. 673 [*Alles widerspricht sich*]. Emphasis original.   [29] Frank (1989), p. 300.

[30] *KFSA* XVIII, p. 416, no. 1108 [den Schein des Endlichen zu vernichten].

[31] *KFSA* XVIII, p. 309, no. 1383 [Polemik gegen die Consequenz].

[32] *KFSA* XVIII, p. 82, no. 637 [antisynthetische Synthesis].   [33] Blanchot (1995), p. 61.

[34] Adorno (1993), p. 74 [Das Bruchstück ist der Teil der Totalität des Werkes, welcher ihr widersteht].

[35] Schelling as quoted in Frank (1989), p. 297, from *SW* I/9, p. 209 [Asystasie, Unbestand, Uneinigkeit].

that of coherence',[36] for '*everything contradicts itself*' since 'the form of consciousness is indeed chaotic', as Friedrich Schlegel asserts.[37] Elsewhere, Schlegel speaks of the 'confusion' and 'characterlessness'[38] which make themselves felt in an art work as a result of the Romantic artist's specific disposition: 'Confusion in poetry is actually a very faithful image of life'.[39] Such 'characterlessness'[40] results in the dialogical nature of the art work: 'A dialogue is a chain or garland of fragments. An exchange of letters is a dialogue on a larger scale, and memoirs constitute a system of fragments.'[41]

The Early Romantic art work consisting of fragments could be said to be merely chaotic, and 'chaos' is indeed a term often used by Novalis as well as Schlegel. However, the tendency towards a greater synthesis, towards the Absolute, is always also present, articulating itself as hope and *Sehnsucht*. As Peter Szondi explains:

> The fragment is conceived as 'the subject embryo of a developing object', i.e. as preparation of the longed-for synthesis. Rather than the not-yet-achieved, or what has remained a detached piece, the fragment is perceived as anticipation, promise.[42]

There are thus two qualities to be recognized in the Romantic fragment: on the one hand, it is a separate entity which stands in constant opposition and contradiction to all surrounding fragments. The reason for this lies in the fragment's individuality, its distinct character. On the other hand, all fragments as they appear in 'striking combinations' and 'surprising turns and configurations' do also, as an ensemble, 'reach out ever further beyond themselves'[43] so as to at least indicate the Absolute. Hence, the fragment is a medium for reflection, a segment of an ensemble whose centre lies outside itself. The fragment system or Early Romantic ensemble cannot be seen to form an absolute whole, since it lacks a centre. Here again, the difference from the aphorism becomes clear: whilst the latter contains in compressed form its core and centre, the peripheral extensions of the fragment system make such concentration impossible.[44] In other words, both aphorism and maxim indeed epitomize the idea of totality, whilst the corelessness of the fragment and the counter-positing of extremes within the fragment ensemble prevents such totality from crystallizing:

[36] Quoted in Frank (1989), p. 298 [Einer der widerstrebendsten Gedanken ist für mich der des Zusammenhanges].

[37] *KFSA* XVIII, p. 86, no. 673, and p. 260, no. 1136 [*Alles widerspricht sich* . . . Die Form des Bewußtseins ist durchaus chaotisch]. Emphasis original. Cf. Frank (1989), p. 299.

[38] *KFSA* XVIII, p. 24, no. 66 [Verworrenheit . . . Charakterlosigkeit].

[39] *KFSA* XVIII, p. 198, no. 21 [Die Confusion in der Poesie ist eigentlich ein treues Bild des Lebens].

[40] See Blanchot (1969), p. 524–525.

[41] *Athenaeum*, p. 112 [Ein Dialog ist eine Kette oder ein Kranz von Fragmenten. Ein Briefwechsel ist ein Dialog in vergrößertem Maßstabe, und Memorabilien sind ein System von Fragmentarischen]. Trans. Firchow (1991), p. 27.

[42] Szondi (1978), p. 20.

[43] *KFSA* III, p. 51 [Merkwürdige Kombinationen . . . überraschende Wendungen und Konfigurationen . . . die stets über sich selbst hinausweisen].

[44] See also my detailed critique of Rosen's theoretically and historically mistaken understanding of the Early Romantic concept of the fragment in Part III, pp. 162–177. The equation of the fragment with the aphorism and with the seventeenth-century French concept of the maxim as developed by La Rochefoucauld and La Bruyère undermines Rosen's attempt (1995) to adequately account for and interpret the fragmentary aspects in Schumann's compositions.

'Totality can never be completed', as Friedrich Schlegel emphasized,[45] and the 'alternative' for the Early Romantic is then 'to constantly contradict oneself, and to combine conflicting extremes'.[46] And to simplify in the extreme: whilst both maxim and aphorism are self-sufficient and self-satisfied in their confident claim to reveal an essence as it were in one stroke, and in the most concise and linguistically most efficient way possible, the fragment depends on other fragments in order 'to make its point' – the 'point' being that through its very opposition and otherness, it denies the system, of which it is a vital part, the articulation of an absolute truth. Here, no one part leads into, or grows out of, the other, and hence there develops no organic whole – the archetypal idea of 'the whole is greater than the sum of its parts'. For the fragment system's centre, the ensemble's core, can never even crystallize, since the fragments themselves are essentially decentred. Because fragments are only 'Bruchstücke des Bewußtseins', they are denied the maxim's or aphorism's 'coherence and reason'[47] and thus cannot possibly generate a totality,[48] but instead represent *ex negativo* the 'gap in our existence'. As Novalis says: 'This Absolute which is only negatively perceived, [realizes] itself through an eternal lack'.[49] This irreducible difference inherent in the form of the fragment is part of the 'negative dialectics' of Early Romantic thought. It is further affirmed through the second Romantic category: Romantic irony to which I now shall turn.

[45] *KFSA* XII, p. 166 [Totalität nie vollenedet werden kann].
[46] *KFSA* II, p. 164, no. 26 [Ausweg [ist] sich selbst immer zu widersprechen, und entgegengesetzte Extreme zu verbinden].
[47] *KFSA* XII, p. 393, no. 402 [Zusammenhang und Begründung].
[48] See also Frank (1989), p. 300.
[49] NO II, p. 269, no. 566 [Jenes negativ zu erkennende Absolute [realisiert] sich durch ewigen Mangel].

3

ROMANTIC IRONY

Like the Romantic fragment, the concept of Romantic irony assumes a crucial position within the Early Romantics' theory of communication. Since is was essentially Friedrich Schlegel who invented the Romantic concept of irony, the most important definitions for this concept can be found in the three collections of his work: the *Critical Fragments* (*Kritische Fragmente*) of 1797, the *Athenaeum Fragments* (*Athenaeum Fragmente*) of 1798, and the *Ideas* (*Ideen*) of 1800.[1] Fragment no. 108 of the *Critical Fragments* names the fundamental paradox the Romantics sought to overcome: 'The impossibility and necessity of complete communication'.[2]

Into these rather dead-locked circumstances, the Romantics introduced Romantic irony as a mediator. In order to avoid terminological confusion, it is important to realize first of all that Romantic irony differs distinctly in function and effect from its traditional version as a rhetorical figure of speech. Rather than occurring at a certain point over the course of speech, and often, as with Heine, at the end of a poem for the sake of reversal as well as a humorous effect, Romantic irony negates the whole idea of an end. For Romantic irony does not posit a counter-statement in order to render the preceding statement invalid – the use of counter-statements which characterizes Heine's mode of irony. Instead, Romantic irony tolerates the coexistence of statement and counter-statement and thus becomes an image of 'the truly contradictory nature in our I'.[3] Used without the intention of generating moments of humour, Romantic irony allows for a series, ensemble, or constellation of logically unconnected statements which never come to a conclusion but which, in interaction with each other, generate a sense of agility, non-decidability and 'chaos'. In this sense, Romantic irony ensures that speech remains in a constant flux of signification, without any primacy assigned to any one statement. While rhetorical irony ensures communication through stating an opposite – a procedure that actually clarifies the message – Romantic irony is the affirmation of an intrinsic non-communicability, in philosophy, but even more so in the arts. One of Schlegel's fragments reads thus: 'Irony is the clear consciousness of an eternal agility, of an infinitely abundant chaos'.[4] It becomes clear here that Romantic irony is an attitude

---

[1] See Behler (1993), p. 142.

[2] *KFSA* II, p. 160 [Unmöglichkeit und Notwendigkeit einer vollständigen Mitteilung]. Trans. Behler (1993), p. 148.

[3] *KFSA* XII, p. 334 [das eigentlich Widersprechende in unserm Ich].

[4] *KFSA* II, p. 263 as quoted in Behler (1993), p. 151.

rather than a momentary gesture. As Frank explains, irony reflects the Romantics' awareness that expression, be it artistic or philosophical, is limited in its capacity to represent the Absolute.[5] Since it was the Romantics' belief that the Absolute was essentially unattainable, it was possible to intuit it but not to represent it: hence, the invention of the fragment system, the openness and inconclusiveness of which contains the potential to evoke and allude to the Absolute. However, the Romantic fragment system in its materiality never escapes its fundamental limitedness as far as its capacity to convey the Absolute is concerned. In order to transcend such limitation, the Romantics invented another, higher, and materially absent means of representation: Romantic irony. In the words of Friedrich Schlegel, it is to be seen as a 'mood that surveys everything and rises infinitely above all limitations, even above its own art, virtue, or genius'.[6]

The significance of irony as a general mood, even as a way of life, is expressed in the following passage:

There are ancient and modern poems that are pervaded by the divine breath of irony through-out and informed by a truly transcendental buffoonery. . . . In this sort of irony, everything should be playful and serious, guilelessly open and deeply hidden. It originates in the union of *savoir vivre* and scientific spirit, in the conjunction of a perfectly instinctive and a perfectly conscious philosophy. It contains and arouses a feeling of indissoluble antagonism between the absolute and the relative. . . . It is the freest of all licenses, for by its means one transcends oneself.[7]

This passage vividly illustrates how the Early Romantics regarded all artistic and intellectual activity: they favoured a non-systematic, contradictory mode of thinking for the sake of fully exploring the human mind. In taking Plato as his model of truly creative thinking, Schlegel writes with admiration:

He is never finished with his thought, and this constant further striving of his thought for completed knowledge and the highest cognition, this eternal becoming, forming, and developing of his ideas, he has tried to shape artistically in dialogues.[8]

I already mentioned the term 'dialogue' a little earlier in connection with Novalis' conception of artistic expression and the idea of 'dialogue' is indeed vital for an un-derstanding of the so-called 'chaotic' structure of the works of Early Romanticism. In a mode of writing which oscillates between the conscious and the unconscious, the artist is able to express the real alongside the unreal, the concrete alongside the abstract. It is as though the artist were in conversation with a group of others whose responses, denials, affirmations and doubts become part of a lively, if 'chaotic' debate. Through this process of self-exploration, the artist traverses all possible areas of life, external and internal. Experiences, both conscious and unconscious, thus

---

[5] Frank (1989), p. 360.   [6] *KFSA* XI, p. 120 as quoted in Behler (1993), p. 148.
[7] *KFSA* II, p. 160, as quoted in Behler (1993), p. 149. Emphasis original.
[8] *KFSA* XI, p. 120 as quoted in Behler (1993), p. 147.

constitute the work, where they follow one another in a loosely arranged stream of images.

The corollary to such a concept of loose poetic concatenation is the sense that freedom is at the centre of all artistic endeavour, that the fragmentariness of its configurations renders art as reflecting the Romantic disposition itself to aim for infinity. Friedrich Schlegel spoke of a 'longing for the infinite' (*Sehnsucht nach dem Unendlichen*),[9] and Schleiermacher of the 'feeling of an unsatisfied longing' (*Das Gefühl einer ungestillten Sehnsucht*), and there are many such sentiments to be found in the literature, attesting to the same spirit.[10] Such was the paradoxical thrust to attain what is unattainable that the numerous testimonies to disintegrative structures in art and philosophy extended beyond theoretical boundaries to capture the actualities of Romanticism – or so one could argue.[11] It is indeed only consistent with Schlegel's orphic thesis of 'self-creation' (*Selbstschöpfung*) and 'self-annihilation' (*Selbstvernichtung*),[12] and his view 'that no one can be a good poet without an inflammation of the spirits and a certain touch of madness',[13] that the aspect of benign insanity is prominent among the Early Romantics. An eternal longing for a world never truly believed to come within reach was a charge powerful enough to generate, certainly in the arts, forms of fragmentation, discontinuation and decay. Elation and melancholy, euphoria and self-criticism are symptoms of the same malaise, a mental disposition that longed for paradisiac states. Such orientation leads to the kind of hypertrophic sensibility which characterizes the work of the Romantic artist.

The dynamic polarities of self-creation and self-annihilation are central to Friedrich Schlegel's definition of irony. He describes naive poetry (as opposed to sentimental poetry) as that which 'to the point of irony or the constant alternation of

---

[9] *KFSA* XVIII, p. 418, no. 1168.

[10] Note in this context another of Friedrich Schlegel's descriptions of Romantic irony given in his very last lecture on 'The Philosophy of Language and the Word' (*Philosophie der Sprache und des Wortes*): 'Irony . . . is love's irony. It originates in the feeling of finality and one's own restrictedness, and in the seeming contradiction inherent in this feeling; [it results from that contradiction] that in every true love is included the idea of endlessness' [Die Ironie . . . ist die Ironie der Liebe. Sie entsteht aus dem Gefühl der Endlichkeit und der eignen Beschränkung, und dem scheinbaren Widerspruch dieses Gefühls mit der in jeder wahren Liebe eingeschlossenen Idee des Unendlichen]. See *KFSA* X, p. 357.

[11] This position is most notably taken by McFarland, an authority on English Romantic poetry and literature. Referring often to early German Romantic writers, McFarland's exploration of the fragmentary in Romantic literary works is connected with an emphasis on the fragmentary lives of their creators. In extending his argument beyond the immediate Romantic context, and thereby reaching a somewhat over-generalizing viewpoint, McFarland states: 'Incompleteness, fragmentation, and ruin – the disaparactive triad – are at the very center of life. The phenomenological analysis of existence reveals this with special clarity. Heidegger's twin conception of *Geworfenheit* . . . and *Verfallen* . . . are ineradicable criteria of existence. In truth, the largest contention of this book can be rendered by Heidegger's formulation that "in existence there is a permanent incompleteness [*ständige Unganzheit*], which cannot be evaded". . . . It can accordingly not be surprising that diasparactive forms, which permeate the human situation, should manifest themselves in the lives and achievements of Coleridge and Wordsworth.' See McFarland (1981), p. 5.

[12] *KFSA* II, pp. 149, 151, 172 and 217.

[13] *KFSA* I, p. 405 [daß niemand ein guter Dichter sein könne, ohne eine Entzündung der Lebensgeister und einen gewissen Anhauch von Raserei].

self-creation and self-annihilation is natural, individual or classic' or as 'the beautiful, individual, idealistic Naive which is at once intention and instinct'.[14] Here, artistic creation is described as a state of ecstasy: it is at once intentional, consciously perceived and controlled, as well as involuntary, inescapable, natural and a sign of genius. Irony as the essential criterion for a poetic work is thus the perpetual alternation of outer and inner forces, of objective and subjective, conscious and unconscious. By means of irony, since its function is that of a constant critique, the artist-as-genius rises above reality and beyond the restrictedness of each work. The work is thus imbued with contrasting expressions which remain structurally independent. Of necessity this goes against the idea of a unified and coherent whole. It can instead be seen to reflect a succession of associated thoughts or a 'series of ideas' (*Ideenreihe*). The atmosphere of an ever-changing series of images, and an overall notion of flux (*Wechsel*) is thus what signifies a truly poetic work of art in the Romantic aesthetics. It follows that the moment of poetic reflection – the ironic interplay of productive action and destructive reaction – is the moment of transcendence. The element of critique, meta-critique and self-reflection is thus an integral part of every new creation.

All these elements – Romantic irony, forms of fragmentation, distance and difference, reflection and transcendence – are what signify a truly poetic work of a naive and 'ingenious' mind. One of the *Athenaeum* fragments draws together these various trains of theoretical thought:

Intention taken to the point of irony and accomplished by the arbitrary illusion of self-destruction is as naive as the instinct that takes [everything] to the point of irony. Just as the Naive plays with the contradictions between theory and practice, so the grotesque plays with the wondrous permutations of form and matter, loves the illusion of the coincidental and the strange and, as it were, flirts with infinite arbitrariness. *Humour* is to do with being and not-being, and its true essence is reflection. Hence its closeness to the elegy and to everything transcendental; hence also its arrogance and its tendency towards the mysticism of wit. Just as genius is necessary for naiveté, so too earnest, pure beauty is a requisite of Humour. Most of all *Humour* likes to hover over the gently and clearly flowing rhapsodies of philosophy or of poetry, and abhors cumbersome masses and disconnected parts.[15]

It is also worth noting that Novalis characterized poetry as an 'art that stirs the soul' (*Gemütserregungskunst*) and as 'inner *painting* and music' able to generate 'inner *moods*

---

[14] *KFSA* II, pp. 172–173 [was bis zur Ironie oder bis zum steten Wechsel von Selbstschöpfung und Selbstvernichtung natürlich, individuell oder klassisch ist . . . was schön, individuell, idealistisch Naive ist, Absicht und Instinkt zugleich].

[15] *Athenaeum*, p. 158 [Absicht bis zur Ironie und mit willkürlichem Schein von Selbstvernichtung ist ebensowohl naiv als Instinkt bis zur Ironie. Wie das Naive mit den Widersprüchen der Theorie und der Praxis, so spielt das Groteske mit wunderlichen Versetzungen von Form und Materie, liebt den Schein des Zufälligen und Seltsamen und kokettiert gleichsam mit unbedingter Willkür. Humor hat es mit Sein und Nichtsein zu tun, und sein eigentliches Wesen ist Reflexion. Daher seine Verwandtschaft mit der Elegie und allem, was transzendental ist; daher auch sein Hochmut und sein Hang zur Mystik des Witzes. Wie Genialität dem Naiven, so ist ernste reine Schönheit dem Humor notwendig. Er schwebt am liebsten über leicht und klar strömende Rhapsodien der Philosophie oder der Poesie und flieht schwerfällige Massen und abgerißne Bruchstücke].

and paintings or visions ... – perhaps also *spiritual* dances'.[16] During the creative process, the poet uses 'objects and words like the *keys* [of a keyboard] and all poetry rests on the active association of ideas – on an autonomous, deliberate, idealistic *production of coincidence*'.[17] It is only a logical consequence that both form and content of such works would be fragmentary:

Novels, without coherence, but with associations, like *dreams*. Poems – merely *melodious* and replete with beautiful words – but yet without meaning and coherence – at most, single comprehensible stanzas – they must be like broken bits of the most diverse things. True Poetry can have only an *allegorical* meaning of a general kind and only an indirect effect, like music etc.[18]

Insofar as feeling is something singular, broken off, and transient, similar to only one single sound which, however, comes from very deep inside and which is therefore something very special indeed, in that sense lyric poetry is fragmentary, objective, and individual.[19]

Romantic irony is capable of communicating, or mediating, this 'sound from very deep inside', for it does not unite statements of truth, but rather conveys the possibility of, and *Sehnsucht* for, a 'yet-to-be-revealed' truth to exist. In this sense Romantic irony is the guardian of continuity for any potentially meaningful encounter. At its most extreme, Romantic irony allows for polymorphous, polyvalent and fractional diction. As a mode of writing, it does the contradictory nature of our thinking justice insofar as it makes room for the endless interplay of statement and counter-statement, primary and secondary thought, aligned and disconnected ideas. In ironically broken speech, the presence of what has been said is as significant as the force exerted by what has remained unsaid. Fulfilled moments and moments of silence are of equal value in the light of Romantic irony.

What are the contemporary implications of these poetic procedures of Early Romanticism? In its function as a constant contradictor, Romantic irony denies the art work as fiction a fixed and finite meaning, thereby highlighting the illusory character of whatever may be total communication. As a method used in order to counteract a compulsion for absolute statements, Romantic irony is like a palliative against the mania of total communication. It is that element of resistance inside language which works against the deceptions of illusion, against the analogy between signifier and signified. It is, therefore, the critical reminder that language

[16] NO III, p. 639 [innere *Malerei* und Musik ... innre *Stimmungen*, und Gemälde oder *Anschauungen* ... – vielleicht auch *geistige* Tänze]. Emphasis original.

[17] NO III, p. 451 [die Dinge und Worte, wie *Tasten* und die ganze Poesie beruht auf tätiger Ideenassoziation – auf selbsttätiger, absichtlicher, idealischer *Zufallsproduktion*]. Emphasis original.

[18] NO III, p. 572 [Erzählungen, ohne Zusammenhang, jedoch mit Assoziationen, wie *Träume*. Gedichte – bloß *wohlklingend* und voll schöner Worte – aber auch ohne Sinn und Zusammenhang – höchstens einzelne Strophen verständlich – sie müssen wie lauter Bruchstücke aus den verschiedensten Dingen sein. Höchstens kann wahre Poesie nur einen *allegorischen* Sinn im großen haben und eine indirekte Wirkung wie Musik etc. tun]. Emphasis original.

[19] *KFSA* XI, p. 67 [Insofern nun aber das Gefühl etwas Einzelnes, Abgerissenes, Vorrübergehendes, gleichsam nur ein einzelner Laut ist, der indessen sehr tief aus dem Innern kommt und etwas durchaus ganz eigentümliches ist, insofern ist die Lyrik fragmentarisch, objectiv und individuell].

finally cannot ground itself. In this modern scenario, Romantic irony becomes a supremely liberating force. Indeed, the Early Romantics owe it to the concept of Romantic irony that, in an enthusiastic, indeed euphoric vein, a vast body of material could be produced. Irony confirms – but in an infinitely delicate, self-effacing manner – that the seemingly tightly woven fabric of images is, in fact, permeable. Irony may thus occasionally pass through it, and stir things up again. It makes all images swirl into the air and reassemble anew.

One could also think of Romantic irony as the third element in a Hegelian chain of signs. Signs, chained together, are engaged in a constant battle for primacy in signification. In this constant battle, irony opens up new prospects of signification. This is never, however, more than a momentary intervention – a glimpse of hope – which manages to untangle the wrestling signs, like two dialectical combatants, in order to expose the Master as the Slave of the Slave.

Frank suggests that this lack of a clear message is equivalent to Derrida's term *'signifié transcendental'*.[20] Since the Romantic work of art as an ensemble of fragmentary images or statements always evokes, but never names, the Absolute, it consists of many 'hints of the infinite'[21] whereby the work becomes 'inexhaustible',[22] and moreover 'all-meaningful', as Novalis said.[23] The Early Romantics' 'romanticization' of the text, so Frank explains, opens up what Schlegel called 'breakaways', 'vistas' or 'glimpses into the infinite'.[24] This is the central criterion of what modernism was then to call the 'endless text' and what led Blanchot to call a book *L'Entretien Infini* – the basis of which is firmly established in the Romantic theory of communication of 1800.

THE EARLY ROMANTICS' CONCEPT OF WORK AND AUTHOR

The new aesthetic principles of Early Romanticism radically revised the Classical mode of expression and communication whereby the concepts of work and author underwent major restructuring. First, the centre of the work – an ensemble of fragments – is absent. The statement, although anticipated, remains unstated. It is, however, made palpable, namely in its very withdrawal, which lies at the heart of the Early Romantic idea of *Sehnsucht*. Second, the fragmentary art work is not autonomous; it is part of an endless stream of voices and counter-voices which intensify, cross, contradict and double each other ironically. Third, the work does not embody the author, nor are there to be found any confessions of personal moods and convictions. These would be better conceived as mere material for Romantic play and chaos into which Romantic irony enters in order to challenge the flux of intention and realization, absence and presence, light and darkness, meaning and vacuity. The

---

[20] Quoted in Frank (1989), p. 365.
[21] *KFSA* XVIII, p. 128, no. 76 [Hindeutungen auf das Unendliche].
[22] NO III, p. 64, no. 603 [unerschöpflich].   [23] NO II, p. 620, no. 402 [alldeutig].
[24] *KFSA* II, p. 200, no. 220 [échappées de vue ins Unendliche].

author is, similar to this ironic inflection, at a distance to all fragments, him- or herself taking an ironic look at their fascinating combinations and transfigurations. What Blanchot once said with regard to literature can thus be transferred to the Romantics' novel concept of how work and author relate:

From this nothing less follows than that literature, beginning to manifest itself thanks to the Romantic declaration, will from now on carry this question – discontinuity or difference as form – within itself. This is a question and task which German Romanticism, and in particular that of the *Athenaeum*, not only divined, but already clearly proposed before it entrusted this question to Nietzsche, and beyond Nietzsche into the hands of the future.[25]

[25] Blanchot (1969), p. 527 [Il n'en reste pas moins que, commençant de se rendre manifeste à elle-même grâce à la déclaration romantique, la littérature va désormais porter en elle cette question – la discontinuité ou la différence comme forme –, question et tâche que le romantisme allemand et en particulier celui de l'*Athenaeum* a non seulement pressenties, mais déjà clairement proposées, avant de les remettre à Nietzsche et, au-delà de Nietzsche, à l'avenir].

4

REFLECTION, LANGUAGE AND MUSIC

The Romantics' speculation on language, both literary and poetic, extended to a general reconsideration of all forms of art. The plastic and visual arts were set against literature, poetry and music within this discussion. The central question was to discover those means in art which are able to 'represent the Unrepresentable' and to evoke the Infinite. Music attained an exceptional status within this highly differentiated discourse because it was conceived of as a system of signs, yet as more abstract than that of poetic language. In the Romantics' perception of language, the idea of a correspondence between signifier and signified had loosened to such a degree that words no longer necessarily referred either to objects or to concepts. This idea was believed to be fully realized in the case of music. In view of its infinite combinatorial possibilities, the musical sign was seen to exceed the word as the 'acoustic configuration of thoughts',[1] for words themselves had become sounds, incomprehensible like a foreign language, like 'Sanskrit . . . which speaks in order to speak, because speaking is its joy and its essence'.[2] This is the basis of a *poésie pure* and of what Foucault, with Nietzsche in mind, calls the definite crossing of 'the threshold between Classicism and modernity':

when words cease to intersect with representations and to provide a spontaneous grid for the knowledge of things. At the beginning of the nineteenth century they rediscovered their ancient enigmatic clarity.[3]

For the Jena Romantics, the autonomy of words, and the resulting sense of freedom as to 'the knowledge of things', was seen to be transcended by the musical system. The Early Romantics believed that no prescribed and generally valid code existed for defining the meaning of any one tone or sound in a piece of music. The musical sign established its function within its own system only. The aspect of such self-referentiality within the musical system, its autonomy, lay at the heart of the

---

[1] Novalis (1962), p. 498. [2] Novalis (1962), p. 105.

[3] Foucault (1970), pp. 128–129. Foucault, although regarding the Romantics' idea of language as the basis for future literary developments, locates the emergence of a language totally freed of signification considerably later than say, 1798, and ultimately at the moment of the 'Nietzschean question "Who is speaking" to which Mallarmé replies – and constantly reverts to that reply – by saying that what is speaking is, in its solitude, in its fragile vibration, in its nothingness, the word itself – not the meaning of the word but its enigmatic and precarious being.' See Foucault (1970), p. 305.

Romantic conception of music and was the very reason for it subsequently being considered the highest form of art.

Another important aspect of the Early Romantics' conception of art and music is their use of a particular terminology which is, thanks to their literary-philosophical rather than technical approach to the subject, replete with poetic, that is metaphorical, speech. Paying attention to a number of expressions found in Schumann's writings on music sensitizes us to certain linguistic idiosyncrasies shared by both[4] and shows Schumann's intellectual affinity with the Early Romantic way of thinking. A brief review of the development and formation of the Early Romantics' aesthetic of music[5] will establish the theoretical backdrop against which a discussion can take place on 'absolute' versus music involving language on the one hand, and Schumann's new concept of the Lied on the other.

The major change in the relationship between words and the world occurred in the late 1700s and early 1800s. Although this dramatic shift coincided with a perceived loss of normative beliefs, of which the French Revolution was a major cause, it was also connected to other related factors which were reflected in the developments of philosophical and religious thought. The key figures of post-Kantian German philosophy – Fichte, Schelling and Hegel – posited in their return to the idea of an absolute subject the source not of a finite (as in Kant) but an infinite cognition (*Erkenntnis*). The gradual abandonment of the doctrine of salvation allowed this assumption to reach its peak: subjectivity was seen as the Absolute itself, the immanent core of the empirical world, of nature, mind and history. From here follows the Early Romantics' fundamental doubt about both the personality and the transcendence of God, which resulted in a new pantheistic metaphysic in close proximity to an atheistic attitude. 'Art raises its head where religions decline', Nietzsche concludes with almost a century of hindsight.[6]

Subjectivity has to be seen, of course, as the central axis for all areas of Early Romantic thought and around which rotates a universe other than reality. 'The mysterious path leads to the inner [within the I]. Eternity is in ourselves or nowhere with its worlds, the past and future',[7] Novalis famously claims when he articulates his generation's reaction to the era's fundamental political and social dislocations, his creed amounting to the almost biblical formulation: 'We shall enjoy more than ever before, for our mind [*Geist*] had been deprived'.[8] This radical move away from immediately experienced external stimuli and the equally radical pursuit of

---

[4] For example Schumann's apologia of a 'new poetic time' in music where he expected the composer to be as much a poet as a musician, and of music that it must always be poetic. The Romantics' concept of 'poetic time' as 'encompassing the future and the present' is a frequent theme in Schumann's writings. So are the Romantics' concepts of irony and wit, contrast and association. See pp. 47–67, below.

[5] Partly based on Frank (1989) and Bowie (1990).

[6] Nietzsche 1878/79 in *Menschliches und Allzumenschliches* [Die Kunst erhebt ihr Haupt, wo Religionen nachlassen] as quoted in Thalmann (1967), p. 26.

[7] *Athenaeum*, p. 52 [Nach Innen geht der geheimnisvolle Weg. In uns oder nirgens ist die Ewigkeit mit ihren Welten, die Vergangenheit und Zukunft].

[8] *Athenaeum*, p. 52 [Wir werden mehr genießen als je, denn unser Geist hat entbehrt].

solutions in the realm of ideas constitutes the basis of an art whose language is the 'imprint of the human mind [*Geist*]'.[9] Truth was no longer seen in God, nor was any God-given truth perceived to reign in nature. In a world increasingly secularized by industrialization and materialism, truth had to come from within.

The main impulse for such exclusive concentration on the Self came from Fichte. In the first version of the *Wissenschaftslehre* of 1794, Fichte developed to the fullest extent the philosophical question of self-consciousness and of reflective thinking. With reflection as its central theme, Fichte's subjective philosophy was enthusiastically received by the two most literary and artistically orientated poet–philosophers of the movement, Friedrich Schlegel and Novalis, who would 'sit together for a few days and philosophize, or as we used to call it – fichtisize!'[10] As Walter Benjamin demonstrates, the Romantics saw in Fichte's thesis of 'thinking about thinking' (*Denken des Denkens*) the proof of the 'intuitive character' of the nature of reflective thinking.[11] Benjamin's discussion of Fichte's concept of reflection brings forward with singular precision the principal characteristic of this celebration of introspection:

Reflection is thus . . . to be understood as the transforming – and nothing else but the transforming – [act of] reflection upon a form.[12]

As Benjamin shows *in extenso*, however, the Romantics modified Fichte's conception of reflection. While for Fichte reflective thinking had no interest other than the interest in itself, and was therefore restricted to its own philosophical medium, thereby attaining an absolute position as a purely intellectual activity, the Early Romantics discovered the Absolute in art.[13] Novalis' engagement with Fichte resulted in the attempt to develop further the proposed theory of imagination within philosophical thinking so as to encompass artistic procedures. For Novalis the poet, it was essential that Fichte's idea of the auto-activity of the mind (*Selbsttätigkeit des Geistes*) could be applied to artistic creation which would include all aspects of life. Rather than remaining within the precincts of pure philosophy, Novalis sought to include the 'curious' and 'special' as it occurred in life and in the mind. He thus drew art into philosophy by giving the artist's self-reflective imagination the greatest status, above that of the philosopher, and arrived at the maxim: 'Spinoza ascended to nature – Fichte to the I, or the person. I ascend to the thesis of God.'[14]

---

[9] A. W. Schlegel (1964) II, p. 226 [Die Sprache ist der Abdruck des menschlichen Geistes, der darin die Entstehung und die Verwandschaft seiner Vorstellungen und den ganzen Mechanismus seiner Operationen niederlegt].

[10] *KFSA* XXIII, p. 363 [beisammen sitzen . . . ein paar Tage und philosophierten, oder wie wir es nannten – fichtisierten!]. See Behler (1992), pp. 55–57, for a more detailed account of Schlegel's and Novalis' reception of Fichte's philosophy.

[11] Benjamin (1973), pp. 14–35 (here 15) [Vielmehr haben die Romantiker in der reflektierenden Natur des Denkens eine Bürgschaft für dessen intuitiven Charakter gesehen].

[12] Benjamin (1973), p. 16 [Es wird also unter Reflexion das umformende – und nichts als umformende – Reflektieren auf eine Form verstanden].

[13] Benjamin (1973), pp. 25 and 29–35.

[14] Quoted in Behler (1992), p. 56 [Spinoza stieg bis zur Natur – Fichte bis zum Ich, oder der Person. Ich bis zur These Gott].

As a result of this rejection of nature and society as the source of truth, the Classical principle of mimesis came to be seen as an inadequate means to reveal what was believed to reign internally. In this sense one can speak of the replacement of world and nature with art, the artistic and indeed the artificial. The emphasis shifted to production itself, to *poiesis*. Yet, signs and symbols still do not '*make* a world' – an attractive, but over-enthusiastic assumption occasionally found in the critical literature on Early Romantic theory and literature.[15] Although there can hardly be any doubt as regards the utopian character of the Early Romantics' aspirations (' – America is right here or nowhere – '),[16] Frank points out that Novalis himself cautioned us against the fallacy of confusing 'the symbol with the symbolized', of a mistaken 'identification' and 'confusion of subject and object'.[17] The notion of truth entails even in its most basic sense the character of anticipation and hope, of longing and desire (*Sehnen* and *Verlangen*). A Novalis fragment from a collection significantly entitled *Faith and Love* makes this defining condition for poetic production quite clear:

All [poetic] representation rests on the Making Present – of what is not present and so forth – (the magic power of *fiction*). My faith and love rests upon Representative Faith. Hence the assumption – eternal peace is already here – God is amongst us . . . – the Golden Age is here – we are magicians – we are moral and so forth.[18]

The Romantics' abandonment of the doctrine of mimesis coincides with their discovery of the potential of language to evoke a world that is non-existent in objective, that is material or natural terms. Aiming at the Beyond, the language of art thus distanced itself from nature in its search for truth/beauty. The historical point of departure was Kant. In the *Critique of Judgement*, Kant seems to conceive of the Beautiful as a form derived from both nature and art. In Frank's careful reading of the relevant passages,[19] it appears to be the case, however, that Kant did in fact prefer natural beauty over its artistically achieved form.[20] Re-evaluating Kant, Schelling in the *Philosophy of Art* of 1802/03 then proposed the opposite: it is not the beauty of nature but the beauty of art that is found superior because – and this is the decisive step towards a truly Romantic aesthetic – art has its origin in the human mind. In its reach beyond nature, art offers us the *potential* of ideas.[21] Schelling ends his chapter on art forms with the assertion that music, as part of 'the Real' (*das Reelle*), does not 'compete' with nature since it is not orientated towards 'the things themselves but only their forms or eternal essences'.[22] On a higher level of truth, music is purified

---

[15] See Thalmann, for example, who asserts 'a reality is being created' [eine Realität wird gemacht]. See Thalmann (1967), pp. 19–21 (here 19).

[16] NO III, p. 421, no. 782 [– hier ist Amerika oder Niergens –].

[17] NO III, p. 397, no. 685 [Verwechslung des Symbols mit dem Symbolisierten . . . Identificierung . . . Verwechslung von Subject und Object]. See Frank (1989), pp. 312–314.

[18] NO III, p. 421, no. 782 [Die ganze [dichterische] Repraesentation beruht auf einem Gegenwärtig machen – des Nicht Gegenwärtigen und so fort – (Wunderkraft der *Fiktion*.) Mein Glaube und Liebe beruht auf Repraesentativem Glauben. So die Annahme – der ewige Frieden ist schon da – Gott ist unter uns . . . – das goldene Zeitalter ist hier – wir sind Zauberer – wir sind moralisch und so fort]. Emphasis original.

[19] *KdU* B, §42, B 167.   [20] Frank (1989), p. 217.   [21] *SW* I/3, p. 622, n. 1.

[22] *SW* I/3, p. 501 [nicht auf die Dinge selbst, sondern nur auf ihre Formen oder ewigen Wesenheiten].

of the material appearance of nature and, appearing as the 'form of the movements of the celestial bodies', music communicates the 'imperceptible harmonies of the spheres'.[23] Two passages in Schelling's *Philosophy of Art* underline what was a central concern for the Jena Romantics: the sublimation of the sensual in the spiritual. First, Schelling's interpretation of the Platonic idea of music:

Socrates says in Plato: That person is a musician who proceeds from sensually perceived harmonies to the non-sensual, the intelligible and *their* proportions.[24]

If the formulation 'proportions' in this context could be interpreted as implying the notion of the symbolic as a form of abstraction of real objects and sensations, another passage brings out more clearly the idea that, in music, the material is '*pure movement*':

Music is the kind of art which . . . sheds the external in that it presents *pure* movement itself; freed from the object [i.e. the material], it [music] is carried on invisible, almost spiritual wings.[25]

Schelling concludes that music is the 'most introverted of all art forms' and – within the spiritual realm of the arts – 'the most boundless of all art forms'.[26] The exploration of the unlimited internal, as opposed to the objective and restricted external, world is the main reason for Schelling's positive evaluation of the expressive potential of music.

A preoccupation with the internal was indeed what demarcated two modern aesthetic positions: one relying on the objectivity of Reason (Hegel); the other finding truth in the inscrutable workings of the Irrational (Schelling). Seen in the light of what may be called the 'absolutist' position of the Early Romantics, Hegel's conception of music, which he put forward in his lectures on aesthetics in Jena in 1822–24, reveals this subtle but crucial difference.[27] Although his conception of music overlaps with that of Schelling, his evaluation differs distinctly. Hegel says:

Subjective inwardness constitutes the principle of music. But the most inward part of the concrete self is subjectivity as such, not determined by any firm content and for this reason not compelled to move in this or that direction, rather resting in unbounded freedom solely upon itself.[28]

---

[23] This is Frank's term, which he derives from Schelling's reference to Plato. The Pythagorean idea of the imperceptible movements of the planets refers to those deafened by life's labour who no longer perceive the chords and sounds of such heavenly music. See Frank (1989), p. 219, n. 1.

[24] *SW* I/5, p. 503 [Sokrates bei Platon sagt: Derjenige ist der Musiker, der von den sinnlich vernommenen Harmonien forschreitend zu den unsinnlichen, intelligibeln und *ihren* Proportionen]. Emphasis original.

[25] *SW* I/5, p. 501 [Die Musik ist insofern diejenige Kunst, die . . . am meisten das Körperliche abstreift, indem sie die *reine* Bewegung selbst als solche, von dem Gegenstand abgezogen, vorstellt und von unsichtbaren, fast geistigen Flügeln getragen wird]. Emphasis original.

[26] *SW* I/5, p. 504 [die verschlossenste aller Künste] and [die grenzenloseste aller Künste].

[27] What is generally known to be Hegel's *Aesthetics* (*Ästhetik*) is a transcription of these lectures based on Hegel's posthumous works by H. G. Hotho, first published in 1835 as *Vorlesungen über die Ästhetik*.

[28] Hegel (1965) II, p. 320 as quoted in Bowie (1990), p. 180.

Subjectivity, in Hegel's thinking, can be articulated only by reference to objects, themselves definable only by conceptual language. Music escapes any reference to objects by virtue of its transitory nature and is thus, as a fleeting phenomenon, unable to articulate conceptual ideas. For Hegel, therefore, music rests 'in unbounded freedom solely upon itself'. Although pursuing the same train of thought, Schelling regarded such freedom from conceptual signification in music as its highest value. He also considered the non-referential mode of expression to be present only in music, for the musical system worked upon its own laws – music turning inside itself, as it were. While the modern reader, in a post-structuralist era, may have little difficulty in understanding the possibility at least of a view of art as strictly self-referential, as 'signifying' rather than 'meaning', it is important to recognize that in Romantic thought, above all perhaps in reaction to Hegel, this turned music aesthetics into an area of problems rather than solutions. Hegel adopts an essentially Rationalist position:

In attempting to grasp the meaning [the listener] is faced with puzzling tasks which rush quickly past, which are not always amenable to being deciphered and are capable in fact of the most various interpretations.[29]

In Hegel's view, it is the transitory nature of music which undermines the possibility of conceptualizing (literally: coming to terms with the music's meaning) through reflection; instead, this transitoriness results in a random multifariousness of interpretation. It should be remembered that reflection was never seen as a goal-orientated activity by the Early Romantics. On the contrary, it was seen as an end in itself. The transitory nature of reflection, due to the progressive flow of ideas and emotions, was seen as a liberating element, precisely because it led away from the restriction to concepts. In this sense, music obviously pertains to the Romantics' concept of reflection. The inherent indeterminacy and ambiguity of music, criticized by Hegel, was perceived by the Early Romantics as its particular and unique value. Bowie remarks correctly that 'Adorno's objections to Hegel's suppression of the "non-identical" in art derive not least from Hegel's failure to see more in the problem of understanding music than a deficit on the part of music itself'.[30]

Hegel's negative evaluation of music becomes most apparent when seen in comparison with other art forms. The plastic arts, Hegel reasons, 'take up the forms of a broad, multiple world of object into themselves' whilst music – 'introverted' as Schelling said – is 'completely abstract'.[31] *Abstract* is the keyword here, for it implies the absence of objects and thus also of concepts. Hegel's preference for music accompanied by a text has its root in this, for it 'gives certain ideas and thereby tears away from that more dreamy element of feeling without ideas'.[32] When Bowie explains that 'feeling [*Gefühl*] was the technical term in Fichte, Novalis and Schleiermacher

---

[29] Hegel (1965) II, p. 320 as quoted in Bowie (1990), p. 181.   [30] Bowie (1990), p. 181.
[31] Hegel (1965) II, p. 261 as quoted in Bowie (1990), p. 182.
[32] Hegel (1965) II, p. 306 as quoted in Bowie (1990), p. 182.

for the pre-reflexive spontaneity of the I',[33] the crucial point lies in the Romantics'
proposition that the spontaneous flow of ideas and feelings originates in the realm
of the unconscious (that which Hegel called the 'dreamy', and to which he ob-
jected) – that is, distinct from an objective world. Operating by its own inscrutable
laws, the unconscious establishes its own system, like music, via reference within
itself. 'Feeling is something singular, broken off, and transient, similar to one sound
only which, however, comes from very deep inside and which is therefore something very special indeed',[34] as Friedrich Schlegel said, carefully avoiding any further
elucidation, for the 'inside' is no longer within the reach of reflection. Thus, the
form these pre-reflexive 'series of ideas' takes is abstract. In this sense, music was
seen by the Romantics as a 'language above language', a means to represent the
Unrepresentable.[35] In this sense, also, the Romantics' conception of music includes
an argument for the thesis that thinking is possible without language:

Here it comes about that one thinks thoughts without that cumbersome detour of words;
here, feeling, imagination and the powers of thinking are one.[36]

---

[33] Bowie (1990), p. 182.   [34] *KFSA* XI, p. 61. See p. 37, above.   [35] Dahlhaus (1978), p. 107.

[36] Wackenroder (1938), in the second part of the *Phantasien über die Kunst*, p. 250 [Es geschieht hier, daß man
Gedanken ohne jenen mühsamen Umweg der Worte denkt, hier ist Gefühl, Phantasie und Kraft des Denkens
eins].

5

THEORIES OF SONG: SCHUMANN'S 'HIGHER SPHERE OF ART'

As I said earlier, Romantic aesthetics sought to systematize the genres of art. At the heart of this enterprise was the question of music and poetry. Initially, the literary-philosophical discourse of the Jena Romantics focused on lyric poetry on the one hand, and 'absolute' (instrumental) music on the other. But efforts such as Clemens Brentano's and Achim von Arnim's collection of hundreds of folk-songs in *Des Knaben Wunderhorn* of 1805 contributed to the increasing interest in Lied composition among composers at the beginning of the nineteenth century. Philosophers as well as music theorists then tried to define the nature of the Lied where music and poetry necessarily interact. The following overview of the main theoretical positions in early nineteenth-century Germany[1] indicates the criteria according to which the Lied was generally conceived, and the gradual formation of the concept of the German Romantic art song. Schumann's thoughts on the matter show him seeking new forms of expression through the Lied, contemplating the setting of words as a 'poetry of song'.

Heinrich Koch may conveniently be taken as a starting-point for the theoretical discussion on the Lied. In 1802, in a general encyclopaedia of music, he explains under the heading 'Lied':

A Lied is essentially any lyrical poem of several strophes which is intended to be sung, and which has a melody that will be repeated with every strophe, and which has the property of being able to be sung by any person who is equipped with healthy and not entirely inflexible singing-organs, and that can be sung without prior artistic training.[2]

Significantly, Koch regarded the Lied as a literary genre. The strophic structure of the poem determines the melody, which is repeated according to the number of poetic strophes. The association with the literary folk-song becomes obvious when

[1] Dürr (1984) provides an excellent historical account of the Lied, which I have consulted for much of my own discussion of the topic.

[2] Koch in the *Musikalisches Lexikon welches die theoretische und praktische Tonkunst, encyclopädisch bearbeitet, alle alten und neuen Kunstwörter erklärt, und die alten und neuen Instrumente beschrieben, enthält* of 1802 [Als Lied bezeichnet man überhaupt jedes lyrische Gedicht von mehreren Strophen, welches zum Gesang bestimmt, und mit einer solchen Melodie verbunden ist, die bey jeder Strophe wiederholt wird, und die zugleich die Eigenschaft hat, daß sie von jedem Menschen, der gesunde und nicht ganz unbiegsame Gesangsorgane besitzt, vorgetragen werden kann]. Quoted in Dürr (1984), p. 8.

Koch emphasizes the Lied's compositional simplicity, which is essential if it is to be sung by an amateur. If the congruence of outer form between text and music was here the focus, and the superiority of text over music was implicit, an article written four decades later demonstrates a significantly different approach. In a music encyclopaedia first published in 1831, the authors Schilling and Nauenburg, under the entry 'Lied', call attention to the primary importance of the 'inner poetic character' of the Lied as 'an imperative result' of the character of the poetry. Noting that 'it is indeed very difficult to determine the true inner and outer character of the Lied, in fact almost impossible' due to the 'hitherto very imprecise use of the word Lied as the name for a genuinely distinct kind of poetic and musical composition',[3] their emphasis on the Lied's dependency on the poetry as the vital factor for its 'inner poetic character' indicates an interest in aspects beyond formal outline. Proceeding from Koch's acknowledgement that the song was 'an important artistic product of the unity of poetry and music',[4] Schilling and Nauenburg continue:

> In order to establish at least to some degree a precise criterion for the musical fabric, the composition of the Lied, it is necessary first of all to examine its inner, poetic character, since the two, music and poetry, are more fused than in almost any other substantial kind of vocal music; the whole genre [of the Lied] is in a certain sense a secondary result of the character [of poetry].[5]

Despite this early mention of inner poetic substance, that is, a semantic and emotive element informing the song, and as such wholly dependent upon the poem, Schilling's and Nauenburg's technical discussion adds nothing new to the traditional conception of a simple melody shadowing the strophic structure of the poem.[6] This essentially formalist theory of the Lied, extending to its so-called 'through-composed' version, can be found in a number of sources.[7] As Dürr points out, behind this conception of a unified strophic Lied structure lies the assumption that a poem contains one emotion which must be rendered musically without any deviation. Schilling and Nauenburg emphasize that the Lied is:

---

[3] In the *Encyclopädie der gesammten musikalischen Wissenschaften, oder Universal-Lexicon der Tonkunst*, 2nd edn of 1841 [Den eigentlichen inneren und äußeren Charakter eines Liedes genügend zu bezeichnen, ist in der That schwer, ja fast ganz unmöglich, und hauptsächlich wegen des bisherigen sehr unbestimmten Gebrauchs des Wortes Lied als Namen einer eigenen Dichtungs- und Compositionsart]. Quoted in Dürr (1984), p. 9.

[4] See Koch (n. 2 above) [ein wichtiges Kunstprodukt der vereinten Poesie und Musik].

[5] [Um jedoch für das musikal. Gewand, die Composition des Liedes, einen nur einigermaßen bestimmten Maßstab aufzustellen, ist es nothwendig, seinen inneren, poetischen Charakter zuvor zu untersuchen, da Beides, Musik und Dichtung, hier so in und mit einander verschmolzen ist, wie fast bei keiner anderen namhaften Vocalmusik, und aus dem Charakter dieser die ganze Gattung jener gewissermaßen als eine unabweisliche Folge hervorgeht]. Quoted in Dürr (1984), p. 9.

[6] 'The song', Koch says, 'is always divided into identical verses and strophes so that it can be sung according to one and the same melody' [Das Lied ist stets in gleiche Verse und Strophen abgetheilt, so daß es nach ein und derselben Melodie gesungen werden kann].

[7] See further evidence in several historical accounts of the Lied in Dürr (1984), pp. 10–11.

a lyrical genre of poetry whose character rests on *one* feeling only which gently moves the soul.... Owing to the fact that emotion is in harmony with itself in the Lied, [the Lied] differs from the ode.[8]

Hegel, in his lectures on aesthetics held in the early 1800s, takes a similar stance:

A song, although it may contain as a poem and a text in itself a wealth of variously nuanced moods, intuitions and ideas, has nonetheless usually this one basic sentiment of one and the same penetrating feeling; it therefore strikes above all just *one single* emotional chord. To convey and reproduce it brings about the chief affect of such Lied melodies.[9]

More than a century later Arnold Schoenberg was to voice his experience of setting poetry to music along Hegelian lines, that is, sharing the conviction that a poem has 'this one basic sentiment of one and the same penetrating feeling'. His essay 'The Relationship to the Text' carries a distinctly combative tone. It was first published in 1912 in Franz Marc's and Kandinsky's journal *Der blaue Reiter*, and Schoenberg's main objective was to defend the aesthetic value of nonconceptual art (such as the expressionist paintings by members of the group *Der Blaue Reiter*) which music, so Schoenberg implies, has always been. Moreover, music outstrips poetry for 'so direct, unpolluted and pure a mode of expression is denied to poetry, an art still bound to subject matter'.[10] The potential of art thus depends, so Schoenberg claims, on the artist's pursuit of an immaterial mode of expression. It follows that the development of music, having reached a certain level of complexity, is rooted in its independence from the often assumed correspondence of musical content with what Schoenberg calls a 'material-subject' (*Stoffliches*), that is, an object. Invoking Schopenhauer's 'wonderful thought' that 'the composer reveals the innermost essence of the world and utters the most profound wisdom in a language which his reason does not understand, just as a magnetic somnambulist gives disclosure about things which she has no idea of when awake',[11] Schoenberg insists first of all on the creative process as a moment of 'inspiration.' The creator speaks in an 'irrational' language and about 'things' of which an otherwise conceptual language (including poetic language) would deny any expression. Thus, the composer knows of no conceptual content

---

[8] Schilling and Nauenburg (see n. 3, above) [eine lyrische Dichtungsart, deren Charakter auf der Darstellung nur *eines* Gefühls beruht, welches die Seele sanft bewegt.... Dadurch daß im Lied das Gefühl mit sich selbst im Ebenmaaße steht, unterscheidet es sich gerade auch von der Ode]. Emphasis original.

[9] Hegel (1965) II, pp. 196–7 [Ein Lied..., obschon es als Gedicht und Text in sich selbst ein Ganzes von mannigfach nuancierten Stimmungen, Anschauungen und Vorstellungen enthalten kann, hat dennoch meist den Grundklang ein und derselben, sich durch alles fortziehenden Empfindung und schlägt dadurch vornehmlich *einen* Gemütston an. Diesen zu fassen und in Tönen wiederzugeben, macht die Hauptwirksamkeit solcher Liedermelodie aus]. Emphasis original.

[10] Schoenberg (1992), p. 10 [weil der noch ans Stoffliche gebundenen Dichtkunst eine so unmittelbare, durch nichts getrübte, reine Aussprache versagt ist]. Trans. (1975), p. 142.

[11] Schoenberg (1992), p. 9 [Der Komponist offenbart das innerste Wesen der Welt und spricht die tiefste Weisheit aus, in einer Sprache, die seine Vernunft nicht versteht; wie eine magnetische Somnambule Aufschlüsse gibt über Dinge, von denen sie wachend keinen Begriff hat]. Trans. (1975), p. 142.

(*keinen Begriff*), and, equally, the composition is not to be reduced to any conceptually definable matters. Further, Schoenberg believes in the artist as 'expressing himself', and in a 'higher reality'. Given this second, decidedly Romantic, premise, Schoenberg's conception of the Lied as relying on the poem's general, rather than specific, content is logical. 'In all music composed to poetry, the exactitude of the reproduction of the events is . . . irrelevant to the artistic value . . .', Schoenberg explains. 'The outward correspondence between music and text . . . has but little to do with the inward correspondence.'[12] One very well-known passage of the essay illustrates Schoenberg's attitude:

A few years ago I was deeply ashamed when I discovered in several Schubert songs, well-known to me, that I had absolutely no idea what was going on in the poems on which they were based. But when I read the poems it became clear to me that I had gained absolutely nothing for the understanding of the songs thereby, since the poems did not make it necessary for me to change my conception of the musical interpretation in the slightest degree. On the contrary, it appeared that, without knowing the poem, I had grasped the content, the real content, perhaps even more profoundly than if I had clung to the surface of the mere thoughts expressed in the words. For me, even more decisive than this experience was the fact that, inspired by the sound of the first words of the text, I had composed many of my songs straight through to the end without troubling myself in the slightest about the continuation of the poetic events, without even grasping them in the ecstasy of composing, and that only days later I thought of looking back to see just what was the real poetic content of my song. It then turned out, to my greatest astonishment, that I had never done greater justice to the poet than when, guided by my first direct contact with the sound of the beginning, I divined everything that obviously had to follow this first sound with inevitability.[13]

Schoenberg's and Hegel's views on the Lied coincide in two points. First, the Lied is conceived of as a separate entity, separate from the poem's own purely poetic content. The poem is Schoenberg's initial inspiration for writing a song, but ceases to have further import. What Hegel called 'this one basic sentiment of one and the same penetrating feeling' and the '*one single* emotional chord', recurs in Schoenberg's

---

[12] Schoenberg (1992), p. 13 [Weil in allen Kompositionen nach Dichtungen die Genauigkeit der Wiedergabe der Vorgänge für den Kunstwert irrelevant ist . . . die äußerliche Übereinstimmung zwischen Musik und Text . . . nur wenig zu tun hat mit der inneren]. Trans. (1975), p. 145.

[13] Schoenberg (1992), pp. 11–12 [Ich war vor ein paar Jahren tief beschämt, als ich entdeckte, daß ich bei einigen mir wohlbekannten Schubert-Liedern gar keine Ahnung davon hatte, was in dem zugrundeliegenden Gedicht eigentlich vorgehe. Als ich aber dann die Gedichte gelesen hatte, stellte sich für mich heraus, daß ich dadurch für das Verständnis dieser Lieder gar nichts gewonnen hatte, da ich nicht im geringsten durch sie genötigt war, meine Auffassung des musikalischen Vortrags zu ändern. Im Gegenteil: es zeigte sich mir, daß ich, ohne das Gedicht zu kennen, den Inhalt, den wirklichen Inhalt, sogar viel tiefer erfaßt hatte, als ich noch an der Oberfläche der eigentlichen Wortgedanken haften geblieben wäre. Noch entscheidender als dieses Erlebnis war mir die Tatsache, daß ich viele meiner Lieder, berauscht von dem Anfangsklang der ersten Textworte, ohne mich auch nur im geringsten um den weiteren Verlauf der poetischen Vorgänge zu kümmern, ja ohne diese im Taumel des Komponierens auch nur im geringsten zu erfassen, zu Ende geschrieben und erst nach Tagen darauf kam, nachzusehen, was denn eigentlich der poetische Inhalt meines Liedes sei. Wobei sich dann zu meinem größten Erstaunen herausstellte, daß ich niemals dem Dichter voller gerecht worden bin, als wenn ich, geführt von der ersten unmittelbaren Berührung mit dem Anfangsklang, alles erriet, was in diesem Anfangsklang eben offenbar mit Notwendigkeit folgen mußte]. Trans. (1975), p. 144.

expression 'truest, inmost essence' (*wahrstes, innerstes Wesen*) later in the passage. Second, both Schoenberg and Hegel are organicists. Both character and structure of the Lied are the result of an inherent sound (*Klang* for Schoenberg) or chord (*Grundklang* for Hegel). Schoenberg explains that 'the work of art is like every other complete organism. It is so homogenous in its composition that in every detail it reveals its truest, inmost essence.' Schoenberg concludes: 'When one hears a verse of a poem, a measure of a composition, one is in the position to comprehend the whole'.[14] Any possible modifications of affect occurring in the course of events in the poem are subsumed into this one 'fundamental sound'. A century before Schoenberg, Hegel claims that the melody:

can remain the same throughout all verses of the poem, even if these are in their content modified in various ways; especially by means of its [the melody's] return, it can heighten its forcefulness instead of weakening the impression . . . Such a tone [i.e. poetic content/expression], may it be fitting for a few verses and not for others, must also prevail in the Lied, because here the particular meaning of the words must not predominate; instead the melody must simply float above the difference.[15]

In contrast to Koch or Schilling and Nauenburg, Hegel significantly affirms the autonomy of the musical composition over the poetic text. The music transcends the poetic content as it simply floats above all (textual) differences. This belief in compositional autonomy is echoed in Schoenberg's closing statement: 'Apparent superficial divergences can be necessary because of parallelism on a higher level'.[16]

With respect to compositional autonomy, E. T. A. Hoffmann's conception of the Lied in the *Writings on Music* sounds conservative:

Inspired by the deep meaning of the Lied, the composer must grasp all moments of the affect as if in a focal point, from which there radiates the melody whose sounds then become the symbol of all different moments of the inner affect which the poet's Lied carries within itself. In order to compose a Lied which agrees completely with the poet's intention, it is indeed necessary for the composer not only to perceive deeply the meaning of the poem, but also and more importantly to become himself the poet of the poem.[17]

---

[14] Schoenberg (1992), p. 12 [Wenn man einen Vers von einem Gedicht, einen Takt von einem Tonstück hört, ist man imstande, das Ganze zu erfassen]. Trans. (1975), p. 144.

[15] Hegel (1965) XIV, pp. 196–197 [Die Liedermelodie kann deshalb auch das ganze Gedicht hindurch für alle Verse, wenn diese auch in ihrem Inhalt vielfach modifiziert sind, dieselbe bleiben und durch diese Wiederkehr gerade, statt dem Eindruck Schaden zu tun, die Eindringlichkeit erhöhen . . . Solch ein Ton, mag er auch für ein paar Verse passen und für andere nicht, muß auch im Liede herrschen, weil hier der bestimmte Sinn der Worte nicht das Überwiegende sein darf, sondern die Melodie einfach für sich über der Verschiedenheit schwebt].

[16] Schoenberg (1992), p. 13 [scheinbares Divergieren an der Oberfläche [kann] nötig sein wegen eines Parallelgehens auf einer höheren Ebene]. Trans. (1975), p. 145.

[17] E. T. A. Hoffmann in a review of Friedrich Wilhelm Riem's *Zwölf Lieder alter und neuerer Dichter* Op. 27 [von dem tiefen Sinn des Liedes angeregt, muß der Komponist alle Momente des Affekts wie in einem Brennpunkt auffassen, aus dem die Melodie hervorstrahlt, deren Töne dann, so wie in der Arie die Worte symbolische Bezeichnung des innern Affekts wurden, hier das Symbol aller verschiedenen Momente des innern Affekts sind, die des Dichters Lied in sich trägt. Um daher ein Lied zu komponieren, das der Intention des Dichters ganz zusagt, ist es wohl nötig, daß der Komponist nicht sowohl den Sinn des Liedes tief auffasse, als vielmehr selbst Dichter des Liedes werde]. See Hoffmann (1988), p. 249.

Hoffmann's stance is 'conservative' because he asks the composer to comply with the text in all its facets, or as he puts it: 'The composer must grasp all moments of the affect as if in a focal point'. In this, Hoffmann suggests what may be seen as an impossibility: emotional multiplicity ('all moments of the affect'), arguably inherent in most poems, is condensed and compressed into the melody. Although the assumption is still that of the one 'deep meaning' of a poem containing one consistent message only,[18] the important point lies in Hoffmann's formulation that the melody becomes a 'symbol' for the feelings expressed in the poem. This entails a transformation of emotional content from one art form into another. Let us note that Hoffmann concentrates exclusively on the melody, the voice being the centre of a symbolic rendition of poetic content. He discusses neither harmony, nor indeed diversity of form.

In the light of these largely restrictive measures for the Lied composer, Hoffmann's final statement is ambiguous. The whole passage builds up to the emphasis that 'not only the meaning' (semantic level) of the poem but more importantly the composer's closest identification with it will result in 'a Lied which agrees completely with the poet's intention'. Were it not for Hoffmann's initial concern that all affects of the poem should be faithfully represented in the Lied's melody 'as if in a focal point', one could mistake the final sentence on the 'composer becoming the poet' as the typically Romantic concept of reading. In that case it would mean an 'immersedness' in the poem, an intuitive feel and understanding of its pulse and sense to the extent of the poem becoming one's own. But reading in the Romantic frame of mind means, above all, reading creatively, that is in a kind of intensive interaction with the object which results in its re-creation on the part of the reader. The Early Romantics also assume, not merely the possibility, but rather the very necessity of 'mis-reading' out of the conviction that a full understanding can never be achieved. The essence then lies in the decidedly liberating act of reading through imagination rather than what Hoffmann expects, which is assimilation. Although the composer begins to enter the poem's realm by becoming its perfect reader, Hoffmann's stance does not extend to the truly Romantic notion of the poem's emanation upon a reader who reflects upon its sounds and meaning in an experience of self-discovery.

SCHUMANN'S HIGHER SPHERE OF ART

With Schumann, after Schubert, the Lied was given a genuine voice. Here, the voice of the poet no longer dominates the musical setting, but rather the poetic text fully becomes part of Schumann's own voice. Neither musical imitation of poetic content nor emotional or stylistic assimilation, the Schumann Lied is the utterance of someone able to make the words he set to music his own. In this regard, the distinction between the role of the voice and the role of the piano should be made

---

[18] Dürr presumes that Hoffmann's statement applies in particular to strophic settings rather than through-composed song. Hoffmann's approach indeed appears problematic, for the implication seems to be that the poem to be set to music does in fact concern only one emotion. See Dürr (1984), pp. 10–11.

very clear. Although Romantically 'intertwined', the relation between the two is complementary as well as contrasting. The voice is the screen on to which 'idealized' sentiment can be projected – the Romantic Other. This involves a dialectic between the voice and the piano.

But I should now admit that the approach I am taking towards little examined material is obviously in the spirit of Schumann's advocate. Nevertheless, as we shall see, Schumann is his own best advocate. A well-read, literary and philosophical mind, he saw clearly what he strove to achieve as a composer of the Romantic song, and he possessed the literary talents to convey his aesthetic programme eloquently and lucidly. It is of great interest therefore to recognize these writings as vivid testimony to Schumann's aims as Lied composer and to listen carefully to the word of Schumann as critic and thinker.

First, we can say that the level at which words and music meet is the melody. Here, through the melody, the nature of language is altered. It differs radically from verbal language, for its phonetic and syntactic functions have become subject to transformation by way of musical sound. Language, especially poetic, that is metrical language, cannot keep its original determinants once music has imbued it with its own laws of signification. In turn, however, music in the form of a sung melody also changes in its semantic capacities. It works along the structural lines of the words and verses which it sings. Hence, by way of the melody's double function situating it somewhere between language and music, it is, hermeneutically, a challenging and intriguing part of the Lied.

The emergence of a voice in Schumann's work was a relatively sudden phenomenon, the reasons for which may be sought in his personal development.[19] The influence of Franz Schubert, whose work Schumann studied very closely during his stay in Vienna in 1838/39, most certainly contributed to his increased interest in song composition, not least in the light of the new edition of Schubert's Lieder having appeared at the same time.[20] This also coincides with the insertion of the famous 'inner' voice into the second movement of the *Humoreske* Op. 20.[21] In the context of Early Romanticism, however, the implementation of a 'poetic voice' in the musical sphere, that is poetry in either the abstract or the literal sense, meant a major source of inspiration, or better stimulation (*Anregung*): the Romantic hero's imagination found here additional material to reflect upon. This was the case with Schumann in a more specific sense. If he had always been able to cast 'moods' and 'characters' in short and fragmentary piano pieces until 1839, this scenario of dialogues between various figures or mental images (Florestan, Eusebius, Raro and many more) achieved a new degree of complexity through the introduction of a vocal melody. Not only horizontally, but vertically, Schumann's text multiplies. In his Lied compositions, Schumann's voice is split into two layers: the voice of the

[19] See below, pp. 111–123.
[20] See a detailed account of Schubert's influence on Schumann in Meissner (1985), pp. 94–100, as well as in Maintz (1995).
[21] Meissner (1985), p. 95.

piano on one level, a human voice on another, higher level. The important point is, however, that the voice in Schumann's Lieder does not grow out of the piano texture, but is superimposed. As a new quality entering Schumann's speech, the voice differs distinctly from the gestures of the piano.

In the language of the Romantics, Schumann's Lied speaks the 'language of the soul'[22] – a soul which has found its imaginary *alter ego*. In the imagination of the composer, the singing voice thus becomes the haunting vision of another, second, 'I' which promises fulfilment. In this sense, the Schumann Lied is the Janus-faced phantasy of the composer's amorous soul: an invocation of the Other as projected in the voice versus the genuine gestures of the piano – yielding and resisting – that signal the Romantic hero's solitude. The Romantic Lied of Schumann symbolizes that constant state of ambiguity, which desire ensures is kept in motion. The piano – leaning forward into the voice and recoiling back on itself – is the space where desire is inscribed, within which the image of the Other is fixed as the pole for identification as well as alienation.

In accordance with the Early Romantics' understanding that nature contained a deeper, supernatural meaning – the 'inner music of nature' or the 'language of the flowers'[23] – in short, what would later be called the unconscious, Schumann conceived of 'the poet's Lieder' as 'the echo of nature's language of flowers'.[24] In the symphilosophical spirit of the Early Romantic poet–philosophers who infused philosophy with poetry, Schumann infused music with poetry and poetry with music. That the 'poetic' characterizes Schumann's instrumental œuvre – either explicitly by way of mottos, literary themes and scenes, or implicitly by way of fictional texts – is well known.[25] His Lieder, however, have usually been evaluated according to criteria which justified blanket comparisons between the underlying poetry and the musical setting in search of analogies. This misses the central idea behind Schumann's compositional processes in the Lied, in which the poem is, as has been mentioned above, always subject to fundamental transformation. Rather than repeating in musical terms what has already been said verbally, the Lied becomes the matrix for endowing the poem with new meaning. The poem is nothing more and nothing less than an object for Schumann's own reflections. I shall now discuss the various aspects that this Romantic procedure entails.

The voice allowed Schumann to infuse the poetic word as well as the musical sign with deeper shades of meaning. Poetic reflection, the Romantic mode of reading and

[22] *GS* I, p. 356 [Seelensprache]. The term appears in Hegel's *Aesthetic* lectures: 'The Poetic in music, the language of the soul . . . – the free resounding sound of the soul in the realm of music is firstly the melody' [Das Poetische der Musik, die Seelenspache . . . – das freie Tönen der Seele im Felde der Musik ist erst die Melodie]. Hegel's emphasis on the melody – regardless of any other structural elements in the Lied – reflects his ultimate preference for reason over emotion, as has been discussed above, pp. 44–46. The limited scope of expression he thereby permits has been made obvious in the above discussion of his concept of the Lied and is therefore not helpful for the central idea behind Schumann's Lied compositions.

[23] See below, pp. 203–206.

[24] *TB* I, p. 78 [die Lieder des Dichters sind nur das Echo der Blumensprache der Natur].

[25] See Dietel (1989) for an interesting discussion of the 'poetic' in Schumann's piano works, and also Lippmann (1964) and Meissner (1985).

'idealizing' the poem's content, thus works in two ways: both music and poetry are 'potentialized' and 'poeticized'. This required no artificial effort since Schumann, as an autobiographical essay reveals, had always seen himself as 'poet and composer in one person'.[26] From adolescence until well into the 1830s Schumann was devoted to, and moved freely between, both forms of expression in the attempt to 'poeticize life' – to elevate life's events to a higher and more meaningful sphere: 'The poet lives in the idealistic world and works for the real world'.[27] In the case of the Early Romantics as well as in Schumann's particular case, the 're-poeticization of life' involved an intensification of the perception of life as it presents itself: ambivalent, mysterious and metaphysical. Hence Schumann's emphasis on 'rare' and 'secret states of the soul'.[28] Hence also his wish that his music would 'reflect here and there perhaps a piece of life'[29] – a statement which may mislead some into rushing to the conclusion that Schumann's work represented a musical biography. Nothing could be further from the truth. If Schumann, more explicitly than any other composer, claims and thematizes a proximity to lived experience, the idea lies firmly within the act of 'poeticizing', a moment of consciousness in which the workings of the Romantic mind are celebrated through means of language – musical language in Schumann's case. With the composition of poetic music, Schumann created for himself a second, imaginary world according to Jean Paul's central thesis regarding the nature of the 'poetic' in the *Vorschule der Ästhetik*: 'Poetry is the only *second* world in the world around us'.[30] This '*second*' world', as Jean Paul describes the 'romanticized' version of the 'real' world, achieves for the Early Romantics a degree of suggestiveness which situates the poetic art work next to lived experience. It portrays an imaginary world, however, as Friedrich Schlegel asserts in one of the *Athenaeum* fragments:

What happens in poetry happens never and always. Otherwise it isn't proper poetry. One shouldn't think that it is actually happening now.[31]

In this Romantic sense of substitution, Schumann aspired to cast the figures of dreams and imagination into music, rather than those found in real life. As Schumann writes in 1828, if 'philosophy is music of the mind, music is philosophy of the soul; philosophy prepares us for a higher life, music brings it to us'.[32]

---

[26] Eismann I, p. 18.

[27] Kreisig GS II (Schumann's central statement in a talk given in September 1827), p. 183 [Der Dichter lebt in der idealistischen Welt und arbeitet für die wirkliche]. Schumann repeats this idea in his diary (*TB* I, p. 78): 'In the soul of the poet is combined the happiest with the purest life; however, he combines the highest life with this [the real, present life] by way of living in the idealistic world and working for the real one' [In der Seele des Dichters verbindet sich das glücklichste mit dem reinsten Leben: das höchste Leben verbindet er aber mit diesen, indem er in der idealistischen Welt lebt u. für die wirkliche arbeitet].

[28] Kreisig GS I, p. 343 [seltene . . . geheime Seelenzustände].

[29] Schumann, in a letter to Simrock concerning his third symphony. Quoted in Floros (1981), p. 97 [vielleicht hier und da ein Stück Leben wiederspiegelt].

[30] JP IX, p. 30 [Die Poesie ist die einzige *zweite* Welt in der hiesigen]. Emphasis original.

[31] *Athenaeum*, p. 116 [Was in der Poesie geschieht, geschieht nie und immer. Sonst ist es keine rechte Poesie. Man darf nicht glauben sollen, daß es jetzt wirklich geschehe].

[32] *TB* I, p. 96 [Philosophie ist Musik des Geistes, Musik Philosophie des Gemüthes; die Philosophie bereitet uns auf ein höheres Leben vor, die Musik bringt es uns].

Schumann's 'poetic consciousness'[33] had to find release in the act of writing, whether musical or literary, for only through poetic speech could a Romantic find self-affirmation.[34] It may be noted here that Schumann's emphasis on poetic consciousness relates directly to his idea of music as a language of the soul. As Meissner admirably demonstrates, Schumann consciously conceived of the creative process as a process of discovering language (*Prozess der Sprachfindung*), as an 'act of unconscious thinking qua poetic consciousness'.[35] The capacity of musical language to convey 'rare states of the soul' is linked to the idea that music is able to 'represent the Unrepresentable'[36] and to convey the enigmatic movements of the unconscious. 'Poetic music' leads us into the 'spirit-world of art'[37] and exercises 'its full power where it extends across into the transcendental, into the spirit-world'.[38] Schumann's Romantic 'I that seeks itself'[39] found full expression in the Lied, for, as he defines the relationship between musical sound and words, 'both are the *ne plus ultra* of Romanticism. Musical sound is above all composed word.'[40] Schumann therefore knew: '*My Lieder*, they are intended to be the true imprint of my own Self'.[41]

The theorist C. F. D. Schubart played a decisive role in Schumann's development as a composer.[42] As Meissner noted, Schumann adopted Schubart's view, as expressed in the *Ideas for an Aesthetic of Music* of 1806, that 'song' was 'indisputably the highest item in the whole of music'.[43] Here, Schubart equates human-kind as 'singing' and 'speaking creatures' which results in the assertion that '*poetry should always be combined with music*'.[44] In Schumann's own early essay, 'On the Intimate Relatedness of Poetry and Music' of 1826, a number of Schubart's ideas reappear in paraphrase, such as Schubart's summary of song as 'the most precise and perfect musical language in the world'.[45] Significantly, Schumann's essay closes with a poem of his own. Its last lines, written in iambic pentameter, are 'And yet 'tis fairer still when the string's sound / Doth raise and glorify the poet's song'[46] – thereby invoking almost literally Friedrich Schlegel's suggestion for the best reading of a poem: 'There is nothing more beautiful on earth than poetry and music mingled in sweet compliance for the greater ennoblement of mankind'.[47]

---

[33] *JB*, p. 282 (Schumann in a letter to Clara in 1838).

[34] Blanchot (1969), p. 524.   [35] See Meissner (1985), p. 24.

[36] NO III, p. 685, no. 671 [Das Undarstellbare darstellen].   [37] Kreisig *GS* I, p. 343 [Geisterreich der Kunst].

[38] Kreisig *GS* I, p. 362 [ihre volle Gewalt... wo sie ins Übersinnliche, in das Geisterreich hinüberspielt].

[39] Friedrich Schlegel, *KFSA* XIX, p. 22, no. 197 [Das Ich, das sich selbst sucht].

[40] *TB* I, p. 96 [beyde sind aber das *Non* [sic] *plus ultra* der Romantic. Ton ist überhaupt componiertes Wort].

[41] *TB* I, p. 112 [*Meine Lieder*; der eigentliche Abdruck meines Ich's sind sie bestimmt]. Emphasis original.

[42] See Meissner (1985), pp. 58–62. See also my discussion of Schumann's 'Characterization of the keys' as influenced by Schubart on p. 145, below.

[43] Schubart as quoted in Meissner (1985), p. 59 [Der Gesang ist unstreitig der erste Artikel in der ganzen Tonkunst].

[44] Schubart (1806), p. 278 [*daß die Poesie immer mit der Musik verbunden sein sollte*]. Emphasis original.

[45] Meissner (1985), p. 60.

[46] Meissner (1985), p. 150, n. 56 [Doch schöner ist's, wenn das Geläut der Saite / Verherrlichend des Dichters Lied erhebt].

[47] These are the closing words of Schlegel's important essay 'On Incomprehensibility' of 1800, which – like Schumann's early essay – ends with a poem. Quoted in translation from Simpson (1988), p. 186.

In his review of Taubert's *An die Geliebte: Acht Minnelieder für das Pianoforte*, Schumann makes both a terminological and a conceptual distinction between wordless piano music originally inspired by words (Heine's poems, as it happens to be in Taubert's case), the genre of *Songs without Words* newly created by Mendelssohn, and the term 'Lied' *per se*, which always implies the presence of a human voice. In contrast to the explicit poetic content underlying Taubert's compositions, Schumann's concluding sentence brings to light his perception of Mendelssohn's works as invoking a less specific poetic content, and instead leading to a general poetic mood:

[This is] a truly real Song without Words, but Mendelssohn gave this genre a name and Taubert carried it out in a different way. I would have . . . , instead of 'Minnelieder', only wished for a more characteristic title; for one can surely say Lieder 'without' words, but the term Lied (without this particular addition) entails the participation of the voice. Perhaps I would have called the music simply 'Music on texts by Heine etc.' Because this is what distinguishes these from the ones by Mendelssohn: they [Taubert's] were inspired by poems, whilst the latter [Mendelssohn's] should perhaps stimulate one to poeticize.[48]

Schumann's concern has naturally always been with those whom we recognize as major poets: Eichendorff, Goethe, Hebbel, Immermann, Kerner, Lenau, Mörike, Platen, Rückert, Schiller, Uhland, besides foreign authors such as Andersen, Burns, Byron and Shelley. The choice of poetic texts for his own settings is testimony to a belief in higher aesthetic achievement through the use of good, if not great, poetry. In a review of songs he writes:

He is even satisfied with poems of lesser substance. But do we have a lack of good [poetry]? A 'yes' as an answer would do an injustice to our poets. How much is there still to be gained in the older German Classicists, how much in the era after Goethe, how much in the most recent [poetry], how much indeed in [poetry] from foreign countries! Why, therefore, reach for mediocre poems which will always take their toll on the music? To crown a true Poet with music – nothing is more beautiful; but to waste it on a mediocre figure, why the effort? – The talented composer expresses himself with greater richness and novelty in better [poems] such as those by Heine. . . . The composer himself will admit that he composed here with greater love.[49]

Schumann's manner of setting a poem to music required that he emancipate himself from formal as well as semantic constraints. To set a poem to music was,

[48] *GS* I, p. 168 [ein recht eigentliches Lied ohne Worte, aber Mendelssohn gab dem Genre einen Namen und Taubert führte ihn in noch andrer Weise aus. Nur hätt' ich . . . statt der Überschrift 'Minnelieder' eine bezeichnendere gewünscht; denn man kann wohl Lieder 'ohne' Worte sagen, aber im Begriff Lied (ohne jenen Zusatz) liegt das Mitwirken der Stimme eingeschlossen. Vielleicht würd' ich die Musik einfach 'Musik zu Texten von Heine u. s. w.' genannt haben. Denn darin unterscheidet sie sich von der Mendelssohnschen, daß sie durch Gedichte angeregt sind, während jene vielleicht umgekehrt zum Dichten anregen sollen].

[49] *GS* III, p. 263 [es genügen ihm selbst Gedichte geringeren Gehaltes. Haben wir denn etwa Mangel an guten? Ein 'Ja' zur Antwort wäre ein Unrecht, was wir den Poeten thäten. Wie viel Ausbeute geben noch die älteren deutschen Classiker, wie viel die Epoche nach Goethe, wie manches die neuste, wie vieles endlich auch das Ausland! Weshalb also nach mittelmäßigen Gedichten greifen, was sich immer an der Musik rächen muß? Einen Kranz von Musik um ein wahres Dichterhaupt schlingen – nichts schöneres; aber ihn an ein Alltagsgesicht verschwenden, wozu die Mühe? – Das Talent . . . äußert sich aber gewiß reicher und frischer in jenen besseren, wie von Heine . . . . Der Componist wird es selbst gestehen, daß er hier auch mit größerer Liebe schrieb].

for Schumann, to discover latent meaning, between lines and within words. To bring these out, the musical setting must, of course, diverge from the immediate expression the poem might contain. In this sense, Schumann conceived of the poem as a stimulus for his musical interpretation, which allowed him to reflect upon the poem freely. This compositional procedure is far removed from the earlier models based on imitation and assimilation. With Schumann, song composition became a means of creatively working on language[50] whereby it was raised to a 'higher sphere of art',[51] as he gave poetry a voice. Hoffmann's model of the composer's assimilation of the text was abandoned by Schumann, as he let imagination become the decisive factor in the musical reading of a poem. Composing a Lied was to become an act of 'fantasizing'[52] in which a poem is the source of inspiration rather than a prescription.

'*Fantasieren*', as Roland Barthes rightly notes, means 'at once to imagine and to improvise: in short, to hallucinate, i.e. to produce the novelistic without constructing a novel'.[53] Accordingly, the poems Schumann chose to set to music may be seen as 'brief fragments' out of which he could 'elaborate ever-new speech'.[54] By way of poeticizing, romanticizing and idealizing poetry, Schumann thus becomes the second, 'extended' poet, in a way a 'meta-poet' of the poem. This is indeed why he would proclaim that his Lieder 'mostly expressed all my feelings musically'.[55] In a different sense from E. T. A. Hoffmann's conception of 'a Lied which agrees entirely with the poet's intention', Schumann saw in the Lied that artistic medium where the deeper meaning of both music and poetry were enhanced:

In *songs* beautiful souls truly get to know each other: the poet meets the composer and vice versa; [songs] must be constituted in such a way that the poet, if he were a musician, would express with musical sounds what he does with word[s]; and the musician, were he a poet, [would express] in words what he does in sounds.[56]

Crucial for Schumann's compositional process in the Lied is what he called 'Anempfinden u. An-denken'[57] – to add his own sentiments and thoughts to a

---

[50] Cf. Barthes' extended use of Kristeva's concept of 'geno-text' for the Romantic song as 'geno-song'. The 'geno-song' is the volume of the speaking and singing voice, the space in which signification can germinate 'from within the language and in its very materiality; . . . it is that culmination (or depth) of production where melody actually *works* on language'. Barthes (1985a), pp. 270–271.

[51] *NZfM* 1 (1834), p. 193.

[52] The term 'Phantasieren' must be seen as one of Schumann's primary compositional concepts. The frequency of the word in Schumann's writings is striking, as is its appearance as the title of compositions: best known is the *Fantasie* Op. 17 of 1836–38, for which Nicholas Marston (1992, pp. 23–24) noted Schumann's sustained efforts to chose between the variants 'Fantasie', 'Phantasien', 'Phantasiestücke' as well as 'Dichtungen'. Other examples include the *Fantasiestücke* Op. 12, written in 1837. The *Kreisleriana* of 1838 bears the subtitle: '8 fantasies'. In 1851 three piano pieces (Op. 111) were again named *Phantasiestücke*, and the *Albumblätter* Op. 124 of 1854 contain a 'Phantasietanz' of 1836 and a 'Phantasiestück' of 1839. Two chamber works, Op. 88 of 1842 and Op. 73 of 1849, are both called *Phantasiestücke*, and the late orchestral pieces, Op. 131 of 1853, bear the title *Fantasie*.

[53] Barthes (1985b), p. 291. Emphasis on '*Fantasieren*' original.   [54] Barthes (1985b), p. 291.

[55] *TB* I, p. 119 [es waren meist meine ganzen Gefühle in Tönen wiedergegeben].

[56] *TB* I, p. 114 [In den *Liedern* lernen sich die schönen Seelen erst kennen, der Dichter den Componisten u. umgekehrt; sie müssen so beschaffen seyn, daß der Dichter, wär' er Musiker, es so in Tönen ausdrükte, wie im Wort, u. daß der Musiker, wär er Dichter es so in Worten, wie in seinen Tönen]. Emphasis original.

[57] *TB* I (May 1831), p. 335.

given text or poem, and hence to make it speak the language of his soul. This is how Schumann wished to raise the Lied to a 'higher art sphere':

Oh composers, become poets, humans, first of all! Learn to get even a little feeling for a poem, to read it and to recite it before you think about raising it to a higher sphere of art.[58]

The idea of music as a 'higher sphere' of artistic expression is, of course, an idea that resonates throughout the writings of the Early Romantics. It finds its echo in Schumann's writings as well as in his compositions. Although perhaps not to be seen as a direct analogy to Schelling's 'harmonies of the spheres', the term in Schumann's usage similarly refers to that level of expression which escapes reflective conceptualization and which is meaningful in the very irreducibility of words to concepts.[59] Hence, Schumann consciously drew the element of poetic music into his settings as he 'fantasized' in his own voice, and through his most personal medium, the piano, when it came to the accompaniment as well as the pre-, inter-, and postludes.

Schumann recognized the sense of an enigma resting within poetic language in the writings of his most admired author, Jean Paul. Like Jean Paul in his synaesthetic orientation, Schumann intended his music to carry a similarly enigmatic quality through an emphasis on non-representational content. In his thinking, the reference to objects and concrete concepts in works of art and music was no longer at issue; in fact, it demonstrated, in Schumann's view, a lack of aesthetic value, if the potentially spiritual essence of music were to be undermined by a representation of objects. 'Poetic consciousness', in the sense of a deeper spiritual level of perception, is what has to inform the work of art. Thus, Schumann criticizes works which 'may represent a flower' whilst he describes his own as a 'so much more spiritual poem. The former is an impulse of crude nature, the latter a work of poetic consciousness.'[60]

One of Schumann's letters of 1828 to the composer Wiedebein clearly reveals his attitude towards the Lied genre. Asking Wiedebein to comment on some of his own early songs, Schumann uses the occasion to explain how a musical setting 'works' on the poetic text, and what kind of poetry attracted Schumann to song composition:

Your songs gave me quite a few happy moments, and I came to understand and decipher Jean Paul's veiled words through them. Jean Paul's dark sounds of mystery became lucid and clear to me only by means of that magic veil of your composition – rather like two negations lead to affirmation, and the entire heaven of sounds, of tears of the soul's joy, drenched in transfiguration all my feelings. . . . Kerner's poems, which engaged me especially because of that enigmatic, supernatural power which one often finds in the poetry of Goethe and Jean Paul, originally stimulated me to try out my poor abilities, because in these poems each word is already a sound of the spheres which must be defined through the musical note.[61]

---

[58] *NZfM* 1 (1834), pp. 193–194 [O Componisten, werdet doch erst Dichter, erst Menschen! lernt ein Gedicht nur ein wenig fühlen, lesen, vortragen, ehe ihr daran denkt, es durch Musik in eine höhere Kunstsphäre zu erheben].

[59] See pp. 54–56, above.   [60] *JB* (Schumann in a letter to Clara in 1838), p. 282.

[61] *TB* I (letter of 15 July 1828 to the composer Gottlob Wiedebein), p. 95 [Ihre Lieder schufen mir manche glückliche Minute u. ich lernte durch diese Jean Pauls verhüllte Worte verstehen u. enträthseln. Jean Paul's

Schumann then asks Wiedebein to write settings of Kerner's Lieder 'to which only through your gentle, soft and melancholy chords is given the most beautiful text and the deepest meaning'.[62] In this last sentence, Schumann articulates his view of setting poetry to music in the most uncompromising terms: a text is *created* by means of the composer's music (voice and piano) — a new, musical text, this is, which supersedes the original poetic text. Text given by chords (that is musical sound in general) means that the poem is idealized or, to use the modern word, interpreted by the composer, and according to his own feelings and views. The important point is that it is the composer who 'writes' the text; it is no longer the poem of the poet, who did nothing more than provide the composer with material for thought and reflection. It becomes clear in this letter that Schumann saw in poetry the material on which he could elaborate and 'fantasize' musically. The musical setting thus becomes the metatext to the poem in the spirit of a 'better understanding' of the material the composer reflects upon. The poem is not seen as having 'the objectivity of gold'[63] but rather as a gem which mobilizes the imagination.

Two *Athenaeum* fragments may be quoted in the context of text in music. In the first, Friedrich Schlegel criticizes the fact that 'many musical compositions are merely translations of poems into the language of music'[64] — the implication being, of course, that the poetic text should in fact be transformed through music. In another fragment, Schlegel suggests the capacity of music to 'create its own text'. Regarding music as part of a greater synaesthetic system, musical language can, by means of reflection, transcend the older concept of a 'naturalness' of expression. Although Schlegel speaks here about 'pure instrumental music', the essential point is his emphasis on 'text' in music as deriving from the composer's ability to 'meditate' and play with his material like a philosopher:

Many people find it strange and ridiculous when musicians talk about the ideas in their compositions.... But whoever has a feeling for the wonderful affinity of all the arts and sciences will at least not consider the matter from the dull viewpoint of a so-called naturalness that maintains music is supposed to be only the language of the senses. Rather, he will consider a certain tendency of pure instrumental music towards philosophy as something not impossible in itself. Doesn't pure instrumental music have to create its own text? And aren't

---

dunkle Geistertöne wurden mir durch jenes magische Verhüllen Ihrer Tonschöpfungen erst licht u. klar, wie ungefähr zwey Negationen affirmiren u. der ganze Himmel der Töne, dieser Freudenthränen der Seele sank wie verklärt über alle meine Gefühle. Kerner's Gedichte, die mich durch jene geheimnisvolle, überirdische Kraft, die man oft in d. Dichtungen Göthe's und Jean Paul's findet, am meisten anzogen, brachten mich zuerst auf den Gedanken, meine schwachen Kräfte zuerst [*sic*] zu versuchen, weil in diesen (Gedichten) schon jedes Wort ein Sphärenton ist, der erst durch die Note bestimmt werden muß].

[62] *Ibid*. [u. ersuche Sie ... uns bald mit d. Composition Kernerscher Lieder zu erfreuen, denen ihre sanften, weichen, wehmüthigen Akkorde erst den schönsten Text u. die tiefste Bedeutung geben können].

[63] Friedrich Schlegel's ironic expression for the written word, which can be given meaning by way of the reader's autonomous reflections upon it.

[64] *Athenaeum*, p. 184 [Viele musikalische Kompositionen sind nur Übersetzungen des Gedichts in die Sprache der Musik]. Trans. Firchow (1991), p. 80.

the themes in it developed, reaffirmed, varied, and contrasted in the same way as the subject of meditation in a philosophical succession of ideas?[65]

The figure of Hans Georg Nägli (1773–1836) is certainly of interest in the context of this ethereal new genre. Also active as a composer of Lieder, Nägli received wider recognition as a theorist in the mid-1820s, lecturing on musical aesthetics extensively throughout Germany. As his decidedly progressive views caused considerable controversy, it can be assumed that Schumann was familiar with Nägli's ideas.[66] In two of Nägli's texts on the Lied we find the term 'higher artistic whole', anticipating Schumann's 'higher sphere of art'. Nägli differentiated between three chronological epochs in Lied composition, declaring the first two to be outmoded. In the first epoch composers tried 'to follow the poet in general' (e.g., C. P. E. Bach); the second was the epoch of the 'declamatory style' when composers aimed at the 'truth of the word's expression' (e.g., Johann Abraham Peter Schulz).[67] For the third epoch 'in which we now live', Nägli emphasized the significance of the instrumental component in the song and as a result welcomed the appearance of pre-, inter- and postludes (e.g., songs by Johann Rudolf Zumsteeg or Karl Friedrich Zelter).[68] In 1817 Nägli defines this 'new era in Lied composition' in more detail. He explains that there must be:

established a higher style of song from which there emerges a new epoch of the art of song, whose distinct character will be a hitherto still unrecognized polyrhythm, i.e. that the rhythm of speech, singing and playing will be interwoven into a higher artistic whole – a polyrhythm which is as vitally important in the vocal arts as is polyphony in the instrumental arts.[69]

Nägli here introduced a new style of Lied composition in which all three components – text, voice and instrument – retain their functional autonomy but at the same time interact simultaneously, resulting in a 'higher artistic whole' (höheres Kunstganzes). He also maintains that the text is the decisive factor on which the nature of all other components depends, 'for all these artistic means, if properly applied, serve to exalt the expression of the word'.[70] Thus, the poetic text becomes

---

[65] *Athenaeum*, p. 199 [Es pflegt manchem seltsam und lächerlich aufzufallen, wenn die Musiker von den Gedanken in ihren Kompositionen reden.... Wer aber Sinn für die wunderbaren Affinitäten aller Künste und Wissenschaften hat, wird die Sache wenigstens nicht aus dem platten Gesichtspunkte der sogenannten Natürlichkeit betrachten, nach welchem die Musik nur die Sprache der Empfindungen sein soll, und eine gewisse Tendenz aller reinen Instrumentalmusik zur Philosophie an sich nicht für unmöglich finden. Muß die reine Instrumentalmusik sich nicht selbst einen Text erschaffen? und wird das Thema in ihr nicht so entwickelt, bestätigt, variiert und kontrastiert wie der Gegenstand der Meditation in einer philosophischen Ideenreihe?]. Trans. Firchow (1991), p. 92.

[66] Schumann mentioned Nägli briefly in the *NZfM* in a review on Bach. See *GS* IV, p. 62 [In der Nägli'schen Partitur stehen die beiden Fugen übrigens ebenfalls so abgedruckt].

[67] Nägli (1811), cols. 629–642 and 645–652 [dem Gange des Dichters im Allgemeinen zu folgen... Wahrheit des Wortausdrucks]. See the discussion of Nägli in Dürr (1984), pp. 15–17.

[68] Nägli, see *ibid.* [in der wir nun leben].

[69] Nägli (1817), col. 765 [ein höherer Liederstyl begründet werden, und daraus eine neue Epoche der Liederkunst... hervorgehen, deren ausgeprägter Charakter eine bisher noch unerkannte Polyrhythmie seyn wird, also dass Sprach-, Sang- und Spiel-Rhythmus zu einem höheren Kunstganzen verschlungen werden - eine Polyrhythmie, die in der Vocal-kunst völlig so wichtig ist, als in der Instrumental-Kunst die Polyphonie].

[70] See *ibid.* [denn alle diese Kunstmittel dienen, wahrhaft angewandt, zur Erhöhung des Wortausdrucks].

musical itself.[71] The composer 'idealizes' the poem 'in its special form' so that the combination of music and language results in what Nägli called 'a new artistic whole'.

The significance of the composer's intensified apperception (*Auffassung*) of the poem's idea [*Gedanke*] in order to achieve this kind of interaction of words and music is evident in one of Schumann's comments on the new developments in song composition. Historically, he locates the shift from the 'dominating taste' of empty phraseology (*Floskelwesen*) towards 'formations full of thought' between 1830–34, and writes:

> In reality the Lied is perhaps the only genre in which real progress has taken place since Beethoven. If one compares in today's Lieder the care taken of apperception [*Auffassung*] intended to render the poem's idea [*Gedanke*] with the negligence of its earlier treatment, where the poem merely ran alongside, and the entire construction there with its shaky formulas of accompaniment which former times were unable to be rid of, only ignorant people could see the opposite.[72]

Considering Schumann's overall affinity with poetry and the application of poetic procedures, it is not surprising that he considered Romantic poetry to have been a decisive factor in the development of a new compositional style in the Lied:

> In order to expedite development, there developed also a new school of poets. With Rückert and Eichendorff, although flourishing earlier, musicians became more familiar [with developments and] set Uhland and Heine to music most of all. Hence originated this more artistic and profound kind of Lied of which earlier composers could, of course, know nothing, because it was the new poetic spirit that was mirrored in music.[73]

The paramount aesthetic principle of 'the new school of poets', the Romantics, is that of evocation and allusion which leads to a fundamental ambiguity, but also generates greater semantic depth. Heine's poetry is on one level exemplary in the deployment of these Romantic means, especially as regards imagery, metaphor and allusion. Indeed, Heine was a master of what he succinctly describes in *The Romantic School* as the characteristics of Romantic poetry:

> People wanted to articulate and sing of these innermost thrills, this endless melancholy which is at once endless sensual pleasure. . . . Thus, there had to be thought up *new images and new words*, and precisely those which, by way of a *secret and sympathetic affinity with these new sentiments*, could at any time *evoke and conjure up these sentiments in the soul*. In this way, so-called Romantic poetry originated, which blossomed at its most radiant in the Middle

---

[71] Dürr (1984), p. 17.

[72] GS IV, pp. 263–264 [Und in Wirklichkeit ist vielleicht das Lied die einzige Gattung, in der seit Beethoven ein wirklicher Fortschritt geschieht. Vergleicht man in den heutigen Liedern den Fleiß der Auffassung, der den Gedanken des Gedichts bis aufs Wort wiedergeben möchte, mit der Nachlässigkeit der älteren Behandlung, wo das Gedicht nur eben so nebenherlief, den ganzen Außenbau dort mit den schlotternden Begleitformeln, wie sie die frühere Zeit nicht loswerden konnte, so kann nur Borniertheit das Gegenteil sehen].

[73] GS IV, p. 263 [Die Entwicklung zu beschleunigen, entfaltete sich auch eine neue Dichterschule: Rückert und Eichendorff, obwohl schon früher blühend, wurden den Musikern vertrauter, am meisten Uhland und Heine componiert. Es entstand jene kunstvollere und tiefsinnigere Art des Liedes, von der natürlich die Früheren nichts wissen konnten, denn es war der neue Dichtergeist, der sich in der Musik wiederspiegelte].

Ages...and which sprang up again in recent times on German soil where it unfolded its most magnificent flowers. It is true, *the images of Romanticism were supposed to evoke more than to signify*.[74]

On another level, Heine was of course also a master of subverting these same sentiments by way of inserting cutting negative irony into the Romantic cast of his poetry. As will be discussed in Part II, the formalism and sophistication in using the model of Romantic poetry is the very basis on which the Heinean reversal of mood and tone (*Stimmungsbruch*) relies in order to achieve its effectiveness. Under such conditions, Heine had to be a stylist.

As is evident from Schumann's reception of Heine's poems,[75] there can be no doubt about his awareness of Heine's 'burning sarcasm' and irony. Schumann also, however, noted 'this great despair' lingering between the lines of Heine's poems.[76] As the exploration of a few central Romantic metaphors and traditional symbols in Heine's poems will show,[77] there is indeed a degree of polyvalency within Heine's poetic language which bestows upon it the privileges of esotericism: on the one hand at a surface level, to communicate stable meaning through modern irony, trivialization, and destruction of the well-known model of folk-poetry, and on the other beneath the surface, to reach a 'secret community' and 'intimate friends' who will 'understand without words'.[78] From one particularly striking comment Schumann made in 1835, but even more so from his musical settings, it is evident that he saw 'the mask of irony' which Heine had put on, and behind which there hid the 'face of pain'. Decidedly in order to prove wrong the 'the whole orientation of the *zeitgeist*, which tolerates a *Dies irae* as a Burlesque',[79] Schumann went about setting Heine's poems in a manner that allowed the tones of vulnerability to come through. No doubt, Schumann was also drawn to Heine's convoluted style on the whole, where the combination of a heightened Romantic sentimentality and modern disillusion increased the sense of ambiguity. With the *Lyrisches Intermezzo*, he was thus provided with what is indeed a whole series of complex Heinean images and sentiments.

But we can further specify Schumann's new conception of the Romantic art song. In reviewing the development in song composition, Schumann had suggested that Lied composers should follow up the development of the 'new school of poets' in

---

[74] B III, p. 399 [die Menschen [wollten] diese geheimen Schauer, diese unendliche Wehmut und zugleich unendliche Wollust mit Worten aussprechen und besingen....Es mußten jetzt *neue Bilder und neue Worte* erdacht werden, und just solche, die, durch eine *geheime, sympathetische Verwandtschaft mit jenen neuen Gefühlen*, diese letztern zu jederzeit im Gemüte *erwecken und gleichsam herauf beschwören* konnten. So entstand die sogenannte romantische Poesie, die in ihrem schönsten Lichte im Mittelalter aufblühete...und in neuerer Zeit wieder lieblich aus dem deutschen Boden aufsproßte und ihre herrlichsten Blumen entfaltete. Es ist wahr, die *Bilder der Romantik sollten mehr erwecken als bezeichnen*]. Emphasis added.

[75] See pp. 124–130, below.

[76] See pp. 125–126, below, on Schumann's reception of Heine and the *Lyrisches Intermezzo*.

[77] See Part III.   [78] *HSA* XXI, pp. 345–346 (Heine in a letter of 1840). See further discussion in Part II.

[79] *GS* I, p. 145 [die ganze Richtung des Zeitgeistes, der ein *Dies irae* als Bourleske duldet]. See also the epigraph of Part III.

terms of their own style.[80] He then characterized the new Lied composer as aiming
for 'more than just better- or worse-sounding music' and praises him for 'rendering
the poem in its incarnate depth. The quietly dreaming and the stimulatingly naive
are thus best achieved' and 'a series of the most diverse images and sentiments is
evoked in this set of songs'.[81]

    This last sentence contains Schumann's compositional aesthetic in a nutshell: ar-
rangements of images, scenes and sentiments. Preferably, these images and sentiments
are 'most diverse'. Hence, a set of songs amounts to an ensemble of 'sentiments' or
'states of the soul' rather than constituting a story. In essence, Schumann's songs
are, like the movements in his piano works, true character pieces, figures of musical representation, 'at the limit, only intermezzi' as Barthes would say, who finds
'the intermezzo consubstantial with the entire Schumannian œuvre'.[82] In his essay
Circle of Fragments, Barthes states what draws Schumann into the realm of the Early
Romantics. In the immediate context of Webern – '*The short pieces* of Webern . . . :
what care he expended *to break up!*' – Barthes makes the historical leap to Schumann:

Schumann was perhaps that composer who (before Webern) understood and practised the
aesthetic of the fragment best. He called the fragment 'intermezzo', he multiplied *intermezzi*
throughout his works: everything he produced was, in the final analysis, intercalated: but
between what and what? What does it mean to have a pure series of interruptions?[83]

    Arnold Schoenberg's remark on Webern's *Bagatelles* may be mentioned in this
context. In distinctly Romantic terms, Schoenberg describes how a poem, gesture
or novelistic scene are musically evoked. In Webern's pieces, just as is the case with
Early Romantic fragments, no story unfolds. That the concentration inherent in
these pieces contributes to the potential of conjuring up these images is worth
noting, not least in view of Schumann's compositional procedures:

Think what self-denial it takes to cut a long story so short. A glance can always be spun out
into a poem, a sigh into a novel. But to convey a novel through a single gesture, or felicity by
a single catch of the breath: such concentration exists only when emotional self-indulgence
is correspondingly absent.[84]

Within the cast of Romantic theory, the song as fragment is 'a part of an extensive
series' and as such is 'the result of earlier, and the seed of later incidents'.[85] What
Friedrich Schlegel's description of the Romantic form clearly implies, however, is
that fragments are situated in relation to each other, that they interact with each

---

[80] See *GS* IV, p. 263.
[81] *GS* IV, p. 264 [will mehr als wohl- oder übelklingende Musik, er will uns das Gedicht in seiner leibhaftigen
    Tiefe wiedergeben. Das Still-träumerische gelingt ihm am besten; . . . auch Reizendnaives. . . . Eine Reihe der
    verschiedensten Bilder und Gefühle erweckt das Liederheft].
[82] Barthes (1985d), p. 300.   [83] Barthes (1975), pp. 96–98. Cf. Pousseur (1993), p. 10.
[84] Schoenberg (1955), p. 15 [Man bedenke, welche Enthaltsamkeit dazu gehört, sich so kurz zu fassen. Jeder Blick
    läßt sich zu einem Gedicht, jeder Seufzer zu einem Roman ausdehnen. Aber: Einen Roman durch eine einzige
    Geste, ein Glück durch ein einziges Aufatmen auszudrücken: zu solcher Konzentration findet sich nur, wo
    Wehleidigkeit in entsprechendem Maße fehlt]. Trans. (1975), pp. 483–484.
[85] *KFSA* I, p. 472 [Glied einer großen Reihe . . . Folge früherer und Keim künftiger Begebenheiten].

other according to the Romantic law of evocation, revocation and anticipation.[86] Schumann's compositional series are thus not simple and arbitrary sequences of thoughts and moods, but rather contain within themselves the tendency towards, although not the achievement of, synthesis. Let us also note here that the resulting instability of a work consisting of a series of characteristic fragments reflects a creative procedure which is typical of the Romantic personality: Schumann's fluctuation between extremes. The fluctuation permeating his work, these changes of direction and disruptive gestures, identify with 'a pulsional body', as Barthes writes of Schumann, 'one which pushed itself back and forth, turns to something else – thinks of something else'.[87] And Schumann does so with conviction: 'By means of extremes one generally achieves more than by keeping to the ponderous golden mean of ordinary men and demi-men'.[88]

'Masses' of impressions and images endow Schumann's narration with the pulsation of diverse and contrasting positions whose origin, as has been noted above, lies in his heightened perceptiveness, his 'poetic consciousness'. A letter of 1838 conveys the power of compulsion under which Schumann produced:

Everything which goes on in the world affects me, politics, literature, people. I think about everything in my own way, which then wants to find a release through music; it wants to find an outlet. That is why many of my compositions are so difficult to understand, for they establish ties with distant interests, often importantly so, because everything that is strange in our times moves me and I must then articulate it musically in turn.[89]

This expresses a real sense of urgency in Schumann's search to find 'release' through the act of writing, whether it be through musical composition or, indeed, through all the other forms of written work, as the thousands of pages of diaries, letters and notes, containing a myriad of ideas, impressions and reflections, demonstrate. It is here, then, through writing itself, that Schumann asserts himself, finding as well as losing himself. Consciously, he was subject to 'the characteristic of our times: this restlessness, the flight and pursuit of all ideas, dreams, opinions, beliefs'.[90]

But Schumann also asserts that 'only he who knows how to control the masses can play with them'.[91] In the language of Friedrich Schlegel, this concept of playful poetic concatenation results in a new kind of 'structure and order which rounds off the free wealth of the power of imagination in ... simple masses, so as to form a loose

---

[86] See pp. 23–32, above.   [87] Barthes (1985d), p. 300.

[88] *TB* I, p. 142 [Mit den Extremen richtet man meist mehr aus, als mit der schwerfälligen goldenen Mittelstraße der gewöhnlichen Menschen und der Halbmenschen].

[89] *JB* (Letter to Clara Wieck of 13 April 1838), p. 282 [Es afficirt mich alles, was in der Welt vorgeht, Politik, Literatur, Menschen; über Alles denke ich nach meiner Weise nach, was sich dann durch die Musik Luft machen, einen Ausweg suchen will. Deshalb sind auch viele meiner Kompositionen so schwer zu verstehen, weil sie an entfernte Interessen anknüpfen, oft auch bedeutend, weil mich alles Merkwürdige der Zeit ergreift, und ich es dann musikalisch wieder aussprechen muß].

[90] *TB* I, p. 310 [Das Merkmal unserer Zeit ist das Unsäte, die Flucht u. Jagt aller Ideen, Träume, Meinungen, Glauben].

[91] *GS* I, p. 137 [nur wer die Massen zu beherrschen versteht, kann mit ihnen spielen].

and light unity'.[92] The metaphors Early Romantic theory applied in order to describe the procedure – 'incessant stream of narration' or 'floating painting'[93] – are, as may be noted, part of Schumann's own vocabulary: 'It is exactly through this confluence of readings, comparison of ideas, perceptions etc. that a solid mass coalesces like Corinthian ore and whereby [the composition] develops into an original painting'.[94] Schumann's creativity indeed depends on, as well as unfolds in response to, stimuli, either coming from without, such as poetry, or coming from within by way of intense self-observation (*Selbstbelauschung*).[95] Imagination is then, as Schumann writes, a matter of 'mediating emotion and reflection' which, via 'Anempfinden u. Andenken', leads artistically to an 'innocence of representation – evocation of the idea by way of external interaction and discharge of one's own [material]'.[96]

Schumann's 'innocence of representation' bears the signs of play, the free play of mind and mood which the Early Romantics were the first to advocate as the primary characteristic of all inner and outer human activity. The proximity to modern psychoanalysis, in particular to the Freudian concept of free association in connection with the unconscious, has its basis here, as has occasionally been noted in the critical literature of Early Romantic poetology.[97] In the context of Schumann's choice of texts, not least the texts for *Dichterliebe*, it is of interest to realize that he chose poems from Heine's *Lyrisches Intermezzo* freely. There was no need to construct a narrative where the play of free imagination was at work. Hence, from the *Lyrisches Intermezzo* Schumann selected whatever enticed his imagination. There was also, as should be emphasized, no effort to construct a narrative where none can be found in the first place, as is demonstrated in Part II. Schumann worked as a true poet in the Early Romantic sense:

The true poem only arises if the poet can choose among the materials which were given to his senses, or which is being transmitted to his memory, and if he can mix, arrange and embellish freely that chosen material for the sensually beautiful pleasure according to the laws of human mood.[98]

Schumann knew that his approach towards the genre of Romantic song meant a departure from current practice. In response to Koßmaly's essay on the Lied published in 1841 in the *NZfM*, he wrote:

---

[92] *KFSA* I, p. 452 [Gestalt und Ordnung rundet die Fülle der Einbildungskraft in . . . einfachen Massen zu einer leichten Einheit].

[93] *KFSA* I, p. 124 [unablässiger Strohm der Rede . . . fließendes Gemälde].

[94] *TB* I, p. 108 [gerade aus jenem Zusammenfluß von Lektüre, Vergleichungen der Ideen, Auffassungen pp. bildet sich eine feste Masse zusammen wie corinthisches Erz u. wird Originalgemälde].

[95] *TB* I, p. 314 [Ueber Selbstbelauschung].

[96] *TB* I, p. 335 [Mitteneinstehen zwischen Empfindung u. Reflexion . . . Unschuld der Darstellung – Erweckung der Idee durch fremde Wechselwirkung u. Absonderung des Eignen –].

[97] See the work of Manfred Frank (1985 and 1990) in particular, who also demonstrates the connection of Early Romantic literary practice to French literary theory.

[98] *KFSA* I, pp. 432–433 [Das eigentliche Gedicht entsteht nur wenn der Dichter unter dem Stoff, der seinen Sinnen gegeben, oder seinem Gedächtnis überliefert wird, schon wählen, und das Gewählte für den sinnlich schönen Genuß nach den Gesetzen des menschlichen Gemüts frei mischen, ordnen und schmücken kann].

In your article about the Lied I was a little aggrieved that you assigned me to the *second* class. I do not request the first, but I believe I am entitled to my *own, separate* class and I like it least to see myself be associated with Reißiger, Curschmann etc. I know that my striving and my means exceed those of the above-mentioned by far, and I hope you can tell yourself that and will not call me vain for it, since nothing could be further from the truth.[99]

Not without hindsight, it seems, did Schumann write the following to a friend in 1842:

I would hope that you will take a closer look at my song compositions. They speak of my future. I do not dare promise more than what I have achieved (especially in the Lied) and I am also pleased with it.[100]

Before we turn to Heine and the *Lyrisches Intermezzo*, here are the stanzas of two poems which Schumann used as epigraphs in the *NZfM*. He did not set these to music, but he certainly seems to have seen in them what Lied composition may mean:

Wem am besten dringen
    most
Liedes Blutström' aus der Brust,
Der wird's beste Lob erringen,
Und sein Weh gibt Andern Lust.[101]

He from whose breast gushes
The song's bloodstream,
Will gain the best praise
And his anguish gives others pleasure.

Wie ein Tollhaus von Tönen!
Und zwischendurch hör' ich vernehmbar
Lockende Harfenlaute,
Sehnsuchtwilden Gesang,
Seelenschmelzend und seelenzerreißend,
Und ich erkenne die Stimme.[102]

Like a madhouse of sounds!
And in between I hear
alluring sounds of the harp,
Singing wild with longing,
Melting souls and tearing them apart,
And I recognize the voice.

---

[99] Wasielewski, *Biographie*, p. 290 (letter in response to Kosmaly) [In Ihrem Aufsatz über das Lied hatte es mich ein wenig getrübt, daß sie mich in die *zweite* Klasse setzen. Ich verlange nicht nach der ersten; aber auf einen *eigenen* Platz glaub ich Anspruch zu haben und am allerwenigsten gern sehe ich mich Reißiger, Curschmann usw. beigestellt. Ich weiß, daß mein Streben, meine Mittel über die Genannten bei weitem hinausgehen und ich hoffe, Sie selbst sagen sich das und nennen mich deshalb nicht eitel, was weit von mir abliegt]. Emphasis as in source.

[100] Wasielewski, *Biographie*, p. 290 (letter of 10 May 1842) [Meinen Liederkompositionen wünschte ich, daß Sie sich sie genauer ansähen. Sie sprechen von meiner Zukunft. Ich getraue mir nicht, mehr versprechen zu können, als ich (gerade im Lied) geleistet, und bin auch zufrieden damit].

[101] Epigraph to the *NZfM* of 16 June 1839.   [102] Epigraph to the *NZfM* of 9 September 1839.

PART II

HEINE'S SIGNATURE OF MODERNITY: THE *LYRISCHES INTERMEZZO*

Das ausgesprochne Wort ist ohne Scham,
Das Schweigen ist der Liebe keusche Blüte.
[The spoken word is shameless, / Being silent is love's chaste blossom].

Heine in 1856. From the final poem in the 'Lamentations' (*Lamentationen*), a collection of Heine's last poems for his beloved, the Mouche. B 6/I, p. 348

6

INTRODUCTION

I discussed the position of the Early Romantics and their new idea of form and expression in the first part of this book, with particular attention to the core categories of reflection, fragment, irony and openness. As visionaries of Absolute Idealism, their exploration of distant lands conjured new forms of art and life. This was short-lived, as the journal *Athenaeum* reflects, appearing for less than three years at the turn of the eighteenth century. Then appeared the Romantic movement's fiercest critic, Heinrich Heine. Born in 1797, at the threshold of a new age and yet constantly exposed to, and deeply involved with, the body of thought of the Romantic generation, he subsequently unmasked and repudiated their ideals in the strongest terms. His critical writings illuminate the other side of Romanticism: the aspects of self-delusion and escapism, of nationalism and bigotry. Since poetry was considered the art form best able to express the Romantic spirit, Heine took issue first of all with Romantic poetry – by producing his own poetry as something of a countermove. There is thus a lot to be learned from Heine's poetic style itself, which absorbs – as much as it seeks to destroy – the Romantic model.

I shall offer a few facts and critical comments on Heine's *Lyrisches Intermezzo* in order to put this cycle of poems into historical, as well as literary-theoretical, perspective. To focus on Heine's poetic procedures, the cycle's formative elements and their function within the poem cycle as a whole will bring some aesthetic ideas to the surface, and may lead to an understanding of its 'poetic logic'. As we shall see, the salient structural characteristic in *Lyrisches Intermezzo*, namely its cyclicity, was in principle preserved by Schumann. Both Heine and Schumann achieved a poetic cyclicity that does not merely assemble particulars in a random fashion, but rather interweaves these thematically and structurally so as to generate evident and intensifying relations. The composer thus set to music what the poet called the 'outer frame of my soul's sick-bay',[1] a tableau of images of inner friction framed and arranged as a poetic cycle. But whereas Heine's poetic procedures have been critically investigated,[2] Schumann's concept of cyclicity still remains – despite various attempts to understand it – the most arcane and analytically challenging aspect of *Dichterliebe*.

---

[1] *HSA* XX, pp. 61–62 [Paßpartout zu meinem Gemütslazarethe].
[2] With greatest sophistication by Norbert Altenhofer (1982).

Heine's *Lyrisches Intermezzo* is a poetic cycle consisting of sixty-five poems and was written at the beginning of the poet's career in the early 1820s. This cycle, however, must be seen as a symptom of estrangement and negativity within the idealist cast of Romanticism. As the textual basis of Schumann's *Dichterliebe*, Heine's poetry exhibits structural and stylistic traits which run counter to the composer's genuinely Romantic aesthetic of form – yet on closer examination this turns out to be too simple an interpretation. Whilst the third part of this book will investigate the ways in which Schumann transforms, 'romanticizes' and 'idealizes' Heine's *Lyrisches Intermezzo*, this part sets out to investigate the poetic cycle critically in view of Heine's oppositional stance towards a Romantic *Weltanschauung*.

In this book I look at cyclicity essentially as an aesthetic modality of modernity. Formally, the artist of the post-Classical era preferred using small forms on the one hand, and to unite these by a central theme on the other. Thus, both Heine and Schumann abandoned the model offered by Goethe, who characterized his own poetic songs as 'the stories of my heart in the form of little paintings'[3] – self-contained, autonomous portraits of a generally positive experience of love. Certainly, the positive tone is missing in both Heine's and Schumann's work; Heine's modern version of love lyric stands apart from its precedent in form and in content as much as Schumann's song cycle does from his musical models by Beethoven and Schubert. Since musical and poetic 'content' is not assumed to represent the same kind of phenomenon here, hermeneutic emphasis is on extrapolating the difference between Heine's and Schumann's view of the modern world. As we shall see, the notion of 'modernity' was conceived of in ideologically opposite ways by Schumann and Heine. Whilst Schumann's cyclicity results from a realization of the Romantic aesthetics of reflection, fragment and irony, Heine's cyclicity defies any sort of 'Romantic progressiveness' in the spirit of Friedrich Schlegel's 'progressive Universalpoesie'.[4] The essence of the *Lyrisches Intermezzo* is not that it is 'eternally evolving, never completed',[5] in Schlegel's words, but precisely that individual poems as well as the cycle do end, and abruptly so, in order to emphasize the significance of an ending itself. As Heine laconically points out twice in the preface of the *Buch der Lieder:*

> Und scheint die Sonne noch so schön,   And however bright may shine the sun,
> Am Ende muß sie untergehn![6]   Ultimately it must set!

The *Lyrisches Intermezzo* is a prime example of Heine's sceptical – as opposed to idealistic – modern stance, which includes the thoroughly negative version of irony. Compared to Romantic irony as developed by the Early Romantics, where it mediates the contradiction between the finite and the infinite as an artistic as well as philosophical procedure, irony undergoes a fundamental change of function in

---

[3] Goethe (letter to Lange of October 1769), quoted in Atkins (1973), p. 721.
[4] The central demand of the Romantics, proclaimed in the *Athenaeum*, Fragment 116. *KFSA* II, p. 182 [Die romantische Poesie ist eine progressive Universalpoesie].
[5] A central thesis on Romantic poetry by the Early Romantics. See Part III.   [6] B I, pp. 12 and 13.

Heine's poetry. If Friedrich Schlegel describes wit as the 'outlooks into the infinite',[7] and irony as the 'evidence of endlessness',[8] Heine's irony cuts through and dismantles the sentiment of endlessness. As a purely rhetorical means, Heine employs irony in order to ridicule the sentimentality many of his poems evoke in the first few lines. It 'breaks the mood' (*Stimmungsbruch*) and thus functions destructively. As opposed to affirming the possibility of a timeless endlessness, the reader is left with sudden nothingness, however comical the effect of Heine's use of irony often may be. Rather than describing an aesthetic attitude signifying the artist's superiority over the work, the contents of Heine's poems are themselves rendered worthless. With Heine, irony has thus become a rhetorical means of relentless negativity and as such is one of the most crucial aspects delineating the essentially antithetical aesthetics of the composer and the poet. We can, then, begin to investigate the relationship of language and music in *Dichterliebe* by way of familiarizing ourselves with the sense of an ending in the poetic cycle on the one hand and the absence thereof in the song cycle on the other. It is thus on a formal level that I shall begin to examine the differences between the two art works, a methodological necessity that will lead to a better understanding of ambiguous musical 'content' at a later stage.

As part of my argument that *Dichterliebe* is aesthetically and semantically guided by non-narrative procedures, an investigation of Heine's idea of poetic form – of what has been called his 'art of arrangement'[9] – will shed light upon a kaleido-scopic spectrum of the modern disposition of forlornness. This means a revision of the frequent assumption that the poems of the *Lyrisches Intermezzo* amounted to a continuous story. As Heine himself calls this poetic cycle a 'psychological picture of myself',[10] we shall further see how it is not external events but an inner state of mind that permeates the poetic cycle. And here, an *imago* of woman serves him as his poetic canvas, appearing as Virgin, Madonna, Sphinx and Beast. Because this *imago* functions as a poetic mirror of Heine's monumental critique of, and personal disposition towards, his time, it becomes the catalyst for Heine's reaction. However, this female *imago*, prominent as it is in all of his poems, serves only as a vehicle for the poet's projections and reflections of his fundamental doubts, his loss of hope, and his inner tornness (*Zerrissenheit*). No woman behind this *imago* ever attains any real presence.

However, Heine's reflections are not only circular, but even static at times. Flashes of images around this same idea make the cycle of sixty-five poems into what Heine described as 'variations on the same little theme'.[11] What seemed true for Heine's world-view becomes the very concept of form in the *Lyrisches Intermezzo*: 'The world does not stay at a rigid standstill, but in an ineffectual cyclical motion'.[12]

---

[7] *KFSA* II, p. 200, no. 220 [*echappées de vue* ins Unendliche].
[8] *KFSA* XVIII, p. 128, no. 76 [epideixis der Unendlichkeit].
[9] Altenhofer (1982), pp. 16–32.   [10] *HSA* XX, p. 280.   [11] *HSA* XX, p. 250.
[12] B IV, p. 49 [Die Welt bleibt nicht im starren Stillstand, aber im erfolglosen Kreislauf].

HEINE, THE ROMANTICS AND DISENCHANTMENT

Heine himself can be seen as showing the way towards a kind of criticism which 'situates Romanticism in the past, but does not *dismiss* it to the past', as McGann suggests.[1] The critical line Heine has taken is reflected in his strikingly sharp and erudite, yet polemical, art–critical prose, and some of his critical writings are just this: a grand testimony of conflicting viewpoints towards works to which he feels emotionally highly attached, since his own early poetry was written in the Romantic spirit. On the other hand, these writings carry a melancholic and at times bitter-cynical tone towards those very works, because they came from 'another world' which can know nothing of present concerns and have therefore lost their credibility, and with it their *raison d'être*. Having produced poetry in the hiatuses of various conventions and traditions, Heine was the first to succumb nostalgically to Romantic spirituality as much as to criticize trenchantly its resurrectionist admiration for ancient and medieval art, and the delusions which such retrograde aestheticism generates.

There was, however, not only a political basis to these indictments (the unmasking of the Romantic movement as reactionary) but – more to the point – a psychological one: Heine felt betrayed. The intoxicating melodiousness of high Romantic poetry (of Brentano and Eichendorff, for example), its excessive rhymes and rhythms, alliteration and onomatopœia, its enigmatic imagery and semi–religious intensity – these all wield such power over the reader's mind that one is compelled to enter worlds and sentiments which stand in stark contrast to the reality this poetry seeks to elevate. Heine was too conscious, perhaps too analytical a contemporary to be able to blind himself to the kind of fatal deceptiveness such illusionary worlds are bound to invoke. He was painfully aware of his lack of faith, which prevented him from seeing art as having healing powers or taking Romantic poetry for what it aspires to create: a kind of mythical respite from the alienating forces of the modern world of materialism, a last residuum of vanished spirituality. The abyss Heine felt yawning between the Romantic disposition and his own comes through in one of his truly remorseless, sardonic passages:

But really what was the Romantic School in Germany?

It was nothing other than the rediscovery of medieval poetry as it manifests itself in its songs, works of art and architecture, and in art and life at large. But this poetry emerged

---

[1] McGann (1985), p. 11.

out of Christianity, it was the passion flower which sprang forth from the blood of Christ. I don't know whether this melancholic flower, which we in Germany call passion flower, is called the same in France, and whether folk tales attribute to it the same mystical origin. It is this strange, ill-coloured flower in whose cup we see the instruments of torture which were used for the crucifixion of Christ, that is hammer, tongs, nails etc. It is a flower which is not necessarily ugly but only ghostly. Indeed, its sight arouses in our soul an atrocious kind of pleasure, similar to these frantically sweet sensations which grow out of pain itself. In this respect, the flower would be the symbol for Christianity itself whose horrific appeal consists precisely of taking delight in this sort of pain.[2]

Heine unmasks the Romantics' passion for medieval forms and Christian values as a kind of pathological obsession with implanting a surrogate profundity into a hopeless, profane age. He imputes a masochistic tendency to the Romantic generation in their adoration of a visually mesmerizing but actually terrifying symbol of Christian belief (the 'passion flower' embodying Christ's martyrdom). Denoting as it does the fundamental tenet of renunciation, Heine rejects such denial and prohibition of sensuality as delirious and perverse ('atrocious pleasure'; 'frantically sweet sensations'). The aspect of suppression is seen by Heine to be the reason for the epoch's defining characteristic of melancholy. Furthermore, the Romantics' avowedly naive reliance on medieval and Christian beliefs is dismissed as deviously anachronistic. Such values, Heine argues, were long lost, and constant efforts to recapture them, via idolizing religious or devotional artefacts, struck Heine as desperate escapism.

The idea of irretrievably lost beliefs as embodied in medieval art – or, more poignantly, Heine's scepticism towards attempts to revive the spiritual substance of works of the past – originates in his doubting the very possibility that this essence is transmissible to later generations. As a consequence, he saw no hope of side-stepping the temporality of his own work. Time, he says, will simply take its toll on art, which was created in and for a particular time and place; this art will mean little or nothing to those of later birth. Ineluctably, its meaning will cease and future generations will perceive his literary and poetic works with eyes that had not seen the world from which they came. Neither motivations nor intentions are communicable once the context for non-discursive understanding has been lost. A letter of condolence written in 1840 to his friend Karl August Varnhagen, whose sister had died, reveals with rare personal openness Heine's pessimistic outlook on the reception of his work:

[2] B III, pp. 361–362 [Was war aber die romantische Schule in Deutschland? Sie war nichts anders als die Wiederentdeckung der Poesie des Mittelalters, wie sie sich in dessen Liedern, Bild- und Bauwerken, in Kunst und Leben manifestiert hatte. Diese Poesie aber war aus dem Christentume hervorgegangen, sie war eine Passionsblume, die dem Blute Christi entsprossen. Ich weiß nicht ob die melancholische Blume, die wir in Deutschland Passionsblume benamsen, auch in Frankreich diese Benennung führt, und ob ihr von der Volkssage ebenfalls jener mystische Ursprung zugeschrieben wird. Es ist jene sonderbar mißfarbige Blume, in deren Kelch man die Marterwerkzeuge, die bei der Kreuzigung Christi gebraucht worden, nämlich Hammer, Zange, Nägel usw., abkonterfeit sieht, eine Blume die durchaus nicht häßlich, sondern nur gespenstig ist, ja, deren Anblick sogar ein grauenhaftes Vergnügen in unserer Seele erregt, gleich den krampfhaft süßen Empfindungen, die aus dem Schmerze selbst hervorgehen. In solcher Hinsicht wäre diese Blume das geeignetste Symbol für das Christenthum selbst, dessen schauerlicher Reiz eben in der Wollust des Schmerzes besteht].

I just learned about the passing away of. I can well imagine your suffering right now. I knew her very well; she always showed the kindest sympathy towards me; she resembled you so much in your calm and gentleness. Even if I did not see her all that often, she certainly counted as one of the *intimate friends*, was part of this *secret circle* in which people *understand each* Other *without words* – Oh God, how has this circle gradually dwindled in the last ten years, *this silent community*! There goes one after another – and we shed fruitless tears over them – until we go ourselves – The tears which will then flow for us will not be as hot because the *new generation knows neither what we aimed at nor what we have suffered*!

And how should they have known us? Our own secret we never spelled out [in words], and we will never spell it out, and we will descend into the grave with our lips closed! *We, we understood each other just through looks, we looked at each other and we knew what was going on in ourselves – this language of the eyes will soon be lost, and our written works left behind, for example Rahel's letters, will be indecipherable hieroglyphs* for those born after us – I know this and I think of it with every new death and departure.[3]

Almost two decades earlier, and directly referring to the *Lyrisches Intermezzo*, we find a comment with similar overtones: 'In truth, it is only very few for whom one writes, especially if one retreats into oneself, as I did'.[4]

Heine's awareness of the limits of communication through his work directly affected his chosen style of writing. Since neither mimetic nor subjective principles are means to secure understanding, Heine developed a more convoluted style. He opts for an open, associative way of communication, characterized by a network of subtle ties between particular ideas or impressions. The concepts of allusion and referentiality create a literary texture of great density on several semantic levels. Altenhofer picks up the striking term 'language of the eyes' (*Augensprache*) from the letter to Varnhagen, and interprets it as corresponding with Heine's preferred literary means of 'association' and 'allusion' as opposed to 'systematic' or 'descriptive' principles. The historical process that causes a gradual deterioration of communication between work and reader – loss of 'Augensprache' – is coupled with a process of paralysis on the side of the text as its messages congeal to 'written, hieroglyphic memorials'

---

[3] *HSA* XXI, pp. 345–346 [So eben erfahre ich von dem neuen Verluste . . . . Ich fühle ganz was Sie jetzt leiden . . . . Ich habe die Hingeschiedene sehr gut gekannt, sie zeigte mir immer die liebreichste Theilnahme, war Ihnen so ähnlich in der Besonnenheit und Milde, und obgleich ich sie nicht allzu oft sah, so zählte sie doch zu den *Vertrauten*, zu dem *heimlichen Kreise*, wo man *sich versteht ohne zu sprechen* – Heiliger Gott, wie ist dieser Kreis, diese *stille Gemeinde*, allmählich geschmolzen, seit den letzten zehn Jahren! Einer nach dem anderen geht heim – Unfruchtbare Tränen weinen wir ihnen nach – bis auch wir abgehn – Die Tränen die alsdann für uns fließen, werden nicht so heiß sein, *denn die neue Generazion weiß weder was wir gewollt, noch was wir gelitten. /* Und wie sollten sie uns gekannt haben? Unser eigentliches Geheimnis haben wir nie ausgesprochen, und werden es auch nie aussprechen, und wir steigen ins Grab mit verschlossenen Lippen! *Wir, wir verstanden einander durch bloße Blicke, wir sahen uns an und wußten, was in uns vorging – diese Augensprache wird bald verloren sein, und unsere hinterlassenen Schriftmähler, z.B. Rahels Briefe, werden für die Spätergeborenen doch nur unenträthselbare Hieroglyphen seyn –* das weiß ich und daran denk ich bei jedem neuen Abgang und Heimgang]. My emphasis. Cf. Altenhofer (1993), pp. 58–75.

[4] *HSA* XX, p. 61 (letter to the poet Immermann on 24 December 1822 when completing the Druckvorlage for *Tragödien, nebst einem lyrischen Intermezzo*, the volume which contains most of the *Lyrisches Intermezzo* poems later to be included in *Buch der Lieder*) [eigentlich sind es ja doch nur wenige für die man schreibt, besonders wenn man, wie ich gethan, sich mehr in sich selbst zurückgezogen].

which are indecipherable for later generations.[5] Heine's remark makes this clear:
'Just don't expect me to write anything systematic; that's the Angel of Death in any
correspondence . . . the associativeness of ideas should always prevail'.[6]

What Altenhofer calls 'palimpsestic procedures' in Heine's prose, an associative plane of meaning evolving over a span of time, is evident in Heine's poetic
output as well. The idea of a 'language of the eyes' and its added sense of resigned acceptance of the condition of estrangement appears again and again as
part of the extensive metaphorical web in *Lyrisches Intermezzo*. The recurring
image of the beloved's eyes or face (in 'Wenn ich in deine Augen seh', 'Dein
Angesicht', 'Im Rhein', 'Allnächtlich im Traume' to mention only poems set in
Dichterliebe)[7] is metaphorically linked to sensations of loss and forlornness. Verbs
such as 'Vergessen', 'Verschwinden', 'Verlorn' [*sic*], 'Verlassen', or 'Wissen'/'Nicht-
Wissen', 'Schweigen', 'Sagen' and 'Sprechen' (to forget, to disappear, to be lost, to
be forsaken, to know/to not know, to be silent, to speak) signify the prevalence of
this. The loss of mutual understanding equals the loss of words ('Und's Wort hab ich
vergessen').[8] It eventually renders the poet's inner world as withheld from others;
his emotions remain unreciprocated because words will not reach the outside world.
There is thus a notion of ineffability to be found in Heine's ostentatiously simplistic
lines and rhymes as much as there is a distinct sense of inner retreat and isolation.

[5] Altenhofer (1993), pp. 58–75.

[6] *HSA* II, p. 10 [Nur verlangen Sie von mir keine Systematie; das ist der Würgeengel aller Korrespon-
denz. . . . Assoziation der Ideen soll immer vorwalten].

[7] See further poems IV (4), V (4a), XI (4b), XIV, XVI, XIX, XXXIX, XLVII (12a), LIII, LV, LVII, LVIII, LXIV.
(Arabic numerals indicate the songs in Schumann's *Dichterliebe*.)

[8] Poem LVII ('Allnächtlich im Traume').

ENDINGS, CUTS, CYCLICITY

Heine's formal and stylistic means attest to a modernist disposition of inner lability and doubt that finds expression in a new kind of lyricism, not based on personal experience as is true for the Goethean *Erlebnisgedicht*, but on modes of reducing experience and emotion to mood and sentiment. Heine's famous *Stimmungsbruch* (breaking of tone and mood) is brought about through irony and reflection, concealed quotations and trivialized Romantic formulas. This and a well-timed use of playfully refined rhetorical or worn-out phrases are the main stylistic components for a Heinean fabrication of deceptively idyllic scenes, whose abrupt disruptions leave a bitter taste of disillusion and alienation.

Since Heine's *Stimmungsbruch* is crucial for an understanding of the underlying tensions in *Lyrisches Intermezzo*, as well as for Heine's emphasis on 'making an end', we shall take a closer look at one representative poem – as it happens, not one included in *Dichterliebe*:

VIII

Es stehen unbeweglich	Standing motionless
Die Sterne in der Höh,	are the stars high in the sky,
Viel tausend Jahr, und schauen	for many a thousand years,
Sich an mit Liebesweh.	and look at each other, longing for love.
Sie sprechen eine Sprache,	They are speaking a language
Die ist so reich, so schön;	that is so rich, so beautiful;
Doch keiner der Philologen	however, not one of the philologists
Kann diese Sprache verstehn.	can understand this language.
Ich aber hab sie gelernet,	But I have learned it,
Und ich vergesse sie nicht;	and I do not forget it;
Mir diente als Grammatik	The beloved's face
Der Herzallerliebsten Gesicht.	served me as my grammar.

Heine's poem begins with an ancient metaphor of the poetic world, an image of grand dimensions: the stars. As often in Heine,[1] the stars, longing unattainably for each other, are heightened representatives of the typical love-scene taking place

---

[1] Cf. poem LX: 'Es fällt ein Stern herunter / Aus seiner funkelnden Höh / Das ist der Stern der Liebe, / Den ich dort fallen seh'.

down on earth. Love is associated with an eternal longing rather than with that of consummation. The exposition of this poem thus adumbrates the Romantic theme. But as the stars speak of this experience in a 'philologically uninvestigated' language, the phenomenon of love as told in their beautiful but cryptic language cannot be communicated to the poet. It is metaphorically defined as far removed from reality and remains unknown to the poet even as a listener because the discourse of love is linguistically incomprehensible to him. The *Stimmungsbruch* occurs after line 6, as Heine introduces prosaic philological pedantry into the atmospheric scene of stellar love. Furthermore, however, the skill with which Heine drops the sentimental tone in order to express the pointlessness of love-poem writing turns Heine into the poet who writes without knowing what it actually is that he is writing about. In the absence of the 'heavenly' experience, in the absence of any knowledge of love, the poet takes the beloved's face as his basic guide and tool for poetic expression. And, in a satirical twist, he reduces his beloved's face to a mundane grammar-book. Whereas the Romantics rendered their object of poetic production as essentially ethereal, Heine's poetry will be tied to his perception of the real. Thus, Heine thematizes his inability to write love poetry spontaneously by reflecting the situation of the Romantically 'uninitiated' poet in this poem.

Fuerst describes the situation well:

Heine's poem plunges with bravura into an especially shallow infinite of fallacy. . . . The felicity of the trifle is not merely in the turning up of 'grammar', but in the whole shift from heavy sentimentality to light witticism. Here, sorrow is overcome by the freedom of the mind. More exactly, a fancy of sentiment is modulated into a fancy of wit.[2]

Adorno adds an important dimension when discussing Heine's idiosyncratic poetic style of *Stimmungsbruch* as part of what was mentioned earlier to be the notion of ineffability in Heine's use of language. He sees in Heine's linguistic virtuosity an act of compensation for the poet's deep-felt powerlessness to express his estrangement and isolation; in Heine's 'failure of Jewish emancipation', Adorno sees the grounds for 'the opposite of a native sense of being at home in language. Only someone who is not actually inside language can manipulate it like an instrument.' Adorno's critique interprets the core characteristic of reification worked into the poetry by the corrupt application of Romantic archetypes as Heine's inability to 'find archetypes of modernity' itself. He then describes Heine's language as 'assimilatory' as a result of being a 'language of unsuccessful identification'. However, there is meaning in such failure:

For the power of the one who mocks impotently exceeds his impotence. If all expression is the trace left by suffering, then Heine was able to recast his own inadequacy, the muteness of his language, as an expression of rupture. So great was the virtuosity of this man, who imitated language as if he were playing it on a keyboard, that he raised even the inadequacy of

[2] Fuerst (1966), p. 76.

his language to the medium of one to whom it was granted to say what he suffered. Failure, reversing itself, turns into success. . . . The figures of this truth are the aesthetic breaks; it forgoes the immediacy of rounded, fulfilled language.[3]

Adorno's sociologically critical perspective perceives the 'stereotypical theme of un-requited love' as 'an image of homelessness, and the poetry devoted to it' as 'an attempt to draw estrangement itself into the sphere of intimate experience'. This is indeed the crux of Heine's intricate metaphorical *écriture*, in which nothing means what it pretends; it infuses the text with a semantic opacity strangely unredeemed by the simplicity of the poems' overt form, rhyme and metre. One agrees with Adorno that the 'intentionally false folk-song' becomes great poetry as a 'vision of sacrifice',[4] for the contrast to be felt between form and content, declared and implied message, signifies Heine's strained relationship to the German language in general and to lyric expression in particular.

The aspect of Heine's unresolved stance towards his Jewish origins is at the core of Adorno's description of Heine's lyric poetry as a 'wound' – a drastic formulation which, however, hits the nerve of the matter. A few remarks may be offered here in addition to Adorno's argument. The stigma, it is suggested, is that of cultural difference, which reappears as the characteristic sting in Heine's language, his mother tongue which reminded him incessantly of his alienation. Around the time of writing the *Lyrisches Intermezzo*, when, for anti-Semitic reasons, Heine was expelled from his fraternity and as a consequence from the University of Göttingen, the bruises he suffered inflamed his aversion for the German language:

I am now experiencing a very special kind of mood, and this may have the greatest im-pact on everything. Everything German disgusts me; . . . The German language splits my ears. . . . Oh . . . , how my soul craves for peace, and how it is yet being torn more and more, day by day.[5]

There is method, then, in Heine's concurrent decision to take the folk-song – the very embodiment of the 'German soul' – as the primary model for his poetry. He applies it *ex negativo*, i.e. not in order to continue the Romantics' intonation of harmony and innocence but to infuse their most cherished artistic medium with his 'inner tornness' (*Zerrissenheit*). A year prior to the appearance of the *Buch der Lieder*, Heine wrote to Wilhelm Müller, the poet of some of Schubert's songs:

---

[3] Adorno (1968), p. 150 [Die Macht des ohnmächtig Spottenden übersteigt seine Ohnmacht. Ist aller Ausdruck die Spur von Leiden, so hat er es vermocht, das eigene Ungenügen, die Sprachlosigkeit seiner Sprache, umzuschaffen zum Ausdruck des Bruchs. So groß war die Virtuosität dessen, der die Sprache gleichsam wie auf einem Klavier nachspielte, daß er noch die Unzulänglichkeit seines Wortes zum Medium dessen erhöhte, dem gegeben ward, was er leidet. Mißlingen schlägt um ins Gelungene. . . . Ihre Chiffren sind die ästhetischen Risse. Sie verzichtet auf die Unmittelbarkeit vollendeter, erfüllter Sprache]. Trans. (1991a), pp. 82–83.

[4] Adorno (1991a), p. 85.

[5] *HSA* XX, p. 50 (letter to his friend Sethe of 14 April 1822) [Ich lebe jetzt in einer ganz besonderen Stimmung, und die mag wohl an allem den meisten Antheil haben. Alles was deutsch ist, ist mir zuwider; . . . Die deutsche Sprache zerreißt meine Ohren. . . . wie meine Seele nach Frieden lechzt, und wie sie doch täglich mehr und mehr zerrissen wird].

From very early on I exposed myself to the influence of the German folk-song . . . ; only in your songs, however, do I believe I have found pure sound and true simplicity. . . . How pure, how lucid are your songs, and all of them folk-songs. In my poems, however, only the form is passably folkloristic, their content, however, belongs to conventional society.[6]

Between these lines of flattery rings a slightly cynical tone. The emphasis on the 'conventional' – that which is 'contemporary' or 'modern' – points to Heine's decided refusal to identify with an aesthetic of euphony for which the folkloric essentially stands. Considering the Romantics' declared objective to salvage potentially troubled times and minds by reviving the healing powers of the folk-song's inherent original melody (*Urmelodie*), the disturbing rupture pervading Heine's poetry belies the Romantic movement's very intent as expressed by Arnim and Brentano:

It will comfort us, in the chaos of our days, to receive a poetry of the folk-song, to search for its remaining sounds; it [the folk-song] descends only on this one celestial ladder whose firm rungs carry the times on which the rainbow-angel descends; they [the folk-songs] greet in conciliation all the antagonists of our days, and heal the great rupture of the world.[7]

Both the title and form of the *Buch der Lieder* are thus laudatory gestures used by Heine to herald sarcastically his own poetic countermove. To thus comply hypocritically with an aesthetic fashion in order to convey its vitiated worth, is in the best tradition of Heine's occasionally bitter irony. The difficulty of Heine's poetry manifests itself precisely at the juncture of poetic appropriation, the moment at which borrowed styles and imagery amount to nothing but a personal lyric arsenal which Heine handles with tremendous sophistication. Heine's creative investment is to be seen in the degree of critical imagination with which he forces these inherited models out of their established realm of harmony by way of confronting them with the harsh tone of a modern society. The famed notion of inwardness to be found in much of Eichendorff's or Brentano's lyric poetry, in the Goethean *Erlebnisgedicht*, or indeed the whole of naive folk poetry, is one of the central aspects with which Heine took issue. The rejection he experienced in his early years made him become an outsider with regard to both his country of birth and his language. Instead of inwardness, the principle that prevails in his poetry is that of self-critical reflection and rationality. Heine's re-reading of the poetic output of a past legacy with the avowed intention of corrupting its ideology presents us with a hermeneutic challenge fairly exceptional within the history of poetry: it is at once an emancipatory act *out* from

---

[6] *HSA* XX, p. 250 (letter of 7 June 1826) [Ich habe sehr früh schon das Volkslied auf mich einwirken lassen . . . , aber ich glaube erst in ihren Liedern den reinen Klang und die wahre Einfachheit, wonach ich immer strebte, gefunden zu haben. Wie rein, wie klar sind ihre Lieder, und sämmtlich sind es Volkslieder. In meinen Gedichten hingegen ist nur die Form einigermaßen volksthümlich, der Inhalt gehört der convenzionellen Gesellschaft an].

[7] Arnim and Brentano (1987), p. 403 [Es wird uns, die wir vielleicht eine Volkspoesie erhalten, in dem Durchdringen unserer Tage, es wird uns anstimmend seyn, ihre noch übrigen lebenden Töne aufzusuchen, sie kommt immer nur auf dieser einen ewigen Himmelsleiter herunter, die Zeiten sind darin feste Sprossen, auf denen Regenbogenengel niedersteigen; sie grüßen versöhnend alle Gegensätzler unserer Tage und heilen den großen Riß der Welt]. Cf. similar statement in Jokl (1991), pp. 26–27.

the models he seeks to expose and a determined act to get inside these same models. The sense of ambiguity is thus a built-in factor in this kind of polysemous poetic texture which one has to try to negotiate.

Obviously, Heine felt intensely out of phase with the generation of poets dwelling on the constituents of a national consciousness by way of adapting a folkloristic style, such as Brentano, Eichendorff and Müller. The notion of illusion that their poetry produces, together with the depiction of dream lands, and the deploying of fairy motifs to stir the reader's imagination, was highly suspect to Heine. Even his ability to simulate an association with this poetic style by writing 'little malicious songs'[8] in the 1820s faltered noticeably in later years. What had once been enough of a vehicle to express contempt towards the deceptiveness of Romantic sentimentality was by 1837 seen as the embodiment of mendacity. It had become entirely impossible for Heine to use it as an artistic means:

I cannot present this new edition of the *Buch der Lieder* to its Trans-Rheinish readers without greeting them in most honest prose. I do not know what strange feeling it is that prevents me from versifying such prefaces by casting it in fine rhythms as is normally the custom for anthologies. For some time now, there has been something inside me that resents all versed forms of speaking, and as I hear, there are many others today who feel a similar aversion. It seems to me that there has been too much lying going on by way of pretty verses, and that the truth shies away from appearing in metrical dresses.[9]

In the same preface some pages later, Heine, however, says that the *Buch der Lieder* was written 'during a time when the flame of truth excited me more than it enlightened me . . .'.[10] On the one hand this was a confession of the Romantic movement's inescapable influence upon a young aspiring poet looking for ideals and models. Initially he found them in poets like Bürger, Goethe and Uhland,[11] as well as in A. W. Schlegel, whose Bonn lectures (1819/20) and encouraging advice he evidently valued at the time of writing the *Lyrisches Intermezzo*.[12] Indeed, Heine was then still under the spell of Schlegelian Romanticism. On the other hand, however, Heine's assertion that Romanticism had for him once been 'the flame of truth' has to do with a shared sense of opposition. Ultimately, Heine's general critical attitude allied him with the movement's main incentive: to defy an unromantic, unfeeling reality with Friedrich Schlegel's programme of a 'progressive universal poetry'.[13] Thus,

---

[8] *HSA* XX, p. 61 [kleine maliziöse Lieder].

[9] *DHA* I/2 *Buch der Lieder*, preface to the second edition [Diese neue Ausgabe des Buches der Lieder kann ich dem überrheinischen Publikum nicht zuschicken, ohne sie nicht mit freundlichen Grüßen in ehrlichster Prosa zu begleiten. Ich weiß nicht, welches wunderliche Gefühl mich davon abhält, dergleichen Vorworte, wie es bei Gedichtsammlungen üblich ist, in schönen Rhythmen zu versifizieren. Seit einiger Zeit sträubt sich etwas in mir gegen alle gebundene Rede, und wie ich höre, regt sich bei manchen Zeitgenossen eine ähnliche Abneigung. Es will mich dünken, als sei in schönen Versen allzuviel gelogen worden, und die Wahrheit scheue sich in metrischen Gewanden zu erscheinen].

[10] *DHA* I/2, foreword to the *Buch der Lieder* [in einer Zeit als die Flamme der Wahrheit mich mehr erhitzte als erleuchtete . . .].

[11] *DHA* I/1, p. 575.   [12] Futterknecht (1985), pp. 198 ff.   [13] Cf. Jokl (1991), p. 27. See Part I.

we find in the early love poetry of Heine a degree of his oft-mentioned *Zerrissenheit* that originates in his attempts at emancipation from at least two unwanted sources of influence: Romanticism as a reactionary force; and the harsh onslaught of industrialization and materialism in a modern world, which degraded the very thought of poetry to an evasive manoeuvre. Heine knew that the times called for other forms of protest, expressive forms more in tune with the epoch's prosaic goals. Somewhat cynically, then, he considered prose more capable than poetry of reaching its audience, of being understood by prosaic minds. Soon after the *Buch der Lieder*, Heine became increasingly adverse to lyricism and his move into higher journalism has to be seen in the light of this disillusioned, yet politically highly motivated, stance.

The fractures in Heine's lyrical language – most obviously inserted through *Stimmungsbruch* – are symbolic of those 'cut feelings' that Heine wanted to express. Heine's stylistic means thus remain true to his ends as he objects to 'fabricating a Catholic harmony of feelings' and decides instead with 'Jacobinical mercilessness' to 'cut and tear feelings apart, for the sake of truth'.[14]

The *Lyrisches Intermezzo* works primarily on the basis of those tensions I have described so far. However, the question of the poet's personal life, his experience of unrequited love, has so often been raised that a few words about such frequently assumed causality seem appropriate. The argument is based on Heine's biographical circumstances over the course of time in which the poems for the *Lyrisches Intermezzo* were written, as ascertained by earlier generations of Heine scholars. Heine, in 1814, fell in love with his cousin Amalie, daughter of the uncle in whose business Heine was, in 1816, trained to become an accountant. The feelings towards Amalie remained unreciprocated, as was the case with her sister Therese, the object of Heine's affection some years later.[15] Heine scholarship has long tried to explain the prominence of the topos of unrequited love in the *Buch der Lieder* in the light of these biographical data. In some cases, this traditional and positivistic approach has led to some amusing 'results' as scholars have tried to establish links between Heine's innumerable love poems and his real or imagined love affairs. Accordingly, scholars have taken pains to identify the myriads of women in Heine's poetry with those he may have met in life, and doggedly established chronologies for both. In the eyes of these critics, Heine's poem–cycle degenerated into a procession of unattainable woman in Heine's life, to each of whom, it was assumed, Heine devoted a poem.

Typical of many others, Elster's biographically orientated investigation[16] along these lines has lost its persuasive power, not only because the certitude of such epistemological dualism between Heine's life and his poetry faltered once sharper forensic eyes challenged Elster's claims as regards Heine's biography.[17] Windfuhr's comment that Heine in his later years, when he was, from all we can know, happily

---

[14] *HSA* III, p. 209 [katholische Harmonie der Gefühle erlügen...jakobinisch unerbittlich, die Gefühle zerschneiden, der Wahrheit wegen...].
[15] Atkins (1973), pp. 721–722.   [16] Elster I, pp. 419 ff., and II, pp. 347 ff.   [17] Rose (1962).

married to Mathilde, still kept writing poetry with the central theme of unrequited love, already points towards the limitations of a biographically based exegesis of the *Lyrisches Intermezzo*.[18] The dubiousness of an approach that concentrates on the poet's personal experience arises primarily, however, from the assumption that poetic content was transmitted and delivered through direct, unfiltered language. Trust in a language whose constituents are in congruence with the images and ideas it names seems to have fed into positivism's mechanistic principle of identifying authorial intention with poetic expression. The various poetic models which Heine's poetic language absorbs, however, and the lack of a genuinely personal lyrical mode as a consequence of this, drain his language of any spontaneity and infiltrate it with a great sense of reserve. Such a conglomerate of styles produces a rather complex situation in which none of the expressive modes – be it the folk-song, Goethe's *West-östlicher Divan*, the Romantics' imagery, or Petrarch[19] – retains its autonomy. Neither the topos of unrequited love nor Heine's cultivation of a stereotypical beauty can be sufficiently interpreted by merely identifying the sources of inspiration, because all meaning inherited from these sources undergoes deformation within the poetic composition itself. If, as in poem XLII for example, the oxymoronic love-model of Petrarch appears simultaneously with a figure of hyperbole of a Romantic image, Heine announces – in the spirit of materialism – the deflation of a nuanced Petrarchic sentiment. Heine thus qualifies the assumed expressive mode of each applied poetic reference by juxtaposing it with others, and speaking through the mask of Petrarch means only that there are other masks waiting which Heine will put on in order ultimately to expose the hollowness of any particular poetic cliché. *Verismo* is thus perhaps the remotest concept that could be said to inform Heine's poetry, since the signs of naturalness are nothing but borrowed ciphers implanted for the sake of disfiguration. The notion of artificiality is then all the more evident when one realizes how Heine plays with the archetypal voice of nature in the folk-song, which is deployed like a traditional requisite amongst a number of others. To adapt to a variety of poetic modes from the literary canon also means to deny his own poetry a sense of belonging. Originality in his poetry is confined to the ways in which Heine appropriates these models for his own uses – a critique of the values his precursors put forward in their work, as well as a critique of poetic truth itself. The honesty of poetic expression is always doubted, for Heine's perception of the world is determined by his own ambivalence. In what he sees, Heine detects the signs of inhumanity, as he does with surgical scrutiny when placing the Blue Flower on his poetic operating table.[20] As Goethe challenged the readers of his autobiography *Dichtung und Wahrheit* to recognize the dialectics between words and the world, Heine

[18] Windfuhr (1966), p. 212.
[19] Windfuhr (1966) can certainly be considered the most thorough and differentiated discussion on the topos of love in the *Buch der Lieder* and elsewhere in Heine's lyrical output. The influence of Petrarch seems, however, overestimated. In contrast to Windfuhr, Prawer (1960) argues for the significance of stylistic over biographical motifs in Heine's early poetry by maintaining the fictionality of the figure of the woman.
[20] See the discussion below, pp. 87–89.

discards this relation altogether and instead puts forward the question of poetry and deception. Heine's overt references to Goethe do not only serve the purpose of reversing his predecessor's statements,[21] as in the case of the last stanza in Goethe's 'Willkommen und Abschied' of 1770:

In deinen Küssen welche Wonne!	In your kisses, what bliss!
In deinen Augen welcher Schmerz!	In your eyes, what pain!
. . .	. . .
Und doch, welch Glück, geliebt zu werden!	And yet, what bliss to be loved!
Und lieben, Götter, welch ein Glück![22]	And to love, Gods, what bliss!

which Heine turns into:

In den Küssen welche Lüge!	In these kisses, what a lie!
Welche Wonne in dem Schein!	What bliss in this illusion!
Ach, wie süß ist das Betrügen,	Oh, how sweet it's to deceive,
Süßer das Betrogensein![23]	Sweeter yet to be deceived!

The critical point lies rather in the sarcastic statement Heine makes about the function of Goethe's poem in principle. After all, the sheer euphoria that defines Goethe's verse could convince the reader of the truth of its statement about the bliss of love. Heine in turn thematizes this power of poetic persuasion: whilst Goethe's poem addresses within the personal ('In deinen Küssen'), Heine speaks about kisses in general ('In den Küssen'). Heine then turns 'eyes' into 'illusion'. Heine not only contradicts Goethe's perception, he ultimately insinuates that believing Goethe's verse means to tune into the game of poetic deception. Goethe, the deceiver ('Ach, wie süß ist das Betrügen') provides his readers with illusions they willingly accept ('Süßer das Betrogensein!'), because it conveniently provides them with a truth sweeter than reality – poetic truth. This example shows that the Goethean principle of depicting the moment of human harmony through poetic language is not the axiom by which Heine's poetry can be tested. Heine's reversal of Goethe's message extends to an exposure of the function of poetry *per se*. The rewriting of Goethe's poem can thus be seen as Heine's attempt to demonstrate how unreliable poetic language can be. The end of the Goethean *Kunstperiode* was for Heine marked by the decay of cultural traditions, a discontinued history of the individual and the loss of fixed aesthetic norms. What guaranteed communication for Goethe's poetry – a reliable aesthetic code of normative tastes, styles and genre – could no longer be taken at face value by someone aware of the disintegrating forces of the modern world.

The quandaries of causation and determinism thrown up by attempting to relate Heine's artistic expression to biography may thus be avoided in the first place by realizing how one-dimensional such an approach really is. It seems clear that such

---

[21] As Windfuhr concludes in (1966), pp. 212–213.

[22] Cited in Windfuhr (1966), p. 213, together with Heine's poem 'In den Küssen, welche Lüge'.

[23] B I, p. 239. Heine wrote 'In den Küssen' around the same time as the poems for the *Buch der Lieder*, and included it in the cycle *Heimkehr* in 1830. See commentary in B I, p. 769, which acknowledges the reference to Goethe's poem, but does not critically discuss it.

accounts are limited to speculation, and much of their force is lost where facts are in such short supply. Moreover, it seems particularly misleading in Heine's case to assume that poetry served as a means to express his views on his own personal life. The living presence we find in these poems, infused with voices from a past poetic tradition, instead confronts us with a degree of stylization that transcends the simple story of unrequited love and performs a monumental critique of current poetic fashion. As Heine commented himself:

One deflowers the poem, so to speak; one tears apart its mysterious veil if such particular influence of a history [i.e. personal history] is proven truly to exist; one disfigures the poem if one mistakenly reads this [the influence of real experiences] into it.[24]

Heine rejects the reader's or critic's aim of constructing a biographical basis as the impetus for artistic expression as much as he doubts the possibility for anyone to be able to discover the underlying motivations for artistic production in the first place. The specificity of any one experience, event or real person behind a particular poem or indeed a whole cycle of sixty-five, deflects from the more general tension that informs his poetry. As we shall see, Heine's efforts at skilfully arranging this large number of poems indicate his move away from depiction of love-situations in the style of Goethe. Arranging his poems so as to put the emphasis on the greater whole as opposed to its parts reflects his conscious decision to take a step away from individual poems altogether; the aspect of rationality features strongly in an attempt to order his poems in the first place and also to order them in such a way that tension increases over the course of the cycle. This, as I shall show later, can be seen very clearly when he prepares the *Buch der Lieder* for publication.

As it is 'a split within himself' that generated poetic 'variations on just one single theme',[25] the strong notion of egocentricity in the *Lyrisches Intermezzo* seems no coincidence. With regard to the origin of his 'torn' condition and its expression in the *Buch der Lieder*, Heine says:

This is the sad secret of my poetic powers; my overall unwellness may have informed my recent poems with something pathological . . . and I would certainly not feel hurt if that which is unknown to me myself would be discovered by others.[26]

Within this rare confessional aside, the underlying emotional force of Heine's poetry becomes clearer. The theme of love is, rather, a thematic focus that allows Heine

---

[24] *HSA* XX, p. 91 [Man entjungfert gleichsam ein Gedicht, man zerreißt den geheimnißvollen Schleyer desselben, wenn jener Einfluß der Geschichte den man nachweist wirklich vorhanden ist; man verunstaltet das Gedicht wenn man ihn fälschlich hineingegrübelt hat]. Cf. also *DHA* I/1, p. 759.

[25] *HSA* XX, p. 91. Letter of 10 June 1823 to the poet Immermann. [Es ist die große Einseitigkeit die sich in meinen Dichtungen zeigt, indem sie alle nur Variazionen desselben kleinen Themas sind]. Cf. *DHA* I/1, p. 758.

[26] *HSA* XX, p. 91 [Das ist das traurige Geheimnis meiner poetischen Kraft; mein Unwohlseyn mag meinen letzten Dichtungen auch etwas Krankhaftes mitgetheilt haben . . . es würde mich gewiß nicht schmerzen wenn man auch das aufdeckte, was ich selbst noch nicht erkenne].

to encompass the facets of his overall psychological disposition that he claims to have driven his poetic enterprise over a span of poetic time which is distinct from a chronological narration of amorous episodes or scenes. Thus, we find certain images and metaphors recur in the course of the poem cycle. As we shall see, they belong to one specific idea: the *imago* of the woman. This *imago* is accompanied by images drawn from the visual, tactile, floral or mineral realms, and these images form perhaps the most intriguing conceptual continuum in the *Lyrisches Intermezzo*.

Syntactically, a paradoxical insistence upon statement versus denial, affirmation and negation, appears with a conspicuously familiar metaphorical language. What Altenhofer describes as 'multiple meaning of text'[27] in Heine's prose holds true for his poetry and is in fact an aesthetic constant in Heine's entire œuvre. In the case of the *Lyrisches Intermezzo*, Heine's ostentatious use of mainstream metaphors and motifs representative of Romantic poetry and folktale, and informed with medievalisms and common imagery, complicates the question of literal and figurative meaning even further. Thus, in the course of sixty-five poems, a complex metaphorical world is created that at once affirms and undermines the Romantic sentiment and ultimately refuses to capture it. A closer look at the semantic meaning of these motifs within the conventional Romantic literary context and the ways in which their destruction is systematically carried out in the *Lyrisches Intermezzo* reveals a degree of subliminal deterioration. Such deterioration signifies an irrevocable break with the values and beliefs of the late eighteenth century. The rationalistic Enlightenment of a modern age became the divide between an idealistic past and a secular present:

Surely, a poet's heart must be torn apart in such miserable times as these. Who ever boasts about himself that his heart remained intact only confesses to have a detached angular heart. Through mine, however, ran the great split of the world.[28]

THE BLUE FLOWER

Heine's *Die Romantische Schule*, written in 1833, is vivid testimony to his unresolved standpoint towards his own heritage. His mordant pronouncement against Romanticism's integrity discloses at the same time an affinity, and even an identification, with a movement that he polemically rejects. The image of the flower – the symbol for the Romantic movement (Novalis' *Blaue Blume*) that Heine so sadistically unmasks as a sign of resignation or chosen renunciation – recurs in one of his last poems, witness to a nostalgic longing for relief in the most Idealist of value systems:

---

[27] Altenhofer (1987), pp. 149–193 (here 178) [mehrfacher Schriftsinn].

[28] Heine, *Bäder von Lucca* (Chapter IV); quoted from *DHA* I/1, p. 757 [Das Herz des Dichters ... muß wohl in jetziger Zeit jämmerlich zerrissen werden. Wer von seinem Herzen rühmt, es sei ganz geblieben, der gesteht nur, daß er ein weitabgelegenes Winkelherz hat. Durch das meinige ging aber der große Weltriß].

Solch eine Blum' an meinem Grabe stand,	Such a flower stood at my grave,
Und über meinem Leichnam niederbeugend,	And bent over my dead body,
Wie Frauentrauer, küßt sie mir die Hand,	Like female compassion, she kisses my hand,
Küßt Stirne mir und Augen, trostlos schweigend.[29]	Kisses my forehead and eyes, dolefully silent.

To allude to the defining symbol of the Romantic spirit, the Blue Flower, as the silent muse on the poet's grave epitomizes Heine's ambivalence towards the Romantic tradition. In the pivotal scene in Novalis' *Heinrich von Ofterdingen*, the hero of ingenious poetic gifts, Heinrich, dreams of the wondrous Blue Flower; as a symbol for his longing and a sign for his poetic destiny, the hero later associates his beloved with the Blue Flower of the dream. The significance of Heine's reference to this seminal passage in one of his more self-defining and conclusive poems lies in the metaphorical superimposition of the Romantic sentiment ('Such a flower') with the female figure of compassion. The Romantics' longing for the absolute is equated with the longing for the eternal feminine. In Heine's case, the Romantic sentiment had touched the poet, but had never really reached him, nor indeed could it have consoled him. Heine's Romantic muse was disconsolately silent.

The referential web around the image of the Blue Flower is evident in poem LXII of the *Lyrisches Intermezzo*, towards the end of the cycle:

Am Kreuzweg wird begraben	At the cross-road will be buried
Wer selber brachte sich um;	He who killed himself;
Dort wächst eine blaue Blume,	There grows a blue flower,
Die Armesünderblum.	Suicide's flower.
Am Kreuzweg stand ich und seufzte;	I stood at the cross-road and sighed
Die Nacht war kalt und stumm.	The night was cold and mute.
Im Mondenschein bewegte sich langsam	By the light of the moon moved slowly
Die Armesünderblum.	Suicide's flower.

The double allusion to the Romantic topos of a wanderer's journey through the world on the one hand, and Christ's progress to Calvary on the other, in connection with the Blue Flower suggests once again Heine's conceptual association of Romanticism with its underlying motivation to escape emotionally from the irretrievable loss of the Saviour. As Heine interprets the Romantics' imagination of distant lands as a compensatory act to replace a lost paradise, he sees such pseudo-religious tendency towards delirium to be nothing short of suicide. The Romantics' lacking a sense of reality as evident in their unwillingness to accept a world devoid of divine providence forces them to flee into the self-fabricated world of illusion. Since the aspect of unreality is at the core of these constructs, life becomes increasingly irrelevant and hence, in Heine's view, resembles death. The parallel to Novalis as the inventor of the Blue Flower in *Heinrich von Ofterdingen* is once again of interest: his development towards highly spiritual poetry (*Hymnen an die Nacht*) follows the

---

[29] B VI/1, p. 437.

death of his beloved Sophie von Kühn. Novalis' initial invocation of Sophie in these hymns eventually turns into prayers to God in which the two images merge into one. Novalis then decides to follow Sophie into death: 'I feel the eternal and un-wavering belief in the heaven of the night, and its light, its beloved'.[30] The aspect of renunciation is obvious when the longing for an imaginary world turns into *The Longing for Death* in the last hymn.[31] Like the hero in Novalis' novel who iden-tifies the Blue Flower of his dream with his beloved, the Blue Flower in Heine's poem is personified. Whilst, in *Heinrich von Ofterdingen*, both woman and flower represent the source of poetic inspiration for the hero as an aspiring poet, she has no such power over Heine. He merely notes the flower in the middle of a cold and mute night; the transcendental quality of Novalis' invention, where love for a woman inspires true poetry as well as a love for God, is not retained in Heine's use of the image of the Blue Flower. Its appearance towards the end of the poetic cycle prepares for the final statement in the *Lyrisches Intermezzo*:

Die alten, bösen Lieder,	The old, vicious songs,
Die Träume schlimm und arg,	The dreams evil and grave,
die laßt uns jetzt begraben,	Let's bury them now,
Holt einen großen Sarg.	Fetch a large coffin.

We have seen Heine use the symbol of the flower in order to allude to two ideas: Christianity and Romanticism. Heine called the former 'this strange and ill-coloured flower', and in view of the context of medievalism and Christ's crucifixion the allusion to the Virgin Mary as the symbol of compassion is fairly clear. Both flowers share the colour blue[32] as the image of a woman merges with the medieval archetype of Christian belief and that of Romantic longing.[33] This *imago* of a woman becomes the central metaphor of the *Lyrisches Intermezzo*:

Doch, Zauberei des Traumes! Seltsamlich,	But, magic of dreams! most strange and odd,
Die Blume der Passion, die schwefelgelbe,	The Flower of Passion, sulphur-yellowish
Verwandelt in ein Frauenbildnis sich,	Turns into an image of a woman,
Und das ist sie – die Liebste, ja dieselbe![34]	And it is her – the beloved, yes, she is the same!

As we will see later in more detail, the poet enlists the sympathy of the reader for his undiminished devotion to a woman who appears many times to be unattainable, and whom he in his fantasies turns into the blessed Virgin, an ephemeron in his dreams. In poem XI ('Im Rhein, im schönen Strome'; Song 6 in *Dichterliebe*), her graces are

---

[30] NO IV, p. 135.   [31] NO I, p. 157.

[32] Heine's description of the flower's colour as 'schwefelgelb' alludes to the 'flame of truth' which – sulphur-poisoned – keeps burning, producing a strange mix of blue and yellow.

[33] 'Blue as the symbol of truth will always remain the sign of human immortality', writes the early nineteenth-century symbol-scholar P. Portal, thus pinpointing what Heine thematizes in the *Lyrisches Intermezzo*: the futile search for truth that has been lost. Quoted in Biedermann (1989), p. 63. The colour blue is often seen as a symbol for the spiritual. In Christian art the colour of the Virgin Mary's robe is typically blue, as in Raphael's *Madonna*.

[34] B IV/1, p. 347.

veiled with gleams of the Holy Mother's azure, the kind light of compassion that shines into the lover's heart as the cathedral's image of the Virgin and that of his beloved's eyes seem to fuse.

Heine's poetry is imbued with such medieval motifs and images which Romanticism had brought to light, and which are evidence for his involvement in the movement. As concerns the *Lyrisches Intermezzo*, its imagery is in the best tradition of Romantic poetry: knights, maidens, stars, flowers, birds and the like. Yet, Heine's early poetry itself is an expression of a refusal to take these Romantic poetic means on their own terms. In this sense, Heine merely *quotes* rather than affirms the Romantics' fascination with the medieval. The 'fantastic obsession with the Middle Ages', as Uhland once called it,[35] is Heine's prime object of critique; he categorically denounces the cultivation of medieval naiveté by confronting it with the tones of modern discourse, as in poem XXV which opens with linden-tree, nightingale and the sun, and closes with 'And then [we] said to each other frostily: "Farewell"!'[36] Inserted into the poetic text is thus the prosaic voice of modern life.[37]

In *Die romantische Schule*, Heine tried to make himself believe that the sentimentality and deliberate illusions of the great Romantics were nothing more than a pathological syndrome which deceptively blinds one to reality.[38] But the main problem lay in Heine's inability to identify emotionally with the Romantic evocation of an ancient world as a promised remedy for troubled modern times. In the *Börne-Nachschrift* of 1840, however, we find a passage that bespeaks Heine's own longing to decipher the Romantic message:

Just who could decipher the voice of the past, these ancient hieroglyphs? Perhaps they do not contain a curse after all, but rather the medicine for the wound of our time! Oh, if one was only able to read [these hieroglyphs]! Who could spell out the healing words which are here carved in the rocks. . . . Perhaps it is written down here where the secret spring is trickling out of which mankind must drink in order to be cured; where the secret of our life is what our nanny told us so much about in her old children's fairy tales, and after which we, the old, are now longing. – Where flows the water of life? We are searching and searching . . .[39]

Here, Heine speaks with a rare, but all the more sincere, tone of melancholy about the potentially healing power of the older scriptures of fairy tales. The strong notion of resentment evident twenty years earlier in the destructiveness of the *Lyrisches Intermezzo* had changed to one of momentary hesitation.

---

[35] In McFarland (1981), p. 8.

[36] [Die Linde blühte, die Nachtigall sang, / Die Sonne lachte . . . Da sagten wir uns frostig einander: 'Lebwohl!'].

[37] In this sense, Ricoeur's term 'emplotment' seems appropriate. See Ricoeur (1989).

[38] Cf. Altenhofer (1987), p. 236.

[39] B IV, p. 140 [Wer enträtselt diese Stimme der Vorzeit, diese uralten Hieroglyphen? Sie enthalten vielleicht keinen Fluch, sondern ein Rezept für die Wunde unserer Zeit! O wer lesen könnte! Wer sie ausspräche, die heilenden Worte, die hier eingegraben. . . . Es steht hier vielleicht geschrieben, wo die verborgene Quelle rieselt, woraus die Menschheit trinken muß, um geheilt zu werden, wo das geheime Wasser des Lebens, wovon uns die Amme in den alten Kindermärchen so viel erzählt hat, und wonach wir jetzt schmachten als alte Greise. – Wo fließt das Wasser des Lebens? Wir suchen und suchen . . .].

9

HEINE'S *IMAGO* OF A WOMAN

The metaphors and their dynamic force across poems in the *Lyrisches Intermezzo* are fascinating. The effect of a highly nuanced use of a small number of central metaphors over the course of sixty-five poems is part of an aesthetic principle which Altenhofer called Heine's 'art of arrangement'.[1] To see how Heine places and displaces these metaphors is to understand the *Lyrisches Intermezzo* not as narrative but as associative in nature; and it is the technique of association that Heine exploits with great skill in order to create a monothematic cyclicity of multiple semantic dimensions.

As to Heine's vocabulary in the *Lyrisches Intermezzo*, deliberately devoted as it is to the imagery derived from archetypal models of love poetry, we distinguish four metaphorical areas. First and foremost, there is the beloved, often invoked via reference to her eyes and face. Appearing in almost every poem in the cycle, Heine presents her as a *type* or *stereotype* because she lacks any signs of individuality. The very parsimony of the information we are offered heightens the effect these few attributes have on the reader's mind. The economic principle works well in presenting a woman who is blond (Prologue and poem LXII), blue-eyed (poems V, XXIX and XXX) and fair-skinned (poems XXX and XLII). The second idea prevailing in the *Lyrisches Intermezzo* is that of pain and death, which, significantly, frequently appears in connection with the woman. Metaphors belonging to the floral and natural realm, and appearing in roughly one-third of the *Lyrisches Intermezzo*, include certain types of flowers and trees. However, these are often personified: they speak in an unknown language, are compassionate, seem to console the lover or appear as the last sign of lost humanity. A fourth metaphorical area concerns the state of dream and the realm of the night. For another third of the cycle, these metaphors are means for Heine to portray his poetic reality.

Yet another, highly convoluted, metaphorical area would concern that of language itself. As was mentioned above in connection with the concept of 'Augensprache', the language topos indicates Heine's doubts about whether art can still be a means of communication in the modern age; in other words, it concerns the question of artistic expression itself and foreshadows what can be called the 'language-crisis' of the nineteenth century. While beyond the concerns of this study of the *Lyrisches Intermezzo* with regard to Schumann's *Dichterliebe*, it would indeed be of interest to

---

[1] Altenhofer (1982), pp. 16–32.

explore this topic of the limits of language; it would have to be treated separately, though, in context with the Romantics' aesthetic of fragmentary expression on the one hand, and the question of nineteenth-century hermeneutics on the other.

With concentration on the *imago* of the woman as an opening into the internal workings of Heine's metaphorical world, it is first of all the beloved's face, and her eyes in particular, that obsess the poet in the *Lyrisches Intermezzo*. But the real metaphorical reach of the woman as *imago* extends far beyond mere poetic imagery. In a virtuoso passage celebrating conceptual and affective reversals, Heine writes with inexhaustible comic energy about the facets that make up his iridescent poetic muse:

I just have this unfortunate passion for the rational! I love it [the rational], despite the fact that it does not bestow me with requited love. I give it everything, and it gives me nothing. But I can't keep from it. And just as the Jewish King Solomon sang the praises of the Church in the *Song of Songs* via the image of a black, ardent girl, so that the Jews would not quite notice, so did I myself do just the opposite in countless songs: I sang the praises of the rational, via the image of a white, cold virgin who pulls me towards her as much as she pushes me away, who smiles in one moment and rages in another, and who finally turns her back towards me. This is the secret of my unrequited love, which I do not disclose to anyone. And it gives you, Madam, a measure to appreciate my folly. You can therefore see that it is of an extraordinary kind, and that it greatly exceeds the usual madness of people. Read my 'Radcliff', my 'Almansor', my 'Lyrisches Intermezzo' – rationality! rationality! nothing but rationality! – and you will be shocked at the high degree of my folly.[2]

This passage is remarkable in many ways, not only because it is one of Heine's most telling accounts of the topos of unrequited love in his poetry. At first sight, Heine seems to go once more into what is known as his 'Madonna cult', forming the background to his poetic œuvre from early on, as I shall show a little later. However, the image of the 'Virgin Mary, this most beautiful flower of poetry' is here reflected back, *via negationis*, on to a biblical text; but not any biblical text, for the seductive powers of the *Song of Songs* derive from the overt sexual overtones and erotic situation it celebrates. This, first of all, and its resulting fame, afford the *Song of Songs* its exceptional status among all other texts in the Bible. It comes as no surprise then that interpretations of the *Song of Songs* have been various and controversial. No doubt, had this text not become part of the canon of Jewish and Christian scriptures, it would be recognized as one of the highpoints of ancient Near Eastern

---

[2] B II, p. 300 (*Reisebilder; Zweiter Teil; Ideen. Das Buch Le Grand*). [Aber ich hab nun mal diese unglückliche Passion für die Vernunft! Ich liebe sie, obgleich sie mich nicht mit Gegenliebe beglückt. Ich gebe ihr alles, und sie gewährt mir nichts. Ich kann nicht von ihr lassen. Und wie einst der jüdische König Salomon im Hoheliede die christliche Kirche besungen, und zwar unter dem Bilde eines schwarzen, liebeglühenden Mädchens, damit seine Juden nichts merkten; so habe ich in unzähligen Liedern just das Gegenteil, nämlich die Vernunft, besungen, und zwar unter dem Bilde einer weißen, kalten Jungfrau, die mich anzieht und abstößt, mir bald lächelt, bald zürnt, und mir endlich gar den Rücken kehrt. Dieses Geheimnis meiner unglücklichen Liebe, das ich niemanden offenbare, gibt Ihnen, Madame, einen Maßstab zur Würdigung meiner Narrheit, Sie sehen daraus, daß solche von außerordentlicher Art ist, und großartig hervorragt über das gewöhnliche närrische Treiben der Menschen. Lesen Sie meinen 'Ratcliff', meinen 'Almansor', mein 'lyrisches Intermezzo' – Vernunft! Vernunft! nichts als Vernunft! – und Sie erschrecken ob der Höhe meiner Narrheit].

love poetry.[3] As Heine draws from the *Song of Songs* with astonishing conceptual and textual precision, a closer look at the connotations this model carries and which Heine creatively exploits opens up more far-reaching levels of meaning than one might at first suspect in this half-serious, half-confessional piece of self-derision.

THE *SONG OF SONGS* AND HEINE'S *IMAGO* OF A WOMAN

On one level, opposition is practised here almost literally, as the two imaginary muses are described as 'black' versus 'white', or 'passionate' versus 'cold', thus evoking the underlying dynamics on which Heine's poetry is based: 'I love her, despite her not returning my love'. On another level, Heine's rather humorous fictitious identification with the legendary poet Solomon, and his rather humour-less, sharp exposure of a readership shown to be devoted to institutionalized ideology and blinded towards sensuality, stand in sharp opposition. Rendered as insoluble paradox, this passage on the *Song of Songs* is no longer just a commentary, but rather an expression of Heine's artistic calculation. As the passionate tone belies any proclaimed rationality, it is indeed language itself that becomes 'a measure to appreciate' a 'folly' that, as Heine makes sure to emphasize, 'greatly exceeds the usual madness of people'. An appreciation of this particular way of using language is at the centre of the following discussion, and the kind of 'unfortunate passion' that it succeeds in expressing.

A hysterical and categorical 'I just have this unfortunate passion for the rational!' throws the issue into focus: rationality. Heine remained devoted to this when he composed seemingly innocent Romantic love songs like those of the *Lyrisches Intermezzo*, where the personification of intellect ('die Vernunft! ich liebe sie') and its transmogrification into the image of an unfeeling, irritating woman leads to an intricate scenario of fatal attraction. For Heine, avowedly deemed to have a reflective, analytical mind, the pull is always towards the rational, admittedly unrewarding and yet irresistible.

And Heine turns the tables – twice. Whilst, as he asserts in the quoted passage, the readers of Solomon's *Song of Songs* were made to believe that the object of devotion was God and thus a tribute to the 'Christian Church', Heine's seemingly simple folk-song poems appeared to many of his readers as genuine love poetry. Its subject matter was assumed to be a real woman and not an abstraction. Whereas in the *Song of Songs* language and theme are of unconcealed sensuousness, Heine's *Lyrisches Intermezzo* is a celebration of Reason. And although the latter is evidently and intentionally adopting the passionate tone of its great old model, Heine's object of passion is not that of sensuous pleasure but that of cold rationality.

The second, perhaps more significant, twist occurs at the level of reception. Heine uses here the opportunity to ridicule what he saw as the aridity of Jewish piety as he portrays the orthodox readers of the *Song of Songs* as ignorant towards its obvious

---

[3] Altenhofer (1982) mentions this passage, although for different reasons, in his brilliant essay on Heine's art of arrangement which has influenced the present studies in many ways.

eroticism. Furthermore, their narrow-mindedness and focus on the externalization of religiousness – the Church – hindered them from even so much as personifying Solomon's poetic object as an embodiment of God. Thus, Heine reduces their devotional aims to mere institutionalism: the Church. And in turning effigy (woman) into institutionalized ideology (Church), Heine dismantles *his own* readers' illusion in turn: blinded by the craze of Romanticism, Heine insinuates that they saw in his poetry only what the Romantic School had taught them to cherish – images and values of the Golden Age. The inversions performed by Heine in his passage on Solomon's *Song of Songs* versus his own poetry are exquisitely clever, to the point of being acrobatic. Passionately describing his passion for rationality, Heine claims to use the traditional form of love poems in order to passionately praise what is traditionally not the topic of love poetry: rationality.

Heine describes his folly to be his fate: whilst, in the *Song of Songs*, Solomon's image of an ardent, dark woman is shown to reciprocate her lover's passion – as the *Song of Songs* is merely a dialogue between two lovers – Heine's image of a virgin of fair and cold appearance shows no signs of affection. Here again, the inversion is perfect: what, by readers of Heine's poems, was perceived as an expression of worldly love (Heine mentions the *Lyrisches Intermezzo*) has at its centre the Divine Virgin, and what by readers of the *Song of Songs* was assumed to represent Solomon's love for the Church was rather, Heine suggests, that for a real woman.

Yet, the implications of Heine's analogy between the *Song of Songs* and the *Lyrisches Intermezzo* reach further. What standard interpretations of the *Song of Songs* identified as a parable of either Solomon's love for Israel, the Church, or for the soul that loves Him, may have missed the point.[4] As Heine suggests, such reading denies the *Song of Songs* its obvious sensuousness by refusing to extend the idea of divine love into human realms. As he said elsewhere, 'Luther had not understood that the idea of Christianity, and the destruction of sensuousness are too much in conflict with human nature to be realized in life'.[5] We may therefore assume that in the case of the *Lyrisches Intermezzo* a certain number of moments of negativity and ridicule directly aimed at the reader had not always been perceived – how else could the *Buch der Lieder* have become such a tremendous success if its readers had been aware of its underlying trenchant critique of prevailing attitudes and society at large? In truth, Heine says, he intended to thwart his audience in their tendency for reverie, their fascination with Romantic love. Heine's critical stance was thus as ardent as what he was about to oppose: the Romantic School and its believers.

---

[4] For this and further information, see the *Encyclopaedia universalis* (1995), pp. 904–906.

[5] The oldest, and today still prevalent, interpretative scheme for the *Song of Songs* transforms human love either into the symbol of a religious reality, that is the bond between God and his people, or discovers in the description of the woman the features of the Virgin Mary. Christian spirituality was thus looking for the image of a powerful mystical union, either with a group (God and Israel; Christ and the Church; Christ and human kind) or with the individual (God or Christ and the human soul; the Holy Spirit and Mary; Solomon and wisdom).

But the analogy with the *Song of Songs* is not only a matter of polemics. The textual and conceptual parallels between the *Song of Songs* and the *Lyrisches Intermezzo* are astonishing and suggest that the *Song of Songs* could be added to the list of works that served Heine as poetic models. Concerning numerous poetic motifs and their manifest biblical fragrance, the commentary in the Briegleb edition already pointed in the direction of the Bible. In addition, as we know today, a Lutheran Bible of 1827 was part of Heine's estate.[6] Finally, Heine's first translators, the French writers Gérard de Nerval and René Taillandier, made an interesting comment in their introduction to the first French edition of Heine's poems[7] which included the *Lyrisches Intermezzo*:

The poem called *Lyrisches Intermezzo* is, in our opinion, the most original work by Heinrich Heine.... To find anything like it, one would have to go back to the *Song of Songs*, all the way back to the greatness of oriental inspiration. Here we find the nuance and the touch worthy of Solomon, the first writer who combined within the same lyricism the feeling of love and the feeling of God.[8]

The following philological exploration, using Heine's copy of the Lutheran Bible, does not pretend to be a systematic comparison between the two works in question; rather it will be limited to the discussion of three isolated and particularly interesting cases of similarity. But these similarities, whether literal or conceptual, are occasion for further thought as they tell us something important about the scale and the tone of Heine's *Lyrisches Intermezzo*. One immediate impression one has is that Heine, by incorporating into his poetic cycle a number of central motifs and phrases from the *Song of Songs*, achieves a paradoxical kind of identification with the legendary poet Solomon. Equal to the grandeur of the gesture of paying homage to the great Solomon is the inverted honour he bestows upon his source by applying a consistent dynamic of negation. Indeed, it seems as if he used the *Song of Songs* for no other reason than to set himself off from it, to imbue the vocabulary of the sensuous *Song of Songs* with a modern feeling of estrangement, and to intone continuous discord over a paradigm of love poetry.

In the first example, the relationship between the *Song of Songs* and Heine's own opening poem of the *Lyrisches Intermezzo*, 'Im wunderschönen Monat Mai', is not literal. It is much more fusionary than that, for it is not only the text that Heine incorporates, but its reach – the ambiance of intense longing.

---

[6] *DHA* VIII/1, p. 27.

[7] This copy has been consulted for the present study. See, in the Nachlaßbibliothek of the Heinrich-Heine-Institut Düsseldorf, *Die Bibel, oder die ganze Heilige Schrift des alten und des neuen Testaments* in the translation of Martin Luther. Frankfurt am Main, 1827.

[8] B VI/2, pp. 265 and 268 [Le poëme intitulé *Intermezzo* est, à notre sense, l'œuvre peut-être la plus originale de Henri Heine.... Pour trouver quelque chose d'analogue, il faudrait remonter jusqu'au *Cantique des Cantiques*, jusqu'à la magnificence des inspirations orientales. Voilà des accents et des touches dignes de Salomon, le premier écrivain qui ait confondu dans le même lyrisme le sentiment de l'amour et le sentiment de Dieu].

Lyrisches Intermezzo	*Hohelied*
	Denn siehe, der Winter ist
	vergangen . . .[9]
Im wunderschönen Monat Mai,	der Lenz ist herbey gekommen. . .[10]
Als alle Knospen sprangen,	die Blumen sind hervor
	gekommen . . .[11]
Da ist in meinem Herzen	
Die Liebe aufgegangen.	
Im wunderschönen Monat Mai,	
Als alle Vögel sangen,	und die Turteltaube läßt sich hören . . .[12]
Da hab' ich ihr gestanden	Stehe auf, meine Freundin, und komm,
Mein Sehnen und Verlangen.	meine Schöne, komm her.

TRANSLATION

In the lovely month of May,	For, lo, the winter is past . . .[13]
When all the buds were bursting,	The flowers appear on the earth. . .[14]
Then in my heart	
love broke forth.	
In the lovely month of May,	
When all birds were singing,	the time of the singing of birds has come . . .[15]
Then I confessed to her	my beloved spake, and said unto me,
My longing and desire.	Rise up, my love, my fair one,
	and come away.[16]

The second example is striking because of its rich textual correspondence between Heine's own poetic creation and its model. Here Heine not only repeats but concentrates as well as amplifies the already overflowing Solomonian act of amorous invocation.

Lyrisches Intermezzo III
Die Rose, die Lilje, die *Taube*, die *Sonne*,
Die liebt ich einst alle in *Liebeswonne.*
Ich lieb sie nicht mehr, ich liebe alleine
Die Kleine, die Feine, *die Reine, die Eine;*
Die selber, aller Liebe Bronne,
Ist Rose und Lilje und *Taube* und *Sonne.* (B I, 76)[17]

Hohelied
liebe Freundin, meine Schwester, meine *Taube*, meine *Fromme . . .*
Aber *Eine* ist meine *Taube*, meine *Fromme*, *Eine* ist . . . die *Liebste*, die *Auserwählte . . .*
Wie schön und lieblich bist du, du *Liebe in Wollüsten.*
Wer ist sie, die hervorbricht wie die Morgenröthe, . . . *auserwählt* wie die *Sonne . . .*

---

[9] See my article (1999) for a more detailed discussion.
[10] See the copy of a Lutheran Bible from Heine's estate mentioned above in note 7.
[11] II, 11.   [12] II, 11.   [13] II, 12.
[14] The English translation of these excerpts from the *Song of Songs* is based on the King James version of the Bible. See II, 11.
[15] II, 12.   [16] II, 12.   [17] II, 10.

TRANSLATION

Lyrisches Intermezzo III
The rose, the lily, the *dove*, the *sun*,
I once loved them all in the *pleasures of love*.
I love them no more, I only love
The little one, the fine one, *the pure one, the One.*
She herself is the source of all love,
Is rose and lily and *dove* and *sun*.

Song of Songs
my sister, my love, my *dove*, my undefiled . . .
My dove, my undefiled is *but one*; she is *the only one* . . . , she is the choice one . . .
How fair and how pleasant art thou, *O love, for delights!*
Who is she that looketh forth as the morning, fair as the moon, clear as the *sun* . . .

The philological accuracy with which Heine approaches the *Song of Songs* is not of primary interest here, but rather the fact that his self-derisory statement in the passage 'I just have this unfortunate passion for the rational!' about the *Song of Songs* in relation to his own 'love' poetry has evidently been made with a conscious awareness of the conflict between explicit eroticism and implicit allegory as presented in the Old Testament.

The third example shows how the two lovers' striking description of each other in the *Song of Songs* – accumulative and freely fluctuating between 'he' and 'she', centring around eyes, lips and cheeks – has been taken up by Heine, distilled and belittled by the German diminutives –chen and –lein, before being woven into the new poetic texture of at least two poems from the *Lyrisches Intermezzo*.

Hohelied	Song of Songs
Deine Augen sind wie Taubenaugen . . .[18]	Thou hast doves' *eyes* . . .[19]
Deine Lippen sind wie . . . . *Deine Wangen* sind wie . . .[20]	*Thy lips* are like. . . *thy cheeks* are like . . .[21]
Deine Augen sind wie Taubenaugen . . .[22]	*His eyes* are like the eyes of doves . . .[23]
Deine Wangen sind wie . . . *Seine Lippen* sind wie . . .[24]	*His cheeks* are like . . . *his lips* are like . . .[25]

Lyrisches Intermezzo XI

Im Rhein, im heiligen Strome,	The Rhine, the holy river,
Da spiegelt sich in den Welln,	reflects in its waves,
Mit seinem großen Dome,	with its great cathedral,
Das große, heilige Köln.	the great holy city of Cologne.
Im Dom, da steht ein Bildnis,	Inside the cathedral there stands a portrait,
Auf goldenem Leder gemalt;	painted on golden leather;

---

[18] The emphases here and later are my own. [19] IV, 1. [20] IV, 1.
[21] IV, 3 and 11. [22] IV, 3. [23] V, 12. [24] V, 12. [25] V, 13.

In meines Lebens Wildnis
Hat's freundlich hineingestrahlt.

into the chaos of my life
it has kindly shone.

Es schweben Blumen und Englein
Um unsre liebe Frau;
Die Augen, die Lippen, die Wänglein,
Die gleichen der Liebsten genau. (B I, 79)

Flowers and cherubs are floating
about our blessed Virgin;
Her eyes, her lips, her little cheeks
are exactly like those of my love.

Lyrisches Intermezzo XIV

Auf meiner Herzliebsten *Äugelein*
Mach ich die schönsten Kanzonen.
Auf meiner Herzliebsten *Mündchen* klein
Mach ich die besten Terzinen.
Auf meiner Herzliebsten *Wängelein*
Mach ich die herrlichsten Stanzen.
Und wenn meine Liebste ein Herzchen hätt,
Ich machte darauf ein hübsches Sonett. (B I, 80)

About my sweetheart's *little eyes*
I make the prettiest canzones.
About my sweetheart's *little mouth*
I make the best tiercets.
About my sweetheart's *little cheeks*
I make the most splendid stanzas.
And if my beloved had a little heart,
I'd make about it a nice sonette.

With poem XI, 'Im Rhein, im heiligen Strome', and its overall idea of singing praises to a female *imago*, Heine transposes the situation he described in the passage about his 'unfortunate passion for the rational!' as 'the Jewish King Solomon sang the praises of the Church' into his own cultural context, and for his own poetic ends. Heine locates the poetic idea of devotion in the centre of German Catholicism: Cologne and its great cathedral – the river Rhine, the cathedral, and the city of Cologne being the three quintessential symbols of the kind of Romanticism which is known still today as 'Rheinische Romantik'. By means of hyperbole, this evocation of the overwhelming power of the Romantic movement draws the reader into the cathedral and further towards the painting of the Blessed Virgin, the ultimate symbol of Catholic devotion, the 'mater credentium'.[26]

The Madonna as the symbol of celestial femininity, beauty and universal, suffering motherhood fascinated Heine for a long time. We come across this image throughout his early poetry and writings. Known in Heine scholarship as Heine's 'Madonna-cult',[27] the poet articulated what seems like an obsession with a female divine figure[28] in the so-called confession letter to his friend Sethe. He wrote in 1816, six years prior to the *Lyrisches Intermezzo*:

As regards my religious views, I may soon be able to tell you something truly astonishing. Has Heine gone crazy? you will exclaim. *But I must have a Madonna.* Will the heavenly replace the worldly? Only in the infinite depths of mysticism can I plummet my infinite pain.[29]

---

[26] V, 13

[27] Heine's reference is to the picture depicting the Annunciation by Stephan Lochner of 1440, still to be seen in Cologne Cathedral. Its background is a golden carpet interwoven with flowers, just as in line 9: 'Flowers and cherubs are floating'. Cf. *DHA* I/1 pp. 789–790.

[28] An acute historical perspective on Heine's 'Madonna-phase' can be found in Sternberger (1976), pp. 181–206.

[29] In this letter (of 27 October 1816), Heine admits his longing to be able to relieve himself of his 'infinite pain' through the image of Christian belief [In religiöser Hinsicht habe ich Dir vielleicht bald etwas sehr

The Madonna as a decisive aspect of Heine's female *imago*, linked with the idea of consolation as embodied in the religious paradigm, is thus at the centre of his writings, and remains so into his last works. Earlier, when I discussed Heine's stance towards the Romantic movement, I referred to one of his late poems where the idea of 'female compassion' finds an equivalent in the Romantic movement's ultimate symbol, the Blue Flower: 'Solch eine Blum' an meinem Grabe stand' (B VI/1, p. 437; 'Such a flower stood on my grave'). The scene in this late poem, however, was that of the poet's own death, and his resigned admission that the movement's belief in transcendence through Idealism did not reach him. In contrast, in the relatively early poems of the *Lyrisches Intermezzo*, the effigy of the Virgin, once equated with the stereotypical image of the beloved, is soon infused with signs of deceit, of pain, and of death. Her fair skin is then reinterpreted as 'pale',[30] and thus carries, with 'white' as a constant in the *Lyrisches Intermezzo*, the connotations of lifelessness and decay. In Heine's *Florentinische Nächte*, for example, an essayistic fragment of biographical origin, we encounter the image of the Madonna innumerable times: a marble statue, white and cold, deceitful and wished to be dead.[31] By way of these repeated representations of a woman with consistently contradictory attributes, yet a good deal of generality, Heine's woman is no longer a simple image. Rather, she is an internalized representation, an entity on to which Heine has projected his conflictual feelings and attitudes. As such, she is no longer a variable, but rather a set piece – an *imago*. Moving through much of Heine's work, the *imago* of a woman followed him like a shadow.

Poem XI 'Im Rhein, im heiligen Strome', however, does not yet add the characteristics of a Fatal Woman to the Virgin's image.[32] Heine's question 'Will the heavenly [Virgin] replace the worldly?' in the confession letter to Sethe, together with the poem's last lines 'The Virgin's eyes, her lips, her little cheeks / are exactly like those of my love' does, however, indicate the superimposition of longing for a spiritual refuge.

In the course of the *Lyrisches Intermezzo*, the *imago* of the woman as painting or as marble statue soon takes on the figure of oxymoron. Poem XII ('Du liebst mich nicht, du liebst mich nicht') plays with the idea of poetic identification. Alluding to King Solomon gazing into the face of his beloved, the poet exclaims (line 4): 'I am as happy as a king' – after 'you love me not'. But here, the beloved is described as in the introductory passage of Heine's analogy to the *Canticles*: the cold woman turns her back towards him: 'you even hate me, you even hate me'.[33]

Verwunderliches mitzuteilen. Ist Heine toll geworden? wirst Du ausrufen. *Aber ich muß eine Madonna haben.* Wird mir die Himmlische die Irdische ersetzen? Nur in den unendlichen Tiefen der Mystik kann ich meinen unendlichen Schmerz hinabwälzen]. HSA XX, p. 22. My emphasis.

[30] See poems V (4a), XXXII and XLII.

[31] See B I, pp. 558–615 (*Florentinische Nächte*), pp. 562–563: 'A wondrous passion for marble statues had developed in my soul . . . painted images of women . . . . I have fallen in love with a painting just once. It was a marvellous Madonna, which I met in the cathedral in Cologne at the River Rhine . . . . I was fascinated with the mysticism of Catholicism . . . . But then I left the Virgin and was taken in by the Greek nymph of a collection of antiques. She had tied me to her marble chains for a long time . . . I was also in love with dead women . . . .'

[32] See Praz (1951).   [33] XII, line 4.

In poem XIV ('Auf meiner Herzliebsten Äugelein'), the sign of beauty (eyes, lips and cheeks) of Solomon's beloved – and with it the expression of admiration – is belittled: diminutives only ('Äuglein', 'Mündchen', 'Wänglein') are cynically enumerated to ridicule the poet's hopeless attempt to write genuine love poetry, which turns out to be mere 'Kanzonen', 'Terzinen' and 'Stanzen'. The writing in the form of the 'sonnet' is dismissed as the poet regrets the absence of the beloved's heart (line 7: 'Und wenn meine Liebste ein Herzchen hätt'' (And if my beloved had a heart)). We find diminutives throughout the cycle as a mirror for Heine's self-deprecating mockery of his own attempts to write 'great poetry' – an impossibility, for the poet lacks conviction in the topos of love itself. Yet again, in poem XXIX ('Und als ich so lange, so lange gesäumt'), Heine invokes the *imago* of the Holy Virgin as seen in Cologne Cathedral: 'My beloved is so beautiful and kind, / her sweet image is still floating before my eyes' (lines 19–20). The stanzas surrounding this isolated thought, however, destroy the illusion.

In poem XVI, Heine confronts his vision of the woman as a tissue of his dreams. By way of negation, Heine affirms the irresistibility of visions in the poet's mind. The imagery of animals together with the scene of the basilisk remind one of E. T. A. Hoffmann's fantastic *Walpurgis Night* stories. There, too, appears a woman-turned-vampire.[34]

Liebste, sollst mir heute sagen:	Sweetheart, today you should tell me
Bist du nicht ein Traumgebild,	Are you not a vision of my dreams,
Wie's in schwülen Sommertagen	Pouring out of the poet's brains
Aus dem Hirn des Dichters quillt?	As happens in muggy summer days?
Aber nein, ein solches Mündchen,	But no, such a little mouth,
Solcher Augen Zauberlicht,	Such magic light of your eyes,
Solch ein liebes, süßes Kindchen,	Such a dear, sweet little child,
Das erschafft der Dichter nicht.	that the poet does not create.
Basiliken und Vampire,	Basilisks and vampires,
Lindenwürm und Ungeheur,	Limeworms and monsters,
Solche schlimme Fabeltiere,	Such terrible mythical creatures,
Die erschafft des Dichters Feur.	those the poet's fire creates.
Aber dich und deine Tücke,	But you and your maliciousness,
Und dein holdes Angesicht,	And your blessed face,
Und die falschen frommen Blicke –	And these fake, sanctimonious looks –
Das erschafft der Dichter nicht.	Those the poet does not create.

Concurrent with the emergence of horror visions out of the *imago* of the beloved, Heine addresses here the concept of poetic imagination on the one hand, and critical self-reflection on the other. As his art of arrangement has the effect of distancing

---

[34] *DHA* I/1, p. 795.

himself from his work,[35] the above poem contains perhaps the most explicit statement Heine makes in the whole of the *Lyrisches Intermezzo* as regards the intrinsic
contradiction that results from a concurrent aim to present a 'psychological picture
of myself'.[36] Instead of denying the psychological function of his poetry, Heine
thematizes the problem within the poetic structure itself. By addressing himself in
the centre of the *Lyrisches Intermezzo* with the over-acted affirmation – 'Those the
poet does not create' – the self-critical message is evident. In another passage of the
Börne postscript, Heine advocates with a real, yet still humorous, sense of urgency
the trusting of the freedom of the poet's imaginary world which is distinct from that
of real experience:

Without the belief in authority no great poet can emerge. As soon as the merciless press
illuminates his private life, and the critics of the day gnaw and worm their way into his words,
the poet's song will no longer find the necessary respect. When Dante walked through the
streets of Verona, the people pointed at him and whispered: 'He was in hell!' Would he
otherwise have been able to describe its tortures so accurately? With so much respect, how
much more profound is the effect of the story of the Francesca of Rimini . . . and of all those
figures of torture, who have poured out of the poet's mind . . . .

No, they did not just pour out of the poet's mind; he did not invent them; he has lived them,
has felt them, he has seen and touched them, he has truly been in hell, he was in the city of
the reprobates . . . he was in exile! – – –[37]

To conclude with the association of the artist in exile is not only a self-referential
reminder of his own exiled existence during the writing of this work; it leads back to
Adorno's perceptive evaluation of Heine's self-understanding as someone standing
outside the world he artistically seeks to grasp. The tensions, horrors and tortures
appearing in a work of art are thus not mere descriptions of an assumed objective
world, but result from a tortured language itself.

   Throughout the *Lyrisches Intermezzo*, one notices Heine's constant reference to
'eyes'. Returning to the so-called 'confession letter' to his best friend Sethe, we find
some indication as to what the focus on eyes entails:

I think I talked to you about this some time ago: that I often detect in your features,
particularly in your eyes Something which repels me in an inexplicable way, and which at
the same time forces me towards you, so that I thought I saw in one and the same moment

---

[35] See Altenhofer (1993)   [36] *HSA* XX, p. 280.

[37] B IV (*Ludwig Börne. Eine Nachschrift. Fünftes Buch*), p. 141 [Ohne Autoritätsglauben kann auch kein großer
   Dichter emporkommen. Sobald sein Privatleben von dem unbarmherzigsten Lichte der Presse beleuchtet wird,
   und die Tageskritik an seinen Worten würmelt und nagt, kann auch das Lied des Dichters nicht mehr den
   nötigen Respekt finden. Wenn Dante durch die Straßen von Verona ging, zeigte das Volk auf ihn und flüsterte:
   'Der war in der Hölle!' Hätte er auch sonst mit allen ihren Qualen so treu schildern können? Wie weit tiefer, bei
   solch ehrfurchtsvollem Glauben, wirkte die Erzählung der Francesca von Rimini . . . und all jener Qualgestalten,
   die dem Geiste des großen Dichters entquollen, er hat sie nicht gedichtet, er hat sie gelebt, er hat sie gefühlt,
   er hat sie gesehen, betastet, er war wirklich in der Hölle, er war in der Stadt der Verdammten . . . er war im
   Exil!– – –].

loving goodwill and then again this most bitter, despicable, icy scorn. And look! this strange, mysterious Something I also found in Molly's glances.[38]

Heine's situation at the time of this letter was that he was leading a fairly miserable existence at his uncle's house in Hamburg, where he was training to become an accountant. He writes further:

But you should really believe me that now, despite everything, the muse pleases me more than ever before. She has become my loyal and comforting girlfriend; she is so secretly sweet, and I love her dearly.[39]

Here again, even within a biographical context, the 'real' beloved called 'Molly' never actually existed. 'Molly' may in one sense be seen as a stylization of Amalie, whom Heine admired in earlier years; in another sense, however, she is the literary heroine featured in the poems of Gottfried August Bürger.[40] The personification of Heine's poetical writing as a woman, as his faithful and consoling beloved, is perhaps the most important statement to keep in mind. In this respect, the sociological element of isolation identifiable with Heine's prosaic surroundings is worth consideration, since these seemed to have generated the need to express his feelings of isolation and despair. Poetry thus serves the purpose of relief, as much as it becomes a mirror of the fairly deep-rooted emotional insecurities in Heine himself. The letter to Sethe shows Heine playing a desperate, as much as a courageous, game in that he confides to his friend on the one hand, laying bare his misery, and therefore inducing a strong sense of trust in Sethe; on the other hand, however, Heine's description of his friend's terrifying, icy and arrogant looks could not be harsher. Heine is intrinsically unsure of the sympathy of others, for he detects in their looks – and here significantly even in the eyes of his best friend – hostility. It is thus essentially a message of total isolation that forces Heine to articulate his feelings and to portray this inner instability in poetry. In his poetry, then, Heine truly creates the *imago* of woman, as in the letter to Sethe, in order to imbue it with his own psychological condition. The retreat we see here is of the kind found in Goethe's *Werther*, when the socially and emotionally deserted hero concludes: 'I am left with nobody but myself'.[41]

The same letter to Sethe contains another, arguably the most telling, remark about Heine's woman in the *Lyrisches Intermezzo*; in the process of writing most of the *Intermezzo* poems, Heine reports to his friend:

---

[38] *HSA* XX, p. 22 ('Confession letter' to Sethe) [Ich glaube Dir…schon längst davon gesprochen zu haben: wie ich oft in Deinen Gesichtszügen und vorzüglich in Deinen Augen Etwas bemerkte was mich auf einer unbegreiflichen Art zugleich von Dir abstieß und zugleich wieder gewaltsam zu Dir hinzog, so daß ich meinte im selben Augenblick liebendes Wohlwollen und auch wieder den bittersten, schnöden, eiskalten Hohn darin zu erkennen. Und siehe! dieses nemliche räthselhafte Etwas habe ich auch in Mollys Blicken gefunden].

[39] *HSA* XX, p. 22 ('Confession letter' to Sethe) [Aber Du sollst es wohl glauben, die Muse ist mir demohngeachtet jetzt noch weit lieber als je. Sie ist mir eine getreue Freundin geworden, die ist so heimlich süß, und ich liebe sie recht inniglich].

[40] As has been noted by Brummack (1980), p. 92.

[41] Brummack (1980), pp. 92–93, with Goethe quotation from p. 93.

Tonight, when I couldn't sleep, I thought about quite a few things, and I have recorded to myself all those things which I love, which are: Number 1, a female shadow which only lives on in my poems.[42]

Heine's woman thus appears in Heine's poetry as something like a poetic spirit. Her image is less ingratiating than Romanticism's Blue Flower, as we have seen; as a shadow she possesses the poet inwardly, populating his mind with dark spectres of an imaginary world.

[42] *HSA* XX, p. 49 [Ich habe mir diese Nacht, als ich nicht schlafen konnte, recht vieles überlegt, und hab mir alles aufgezählt, was ich liebe; und das ist: Nr. I. ein weiblicher Schatten, der jetzt nur noch in meinen Gedichten lebt].

10

THE GENESIS OF THE *BUCH DER LIEDER*

I intend to discuss the publication and reception history of the *Buch der Lieder* only insofar as this is relevant to an understanding of Schumann's reception of Heine's poetry. That it should be of any interest at all, in a study ultimately focusing on Heine's text as assimilated in a piece of music, emerges from two aspects of its history. First, Heine's aesthetic objectives come to the fore as we see him prepare and comment on a complete edition of his early poems. Secondly, a few striking parallels seem to suggest themselves between the rising success of the *Buch der Lieder* and the evolution of *Dichterliebe*.

The *Lyrisches Intermezzo* is one of four poetic cycles in a volume which Heine intended to comprise 'the beginning and end of my lyrical youth'.[1] A large proportion of these poems had already appeared in preceding years. For Heine, who was not yet thirty years of age, to prepare a 'complete edition of [his] known works'[2] shows his aim to assemble and preserve, as well as to bring to a close the period of life in which these lyrics were produced. By publishing them in book form and by deliberately including the dates of composition in the cycles' titles,[3] the poetry is rendered 'dated'; print makes them become 'out-dated'. What had once grown out of momentary feelings and experience is made into documentation. However, the distance between past motivations and aesthetic presentation introduces a new, self-critical, poetic dimension to the work. When Heine later speaks of 'horrific sullenness' that befalls him at the sight of 'printed juvenile poetry', he is acknowledging his detachedness from this particular productive phase. To attach an exact date to each of the poetic cycles in the *Lyrisches Intermezzo* also carries a sense of *vraisemblable*: it is an attempt to locate these poems within the present world, within the reality of their readers.[4] Heine's desire to correspond with his readers can be seen in the Foreword to the second edition of the *Buch der Lieder* which reads:

Not without a feeling of diffidence and awkwardness do I hand this edition of the book over to its readers. . . . I feel the kind of uneasiness which overcame me ten years ago at the time of its first publication and which weighs upon one's soul. This feeling will only be understood by that poet and poetaster who has seen his first poems in print. First poems!

[1] Letter to Varnhagen, 24 October 1826. *HSA* XX, p. 272 [Anfang und Ende meines lyrischen Jugendlebens].
[2] Letter to Moses Moser, 30 October 1827. *HSA* XX, p. 33 [Gesamtausgabe meiner bekannten Gedichte].
[3] *Junge Leiden, 1817–1821; Lyrisches Intermezzo, 1822–1823; Die Heimkehr, 1823–1824; Die Nordsee, 1825–1826.*
[4] See Culler (1975), pp. 137–152.

They should be written on slip-shod, faded paper, in between, here and there, must be a pressed flower or a curl of blond hair, or a discoloured piece of hair ribbon; and in some places there should still be visible the trace of a teardrop . . . But first poems which are printed in brilliant black on horribly smooth paper, they have lost their sweet, virgin-like charm and arouse in their author a horrible feeling of sullenness.[5]

As Altenhofer has argued, this statement thematizes the dichotomy of the Goethean model of *Erlebnislyrik*[6] and Heine's own self-critical poetry. Heine quotes the paraphernalia, the local colour which traditionally spoke for the topical uniqueness of lyric production, only to realize – as all non-literary traces of this moment are wiped out by the representational perfection of print – that his conscious interventions into a past creative process whose motifs he cannot emotionally duplicate inevitably undo the last scintilla of expressive immediacy. Heine – by his own intention – leaves the 'experience model of love poetry' (*Erlebnismodell der Liebesdichtung*)[7] behind when working towards a cyclic arrangement, an aesthetic more in accord with his leanings towards Petrarch than Goethe. The poetry becomes more artistic, more artificial in a way, less representative of its particularity. Thus, the Classical love-poem matrix does not accord with the structure of the *Lyrisches Intermezzo*. The cyclic arrangement introduces a self-reflexive element that replaces the text's correspondence to an outward situation by an inner literary connection to its surrounding texts.[8]

This fact is important. It means that the cycle's greater structure takes precedence over the single poem. In the course of revising the *Buch der Lieder* for succeeding editions, Heine's aim to perfect its epigrammatic and correlative style comes to the fore: superfluous diminutives, archaisms, dissonances, word-repetitions and thematically distracting elements were removed[9] so as to strengthen the cycle's internal links, links which generate the special kind of leitmotif continuum present in the *Lyrisches Intermezzo*.

The emphasis on the whole over its parts was Heine's main concern when considering whether to publish poems which had either originally been interpolated within the prose sections of *Tragödien, nebst einem lyrischen Intermezzo* (1823) or published in various journals such as the *Gesellschafter*.[10] Here, his task was to achieve poetic

---

[5] B I, p. 9 [Nicht ohne Befangenheit übergebe ich der Leserwelt den erneuten Abdruck dieses Buches. . . . Bei seinem Anblick erwachte in mir all jenes Unbehagen, das mir einst vor zehn Jahren, bei der ersten Publikation, die Seele beklemmte. Verstehen wird diese Empfindung nur der Dichter oder Dichterling, der seine ersten Gedichte gedruckt sah. Erste Gedichte! Sie müssen auf nachlässigen, verblichenen Blättern geschrieben sein, dazwischen, hie und da, müssen welke Blumen liegen, oder eine blonde Locke, oder ein verfärbtes Stückchen Band, und an mancher Stelle muß noch die Spur einer Träne sichtbar sein . . . Erste Gedichte aber, die gedruckt sind, grell schwarz gedruckt auf entsetzlich glattem Papier, diese haben ihren süßesten, jungfräulichsten Reiz verloren und erregen beim Verfasser einen schauerlichen Mißmut].

[6] 'Erlebnisdichtung' is a standard term in German studies for the poetry of Goethe and his contemporaries. It describes poetry that captures a particular moment in its *entirety* – and usually happiness, in the case of most of Goethe's love poems.

[7] Windfuhr (1966), pp. 266–285.   [8] Altenhofer (1982), p. 18.

[9] Atkins (1973), p. 705. These variants are best documented in *DHA* I as edited by Pierre Grappin.

[10] See *DHA* I, pp. 748–753.

continuity between many dispersed poems by strengthening their ties for the sake of a perfected greater whole. His desire to see these early love poems eventually appear collectively indicates that Heine conceived of them as what he later called 'variations on the same little theme', thus revealing that it is essentially one single pervasive idea that speaks for his poetic intentions. Heine wrote to his friend Moses Moser on 15 December 1825:

By next Easter, I feel like having something printed called 'Wanderbuch Part I', which would be the following pieces: I. a new Intermezzo, approximately 80 little poems, mostly travel-pictures, and which you already know about. I would have to discuss with Dummler [publisher of *Tragödien*] whether it would not be advisable to print the *Lyrisches Intermezzo* once again, the new Intermezzo (I.) in order to separate it from the *Tragödien*. The whole thing would be published separately as a book of 10 to 11 gatherings under the title 'The Great Intermezzo'. This book would form a most original whole and would find many admirers.[11]

That Heine was conscious of the fact that his art of arrangement[12] represented a novel and stylistically unprecedented kind of poetry *in extenso* comes through in his phrase 'most original whole', or his later comment about the *Buch der Lieder*: 'It would be a book that could not easily be compared to anything else'.[13]

The enormous success of Heine's *Reisebilder* ('The book that caused a commotion, and sold well'), published in 1826, strengthened the poet's confidence, and the plan of 'a grand collection of all my poems' materialized with the first edition of *Buch der Lieder* in 1827.[14] All but seven poems for the *Buch der Lieder* had already appeared in journals and newspapers. Not surprisingly, the publisher Campe asked sardonically: 'But tell me, my dear Heine, just how should this book surprise anyone? Do you still have so much unpublished material which would be added to it?'[15] However, Heine justified a complete edition by stressing its historical value and documenting what we earlier heard was the 'beginning and end of my lyrical youth'.[16] With the *Buch der Lieder*, Heine calculated further to impress the public and to heighten his popularity as he writes: 'a few friends are pressing me to publish a select poem collection, chronologically ordered, and fastidiously selected; it would become as

[11] Heine to Moser. Quoted in Atkins (1973), p. 712 [Variazionen desselben kleinen Themas]. [Ich habe nämlich Lust, nächsten Ostern unter dem Titel 'Wanderbuch, I. Teil' folgende Piècen drucken zu lassen: I. Ein neues Intermezzo, etwa 80 kleine Gedichte, meist Reisebilder, und wovon du schon 33 [in *Gesellschafter* of March 1824] kennst. . . . Zu besprechen wäre mit Dumler ob es nicht ratsam wäre das lyrische Intermezzo, welches zwischen den Tragödien steht, nochmals abdrucken zu lassen, das neue Intermezzo (I.) damit zu verbinden, und das ganze als ein Büchlein von 10 bis 11 Bogen, unter dem Titel 'Das große Intermezzo', besonders erscheinen zu lassen. Dieses Büchlein würde ein höchst originelles Ganzes bilden, und viele Gönner finden].

[12] Altenhofer (1982), p. 29.

[13] *HSA* XX, p. 228 [Es wäre ein Buch das nicht so leicht seines Gleichen fände].

[14] Letter to Varnhagen, 24 October 1826. *HSA* XX, p. 272 [Das Buch hat viel Spektakel gemacht und viel Absatz gefunden].

[15] *HSA* I, p. 639 [Sie sagen, lieber Heine, das Buch würde überraschen, wodurch? Haben Sie denn soviel Ungedrucktes noch was dazu kommen soll?].

[16] *HSA* XX, p. 272 [Anfang und Ende meines lyrischen Jungendlebens].

popular as those by Bürger, Goethe, Uhland etc. . . . Inexpensiveness and all other necessities to become popular would be my only considerations.'[17]

The first edition of the *Buch der Lieder* sold slowly, and Campe wrote to Heine in 1833: 'The stock went down from 2000 to 800, and the book is selling for the last two years only in connection with the *Reisebilder*'. The following remark concerning the group of buyers includes Schumann, who in 1828 had become a university student in Leipzig: 'Your book is sold to the universities, to young men and people like that – who have no money'.[18]

However, a second edition of the *Buch der Lieder* was published in 1837 and this led to a third edition two years later. The fourth edition followed in 1841. In 1843, Campe writes to Heine: '[*Das Buch der Lieder*] is the only thing that sells',[19] and eventually a fifth edition came out in 1844, the year *Dichterliebe* was first published. During Heine's lifetime, a further eight editions were published, thus documenting the triumphant success of this collection.[20]

---

[17] Letter to Friedrich Merckel, 16 November 1826 [Einige Freunde dringen darauf, daß ich eine auserlesene Gedichtesammlung, chronologisch geordnet und streng gewählt, herausgeben soll, und glauben, daß sie ebenso populär wie die Bürgersche, Göthesche, Uhlandsche u.s.w. werden wird. . . . Die Wohlfeilheit und die anderen Erfordernisse des Popularwerdens wären meine einzigen Rücksichten].

[18] *DHA* I/1, p. 605; letter from Campe to Heine, 12 July 1833 [Der Vorrath von diesen 2000 ist bis auf 800 geschmolzen, und seit 2 Jahren beginnt das Buch erst regelmäßig, durch wiederholte Versendung mit den Reisebildern, gangbar zu werden]. [Ihr Buch geht nach den Universitäten, an junge Männer und derg. – die kein Geld haben].

[19] *DHA* I/1, p. 617; letter from Campe to Heine, 2 May 1843 [[Das *Buch der Lieder* ist] das Einzige, was seinen Gang geht].

[20] The sixth edition appeared in 1847 and was followed by further editions up to the thirteenth edition in 1855.

PART III

THE POETICS OF *DICHTERLIEBE*

. . . Byron, Heine, Victor Hugo und ähnliche . . . Die Poesie hat sich, auf einige Augenblicke der Ewigkeit, die Maske der Ironie vorgebunden, um ihr Schmerzensgesicht nicht sehen zu lassen; vielleicht, daß die freundliche Hand eines Genius sie einmal abbinden wird.

[. . . Byron, Heine, Victor Hugo and others . . . Poetry has, on occasions in eternity, put on the mask of irony so as not to show its face of pain; perhaps the kind hand of a genius will take it off someday].   Schumann in 1835 *GS* I, p. 145

11

INTRODUCTION

As one of the most significant compositions in the musical repertoire, *Dichterliebe* has received sustained and ongoing analytical attention.[1] Without exception, critics have attempted to explain its formal and harmonic complexity, especially the intricate relationship of its parts, according to the laws of the Classical model, that is, in essence, in the light of coherence and structural unity. These attempts have generally remained unconvincing. This study attempts to reconsider the enigmatic form of *Dichterliebe* by introducing the Early Romantics' conception of form in general, and Schumann's highly idiosyncratic compositional procedures in particular. Friedrich Schlegel's assertion that 'all Classical forms of poetry in their strict purity are now laughable' indicates the Romantics' new understanding of the form of the art work.[2] According to the Romantics' own conception, then, we can say that Romanticism in its *early* form means, ultimately, a celebration of the absence of finished works and a celebration of the poetic act itself:

Other kinds of poetry are finished and are capable of being fully analysed. The romantic kind of poetry is still in the state of becoming; that, in fact, is its real essence: that it should forever be becoming and never be perfected. . . . It alone is infinite, just as it alone is free.[3]

The creative and poetic act could be viewed as the spontaneous signature of a state of mind, and the gesture of a momentary cognisance of, and reflection upon, the movements of that mind. In this sense one may speak of 'inspiration', which, indeed, characterizes Schumann's mode of writing – music as well as prose or poetry. The following diary entry written in the spring of 1846, six years after composing *Dichterliebe*, is testimony to such a creative process. By referring directly to *Dichterliebe*

---

[1] The analytical accounts of *Dichterliebe* that I have considered in some detail in this study, also including those concerned with a single song or parts of the cycle, are primarily Benary (1967), Komar (1971), Moore (1981), Neumeyer (1982), Agawu (1984), Sams (1993) and Pousseur (1993). The central issue preoccupying these analyses, namely that of unity and narrativity, is debated in the course of this Introduction as well as in the following analytical essays.

[2] *KFSA* II, p. 154, no. 60 [Alle klassischen Dichtarten in ihrer strengen Reinheit sind jetzt lächerlich].

[3] Fragment no. 116, the manifesto of the Romantics, in the *Athenaeum* [Andere Dichtarten sind fertig und können vollständig zergliedert werden. Die romantische Dichtart ist noch im Werden; ja das ist ihr eigentliches Wesen, daß sie ewig nur werden, nie vollendet sein kann. . . . Sie allein ist unendlich, wie sie allein frei ist]. *Athenaeum*, p. 119. Trans. Firchow (1991), p. 31.

as a 'a song cycle of twenty pieces', Schumann speaks of 'inspiration' in terms of his spontaneous and rapid mode of composing:

I have written most, almost everything, [even] the smallest of my pieces, in inspiration; most [was written] at an unbelievable speed – my first symphony in B-flat major in four days, likewise a song cycle of twenty pieces, [and] the Peri in a relatively similar short period of time. Only from the year 1845 onwards, when I began to invent and work out in detail everything in my head, did an entirely different mode of composing begin to develop.[4]

The 'inspired' Romantic art work was created in the spirit of a heightened self-consciousness, was an experimentation with the Self, and was, therefore, conceived of as inconclusive. Handed over to future generations, it does not lose its non-representational and provisional character, as Friedrich Schlegel observed:

A project is the subjective embryo of a developing object. . . . The sense for projects – which one might call fragments of the future – is distinguishable from the sense for fragments of the past only by its orientation, which is progressive in the former, but regressive in the latter. It is essential to be able to at once idealize and realize objects immediately, to complement them and partly execute them within oneself.[5]

Yet, if the emphasis was on the momentary, and if the intention truly was to come to consciousness through the act of creating whilst the content of the unfinished result was absent, then, in Blanchot's phrase, the Romantic artist has 'failed twice over'. As Blanchot points out with regard to the case of Novalis:

The Romantic author fails twice, because he cannot really disappear . . . and because the works, through which he cannot help pretending to fulfil himself, remain – as if intentionally – unfinished. Thus, Novalis will die, almost symbolically, without having written Part II of *Heinrich von Ofterdingen*, that part which would have been called 'Fulfilment' (*Erfüllung*).[6]

In the case of *Dichterliebe*, the situation could be seen as even more extreme: before appearing in print, it first disappeared immediately after 'completion' in 1840 for four years. And when it actually did appear in print in 1844, four songs had disappeared. The first circumstance seems unusual for the restless Schumann of 1840, who created

---

[4] *TB* II, p. 402 [Ich habe das Meiste, fast Alles, das kleinste meiner Stücke in Inspiration geschrieben, vieles in unglaublicher Schnelligkeit, so meine 1ste Symphonie in B Dur in vier Tagen, einen Liederkreis von zwanzig Stücken ebenso, die Peri in verhältnismäßig ebenso kurzer Zeit. Erst vom Jr. 1845 an, von wo ich anfing alles im Kopf zu erfinden und auszuarbeiten, hat sich eine ganz andere Art zu componiren zu entwickeln begonnen]. See Nauhaus' commentary identifying *Dichterliebe* as the composition to which Schumann refers here, in *TB* II, p. 549, n. 718.

[5] *Athenaeum*, p. 103 [Ein Projekt ist der subjektive Keim eines werdenden Objekts. . . . Der Sinn für Projekte, die man Fragmente aus der Zukunft nennen könnte, ist von dem Sinn für Fragmente aus der Vergangenheit nur durch die Richtung verschieden, die bei ihm progressiv, bei jenem aber regressiv ist. Das Wesentliche ist die Fähigkeit, Gegenstände unmittelbar zugleich zu idealisieren und zu realisieren, zu ergänzen und teilweise in sich auszuführen].

[6] Blanchot (1969), pp. 517–518 [L'auteur romantique échoue deux fois, puisqu'il ne réussit pas à disparaître vraiment . . . et puisque les ouvrages par lesquels il ne peut s'empêcher de prétendre s'accomplir, restent, et comme par intention, inaccomplis. Ainsi, Novalis va-t-il mourir presque symboliquement sans avoir écrit la seconde partie de *Heinrich von Ofterdingen*, celle qui aurait dû s'intituler 'Accomplissement' (*Erfüllung*)].

'at an unbelievable speed' and in great quantity, eager to get his scores to the publisher as soon as they were written, in order to make a name for himself. The second circumstance, however, seems indicative of a mode of writing whose only meaning resides in the act itself. The work's power lies nowhere other than in the moment of its creation, and represents nothing other than the pure movement of writing. Once that poetic moment (that 'rare' and 'secret state of the soul' as Schumann would say[7]) has ceased, the work ceases with it. The artist becomes detached.

Dichterliebe is an abstract piece of music. It is also – quite apart from the actual poetry by Heine – an example of abstract poetry in the Early Romantic, and arguably modernist, sense. It structurally reflects itself and realizes itself through reflection. The issue in *Dichterliebe* is thus, as Blanchot notes with regard to Early Romantic poetry in general, no longer one 'of poetic art' as 'subsidiary knowledge: it is the very heart of poetry which is knowledge; its essence is to be both a quest and a quest for itself'.[8] Hence Schumann's title: *Dichterliebe* – a celebration of being a poet and a celebration of the amorous state at once, that is, the highest state of subjectivity.

So Schumann is subject. Which Schumann? Not the aphasic Schumann of 1850, but the one of 1840 who spoke for the sake of speaking: 'a writer by destiny, for a writer is probably nothing but a language enthusiast?' as Novalis says in his important essay on the nature of poetry, asserting that 'to talk for the sake of talking – that is the liberating formula.'[9] But again, which Schumann? There is no single Schumann. Instead there are characters – Eusebius, Florestan, Raro, and many others. This results in what one could call Schumann's Protean characterlessness, his instability, divided into various personae:

The more specific music is, the more separate images music will expose to the listener; the more also will it grasp, and the more eternal will music be, and new for all ages. . . . This is the spirit of particularity.[10]

Schumann thus fantasizes and imagines, for example, hearing the voice of one of his characters, Florestan, say to him:

Indeed there are more figures and speaking characters in your way of composing; arrangement and shape (form) are also different. Good heavens! I could reply, this seems to me the first thing inscribed into my style which leans towards the Romantic.[11]

---

[7] Kreisig *GS* I, p. 343 [seltene . . . geheime Seelenzustände].

[8] Blanchot (1969), p. 518 [Naturellement, il ne s'agit plus ici d'art poétique, savoir annexe: c'est le cœur de la poésie qui est savoir, c'est son essence d'être recherche et recherche d'elle-même].

[9] Novalis as quoted in Frank (1989), p. 283 [ein berufener Schriftsteller, denn ein Schriftsteller ist wohl nur ein Sprachbegeisterter? . . . Reden um der Rede willen, so lautet die befreiende Formel].

[10] *TB* I, p. 410 [Je spezieller eine Musik ist, je mehr einzelne Bilder im Ganzen sie vor dem Hörer ausbreitet, desto mehr erfaßt sie, u. desto ewiger wird sie seyn u. neu für alle Zeiten. . . . Dies ist der Partikulargeist].

[11] *TB* I, p. 361 [so sind doch in deinem [Compositionsstil] mehr Gestalten und sprechende Charaktere; auch Anordnung und Gestalt (Form) wären anders. Beym Himmel: könnt' ich erwidern, dies scheint mir wie das erste in meinem Styl geschrieben, der sich zum Romantischen neigt].

By his own account, Schumann thus produced 'nothing big, but much that is fragmentary and good'.[12] His writing of short pieces derived, as I discussed earlier,[13] from a compositional process whose central dynamic was to 'fantasize' – to speak the 'language of the soul', as Schumann would have it.[14] In this, he explored the movements of the unconscious, if one were to translate such Romantic formulations into modern terms. As regards Schumann's heightened apperception of events which he experienced as coming from outside and inside, Barthes offers a good description of how Schumann's 'Romantic soul' reacted:

'Soul', 'feeling', 'heart' are romantic names for the body. Everything is clearer, in the romantic text, if we translate the effusive moral term by a pulsional corporeal one – whereby there is no harm done: romantic music is saved, once the body returns to it – as soon as, through music, in fact, the body returns to music. By restoring the body to the romantic text, we correct the ideological reading of this text, for this reading, that of our current opinion, never does anything but *invert* ... the body's motions into movements of the soul.[15]

When discussing the literary theme of the *Carnaval* in Schumann's piano music, Barthes notes that it is 'truly the theatre of [a] decentering of the subject (a very modern temptation) which Schumann expresses in his fashion by the carousel of his brief forms'.[16] One can thus, in recognizing the full extent of Schumann's fantasizing, imagine his compositions as taking the form of visual images, which rise up from an inner, rather archaic realm. Representing the Early Romantics' 'inner plurality'[17] and realizing Novalis' idea about 'the perfect human being' who 'must virtually live in several places and inside several human beings',[18] Schumann succeeded in giving a 'representation ... of the inner state, of inner transformations'.[19] *Fantasizing* as Schumann did was, indeed, what Friedrich Schlegel had called the 'free play of thought itself' (*freies Selbstdenken*) – an 'ensemble' of ideas reaching nothing but an 'antithetical synthesis'[20] that is capable of representing 'the fragmentary character of the human consciousness'[21] and 'the essentially contradictory nature of our I'.[22] These ideas, each itself a 'fragment of consciousness', appear in 'striking combinations' and 'surprising turns and configurations' to 'reach out ever further beyond themselves'.[23] They may contradict each other, as much as they interact with each

---

[12] *TB* II (April 1838), p. 54 [Nichts Großes gearbeitet, doch viel fragmentarisches Gute].

[13] See p. 53.   [14] Kreisig *GS* I, p. 356 [Seelensprache].

[15] Barthes (1985d), p. 308. Emphasis original.

[16] Barthes (1985c), p. 296.   [17] NO III, p. 662, no. 598 [innere Pluralität].

[18] NO III, p. 560, no. 34 [Der vollendete Mensch muß gleichsam an mehreren Orten und in mehreren Menschen leben].

[19] NO II, p. 283, no. 637 [Darstellung ... des inneren Zustandes, der inneren Veränderungen].

[20] *KFSA* XVIII, p. 82, no. 637 [antithetische Synthesis].

[21] *KFSA* XII, p. 392 [der fragmentarische Character des menschlichen Bewußtseins].

[22] *KFSA* XII, p. 334 [das eigentlich Widersprechende in unserm Ich].

[23] *KFSA* III, p. 51 [Merkwürdige Kombinationen ... überraschende Wendungen und Konfigurationen ... die stets über sich selbst hinausweisen].

other, to generate a real sense of 'agility'.[24] The whole constellation of ideas finally turns into what Friedrich Schlegel called a 'polemic against consistency'.[25]

With regard to form, *Dichterliebe* has received a great amount of attention, since inner coherence cannot easily be detected here.[26] The criteria most analytical enquiries have sought to adopt for *Dichterliebe* never seem to suit the object. The definition of a tonal centre has usually been as great a concern as it has become an obstacle. As will be argued in response, on the basis of analysing a number of songs from *Dichterliebe*, the absence of resolution and formal integration in the Classical sense is precisely what denied to these earlier analyses truly convincing conclusions.

There is good reason, however, for giving the question of rationale some thought in a musico-poetic analysis of *Dichterliebe,* for most earlier enquiries have sought a particular reason or principle on which the cycle's tonal system is based. For example, a 'general compositional plan' and 'integrated musical totality' have been proposed as resulting from a 'coherent key scheme' or from considering the songs as 'interdependent movements governed by a single key'.[27] Motivic and rhythmic interrelations have been pointed out to underscore this idea. But Heine's poems and poetic style have hardly been considered in any detail, if they found any attention at all.[28] In the rare cases where the poems were taken into account, more often than not a narrative has been presumed and the analysis in question has found itself trapped in an argument of tonal narrativity or narrative tonality.[29] The analysis offered by Henri Pousseur must, however, be called an exception, as the composer provides a detailed and imbricated analytical discussion which follows, strikingly, a quasi-serial path.[30] This is made obvious from the start, when he quotes Barthes'

---

[24] *KFSA* II, p. 263 as quoted in Behler (1993), p. 151.

[25] *KFSA* XVIII, p. 309, no. 1383 [Polemik gegen die Consequenz].

[26] For a particularly adamant approach, see Komar (1971), whose aim it was to present 'an extensive study of the coherence of the sixteen songs of *Dichterliebe* as a totality' (pp. vii–viii). Neumeyer (1982) has argued against Komar's approach in favour of 'narrative and dramatic progressions' as 'generators of organic unity'. Neumeyer also suggests that 'key unity is not necessary to an integrated song cycle; whatever the manner of tonal integration may be, it has not been identified yet'. See Neumeyer (1982), pp. 104–105 as well as (1997), 197–216.

[27] Komar (1971), pp. 65–66.

[28] The exception is Hallmark (1979) who takes Heine's poetry into account. For an overt refusal to consider the poetry, see Komar (1971, pp. 8–9): 'The main point is that one can appreciate the music of a song without understanding the words, while one can receive little idea of a song at all from the words alone. I am inclined to think that the more a song depends upon textual interpretation by a singer, the less good it is'. Komar offers a second argument by proposing (p. 11) that 'the postludes indicate how little the words count – else what purpose in so much non-verbal music?', to finally make his stance abundantly clear (p. 11, n. 20): 'In fact, the words actually impede my enjoyment of the whole cycle – to the extent that I heed them. The moping, distraught lover portrayed in German song cycles bores me, but this feeling in no way detracts my enthusiasm from the music of the great song cycles by Beethoven, Schubert and Schumann.'

[29] Hallmark (1979, pp. 149–150) states: 'Analysis of the musical cycle as a whole must also be considered in conjunction with the poetry. In *Dichterliebe* the tonal plan and the narrative sequence support one another.' Neumeyer (1982, p. 97) – in following Hallmark's remarks on poetic 'narrative' – finds that 'the combination of the harmonic-tonal with narrative-dramatic aspects should potentially allow an adequate interpretation of organic structure'.

[30] The analysis was first conceived in 1975 and has appeared in a French edition (1993) which contains a lengthy postscript.

remark that 'Schumann was perhaps that composer who (before Webern) understood and practised the aesthetic of the fragment best'.[31] The line of serialism is indeed pursued throughout, by way of suggesting 'a virtual row'[32] as well as by asserting that *Dichterliebe* is, 'in the last analysis', governed by certain 'figures' or 'groupings' 'even on the level of the "series" of (16) tonics'.[33] Finally, Pousseur asserts that it seems beyond doubt that these figures are the result of a general 'serial organization'. Pousseur concludes: 'I hope to have demonstrated, that this [serial organization] was intended by Schumann'.[34] Clearly, Pousseur has not worked in the name of 'authenticity'. However, his own orientation as a composer has led to a kind of analysis that is inspired, individualized and very creative, as it draws a work of 1840 right into the present. Pousseur thus truly champions his cause, and with conviction, as well as by imbuing his dense analytical text with a beautiful, highly expressive poetic diction. In this sense, Pousseur's contribution can be said to carry an admirable *esprit de large envergure*. That *Dichterliebe* exerted a special influence upon Pousseur, across all historical boundaries, has been acknowledged openly through his own composition called *Dichterliebesreigentraum*, translated by Michel Butor as *Les amours du poète tournent en rêve*.

In view of the main tendency perceptible in most analyses of *Dichterliebe*, namely that of coherence, a few additional remarks should be made. Aside from the problematic contention that either Heine's original poem-cycle or Schumann's condensed version should be regarded as a narrative, and aside from the even more problematic equation of poetic and tonal meaning, it must be obvious that any analysis which takes the four deleted songs into consideration would have to be able to identify these songs as also conforming to some such musical totality in order to sustain the argument. In this regard, a certain lack of rigour within the purely organicist argument is emphasized by the fact that none of the four deleted songs has been analysed in any detail at all.[35] In the last instance, one would wish to see some demonstration that the four songs were removed specifically in order to tighten up the surface coherence of the cycle. This, however, still remains to be done. For the time being, and in the absence of more conclusive evidence as regards the composer's reasons for the exclusion of these four songs, it can be submitted that their *inclusion* expands the structure of the cycle as it is known, which, in turn, imposes upon the published version a former, original order which may or may not accord with the analytical findings established thus far.

As far as the compositional process of *Dichterliebe* is concerned, however, there is every reason to believe that Schumann conceived the work as perfectly valid in its original form of twenty songs – at least until 1844. Nothing in the sketches,

---

[31] Pousseur (1993), p. 10. For a discussion of this quotation from Barthes (1975), pp. 64–65, see also pp. 114–115, above.

[32] Pousseur (1993), pp. 21–28.   [33] Pousseur (1993), p. 180.   [34] Pousseur (1993), p. 180.

[35] Both Sams (1993) and Hallmark (1979) offer a hasty treatment of the four deleted songs. Pousseur (1993), in his post-scriptum of 1993 to his analysis of *Dichterliebe* dating from 1975, remarks of the four songs that their removal served a 'purifying purpose' as regards narrative as well as formal procedures. Unaware, as he acknowledges, even of the existence of the four songs until 1993, he does not offer a detailed analytical account of any of them.

as Hallmark's study shows, indicates hesitation or a lesser degree of compositional conviction when it comes to the four songs: they seem to have been written in the same spirit and productive continuum as all the other songs within a span of nine days in May 1840. Conceived and carried by the same kind of remarkable *élan*, no changes were made to the twenty songs during the next four years. Hence, if Schumann *did* have an overall compositional plan in mind for *Dichterliebe*, then it must have encompassed the four discarded songs as well. It makes little sense to believe that a certain premeditated compositional conception came to a halt twice (between Songs 4 and 5, and Songs 12 and 13) in the middle of the flow of writing. However, even in the hypothetical case of Schumann regarding these four songs as inferior to the others at the time of preparing for their publication in 1844, the reason for their exclusion cannot be found in any lack of musical logic with regard to the rest of the work, *if* the argument for an overriding compositional plan were to hold water. In other words, as part of the same compositional process, either the four songs will demonstrate ties that render them part of the whole, or the whole organicist argument has to be reconsidered, perhaps even rejected.

To date, there exists no evidence from which final conclusions could be drawn in order to answer convincingly the vexed question as to why these four songs were excluded from the first edition of *Dichterliebe*. However, a letter from the composer to the publishers Bote & Bock written on 2 June 1840, that is, a day after the completion of *Dichterliebe*, clearly suggests that Schumann intended it to be published in its entirety:

Esteemed Sirs,

During your stay here in connection with the take-over of the publishing house, [you] were so kind as to make an offer regarding one of my compositions. At the time when you spoke to me about this, I had already made arrangements for my manuscripts, and other things were not yet put in order. Now, I am finished with a more extensive song composition and have the honour of enclosing for you the complete title, which could be followed by the work itself within the next fortnight.

I would like to see the collection, which forms a whole, appear unseparated. But since this may perhaps not seem advisable to you, I take the liberty of asking whether it is possible for you to prepare one set of copies which comprises the whole *cycle*, and another set which you could divide *into two halves*. . . .

As regards the public success which the songs might gain, it is not for me to pass judgement. I allow myself only to say that I have almost never written with as much love as I did during the composition of this collection. With my numerous connections, it will also be easy for me to obtain rapid dissemination and recognition of the songs.[36]

---

[36] See the first, and to my knowledge only, publication of this letter in Altmann-Berlin (1923), pp. 865–866 [Ew. Wohlgeboren / waren so gefällig, mir bei Ihrem Hiersein wegen Verlagsübernahme einer meiner Kompositionen einen Antrag zu stellen. Im Augenblick, als Sie davon zu mir sprachen, hatte ich über meine Manuskripte schon disponiert, und anderes war noch nicht geordnet. Jetzt bin ich mit einem größeren Liederwerke fertig und beehre mich, Ihnen den vollständigen Titel beizulegen, dem das Werk binnen vierzehn Tagen nachfolgen

Schumann's 'complete title' had been enclosed on a separate page and reads:

Gedichte

von Heinrich Heine

20 Lieder und Gesänge
aus dem lyrischen Intermezzo im Buche der Lieder
für eine Singstimme und das Pianoforte
componirt
und
Hrn Dr. Felix Mendelssohn Bartholdy
freundschaftlich zugeeignet
von
Robert Schumann

2ter Liederkreis
aus Heines Buch der Lieder
Op. 29 [Op. 48] Hft. 1. u. 2.[37]

From Schumann's letter and title page, it is obvious that Schumann indeed wished all twenty songs to be published as a whole. What is also apparent is, however, that he seemed to have anticipated difficulties in achieving this goal with the publishers in the first place, for which reason he suggests a compromise solution that would involve the publication of *Dichterliebe* in one volume, as well as divided into two volumes. In both cases, however, Schumann expected all twenty songs to be included. Noteworthy is also Schumann's vacillating use of the terms 'collection' (*Sammlung*), 'cycle' (*Zyklus*) and later also 'song composition' as well as 'song cycle' (*Liederwerk* and *Liederkreis*, see below) which indicates at once a loose conception of cyclicity, as well as a somewhat stricter idea of the collection to be more than a random assemblage of unrelated pieces of music.[38] In this regard, one could make the suggestion that Schumann had, with Op. 48, invented a new genre which he did not have the vocabulary to describe other than in conventional, and perhaps inappropriate, terms. Novalis' concept of 'a dream image – without coherence – an

könnte. / Gern sähe ich die Sammlung, die ein Ganzes bildet, auch ungetrennt erscheinen. Da Ihnen vielleicht dies aber nicht ratsam schiene, so erlaube ich mir die Frage, ob es nicht ginge, daß Sie eine Anzahl Exemplare, die den ganzen *Zyklus* umfaßte, und eine andere Anzahl, wo sie *in zwei Hälften* getrennt würde, anfertigen lassen könnten. . . . Über den Erfolg, den die Lieder im Publikum haben könnten, steht mir kein Urteil zu. Ich darf Ihnen nur sagen, daß ich fast noch nie mit soviel Liebe geschrieben habe als während der Komposition dieser Sammlung. Bei meinen mannigfachen Verbindungen ist es mir auch leicht, den Liedern schnell Eingang und Wirkung zu verschaffen]. Emphasis original. This letter was brought to my attention by Renate Hilmar-Voit who is aiming, together with the singer Thomas Hampson, to prepare a new edition of *Dichterliebe* on the basis of new archival material related to the sketches of the cycle. Thomas Hampson, with Wolfgang Sawallisch on the piano, recorded the 1840 original version of *Dichterliebe* in 1994 (released in 1997 by EMI 7243 5 55598 2 1) including in the booklet a succinct summary of the genesis of the work's complex publication history by Hampson and Hilmar-Voit under the title *20 Lieder und Gesänge aus dem Lyrischen Intermezzo im Buch der Lieder*. Since this letter appeared in print only once, and as long ago as 1923, no notice has been taken of it in the critical literature on the publication history of *Dichterliebe*.

[37] See Hallmark (1979), p. 124.   [38] See also Ferris (2000).

ensemble of wondrous things and incidents – e.g. a *musical fantasy*',[39] or Jean Paul's idea about poetic writing to be able to render 'constellations of a subterranean firmament',[40] may perhaps be more apposite ways of characterizing *Dichterliebe* – not least with regard to Schumann's confessed aim to render audible what can be called the irrational and the unconscious.[41]

Bote & Bock's response to Schumann's enquiry, dated 22 July 1840, is a politely phrased rejection. This may or may not explain Schumann's hesitation, which seems to have lasted until late in 1843, when he ventured to approach other publishers again. The rejection by Bote & Bock reads:

As regards your most kind offer, it was most delightful for us to see that you are not opposed to allowing works of your valued talent to appear in our publishing house. After due consideration of the publication of your 'Liederkreis' Op. 29 [*recte* Op. 48], we feel obliged, however, to desist. We understand very well what an honour such an undertaking is for the publisher – but this work is indeed too significant for us beginners, and not suitable from the viewpoint of our business. Should you however have ready, now or later, a smaller composition for piano. . . .[42]

Only in August 1843, after more than three years, for which no further significant documentation has come to light, did Schumann eventually approach Breitkopf & Härtel about the publication of *Dichterliebe*. The letter, dated 6 August 1843, and now housed in the University Library of Darmstadt, shows Schumann trying out a different strategy in order to make the composition appear worthy of publication. The introductory remarks are particularly interesting in contrast to Schumann's later statement of 1846 about 'inspiration' and 'unbelievable speed' of composition:

At the same time I allow myself to enquire whether you would be inclined to publish a song composition of mine. I have worked on it and polished it for 2 [*sic*!] years, and wish to thereby end my role as a song composer for the time being. It is a cycle of 20 songs, which form a whole, but each of which is also self-contained. The best would be to divide it into two booklets where each one comprised 20–22 plates. There is no rush with the publication, if you were not to explicitly wish it.[43]

---

[39] NO III, p. 454 [ein Traumbild – ohne Zusammenhang – Ein *Ensemble* wunderbarer Dinge und Begebenheiten – z. B. eine *musikalische Phantasie*]. Emphasis original.

[40] JP IX, p. 58 [Sternbilder eines unterirdischen Himmels].

[41] See Meissner (1985) who demonstrates this aspect of Schumann's creativity with exceptional clarity.

[42] See the first and only publication of this letter in Altmann-Berlin (1923), p. 867 [Was nun Ihre sehr geehrte Offerte anbelangt, so war es uns höchst erfreulich, zu ersehen, daß Sie nicht abgeneigt, Werke Ihres geschätzten Talents in unserem Verlag erscheinen zu lassen. Nach gehöriger Erwägung der Herausgabe Ihres 'Liederkreises' op. 29 [*recte* Op. 48] sehen wir und indes veranlaßt, hiervon abzusehen. Wir sehen sehr wohl ein, wie ehrenwert ein derartiges Unternehmen für einen Verleger ist – doch ist das Werk für uns Anfänger doch zu bedeutend und dem Standpunkte unseres Geschäfts nicht angemessen. Sollten Sie jedoch jetzt oder später eine kleinere Klavierkomposition fertig haben . . .].

[43] Brought to my attention by Renate Hilmar-Voit who kindly permitted the quotation of parts of the letter from her personal notes. The original German reads: 'Zugleich erlaube ich mir anzufragen, ob Sie geneigt wären, ein Liederwerk von mir zu drucken. Seit 2 [*sic*!] Jahren habe ich daran gearbeitet u. gefeilt, und möchte damit meine Bahn als Liederkomponist auf eine Zeitlang beschließen. Es ist ein Zyklus von 20 Liedern, die ein Ganzes, aber

This letter would perhaps be the most significant single document to consider in the scholarly aim of determining a definitive edition of *Dichterliebe*, for it addresses as well as leaves open precisely those two aspects – the original conception as a cycle containing twenty songs, and Schumann's supposed editorial act of 'purification'[44] prior to the first edition – on which the argument for or against a new edition of *Dichterliebe* ultimately rests. On the one hand, Schumann claims to have 'worked on' and 'polished' the composition over a period of two years; on the other hand, this polishing does not seem to have embraced the alteration of the original conception of *Dichterliebe* as consisting of twenty songs. In other words, it leaves the issue, if not positively open, at least leaning in favour of a version consisting of twenty songs.

However this may be, the letter quoted above to Breitkopf & Härtel (6 August 1843) indicates a change of mind nonetheless, albeit of a different kind. Schumann was no longer in a rush to publish *Dichterliebe*, as had been the case shortly after finishing the composition. By 1843, with three years separating the enraptured Schumann of Lieder from the more settled composer of symphonies and much chamber music, a certain degree and kind of indifference seems to have set in. Having sensed to be 'embarking on completely new paths in music' just prior to completing *Dichterliebe*,[45] and once the particular 'state of the soul' sustaining its compositional process in May 1840 had ceased, the immediate significance of *Dichterliebe* – its urgency – had ceased with it. Schumann had, inevitably, become detached.

Yet another letter, written on 6 October 1843 to the publishers Böhme & Peters, supports the contention that for a considerable period of time Schumann maintained his aim of seeing *Dichterliebe* published as it was originally conceived:

> I allow myself to offer the publishing house . . . three compositions, together with the request to let me know whether you would be inclined to publish one or the other, or all three . . . 20 Lieder and Gesänge [set] to H. Heine's Buch d. Lieder for solo voice plus piano accompaniment, Op. 47 [*recte* Op. 48] (approximately 44–48 plates).[46]

The first mention of the composition's title appears in a letter of 27 December 1843, to the publisher Peters: 'Since I will be taking a longer trip in 12–14 days, I would be pleased to receive the corrections of my Liederkreis "Dichterliebe". . . .'[47] From this date onwards until August 1844, when *Dichterliebe* appeared in its presently fixed form, no further correspondence has surfaced.[48] Final uncertainty as to the

---

auch einzeln für sich ein Abgeschlossenes bilden. Am besten ließe es sich in 2 Hefte teilen, wo auf jedes ungefähr 20–22 Platten kämen. Mit der Herausgabe hat es keine Eile, wenn Sie es nicht gerade wünschten.'

[44] See Pousseur (1993), p. 177.

[45] See Schumann's letter of 31 May 1840 to Clara Schumann, *Briefe einer Liebe*, p. 279.

[46] Quoted, with the kind permission, from private notes of Renate Hilmar-Voit [erlaube ich mir die . . . drei Compositionen zum Verlag anzubieten, mit der Bitte, mir mitzutheilen, ob Sie die eine oder andere, oder alle drei herauszugeben geneigt sein würden. . . . 20 Lieder und Gesänge a. H. Heines Buch d. Lieder für 1 Singstimme m. Begleitung d. Pianofortes. op. 47 [Op. 48] (ca 44–48 Platten)].

[47] Quoted, with kind permission, from the private notes of Renate Hilmar-Voit [Da ich in 12–14 Tagen eine größere Reise antrete, so wäre es mir lieb, vorher noch eine Correctur meines Liederkreises 'Dichterliebe' zu erhalten. . . .]

[48] Cf. Nauhaus' corrective comments as to the date of publication in *TB* II, p. 536, n. 609.

'authentic' version derives from a statement made by Erler, as he recounts his conversation with the proof-reader of *Dichterliebe*, Roitzsch:

> He told me that Schumann had incessantly polished and altered his works at proof stage. With the song cycle Op. 48 it seemed odd to [Roitzsch] that Schumann had changed much in the first set of proofs and eventually restored the original readings in the final revision.[49]

If these documents may at first sight seem to raise questions worth considering in an attempt to challenge the validity of the presently accepted version of *Dichterliebe* as sixteen rather than twenty songs, it needs to be clarified that my aim lies elsewhere. Although considering *Dichterliebe* may for some be an obvious and perhaps ideal occasion to reopen matters such as intentionality, or the contingency of an authorial edition, or the idea of a 'Fassung letzter Hand', my enquiry meditates on 'genesis' only in passing. It does so, however, not by way of adding to the celebrations of the identity of the 'work' or the author – occasionally to be found in the rhetoric of manuscript studies – but by viewing Schumann's *Dichterliebe* sketches as a necessary complement to an argument of a different sort. The relation of a presumably authoritative score and its substantially divergent sketches may, rather, be thought of as indicative of a compositional procedure that opposes, rather than aims to achieve, systematic unity. The learned urge to systematize, which seems so prevalent in most enquiries into *Dichterliebe*, exhibits a general and possibly excessive solicitude for harmoniousness and, above all, coherence.

Ultimately, editorial aspirations towards an authoritative score as well as the aim to construct a coherent poetic narrative on the basis of both text and music seem like auxiliary measures taken in order to accommodate a compositional structure which no longer accords with the Classical model. *Dichterliebe* can be viewed, I believe, as demonstrating the opposite of wholeness and still be aesthetically entirely convincing. What we may well be dealing with is discontinuity, rupture, thoughts and 'states' not perfectly ordered and harmoniously linked. I have attempted to redefine the unanswered question of a score's conclusiveness or inconclusiveness by doubting whether Schumann adhered to the idea of completeness in the first place. Rather, *Dichterliebe* may point to a compositional conception that not only tolerates, but elevates, and indeed celebrates, the notion of the Romantic fragment system to the extent that its integrity, let alone its beauty, is not at risk, even if parts of its text are missing or dismissed. Such is the case of *Dichterliebe* – a masterpiece not despite, but by virtue of, its disintegrative forces and open-endedness. It need not be interpreted in respect of any hypothetical completeness.

In the present study, I explore this opposite position from a variety of angles, one of which is the poetic text underlying *Dichterliebe*. As I have said earlier, Heine's words themselves constitute a plane of disjointed reflections, which cannot adequately be

---

[49] Erler (1887) II, p. 124 [Er erzählte mir, daß Schumann unaufhörlich während der Correcturen an seinen Werken gefeilt und geändert habe. Mit dem Lieder-Cyclus op. 48 sei es ihm [Roitzsch] merkwürdig gegangen; Schumann habe viel in der ersten Correctur verändert und schließlich in der Schlußrevision die erste Lesart wieder hergestellt].

evaluated on the basis of continuity and narrativity. A second angle would be to find in the form of *Dichterliebe* the kind of poetic fragmentation that gains meaning by its unconcealed renunciation of completeness, its lack of ultimate closure, its very suggestiveness. In this sense, *Dichterliebe* may perhaps be seen as an expression of Schumann's awareness that the emotive space he tried to capture was, in fact, open and elusive. For the expression of a poet's love, there is no need to spread behind it a canvas or scenario crowded with action, a succession of events and a logical ending. Finally, there may not be an absolute need to draw a direct parallel between the events of *Dichterliebe* and those of Schumann's life, as has been suggested in most critical accounts of this composition.[50] Instead of assuming a biographical subtext, *Dichterliebe* may be viewed as the Romantic variant of a *discours d'amour*, which captures the poetic, illusory as well as intensified relation to the world by employing a diction whose 'images are able to rise above the rest of the world', since poetic language has lost 'the standards of reality', as Schelling said. Poetry 'moves rapturously to the limit of things . . . as far as its wings intend to take it, without being aware of any kind of aberration.'[51]

I have attempted to explore in four analytical essays the expressive possibilities of *Dichterliebe* in the light of those creative procedures developed by the Early Romantics. But first I will briefly discuss Schumann's reception of Heine and his *Lyrisches Intermezzo* in order to appreciate on the one hand the composer's long-standing involvement with Heine's work, and on the other that Schumann was well aware of Heine's sharp, hence modern, type of irony. Yet, such perceptive reading on Schumann's part did not prevent him from making the poems he chose for *Dichterliebe* his own. He thus became the 'second poet' of these poems.[52] The first analytical essay discusses the Early Romantic conception of 'poetic time' by way of comparing Song 13, 'Ich hab' im Traum geweinet', with the late and almost unknown song 'Der schwere Abend' on poetry by Nikolaus Lenau. The second essay analyses the cycle's famous first song, 'Im wunderschönen Monat Mai', in the light of one of the core concepts of Early Romantic poetics, the fragment. The third essay establishes structural and semantic links between Songs 4, 4a, 12 and 16 by way of investigating Schumann's striking use of one of the three possible transpositions of the diminished-seventh chord. Here, Heine's idiosyncratic gesture of the *Stimmungsbruch* and the thematic opposition of love and death characterizing the four songs are analytically shown to have been treated with great compositional sophistication. Every time the diminished-seventh chord appears, the topos of unrequited love is named and rendered ambiguous. In these isolated and structurally exposed instances, the diminished-seventh chord functions essentially as a deflection from, if not disruption within, the overall flow of the music. The fourth essay offers a new

---

[50] See Neumeyer (1982), Haesler (1982 and 1987), Pousseur (1993) and Sams (1993).

[51] AWS *SW* VII, pp. 94–95 [Bilder die sich über die ganze übrige Welt erheben. . . . Poesie hat den Maßstab des Wirklichen verloren. . . . Sie schwärmte bis an die Grenzen der Dinge . . . soweit die Flügel der Phantasie sie nur tragen wollen, ohne sich einer Verirrung bewußt zu werden].

[52] See my discussion of Schumann's concept of the Lied on pp. 47–67.

interpretation of the meaning of the cycle's famous last postlude. As it refers back to Song 12, as well as to other musical material both from within and from without *Dichterliebe*, Schumann takes a retrospective glance at a few significant earlier events in the cycle or in other works. It is in terms of Romantic irony, so central to Early Romantic theory, that the exceptionally enigmatic compositional procedure of the last postlude of *Dichterliebe* can be re-experienced in new ways.

12

SCHUMANN'S RECEPTION OF HEINE
AND THE *BUCH DER LIEDER*

Schumann bought his copy of the *Buch der Lieder* in 1828, that is at a time when the poem collection had just about appeared and long before it reached any kind of popularity, let alone fame. This speaks for Schumann's acute literary instinct as much as for his overall familiarity with the developments in literature.[1] Two more reasons, however, explain Schumann's interest in Heine's poetry and his acquisition of Heine's poem collection as early as 1828.

First, 1828 coincides with the period in Schumann's life which was marked by continuous doubts as to what he felt his vocation should be – poetry or composition. Schumann's father, a writer of sorts, Byron-translator, publisher and bookseller, very possibly acted as a role model which gave rise to many of Schumann's first literary attempts in verse, prose and dramatic scenes. During the years between 1823 and 1828 in Zwickau, Schumann shows a clear preoccupation with literature rather than music and these were no doubt formative with regard to his literary tastes. In 1825 he set up a reading group called 'Litterarischer Verein' (Literary Club) which demanded by statute that 'it is the duty of all educated persons to know their mother country's literature . . . not to neglect German literature and to strive with great zeal to get to know it'.[2] This introduction to German literature included a number of major works, aesthetic-philosophical texts such as Schlegel's *Ueber die altdeutsche Litteratur* and *Ueber die Volksbildung* and Fichte's *Reden an die deutsche Nation* as well as purely literary works by Schiller, Wieland and, of course, Jean Paul (*Der Traum eines Wahnsinnigen* and *Die Neujahrsnacht eines Unglücklichen*, for example). It comes as no surprise that Schumann, in his *Musikalischer Lebenslauf* of 1840, asserted he had been 'familiar with the most important poets of almost all countries'.[3] Schumann's

---

[1] Schumann's friend Flechsig notes in his biography: 'But all the more enthusiastically he [Schumann], now [1828 in Leipzig] that all restraints of school had gone, went to freely advance his life's work. He took piano lessons with Wieck. . . . Alongside always the most recent things in literature – Heine's Reisebilder, Menzel's Deutsche Geschichte – especially much reading of Jean Paul. . . .' [Aber um so eifriger ging er [Schumann] jetzt, [1828 in Leipzig] wo aller Schulzwang gefallen, freiwaltend an sein künftiges Lebenswerk. Er nahm Klavierunterricht bei Wieck. . . . Daneben immer das Neueste in der Literatur – Heines Reisebilder, Menzels Deutsche Geschichte – besonders viel Lektüre von Jean Paul . . . .] Quoted in Schneider (1970), p. 253. For a good overview of Schumann's early literary interests and activities, see Daverio (1997) and Tadday (1999).

[2] Schoppe (1991), pp. 17–32 (here 17) [[es ist] jedes gebildeten Menschen Pflicht, die Literatur seines Vaterlandes zu kennen . . . die deutsche nicht zu vernachlässigen und mit allem Eifer danach zu streben, sie kennen zu lernen].

[3] Schumann as quoted in Schoppe (1991), pp. 17–32 (here 17) [Die bedeutendsten Dichter ziemlich aller Länder waren mir geläufig].

own literary aspirations may well have played a decisive role in the formation of his library. At the same time, he may well have been seeking literary models, and among them Heine's *Buch der Lieder*.

The second reason for Schumann's interest in Heine around 1828 is, of course, that this is the year when he actually met Heine. In May 1828, Schumann, together with his friend Gisbert Rosen, undertook something rather common at the time: an 'educational journey' or 'a tiny tour of genius', as Schumann put it.[4] On this journey, Schumann also visited the grave of his admired Jean Paul in Bayreuth where he received a small Jean Paul portrait from the poet's widow.

The connection with Heine was established through Heinrich Kurrer, a friend of Schumann's father, whose daughter was friendly with an actor called Carl Krahe; Krahe knew Heine and wrote an introduction for Schumann and Rosen to meet the poet.[5] Schumann recorded his impression of Heine several times and the result is a number of very fascinating statements indeed, extremely sharp in observation and noteworthy for their consistency. First, the diary entry of 8 May 1828:

Heine – witty and intelligent conversation – ironic little man – charming play-acting – walk to the Leuchtenbergische Gallerie.[6]

Characterizing the man Heine in this way – 'witty', 'ironic' and 'play-acting' – gives a concise as well as consistent picture of the poet. Six months later Schumann summarized his impression of Heine's lyrical tone in connection with a critical evaluation of Grabbe's *Herzog Theodor von Gothland*. After criticizing the author's 'atheistic, desperate agony' and 'unresolved dissonance, . . . his destructivism', Schumann concludes:

But after all, Gothland is a tragedy with which nothing compares; a singular phenomenon that had never been written before – oh, this Grabbe must have sunk low in his life and must have experienced a good deal – he reminds one often of the *bizarre things in Heine's songs, that burning sarcasm, that g r e a t despair, all those caricatures of majesty and dignity he shares with Heine.*[7]

In his letter of thanks to Krahe of 9 June 1828, we find another eloquent account of the impression Heine made on Schumann, worth quoting in full:

I did not feel comfortable and at home in Munich as I perceived the cold, sharp tone of this capital city only too soon. The meeting with Heine . . . which I owe Krahe whom I ask you to send my warm regards, made my stay to some extent interesting and likeable. After

---

[4] See Schumann's letter of thanks to Krahe [Bildungsreise; winzige Geniereise] in Schnapp (1924), p. 16.

[5] Schnapp (1924), p. 4. See also *TB* I, p. 57 (31 May 1828) [Empfehlungsbriefe an Heine nach München].

[6] *TB* I, p. 64. For 5 May, Schumann noted 'Heine's Frühlingswohnung' which may mean that he and Rosen went to find out Heine's address. [Heine – geistreiche Unterhaltung – ironisches Männchen – liebenswürdige Verstellung – Gang mit ihm auf die Leuchtenbergische Gallerie].

[7] *TB* I, p. 129 (31 October 1828) [Und doch trotz Allen ist dieser Gothland ein Trauerspiel ohne Vergleich, ein einziges, wie es noch nicht geschrieben worden ist – o dieser Grabbe muß einmal schon sehr, sehr tief gesunken seyn u. Manches erfahren haben – er erinnert oft an die *Bizarrerie in den Heineschen Liedern, jenen brennenden Sarkasmus, jene g r o ß e Verzweiflung, alle die Caricaturen von Hoheit u. Würde hat er mit Heine gemein*]. My emphasis, except for 'g r o ß e'.

Mr Krahe's description I had imagined Heine to be a grumpy, misanthropic man, who would be already too superior over all people and life to be able to still feel sympathetically close towards them. But how different did I find him! and how entirely different was he than I had imagined him to be. He approached me with all kindness and like a human, Greek Anacreon. He pressed my hand amicably and gave me a tour of Munich for several hours – all this I had never expected from a man who had written the *Reisebilder; only around his mouth was there a bitter, cynical smile, but a noble smile about the trivial matters of life, and scorn about the narrow-mindedness of people; but even this bitter satyr, whom one can perceive in his Reisebilder only too often, this profound inner resentment at life which goes right through the core, rendered the conversation very charming.*[8]

Schumann's characterization of Heine's *Reisebilder* and lyric poems stands in stark contrast to the impressions he recorded when meeting the author in person. However pleasant the encounter with Heine may have been, Schumann sensed an aura of estrangement and *Weltschmerz* in Heine's 'bitter, ironic smile' and 'scorn' about the world. It needs to be stressed, then – in anticipation of my analysis and interpretation of Schumann's settings – that Schumann did not at all miss the sharp edges in Heine's poetry. In fact, he talks about no other aspect than this when describing Heine's *Lieder* (i.e. the *Buch der Lieder*) as an expression of the 'bizarre', of 'burning sarcasm' and 'agony'. Heine's 'scorn', his 'inner resentment at life' and a sense of 'satire' seems to have fascinated Schumann.

It is interesting that Schumann's perceiving of Heine's 'burning sarcasm' and 'inner resentment' as an expression of the poet's fundamentally antagonistic stance towards the world did not lead to the kind of irritation that this very idiosyncrasy at times inspired even among recent critics who reduce Heine's sharpness to an expression of morbidity stemming from an unstable sufferer.[9] An early review of the *Lyrisches Intermezzo* written in 1822 by Karl Immermann accords with Schumann's own evaluations:

Heine's energetic nature seems to cultivate in particular that bitter rage about a dry and irre-sponsive present, that profound animosity towards the times; and this makes it understandable

---

[8] Schnapp (1924), pp. 17–18 [In München [befand ich mich] nicht ganz wohl und heimisch und ich merkte den kalten, schneidenden Residenzton nur zu bald. Die Bekanntschaft mit Heine, welche ich Krahe, den ich Sie herzlich von mir zu grüßen bitte, zu verdanken habe, machte meinen Aufenthalt einigermaßen intereßant u. anziehend. Ich stellte mir nach der Skizze des Herrn Krahe, in Heine'n einen mürrischen, menschenfeindlichen Mann vor, der schon zu erhaben über den Menschen und dem Leben stünde, als daß er sich noch an sie schmiegen könnte. Aber wie anders fand ich ihn und wie ganz anders war er, als ich mir ihn gedacht hatte. Er kam mir freundlich, wie ein menschlicher, griechischer Anacreon entgegen, er drükte mir freundschaftlich die Hand u. führte mich einige Stunden in München herum – dies alles hatte ich mir nicht von einem Menschen eingebildet, der die Reisebilder geschrieben hatte; *nur um seinen Mund lag ein bittres, ironisches Lächeln, aber ein hohes Lächeln über die Kleinigkeiten des Lebens u. ein Hohn über die kleinlichen Menschen; doch selbst jene bittere Satire, die man nur zu oft in seinen Reisebildern wahrnimmt, jener tiefe, innere Groll über das Leben, der bis in das äußerste Mark dringt, machte seine Gespräche sehr anziehend*]. My emphasis.

[9] See Futterknecht (1985, p. 310) who finds: 'Heine is that type of a progressive who makes a taboo of the origin of his own suffering and who dreamed up a reality for himself which suited his own needs for mental nursing but which does not reflect what one sensibly could call the problems of the times.' See the comment by Jokl (1991), p. 10.

why this young poet was unable to produce amongst 58 poems not a single one expressing joy and cheerfulness.[10]

Given Schumann's interest in literature and his awareness of the contemporary literary scene, and Heine's work in particular, we may assume that a certain dynamic developed between the growing public success of the *Buch der Lieder* and the conception of *Dichterliebe*. Thus Schumann, after some ten years of devoting himself compositionally almost exclusively to the piano, felt at once ready to explore the special complexities of song composition as well as to explore Heine's poetry at a time when the poem collection enjoyed growing public impact. But already by 1833 it was Heine's so-called *Lieder* that had inspired Schumann to write what may be called 'Songs without Words'. He noted in his *Leipziger Lebensbuch*:

Musical poems with underlying Lieder by H. Heine, composed and dedicated to Heine.[11]

Schumann began setting Heine's poems to music in 1840 with *Liederkreis* Op. 24, and *Dichterliebe* Op. 48, the year in which Heine's *Buch der Lieder* had become one of the most popular poem anthologies of the time. *Dichterliebe* was published in 1844, the year the *Buch der Lieder* went into its fifth edition. This is not to suggest any particular strategy or pragmatism on Schumann's part, in the sense that he can be supposed to have speculated on an increasing success rate for the Heine settings, since Heine had already become a household name. Rather it demonstrates the sensitivity to feel the pulse of his times and to respond to it. While there are indeed reasons to do with his individual artistic development that explain why Schumann turned to song composition in 1840 rather than at any earlier point,[12] it is also true that Schumann chose a poetic text whose influence on him goes back more than a decade, showing a fairly intense and long-standing fascination with Heine.[13]

For textual reasons we need to determine which edition of Heine's *Buch der Lieder* it was that served Schumann as his text at hand. It is certain that he used the first edition of 1827 (Hamburg: Hoffmann und Campe) for two reasons. First, Schumann owned a copy of the *Buch der Lieder*.[14] This copy was acquired by the

---

[10] Karl Immermann in the *Rheinisch-Westfälischer Anzeiger Hamm*, supplement 'Kunst-und-Wissenschaftsblatt' no. 23 of 31 May 1822, as quoted in Galley and Estermann (1981), p. 35 [Jenen bittren Grimm über eine nüchterne, unempfängliche Gegenwart, jene tiefe Feindschaft gegen die Zeit scheint nun die kraftvolle Natur unsers Heine ganz besonders zu hegen, und daraus wird es mir erklärlich, warum ein Jüngling unter 58 Gedichten auch nicht ein einziges zu geben vermochte, aus dem Freude und Heiterkeit spricht].

[11] *TB* I, p. 417 (8 March 1833) [Musikalische Gedichte, mit unterlegten Liedern von H. Heine, verfaßt u. Heine zugeeignet].

[12] See Kapp (1984) as well as my own comments below, pp. 160–167.

[13] In this context, Sams' statement sounds rather off-hand when he writes that the source of Schumann's Heine settings were 'the first edition of the *Buch der Lieder* – thirteen years, two editions, and several revisions out of date. . . . Out of twenty-five years of composing he [Schumann] devoted some twenty-five days, spread over a year or two at most, to setting a few pages of one single volume; there is no evidence that he even so much as glanced at another Heine lyric for the rest of his life.' Sams (1993), p. 3.

[14] Although Hallmark did not know of the existence of Schumann's personal copy he rightly figured: 'Because he [Schumann] often quoted Heine poems in the *Neue Zeitschrift für Musik* and because neither he nor Clara copied any Heine poems into their "Abschriften verschiedener Gedichte zur Composition" notebook, it seems

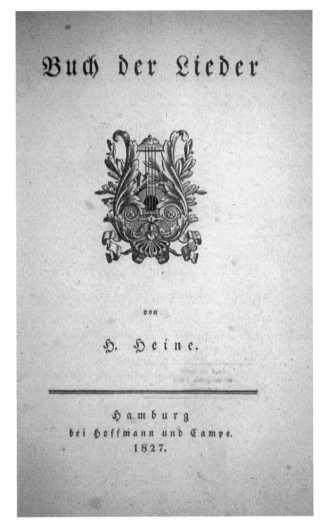

Fig. 1.   Title page of Schumann's personal copy of
the first edition of Heinrich Heine's *Buch der Lieder*
of 1827.

Heinrich-Heine-Institut in Düsseldorf in 1983 and the title page, showing 1827
as the year of publication, is reproduced here (see Fig. 1). Two inscriptions in
Schumann's own hand indicate the date when he received the book. The first is on
the page prior to the title page (see Fig. 2). It reads: 'Von W. Ulex geschenkt erhalten

likely that Schumann had a personal copy of the *Buch der Lieder*.' Hallmark noted that the second edition of
1837 contains a textual change in the eleventh poem, 'Im Rhein, im heiligen Strome', which does not appear in
Schumann's autograph manuscript and also concludes that Schumann must have used the first edition of 1827.
See Hallmark (1979), p. 16.

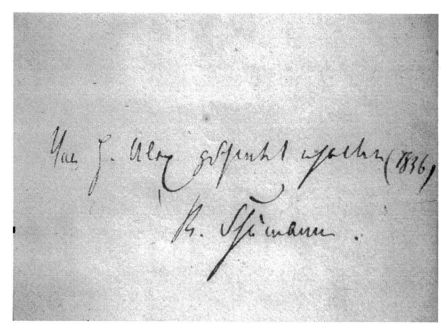

Fig. 2.   Page prior to title page of Schumann's personal copy of the first edition of Heinrich Heine's *Buch der Lieder* showing the inscription: 'Von W. Ulex geschenkt erhalten (1836): R. Schumann'.

(1836) R. Schumann' (Received as a present by W. Ulex (1836) R. Schumann). Wilhelm Ulex was one of Schumann's friends from school, with whom he also visited Clara in Dresden in February of the same year. The second inscription, on page 114, towards the beginning of the *Lyrisches Intermezzo*, suggests it was on this occasion that Ulex presented Schumann with this copy of Heine's *Buch der Lieder*, for the date in Schumann's own hand next to the poem *Wenn ich in deine Augen seh'* reads: '8 Februar 1836.' (see Fig. 3). As this copy contains further indicative markings in Schumann's own hand regarding a number of poems used for *Dichterliebe*, this manuscript has been taken into consideration in the following musico–poetic analysis. The underlining, presumably in Schumann's hand, of various lines and passages clearly demonstrates the composer's particularly involved reading of Heine's poems even prior to the compositional stage.

The second reason indicating Schumann's use of the first, rather than any later, edition of the *Buch der Lieder* derives from a diary entry of 23 August 1828 which reads: 'Heines Buch der Lieder'.[15] This suggests that eight years before Ulex presented Schumann with the copy in which we now find Schumann's markings, Schumann had had access to a volume of Heine's *Buch der Lieder*. But considering Schumann's overall knowledge of literature and poetry and his reference to Heine's 'Lieder' in

[15]   *TB* I, p. 123. Hallmark (1979, p. 21) mistakenly takes 8 August 1828 as the day of acquisition.

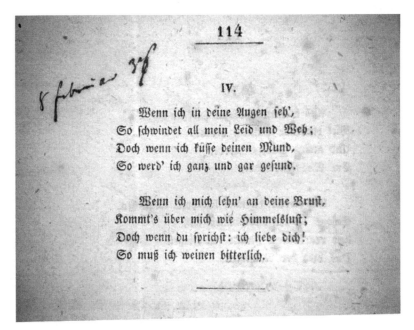

Fig. 3. Page 114 of Schumann's personal copy of the first edition of
Heinrich Heine's *Buch der Lieder* showing in the upper left-hand
corner the inscription: '8 Februar 1836'.

his letter to Krahe, we can assume that he was familiar with Heine's poetry even
earlier than 1828, the diary entry simply referring to a repeated reading of Heine's
poems. In 1836, thanks to Ulex's present, Schumann finally owned a copy of Heine's
Buch der Lieder, and four years later, when setting out to compose *Dichterliebe,* he
concerned himself with these poems again and in detail, as various markings in the
hand copy indicate.

13

MUSICO-POETIC ANALYSIS

(I) THE ROMANTIC CONCEPT OF 'POETIC TIME' IN *DICHTERLIEBE*

> Dichterleben.
> 'In die See möcht' ich hinaus'
> Eine grosse Heimat hab' ich – die Welt.
> Die Wahlfahrt nach dem Ozean –
> Und knüpfst freundlich die Gegenwart
> An die Vergangenheit u. Zukunft –
> Warum? –
> Warum ich weine?
> Warum ich dichte?
> Warum ich liebe? –[1]

This entry from Schumann's diary is revealing. As a self-referential statement it essentially asserts that being a true Romantic means being a poet, forever longing for the unattainable – a *Heimat* which, in truth, is no *Heimat* for it is the whole world, and as such a no-man's-land, as much as it is the inner self. These lines devoted to 'Dichterleben' evoke *Dichterliebe* in their strong assonance and read like a presentiment of its inward idea: a kind of floating quest, where time and place remain unfixed, the present merging past and future, the immediate expanding both backwards and forwards.

Thoughts on how the present merges with the past and future occur frequently in Schumann's writings.[2] These passages, written in fragmentary style, show the

---

[1] *TB* I, p. 322 (28 September 1830) [Poet's life. / Into the sea I long to go / A great homeland I have – the world. / The pilgrimage to the ocean – / And kindly you are connecting the present / to the past and to the future – / Why? – / Why am I crying? / Why am I composing [music/poetry]? / Why am I in love? –]

[2] Especially in earlier years, roughly between 1827 and 1835 that is, Schumann's concern for the concept of time is particularly prevalent. Here, significantly, we find most references in the form of diary entries, the place where Schumann noted down his ideas in order to 'return to them in later years . . . so as to be able to compare my views and feelings with those earlier ones, and to see whether I remained true to myself' (*TB* I, p. 22). Meissner (1985, p. 17) notes the articulateness and consistency with which Schumann develops his own aesthetic viewpoint in these diaries. 'Poetic time' as the central parameter of Schumann's conception of 'poetic music' appears throughout his writings. A few relevant quotes may be given here: *TB* I, p. 304: 'The future shall be the higher echo of the past' [Die Zukunft soll das höhere Echo der Vergangenheit sein]; *TB* I, p. 130: 'A clock without a hand is like chaos with no beginning and no end – time smashed – inestimable eternity' [Eine Uhr ohne Zeiger ist wie ein Chaos

composer meditating on one of the central aspects of Romantic aesthetics, the concept of 'poetic time'. Schumann's descriptions of 'poetic time' are consistent with those we find in the writings of some of the leading Early Romantic poet-philosophers. Such preoccupation with the idea of poetic time may be of interest on the level of Schumann's compositional procedures. I shall thus take a look at the literary-aesthetic sources which advanced the concept of 'poetic time' and which Schumann evidently read. In tracing Schumann's understanding of this idea, Jean Paul's *Vorschule der Ästhetik* of 1804 is of particular value. Not only the novels of his favourite writer,[3] but also this influential theoretical treatise, had a profound impact on Schumann's aesthetic thinking. The ramifications of this concept with regard to early nineteenth-century musical thought will be considered as will its specific manifestation in *Dichterliebe*. A musico-poetic analysis of the song 'Ich hab' im Traum geweinet', seen in relation to Schumann's late song 'Der schwere Abend' Op. 90 no. 6, finally explores how *Dichterliebe* is imbued with the idea of an open, poetic temporality.

GENERAL CONSIDERATIONS

The Romantics' concept of poetic time includes the case of musical expression. Here, the Romantics were intrigued by the way in which musical sound created a sense of time that differed from that of 'real time'. The listener perceives and is moved by music at the moment it 'resounds', whilst the effect of that musical moment is determined by what was heard earlier in time as well as by what is yet to come. This ephemeral quality of music led the Romantics to hold it in high esteem. Thus, in their speculative evaluation of the artistic genres, music ranked highest together with poetry. One reason for the assumed correspondence between these two genres was their shared property of rhythm and metre. Another, more important, one, however, lay in the way in which words in poetry rely upon each other in sense and rhyme, a situation similar to that of music. In music too, motives, phrases or melodies are semantically dependent on what occurs before or after them. What has often been described as a sense of magic, namely that a word or tone never stands alone, but that its meaning is acoustically and thus semantically determined by preceding or future events, was thought to be immanent in both poetry and music.

Another important aspect to consider here is the Romantics' orientation towards synaesthesia. This, together with the designation of music as superior amongst the artistic forms, is well described in W. H. Wackenroder's influential novel *Herzensergießungen eines kunstliebenden Klosterbruders*[4] – a pioneering piece of

---

ohne Anfang u. Ende – die zertrümmerte Zeit – die unübersehliche Ewigkeit]; *TB* I, p. 337: 'Venice moves one so much because all memories of time are mirrored back within a small place – St. Mark's Square' [Venedig ergreift deshalb so, weil alle Erinnerung der Zeit in einem kleinen Raum beschränkt sich zurückspiegeln – dem Markusplatz].

[3] As noted throughout the Schumann literature, but discussed more extensively only by Jacobs (1949), Lippmann (1964) and Daverio (1993).

[4] 1798 anonymous, ed. Ludwig Tieck.

Romantic literature whose hero, a poet and musician, enacts a *Weltanschauung* with which many artists of the generation identified.

The Romantics' preoccupation with synaesthesia influenced Schumann's conception of song. His treatment of language in *Dichterliebe* shows this concern to bring the two, music and poetry, close together so as to form an expressive, synaesthetic whole. It is, however, always the emotive core of a poem, in a Jakobsonian understanding of the lyric,[5] that Schumann tried to capture musically. Schumann's reading of a poem was therefore not grammatical in nature, and the concept of synaesthesia within his genuinely Romantic stance implies, above everything else, the act of imagination. In opposition to either poetic ignorance on the one hand, or musical realism on the other, Schumann's settings demonstrate the kind of imaginative reading that increases the poetic function of the poem such that its potency is realized through the language of music. This idea is described in Schumann's dictum 'music is the highest potential of poetry'. Music oversteps the limits of certain characteristics inherent in a poem and intensifies – formally and semantically – the poetic content. The autonomy of the poem thus dissolves into an equal autonomy of song, which itself becomes poetic. No longer does the song necessarily reproduce the content of the poem, and although one may recognize a dependency between poetic and musical material, the simultaneous difference between the two is just as significant. Schumann's settings carry this contradiction within them and exhibit with idiosyncratic ambiguity the mutable relationship between representation and possibility. Contained in these songs is always the moment of critique, a hermeneutic that turns the act of reading into an artistic act itself.[6] In light of this, the question invariably raised by earlier critics[7] as to whether Schumann 'understood' the poems he set to music, or – in the case of *Dichterliebe* – whether he failed to grasp Heine's ironic or cynical twists, loses much of its significance. Schumann's Romantic reading of poetry leaves behind the letters on the page and recognizes instead an autonomy of the text that is not concerned with an author's intention. This is certainly in the spirit of Schleiermacher's dictum 'first to understand the narration and then to understand it ever better than its author' for the sake of 'trying to revive everything that [the author] can be unaware of'.[8] What features strongly in many discussions of music that involves words – certainly in the literature on *Dichterliebe* – is what Friedrich Schlegel ironically called the dream of a 'real and genuine language', a language which would have the 'objectivity of gold'. A language printed in 'bas-relief' and 'with gold letters on silver tablets' would be too beautiful, Schlegel jests, 'to be rejected with the vulgar remark that it doesn't make any sense'.[9] Since poets only use ordinary pen and paper, however, the meaning of their words never attains

---

[5] Jakobson (1987a).   [6] See Benjamin (1973), Frank (1985), pp. 358–364, and Behler (1992), pp. 271–277.

[7] Hallmark (1979), Moore (1981) and Sams (1993).

[8] Quoted in Behler (1992), p. 271 [die Rede ebensogut und dann besser zu verstehen als ihr Urheber . . . vieles zu Bewußtsein zu bringen, was ihm unbewußt bleiben kann].

[9] In his essay 'On Incomprehensibility' [Über die Unverständlichkeit], *KFSA* II, p. 365 [reelle Sprache . . . Objektivität des Goldes . . . seine Werke im Basrelief zu schreiben mit goldenen Lettern auf silbernen Tafeln . . . eine so schön gedruckte Schrift mit der groben Äußerung, sie sei unverständlich, zurückweisen wollen?].

golden certainty. An analysis of the poem on the one hand and its participation in the new poetic creation of the song on the other demonstrates this kind of semantic difference. An awareness of these main philosophical conceptions of the Romantics within the analytical process leads to a fuller understanding of the fact that theory and practice – be it epistemological (critic) or creative (artist) – are no longer separate activities. Instead, these activities are a constant interplay, just as it can be observed how Schumann's practice of song writing grew out of his concern for contemporary aesthetic tenets. Concurrently, his songs shed further light on these theoretical propositions and offer validation, as much as enrichment, for an all-embracing Romantic theory of the arts – literature, poetry and music at its centre.

JEAN PAUL'S SYNONYMY OF 'ROMANTIC' AND 'POETIC'

Schumann's notably early and sustained interest in Romantic literature and aesthetics was, one may assume, pursued in an attempt to clarify and formulate his own artistic position. He then advocated this theoretically and compositionally as 'a new poetic future'.[10] The ideas promoted in certain Romantic texts can be shown to have had a formative effect on Schumann's development of his 'musical poetics'. In this sense, Schumann realized and elevated in music what the Romantics had advanced in poetry, literature and philosophy: that is the ideal to 'represent the Unrepresentable'.[11] And Schumann even fulfilled the Romantics' highest aim: he conveyed the ineffable, but through a medium that elevated the abstractions of Romantic philosophy to art. Through art – by intertwining language with music – Schumann succeeded in exemplifying the philosophical claims of Romantic theory.

Music was considered to be the least representational among the artistic genres. The Romantics thought music to be the highest form of art because it was not restricted to expressions previously given in any symbolic form. Since language ultimately remains denotative and conceptual, and the visual arts remain descriptive, music was believed to 'speak' without the burden of concrete and manifest meaning.[12] Music was thus believed to be the ideal language, able to express inner feelings. Music revealed unconscious contents, was therefore part of the idea of the 'language of the souls' (*Seelensprache*):[13] universal and ethereal, natural and therefore true (Fr. Schlegel, Novalis).

Of course the term 'romantic' is, has been and will always be much debated. Although it has been very much a part of critical parlance since the beginning of

[10] *NZfM* 2 (1835), p. 3.

[11] See Part I for an extensive discussion of this central claim of the Early Romantics, here given in Novalis' famous formulation in NO III, p. 685, no. 671 [Das Undarstellbare darstellen].

[12] In this respect, the emergence of *Lieder ohne Worte*, and Mendelssohn's in particular, is striking. Schumann reviewed several works of this new genre in the *NZfM*, and often used this opportunity to discuss the relevance or irrelevance of titles for these short piano pieces.

[13] *GS* I, p. 45. A valuable discussion can be found in Meissner (1985), pp. 19–20 and 23–24.

the nineteenth century, it famously has never been strictly defined.[14] In Schumann's case, however, 'romantic' appears to be synonymous with 'poetic' – a term equally arcane but crucial for an understanding of Schumann's aesthetics.[15] Both concepts, 'romantic' and 'poetic', were vital parts of the aesthetics of Jean Paul, whose definition of 'romantic' extended beyond poetry to include music. As has been noted before, Jean Paul exerted the greatest impact on Schumann's aesthetic thinking among the Romantic poet-philosophers he read.[16] Plantinga's belief in Schumann's 'naiveté about philosophy and philosophers',[17] together with the assumption that Schumann ignored Jean Paul's *Vorschule der Ästhetik*, has been convincingly challenged by Meissner. Several quotes and paraphrases in Schumann's diaries and elsewhere indicate a keenly sensitive preoccupation not only with Jean Paul's novels but also with his philosophical system.[18] One quote in Schumann's *Mottosammlung* of 1834 is especially pertinent. Extracted from the *Vorschule der Ästhetik*, Schumann made note of Jean Paul's definition of 'romantic':

Romantic is the Beautiful without limits, or beautiful Endlessness, just as there is also a Sublime.[19]

Schumann must have considered these words significant. They reappear twice as epigraphs in the *NZfM*: first, when he proclaimed a 'new poetic age' in the second issue of the *NZfM* in 1835,[20] and again in 1841, a year after composing *Dichterliebe*.[21] Schumann also took note of Jean Paul's definition of 'romantic' when it appeared in connection with music. Originally only offered in connection with poetry[22] in the *Vorschule der Ästhetik* (1804),[23] the later *Kleine Nachschule zur ästhetischen Vorschule* (1825) included the case of music, describing it as 'Romantic poetry through the ear'[24] and again as the most adequate medium for the 'The boundlessly Beautiful'.[25] Schumann was also familiar with the following passage:

Every kind of poetry has its own image amongst the bodily parts. Thus, music, for example, is Romantic poetry through the ear. This [poetry] as the boundlessly Beautiful is less mirrored before the eye whose boundaries vanish not in such an indefinable way as those of a dying

[14] Blume (1974), pp. 307–385. See also Part I.   [15] See Meissner (1985), pp. 13–14.

[16] First stated by Kretzschmar (1906), pp. 49–73, and confirmed by Meissner (1985), pp. 12ff.

[17] Plantinga (1966), pp. 112–113.

[18] See Meissner (1985), pp. 12–13 and pp. 130–131, n. 18. Plantinga's assumption that Schumann ignored Jean Paul's *Vorschule der Ästhetik* resulted from a misinterpretation of a critique by Schumann in the *NZfM* of 1834. Under the title *Das Aphoristische*, Schumann indirectly refers to Jean Paul's *Vorschule der Ästhetik* as well as to the *Kleine Nachschule der ästhetischen Vorschule*.

[19] Boetticher, *Einführung*, p. 352 [Das Romantische ist das Schöne ohne Begrenzung, oder das schöne Unendliche sowie es ein Erhabenes gibt].

[20] *NZfM* 7 (23 January 1835), p. 25.   [21] *NZfM* 50 (21 June 1841), p. 199.

[22] 'Dichtkunst', literally to be translated as 'composition'.

[23] Jean Paul, *Vorschule der Ästhetik* (1804). Cf. Meissner (1985), p. 12.

[24] Jean Paul, *Kleine Nachschule zur ästhetischen Vorschule* (1825) [romantische Poesie durch das Ohr].

[25] JP IX, p. 466 [Schönen ohne Begrenzung]. Here, Jean Paul's definition of 'the romantic' is again part of a general evaluation of the art forms. A variant of the same idea can be found in one of the *Athenaeum* fragments; here, 'the poetic' is described by way of an approximation to music and the visual arts: 'Poetry is music for the inner ear, and painting for the inner eye; but soft music, and floating painting' [Die Poesie ist Musik für das innere Ohr und Malerei für das innere Auge; aber gedämpfte Musik, aber verschwebende Malerei]. See *Athenaeum*, p. 131.

tone. No colour is as Romantic as a sound, simply because one is no longer aware of those tones having vanished earlier at the moment that the last tone is dying away; and because sound never resounds alone, but only threefold, just like the Romantic of the future and the past merging with the present.[26]

Schumann's repeated references to Jean Paul demonstrate an affinity with the writer that eventually extended into his aesthetics of composition, most strikingly in the *Papillons* of 1829/30. Here, Schumann avowedly wrote music to capture the pivotal scenes of Jean Paul's novel *Flegeljahre*.[27]

The significance of Jean Paul's definition of 'romantic' quoted earlier lies in its proposed concept of time: present poetic expression encompasses the past and anticipates the future. Although Jean Paul's concept of an aesthetic union of music and poetry included an implicit ranking of the artistic genres, Schumann gives them equal weight. As the highest forms of art, Schumann calls both poetry and music the 'Ne plus ultra of the Romantic. Sounds are above all nothing but composed words.'[28] The concept of 'romantic' therefore appears as an affirmation of the unity of the two art forms. By apostrophizing music as 'romantic poetry through the ear', his category 'poetic' bears primary importance for the integrating force of 'romantic' in both music and poetry. Thus, the two terms 'romantic' and 'poetic' are *per definitionem* in congruence.[29] Schumann was a true apologist of what he called a 'young poetic future' and a 'new poetic age'.[30] The essential supposition of this expression is that Schumann envisioned a future in which poetic art and real life might interact constantly. Efforts to achieve this kind of interaction were formidable,

---

[26] JP IX, p. 466 [Jede Dichtart hat unter den Körpern ihre Ebenbilder, die uns anregen. So ist z.B. die Musik romantische Poesie durch das Ohr. Diese als das Schöne ohne Begrenzung wird weniger von dem Auge vorgespiegelt, dessen Grenzen sich nicht so unbestimmbar wie die eines sterbenden Tons verlieren. Keine Farbe ist so romantisch als ein Ton, schon weil man nur bei dem Sterben des letztern, nicht der erstern gegenwärtig ist, und weil ein Ton nie allein, sondern immer dreifaltig tönt, gleichsam die Romantik der Zukunft und der Vergangenheit mit der Gegenwart verschmelzend]. According to Boetticher, *Einführung*, p. 353, Schumann partly underlined this passage.

[27] In a letter to a critic who was to review Op. 2, Schumann, after giving the titles of some scenes, adds: 'I kept turning over the last page, for the end seemed like a new beginning – almost unconsciously I went to the piano, and so one Papillon after another appeared.' In *Jugendbriefe*, p. 167. Schumann's crucial remark on Jean Paul's literary style is as follows: 'Jean Paul himself is mirrored in all his works, but each time as two persons: He is Albano, and Schoppe. . . . Only the one and only Jean Paul was able to combine within himself two people at once. He is super-human: and yet he is himself: always stark contrasts, even if he does not combine extremes within his works and within himself – and yet, he is alone' [In allen seinen Werken spiegelt sich Jean Paul selbst ab, aber jedesmal in *zwey* Personen: er ist der Albano u. Schoppe . . . Nur der einzige Jean Paul konnte in sich zwey solche verschiedenen Charactere in sich allein verbinden; es ist übermenschlich: aber er ist es doch – immer harte Gegensätze, wenn auch nicht Extreme vereint er in seinen Werken u. in sich – u. er ist doch allein] in *TB* I, p. 82, emphasis original. As is demonstrated in Part I, the role of contrast in Romantic irony is evident in Schumann's description of Jean Paul's style. See also John Daverio's remarks as regards the formal consequences for Schumann's Jean Paul-inspired *Papillons*. Daverio (1993), pp. 51 and 55–56.

[28] *TB* I, p. 96 (13 July 1828) [Töne sind höhere Worte . . . beyde sind das Non plus ultra der Romantik. Ton ist überhaupt komponiertes Wort].

[29] Dahlhaus (1969a), pp. 261–276. See also Meissner (1985), pp. 12–18.

[30] Schumann announced the advent of 'a new poetic age' most enthusiastically in 1835 in the *NZfM* 2, p. 3. A valuable discussion of Schumann's progressive stance as a Romantic can be found in Dahlhaus (1988), pp. 258–261.

as was the Romantics' aim to poeticize the world at large. Schumann writes: 'The whole undertaking is attractive, however difficult it seems; poetry must shine through everywhere in order to cover over as much as possible the prosaic aspects of life.'[31]

This last statement very clearly shows Schumann's intellectual and temperamental affinity with the Early Romantics, in that it reflects their prime demand for a 'universal poeticization' in which art becomes life, and vice versa. No longer is there a divide between the two, once a prosaic life is imbued with poetic moments. The aim was to elevate one's life by 'poeticizing' it. A. W. Schlegel states: '[poetry] elevates us above an ordinary reality into the world of phantasy and imagination'.[32] Transcendence was thus thought to lead the mind in two directions: it takes on the form of an elegiac reminiscence of the lost past, and at the same time provides a view into utopian idylls. Most of all, however, it is an emotional super-elevation of a moment in the present, a transfiguration of normal life. In every case, however, there is a strong affinity with dreams and fairy-tales. The aim to 'poeticize' life is closely connected with Schumann's idea of 'poetic time', for the conceptual emphasis on a moment of the present that fuses past and future derives from Schumann's concentration on what he calls 'rare' and 'secret states of the soul'.[33] Schumann sought to project these in his music in order to emphasize its reference and relevance to life, a 'poetic life' reflected in music.[34] To introduce into his compositions present psychic conditions, bizarre, torn or extreme in nature, meant for Schumann to represent a present which embodies the past as much as it anticipates the future. This concept was new, but Schumann readily acknowledged signs of it in a young composer's work, emphasizing that the aim of merging life and art would necessarily result in a display of decidedly bizarre musical moments:

This hitherto unknown, probably young, composer [lit.: *Tondichter* or sound-poet] is one of the rarest phenomena of our times. He belongs to no school, creates out of himself . . . ; he created for himself a new, ideal world which he almost wilfully – at times with most original bizarreness – fantasizes about.[35]

---

[31] *TB* I, p. 140 [Die ganze Arbeit ist anziehend, so schwierig sie auch scheint; die Poesie muß überall hervorguken, um die Prosa im Leben so viel wie möglich zu übertünchen].

[32] A. W. Schlegel (1964), pp. 95–105 (here 99) [Das Poetische ist das, was uns über die gewöhnliche Wirklichkeit in eine Welt der Phantasie erhebt].

[33] Kreisig *GS* I, p. 343 [seltene . . . geheime Seelenzustände]. That Schumann believed 'that music is affected by every occasion in life' has been well demonstrated by Lippmann (1964), p. 314. The influence of the composer's life on the nature of his aesthetic outlook and creative output has so often been stated in Schumann scholarship that is has become a commonplace. In its non-specificity, it is, however, of little critical consequence, and only hints at what I hope to demonstrate here in more specific terms. It may be pointed out that Schumann's notion of 'rare' and 'secret states of the soul' is not to be investigated in an explicitly psychologizing fashion, for its importance lies in the aesthetic realization of the idea.

[34] 'That would be small art, if it only sounded and had no language nor signs for the states of the soul! –' exclaims Florestan in *Aus Meister Raro's, Florestan's und Eusebius' Denk- und Dicht-büchlein* (see *GS* I, p. 35 [Das wäre eine kleine Kunst, die nur klänge, und keine Sprache noch Zeichen für Seelenzustände hätte]).

[35] *TB* I, p. 426 (1836) [Der uns zum erstenmal begegnende, wahrscheinlich noch jugendliche Tondichter gehört zu den seltensten Erscheinungen der Zeit; er hängt an keiner Schule, schöpft aus sich selbst, prunkt nicht mit fremden, im Schweiß des Angesichts zusammen gelesen[en] Federn; hat sich eine neue ideale Welt erschaffen, worin er fast muthwillig, zuweilen gar mit origineller Bizarrerie herumschwärmt].

To summarize, Schumann's aesthetics rest on these two pillars: on the one hand a specific concept of time, and on the other, the intent to represent in music decidedly 'rare' and 'secret states of the soul', made of 'poetic material'[36] from a 'language of the soul' (*Seelensprache*).[37] As a highly idiosyncratic term in Romantic theory, *Seelensprache* is conceptually related to that of 'language of the flowers' (*Blumensprache*) of which Schumann says: 'A musical language of the flowers was one of my earliest ideas'.[38]

THE ROMANTICS' SEARCH FOR A *LANGUAGE OF THE SOUL*

Schumann's fascination with, and wish for, a musical language of flowers was probably partly inspired by Novalis, in whose unfinished novel *Heinrich von Ofterdingen* (1802) the topos of 'a high, radiant blue flower' ('eine hohe lichtblaue Blume') – appearing in the hero's dream – symbolizes the longing for Romantic love. Containing extensive passages evaluating the role of the Romantic poet in opposition to his Classical predecessor (Goethe's *Wilhelm Meisters Lehrjahre*), the Blue Flower became the emblem of the Romantic age.[39]

The Romantics' systematic reassessment of the artistic genres concentrated on this concept of *Seelensprache* in their search for an ideal artistic language. In music theory, as I discussed earlier, this idea culminated in a new concept of the Lied. Schumann, for one, demanded that a song composer firstly fathom the transcendental core of a poem in order to let music and poetry coalesce at the highest level. Ideally, the Lied was for Schumann *the* Romantic medium of poetic sublimation, able to raise musical and literary poetics to the highest order: to what Schumann called a 'higher sphere of art'.[40] The three artistic idioms – poetry, voice and instrument – would no longer exist independently, but instead condition each other mutually. The relationship between text and music therefore became a dialectical one.

[36] *GS* I, p. 300 [poetischen Grundstoff].

[37] See Schumann's letter to Clara of 8 February 1838 in *NF*, p. 110: 'Often strange in appearance is the human heart, and pain and joy intermix in wild disorder. But you must still hope for the best; I feel there is much in me still, indeed often I am so rash as to believe that music as the language of the soul is still in its beginnings.'

[38] *TB* I, p. 400 (26 May 1832) [Eine musikalische Blumensprache war eine meiner frühesten Ideen]. The concept of 'Blumensprache' is particularly pertinent for Song 8 ('Und wüssten's die Blumen die kleinen') and Song 12 ('Am leuchtenden Sommermorgen'), the latter of which is discussed in more detail on pp. 200–206, below. As a central idea of Romantic poetics, the personification of flowers originates in the Romantics' assumption that true art speaks in the language of nature. The 'Universalgeist' is assumed to rest in flowers who have a soul, express human emotions, and are compassionate. This topos first appears as part of Schumann's literary imagination when he is following the style of Jean Paul and Novalis. See for example Schumann's novelistic pieces *Mitternachtsstück aus Selene* in *TB* I, p. 135: 'the flowers were softly speaking to each other' [die Blumen sprachen mild miteinander] and *Mitternachtsstück*: 'the willow and the cypress were whispering softly in their own language ...' [die Tränenweiden u. die Cypressen flüsterten sich leise ihre Sprache zu ...]. In *GS* I, p. 356, Schumann defines 'Seelensprache' as the 'language of the heart before all others' [Herzenssprache vor allen andern]. Here, Schumann's concept of 'Seelensprache' elevates music to the 'poetic' in the sense of a 'Sprache über der Sprache' (Dahlhaus (1978, p. 15)). In Schumann's Reisenotizen I, 'Michälis' 1828 (*TB* I, p. 41) he says: 'Every composer [lit.: sound-artist] is a poet, only a higher one' [Jeder Tonkünstler ist ein Dichter, nur ein höherer].

[39] Although Schumann only mentions the writer Novalis and not the title of this work (*TB* I, pp. 97 and 111), the notoriety of *Heinrich von Ofterdingen* at the time gives weight to the assumption that Schumann knew it.

[40] *NZfM* 1 (1834), p. 193 [höhere Kunstsphäre].

HEINE'S 'ICH HAB' IM TRAUM GEWEINET'
IN POETIC TERMS

The song 'Ich hab' im Traum geweinet' is a good example of how Schumann tried to capture a 'special mood', one of those 'rare states of the soul' that he felt compelled to express musically. When compared with a later setting of a Lenau poem (Op. 90/6), it is also a good example of Schumann's aesthetic of 'poetic time'.

At first sight, Heine's metaphorical language in 'Ich hab' im Traum geweinet' is simple, as is the poem's formal outline and metre. In this, it is even more straightforward than most of Heine's early poetry, and it demands little analytical skill to understand its structure – a conventionally constructed tripartite form, the three stresses in the first two lines form an iambic metre, which then changes into an anapaestic one in line 3 at 'und die Träne' with two short syllables followed by a long one. The enjambment between lines 3 and 4 in each verse causes a looser metrical continuation, which also ensures that the sense is carried over from one line into the next. This is well in accordance with the imagery centring on flowing tears and weeping ('Träne' 'flows' into 'Floß' and likewise in the other two verses).

Ich hab' im Traum geweinet,	I wept in my dream,
Mir träumte, du lägest im Grab.	I dreamed that you lay in your grave.
Ich wachte auf, und die Träne	I awoke, and the tear
Floß noch von der Wange herab.	Still ran down my cheek.
Ich hab' im Traum geweinet,	I wept in my dream,
Mir träumte, du verließest mich.	I dreamed that you had forsaken me.
Ich wachte auf, und ich weinte	I awoke and I went on weeping
Noch lange bitterlich.	Still long and bitterly.
Ich hab' im Traum geweinet,	I wept in my dream,
Mir träumte, du wärst mir noch gut.	I dreamed you were still kind to me.
Ich wachte auf, und noch immer	I awoke, and still
Strömt meine Tränenflut.	The flood of my tears is streaming.

The repetition of the first line of each stanza ('Ich hab' im Traum geweinet') achieves a declamatory effect. But declamation here is introverted in nature, since the poet is speaking to himself, slowly recounting an inner experience as his dream re-emerges three times before his eyes. Thus, it is an inner world that is mapped out, and in the state of dream, feelings are more enhanced and anxieties more pronounced. The theme of introspection rests in this poem with the use of the lyrical 'I' which speaks throughout the poem, 'ich' and 'mir' being stated at the beginning of three out of four lines in each stanza, and altogether (including the 'mich' in II/2) appearing twelve times. Thus, the poet is at the poem's centre and the two defining spheres of being, say dreaming and wakening, or subconsciousness and consciousness, are presented through the poet's agency only.

The emotional intensity of this poem exceeds that of most other poems from the *Lyrisches Intermezzo* by concentrating on just three motifs: dream, weeping and awakening. This brings about an unusual continuity of scene which is – like the lyrical 'I' – mainly achieved through the triple repetition of the first and part of the second and third lines in each stanza. After establishing 'Ich hab' im Traum' as a leitmotif, 'Mir träumte' consolidates the poem's nocturnal theme. The inevitability of this state taking hold of the poet is indicated by the passive form '*mir* träumte'[41] (as opposed to '*ich* träumte'); thus it is some *external* power that 'makes' the poet dream, and which forces these visions on to the dreamer.

The shift from dream to reality corresponds to a sudden change of metre: 'Ich wachte auf' not only departs from the preceding dactyls, but its tentative iambic metre breaks up altogether after 'und' cuts the line in half. The emphasis thus shifts to 'Träne':

> Ich hàb' im Tràum gewèinet.
> Mir träumte, du lägest im Grab.
> *Ich wachte auf*, und die **Träne**
> Floß noch von der Wange herab.

Although Heine often portrays the central Romantic theme of love as a decidedly painful and isolating experience,[42] the familiar means to convey that message – *Stimmungsbruch* (i.e. trivialization, malicious overtones, unanticipated renunciation of initially positive sentiments) – are missing in 'Ich hab' im Traum geweinet'. However, the notion of a fatal forlornness – a quiet submission to incurable despair – is communicated through an inversion of cause and effect: whilst the first stanza still enables the reader to follow and possibly empathize with what the poet experiences, the second stanza already introduces a subliminal degree of confusion which then turns into a real loss of comprehension in the third stanza. The narrative remains ambiguous because there seems to be no logical correspondence between the woman's apparent fondness of the man ('Mir träumte, du wärst mir noch gut') and the lover's disconsolate reaction ('noch immer/Strömt meine Tränenflut').

Visually, the image of the woman is the focus of the poet's dream. However, through emphasis on the emotional state of the lyrical 'I', the woman obtains no real presence. She has no effect on the poet who remains inexplicably desolate, irrespective of how the woman acts in his dream. In this, she has no claim to be of the essence of the poem. The persistence in the lyrical 'I' and his unchanged sentiment leaves no room for the woman ever to come to the fore. What in narrative-orientated interpretation could then be called a lack of common sense is here an absolute necessity: visions of dreams are flashes of emotions, and objects or actions are mere vehicles to portray an inner situation. Thus, Heine uses the image of the woman to underscore a constancy that defies the teleological plot. Despite these images unfolding over the course of three rhythmic stanzas, the poem works at some level above that of temporality: the state of dream and that of waking interchanging.

The poet's deeply felt and overwhelming despair also has no external cause, since the poet knows no reason for this sorrow. The figure of the woman is ultimately

---

[41] A literal translation would read 'it came to me in a dream'.   [42] See Part II, pp. 74–90.

not the object over which the poet grieves, because her different appearances –
seeing her dead, seeing her leave or seeing her sustained fondness – have no effect
on the poet's state of mind.[43] What has been lost is ultimately unknown. Forlorn in
innermost uncertainty, the sentiment is that of melancholy, the defining disposition
of a modern age that found in Freud an analyst who distinguished it from sadness
by its added phenomenon of an 'unknown loss'.[44]

By means of repetition, Heine fixes the lyrical 'I' within the centre of the poem,
which also emphasizes the focus on an inner world. Thus, the poem's principal
metaphors of *Traum* (dream) and *Tränen* (tears) merge into one, for the flow of tears
(visible and real) grows out of dreams into the moment of awakening to reality as
the poet becomes aware of the tears' existence. These two metaphors are linked by
alliteration as the initial consonants are the same and the following vowel is altered
by an Umlaut only. 'Tränen' is connected to 'weinen' (weeping) – the dominant
emotion of the poem. These three images, 'Traum', 'Tränen' and 'weinen', appear
twelve times.

One could maintain that the 'content' of the poem runs in two, opposite, directions: the lover dreams that, first, his beloved lies in the grave (first stanza), then that
she has left him (second stanza), and finally that she is still kind to him. But contrary
to expectation, the better the dreams get, the more distressed the lover feels. First, the
tears run down his cheek, then he weeps bitterly, and finally it is a flood of tears. Two
oppositional realities would then be at play here: the dream of a woman, and the
poet's emotional response when he awakes. But the way in which the words 'Traum'
and 'Tränen' interlock in sense and metre contributes to the sense of one stream of
consciousness merging with the other. Poetry as *Dichtung* (poiesis) and *Verdichtung*
(condensation) manifests itself and leaves behind the processes of development and
change that characterize narrative strategies. Here, the ceaseless invocation of dream
and flowing tears becomes absorbed into a stasis of inward-looking constancy.

SCHUMANN'S 'ICH HAB' IM TRAUM GEWEINET' IN MUSICO-POETIC TERMS

The formal simplicity of the poem contributes to the singular conciseness with
which Heine expresses a complex psychological mood of some highly nuanced kind
of melancholy. In his setting Schumann follows closely the simplicity of structure
and metre in Heine's poem.

The song – like the poem – is in tri-partite form (bb. 1–11; bb. 12–22; bb. 23–33;
followed by a postlude bb. 34–38), the $^6_8$ time recasting the iambic metre of the
poem. If this seems predictable, Schumann nevertheless applies two exceptional
musical means whose striking effect makes this song the still point of the turning

---

[43] The same idea of portraying a woman whilst actually aiming to convey Romantic longing is to be found in
Heine's most famous poem on the Loreley 'Ich weiß nicht, was soll es bedeuten, / Daß ich so traurig bin' of
Die Heimkehr (1826).

[44] Freud, 'Trauer und Melancholie' (1917), SA 3.

1 *Ich hab' im Traum geweinet* Op. 48, no. 13

Ich hab' im Traum geweinet

1 (*cont.*)

world of *Dichterliebe*. First, he chooses a highly unusual key – Eb minor; only two other songs, among some 250 that Schumann wrote, are set in this key.[45] And secondly, Schumann denies the voice the close and embracing accompaniment so typical of his song compositions. In fact, 'Ich hab' im Traum geweinet' is the only song in which Schumann uses such strikingly sparse accompaniment. The voice appears on its own, devoid of any harmonic support – a psalm-like intonation, a lamento.[46] The voice declaims the words 'Ich hab' im Traum geweinet' on the pitch Bb and stresses the word 'weinen' by moving up a minor second (b. 2). This rhythmically characteristic insistence on Bb pressing into Cb only to revert to Bb constitutes and articulates the vocal 'identity' level of this song. Stated without any accompaniment at this opening stage, and viewed without reference to the song's key signature, the harmonic meaning of this pitch is indefinite. The piano's statement in bb. 3–4 – in many ways a strikingly different, yet equally characteristic motive – constitutes the second identity level. It is by dint of the piano, no doubt, that the harmonic function of the opening vocal line is determined as a dominant. In this, the piano asserts its superior role as the governing structural force here, for it is the piano which defines the harmonic status of the voice, and not the other way around. Let us note that this is not even a dialectical relationship, for the voice is, as has been said above, functionally indefinable when it first occurs, whilst the piano – much in contrast to the voice – is actually quite self-sufficient as far as harmonic function is concerned: it is a cadential commonplace (or 'trope'). The point to be made here is that the hierarchical relationship between voice and piano which Schumann establishes in this marked fashion at the beginning of the song (bb. 1–4) illustrates the central idea of his conception of Romantic song: the voice is superimposed on the 'genuine' musical matrix of this song, the piano.[47]

One could argue that the source of the pitch Bb lies in the music preceding Song 13. Interestingly, regardless of which version of *Dichterliebe* one chooses to consider, either song is firmly grounded in a Bb tonality: as regards the original conception of *Dichterliebe*, it is Song 12b ('Mein Wagen rollet langsam') in the key of G minor; in the version which was eventually published, it is Song 12 ('Am leuchtenden Sommermorgen') in the key of Bb major. In both cases, however, the significance of a tonal relation to be observed between Song 13 and the music preceding it lies in the fact that the Cb in the lamento (b. 2) is a shock, and the Fb in b. 5 is a second one.

The intensity exuding from the vocal lamento is heightened by the piano's contrasting gesture. It breaks through after a significant void (created by the pause in b. 3) with characteristics diametrically opposed to the voice: rhythm and texture, articulation (staccato) and dynamic (*pp* instead of *p*). Hence, a common melodic

---

[45] Sams (1993, pp. 41 and 120), referring to 'Lieb Liebchen' (Op. 24/4), suggests that Eb minor here is associated with the idea of death.

[46] Agawu (1984, p. 170) calls this passage a 'recitative', although the term 'lamento' may perhaps seem more appropriate in view of the continuous rhythm, and in view of the fact that the entire atmosphere of this music does not display the kind of freedom one associates with recitatives.

[47] See the model for Schumann's conception of the Romantic song as proposed on pp. 5–7 and 52–67.

shape or even melodic development does not obtain. However, viewed analytically in terms of voice-leading, the lamento's B♭ passes into the piano as a link between the first and second vocal utterance. As a result of the piano forming the line A♭ – G♭ – F – G♭ (bb. 3–4), the F♭ in the lamento (b. 5) is literally 'outstanding'.[48]

Returning to the main characteristic of this song's musico-poetic relations, one notes that the intensity of feeling portrayed in the poem stands in stark contrast to the song's structural simplicity and stylistic purity. Thus, Schumann chose the key of E♭ minor most carefully in order to reflect a specific mood, not least perhaps in view of the overall musical context.

The issue of key relations in *Dichterliebe* has often received critical attention,[49] and rightly so, for one senses a deliberate and significant employment of tonal centres in the cycle. As is well known, there was an increased awareness of this matter in nineteenth-century music theory and compositional technique, which Schubart in his *Ideen zu einer Ästhetik der Tonkunst* addresses in great detail.[50] As probably one of the first theoretical works read by Schumann, he took great interest in this treatise for, in 1823, he copied long passages from it into a note book.[51] In the search for epigraphs for the *NZfM*, Schumann took up Schubart's *Ästhetik* again in 1838,[52] writing to his friend Fischof: 'Here follows Schubart in whom I found a lot'.[53] Responding to the passage on the character of keys in Schubart's treatise, Schumann, when addressing the issue in the *NZfM*, makes a striking point:

Simple feelings require simple keys. Complex ones require those that rarely meet the ear. Thus one might observe the rising and falling of emotions by means of the interwoven circle of fifths. The tritone, the midpoint of the octave, F♯, that is, seems to be the highest point, the pinnacle, which then descends through the ♭ keys down to simple, unadorned C major.[54]

'Complex moods' are thus musically rendered by distant and unusual keys that are rarely encountered. Furthermore, in a circle of increasing intensity, Schumann determines the tonal equivalent of an emotional peak as the tritone F♯. In this perspective of ultimate distance as well as ascendancy, the thirteenth song assumes exceptional symbolization: an enharmonic change renders F♯ as G♭ whose relative key is E♭ minor – the key of 'Ich hab' im Traum geweinet'. Thus, tonally and

---

[48] This is a significant aspect as regards the interaction between voice and piano in this song. However, the main concern at this stage of the discussion is with the key only.

[49] Most specifically by Komar (1971), Neumeyer (1982) and Pousseur (1993).

[50] Schubart (1806), pp. 377–382.

[51] See the reference made by Köhler (1994, p. 193, n. 8) regarding the autograph of Schumann's *Blätter und Blümchen aus der goldenen Aue, gesammelt und zusammengebunden von Robert Schumann, genannt Skülander.*

[52] See *TB* II, p. 84 [Schubarts Aesthetik angefangen . . . Schubarts Aesthetik beendigt]. See also Schubart-epigraphs in *NZfM* 10, nos. 20, 40, 47, and 11, nos. 20, 25, 29, 32 and 38, as stated by Nauhaus in *TB* II, p. 492, n. 319.

[53] See *NF*, Letter to Fischof, no. 146, p. 145.

[54] 'Charakeristik der Tonarten', originally published in the *NZfM* and now to be found in *GS* I, pp. 180–182 (here 182) [Einfachere Empfindungen haben einfachere Tonarten; zusammengesetzte bewegen sich lieber in fremden, welche das Ohr seltener hört. Man könnte daher im ineinanderlaufenden Quintenzirkel das Steigen und Fallen am besten sehen. Der Tritonus, die Mitte der Octave zur Octave, also Fis, scheint der höchste Punkt, die Spitze zu sein, die dann in den B-Tonarten wieder zu dem einfachen, ungeschminkten C-dur herabsinkt].

otherwise this song becomes the polar centre – in the circle of fifths as well as in the circle of emotions.[55]

Once the voice has sung 'Ich hab' im Traum geweinet', the piano states its own motive in the low, tenor register (bb. 3–4). Thereafter, the voice continues in a lamento (bb. 4–6). Voice and piano remain in alternation for stanzas 1 and 2, but the situation changes in anticipation of the momentous statement made in the poem's third and last stanza. Whilst the first stanza closes with two brief cadential chords in the piano and a fermata (b. 11), the second stanza's ending seems at first to follow this pattern, only to depart from it in b. 22. Here, when the voice is about to recite 'Ich hab' im Traum geweinet' without accompaniment for the last time, the piano pre-empts the repeated declamation on Bb (bb. 22–23). With the voice entering in b. 24, the compelling nature of the unaccompanied voice up to this moment is manifest retrospectively: now that voice and piano begin to merge (bb. 26 onwards), the gradations of emotional intensification form a transition from sadness, through sorrow, into despair. The last awakening ('Ich wachte auf, und noch immer/Strömt meine Tränenflut') is recited on Db alone, at first underscored by unison Dbs in the piano accompaniment (b. 28) but then inexorably dissolving into dissonant clusters (bb. 29–30).

At this very moment, the voice reaches its highest pitch, Fb[1], on 'Tränen (-flut)' (b. 31) – a 'dramatic moment', and indeed *the* dramatic moment of this song as it recalls the unaccompanied low Fb, the 'shock', in b. 5 (see Ex. 1).[56] Thus returning to the song's beginning, the rhythmic pattern pushing the long series of Dbs into motion (b. 28) is identical with that of the rhythmic pattern of the Bb in the lamento (b. 1, including its upbeat). The final statement of the vocal motive not only shares, but intensifies, the sense of insistence on one pitch at the opening of the song, for it occurs with doubled force in the voice and the piano, and continues over a longer period of time (instead of two bars, it is prolonged over five bars), and most importantly is marked by the increasing dissonances in the piano. It thus appears like a heightening of the first statement's power in the Early Romantic sense of *Potenzierung* within a series of poetic ideas (*Ideenreihe*) or moods.

The descent downwards, from Fb to Eb in the voice (b. 32), then to Db, Cb and Bb in the piano (bb. 32–33), carries a specific meaning: it forms the tritone which we

---

[55] Schumann knew that compositions written in remote keys posed a problem as regards the general understanding of such a means. Reviewing a cycle of etudes by Goldschmidt (who uses the 'strange keys' [fremdartige Tonarten] Db or F♯), Schumann says: '. . . ein junger Componist, zu dem man sich erst durch 5 bis 6 Kreuze durcharbeiten muß, braucht noch einmal so viel Zeit zur öffentlichen Anerkennung' [it will take extra time for a young composer to gain public appreciation, if, in order to understand him, we have to work our way through 5 and 6 sharps]. However, Schumann also asserts: 'Die Hauptsache aber ist, er bewahre sich seine Natürlichkeit und schreibe dann, in welcher Tonart er wolle' [the main thing is, however, he retains his personality for then he may write in whatever key he pleases], in GS IV, p. 203. For a historical discussion of the significance of rare keys, see MacDonald's most informative and interesting article titled 'Gb', in which he points out that 'remote, especially flat, keys were eventually given the attributes of sensuousness and mysterious ecstasy. . . . On the keyboard these keys have a physical feeling which may be regarded as sensual and which, therefore, may have been shunned by composers of a puritanical cast of mind.' MacDonald (1988), pp. 221–237 (here 226). Further and subtle discussion of the 'spectral Gb' is to be found in Richard Kramer (1994), pp. 13–17.

[56] See above, p. 144.

Ex. 1 'Ich hab' im Traum geweinet' (Op. 48, no. 13), conclusion of
vocal line and postlude

know was of singular significance within Schumann's conception of keys. The way
in which Schumann assures a clear articulation of 'a complex feeling' is indicated
by the registral transfer in the piano so as to continue the descent in a continuous
line downwards (bb. 32–33). The piano's sudden *sforzato* affirms the tritonal rupture
as the song's final gesture, followed by a bar of silence (b. 34). The song fades
away, without a definite resolution in the top line of the texture in the closing bars
(bb. 35–38).

Striking as a musico-poetic, as well as semantic, entity are bb. 20–25, for the
content of 'Ich weinte noch lange bitterlich' is first echoed by the piano (b. 22)
but then continued (bb. 23–25) in the sense that these words foreshadow a continuation. 'Ich weinte...noch lange' is best translated with 'I kept crying for a long
time' – words that forecast the never-ending stream of tears ('Tränenflut'). The grav-
ity of feeling is indicated in the piano: the main motivic idea is now set in full and
heavy chords, and the shift towards a darker mode is instantly perceptible as these
bars' contrast with the previous few and exclusively short chords in *pianissimo* and
staccato.

When the piano thus intones the main motive, the texture seems to become
'grounded' for the first time in the entire song. This sensation is particularly prominent at the height of the crescendo when the right hand moves up one step (which
mirrors the move in the voice on 'geweinet'), while the left hand descends into the
lowest register. Like the sense of sustained desperation introduced in the poem, the
piano's long chords let this sense 'sink in' as the meaning of 'lange' ('long-lasting')
is literally lowered and thus 'deepened'.

As discussed above, the piano also pre-empts what the voice will continue to sing ('I wept in my dream'), but the voice is now (bb. 25–26) embedded in chords on 'geweinet' – the central emotion of poem and song. Thus, the function of the piano in bb. 22–24 works backwards (intoning the voice's part from before), synchronically (a statement on its own imbued with the words of the voice) and forwards (pre-stating the voice-part of bb. 25–26). This procedure, the lyricization of the piano bending backwards and forwards, marks the structural turning-point of Song 13.

We see in 'Ich hab' im Traum geweinet' how inextricably intertwined music and language have gradually become as the tellingly sparse chordal accompaniment turns lyrical (b. 22), and hence loses its original identity, in anticipation of the poetic meaning in the last stanza. Whilst the two levels, voice and piano, consistently keep apart for the first two stanzas (bb. 1–21), they temporarily fuse when the emotional drama of the poem draws near its poetic 'resolution' (bb. 22–33). Let us note, too, that the piano, from b. 35, resumes its original role of counteracting the lyrical level to leave no trace of the voice's expressive, subjective lamento behind; after a moment of stillness (b. 34), it reasserts itself as the objective, controlled and solitary voice – Schumann's genuine voice.

Schumann's musical assimilation of the poem thus works on two semantic levels: the instrumental one forming the critical counterpoint to the vocal rendition of the poem's dramatic development. Furthermore, the musical reading of the poem's intricate sense proceeds on several temporal levels. Perceived without an awareness of the poetic structure, this kind of music does not disclose the sensitivity of Schumann's reading. Finally, the stylistic deviation evident in the setting of this poem, markedly different to those surrounding it in *Dichterliebe*, indicates a particular involvement with Heine's poem on Schumann's part. The 'state of the soul' here described seems to have called for exceptional musical means: in the key chosen, and in the complex interaction between an insistently lamenting voice and a resistingly reserved, eventually yielding, but lastly 'composed' piano accompaniment.

MUSICO-POETIC INTERTEXTUALITY: 'DER SCHWERE ABEND'

Ten years later, six years before his death and in one of his very last compositions, Schumann returned to a similar emotive space. Although *Dichterliebe* contains some remarkable interrelationships within itself, the most remarkable of all lies outside this cycle. It is the striking paraphrase of 'Ich hab' im Traum geweinet' in 'Der schwere Abend' (Op. 90/6), a setting of a poem by Nikolaus Lenau.

Where do we situate Lenau within the Romantic literary scene? And how did Schumann come across his poetry, and when? 'Der schwere Abend' is the last of Schumann's *Sechs Gedichte von Nikolaus Lenau und Requiem*, composed in Dresden within three consecutive days of August 1850, shortly before moving to Düsseldorf.[57]

---

[57] *TB* III/2, pp. 533–534.

2 *Der schwere Abend* Op. 90, no. 6

Der schwere Abend
(Lenau)

2 (cont.)

On 26 August 1850, Schumann asked his publisher to assist him in 'erecting a small monument' to Lenau, 'the sad but ever so marvellous poet'.[58]

As one of the great German poets of *Schwermut*, Lenau (1802–50) is mainly associated with the late Romantic attitude of *Weltschmerz*. Immensely popular during his life-time,[59] his highly rhythmical poetry exhibits his belief in pantheism almost exclusively through the agency of nature. In strong opposition to realism, Lenau saw the function of modern nature poetry as:

causing conflict between nature and human life, and to gain, as a result of this conflict, a third, organically living element which represents a *symbol* of that higher unity within which nature and human life is comprised.[60]

What is often described as the development of 'an impulsive, depressive and deeply disturbed personality'[61] led to Lenau's complete physical and mental breakdown in 1844 and his committal to an asylum, where he remained until his death on 22 August 1850 – just when Schumann had finished setting the *Sechs Gedichte von Nikolaus Lenau und Requiem*.[62]

Schumann's interest in Lenau's poetry goes back to the late 1830s, when he was seeking poems suitable for publication in the *NZfM* in the spirit of a 'new poetic age', or, in fact, for song-settings.[63] During his largely disappointing stay in Vienna in 1838, Schumann makes several references to Lenau in his diary: 'Saw Lenau in the café house, but didn't go and speak to him'[64] and 'Read Lenau's poems at home'.[65] Among the frequent mentions of his apparently depressed mood, Schumann writes some weeks later: 'deep melancholy. . . . Read and excerpted epigraphs from: . . . Lenau's and Heine's poems'.[66] After being introduced to Lenau, Schumann noted in his diary: 'He has a melancholy, very gentle and engaging trait about lips and eyes'.[67]

---

[58] [Es soll mich freuen, wenn Sie mir die Hand reichten, dem unglücklichen, aber so herrlichen Dichter mit diesem Werke ein kleines Denkmal zu setzen . . .]. Letter to the publisher Kistner, in Jansen (1904), pp. 467–468.

[59] Lenau's first collection of poems, *Gedichte* of 1832, supplemented in 1838 by a further volume entitled *Neuere Gedichte*, reached seven and five editions respectively between the years of 1832 and 1844 alone. See also the commentary by Hartmut Steinecke in Lenau (1993), p. 156. In comparison, Heine's *Buch der Lieder* reached a second edition ten years after its first appearance in 1827. See p. 107, above.

[60] Lenau (1993), p. 159 [die Natur und das Menschenleben in einen innigen Konflikt bringen, und aus diesem Konflikte ein drittes Organisch-lebendiges resultieren zu lassen, welches ein *Symbol* darstelle jener höhern geistigen Einheit, worunter Natur und Menschenleben begriffen sind]. My emphasis.

[61] Garland (1986), pp. 547–548.

[62] For the Requiem, as is evident from Schumann's *Abschriftenbuch*, Schumann set August Heinrich Theodor Sieverses' German translation of an anonymous Latin text ('Requiescat a labore') describing Heloïse's lament for Abelard. Cf. also Kaldewey (1991), pp. 91–92.

[63] To a correspondent in Vienna, Schumann writes on 14 January 1838: 'Do you know Lenau a little better? Should he not be prepared to submit for publication in the journal a few shorter poems, suitable for composition?' [Kennen Sie Lenau genauer? Sollte er sich nicht bereit finden lassen, mir ein paar kleinere Gedichte, die sich zur Komposition eignen, in die Zeitschrift zum Druck zu geben?]. Jansen (1904), pp. 107–108.

[64] *TB* II, p. 78 (entry for 29 October 1838) [Lenau sah ich auf dem Kaffeehaus, sprach aber nicht mit ihm].

[65] *TB* II, p. 74 (entry for 14 October 1838) [zu Hause Lenau's Gedichte gelesen].

[66] *TB* II, p. 83 (entry for 6 December 1838) [tiefe Melancholie . . . Gelesen und Mottos geschrieben aus . . . Lenau's und Heine's Gedichten].

[67] *TB* II, p. 83 (entry for 12 December 1838) [er hat einen melancholischen sehr sanften u. einnehmenden Zug um Lipp u. Auge].

For the composition of Op. 90 in 1850, Schumann returned to the transcribed selection of Lenau poems contained in his and Clara's *Abschriftenbuch*.[68] Its first performance took place a few days before the Schumanns departed for Düsseldorf. Litzmann reports:

Official Dresden and the local, permanently appointed [*beamtet*] musicians took no notice of Robert Schumann's leaving Dresden. However, a farewell evening had taken place a few days earlier at Bendemann's on 25 August, at which Clara played and Miss Jacobi sang from the newly composed Lenau songs by Robert 'which were all very melancholy'. 'How strange', Clara writes, 'these songs close with a Requiem, of Heloïse, which Robert had been looking for in order to conclude in a somewhat moderate/soothing tone . . . , and in the belief as well that Lenau was dead. The latter was not the case but, how miraculously, just today Robert read that he had passed away, and thus the first Requiem was sung for him by Robert. This [the Requiem] as well as the composition of the songs put everyone in a particular, sad [*wehmütig*] mood.'[69]

Schumann's reference in 'Der schwere Abend' to the earlier setting of Heine's 'Ich hab' im Traum geweinet' is as obvious as it is significant. The opening chords alone make us revisit the moment in *Dichterliebe* where they hauntingly permeate the song's bare matrix. There, it is the acoustic stillness into which these chords distantly enter after what seems to be an indefinite pause (bb. 33–34) and as the song's last wordless words (see Ex. 2). Frozen in time and space, a final shadow of sound casts the silence into eclipse (bb. 36–38), so as to reverberate into eternity.[70]

'Der schwere Abend' thus sustains the starless atmosphere of 'Ich hab' im Traum geweinet', and it does so compositionally as well as textually with 'Und sternlos war die Nacht' meaning, literally, 'and starless was the night'. 'Der schwere Abend' resumes the never-ending stream of solitude by taking up in the piano the fragmentary theme of a song of the past, 'Ich hab' im Traum geweinet' (Op. 48, no. 13, b. 3). There, the piano foreshadowed the words 'mir träumte, du' rhythmically (see Ex. 3).

---

[68] The volume, now held in the Robert-Schumann-Haus Zwickau (unpublished autograph D-ZSch, Sign. 4871/VIII, 4–5977 A3) is entitled *Abschriften von Gedichten zur Composition. / Gesammelt von Robert und Clara Schumann / vom Jahr 1839 an*. It contains 169 poems by 34 different poets, 101 of which were set to music in 94 compositions, 7 of which were by Clara Schumann. See Kaldewey (1991), p. 88.

[69] Litzmann II, p. 221 [Das offizielle Dresden und die einheimischen beamteten Musiker nahmen von dem Scheiden Robert Schumanns aus Dresden keine Notiz. Dagegen hatte wenige Tage zuvor am 25. August bei Bendemann im Freundeskreise eine Abschiedsfeier stattgefunden, wo Clara spielte, und Fräulein Jacobi aus den neuen eben komponierten Lenauschen Liedern von Robert, 'die alle sehr melancholisch sind', sang. 'Wie eigen', schreibt Clara, 'die Lieder beschließen mit einem Requiem, von der Helise, das Robert gesucht hatte, um doch einigermaßen mildernd anzuschließen . . . und in der Meinung zugleich, Lenau sei tot. Letzteres war nicht der Fall, aber, wie wunderbar, gerade heute las Robert, daß er verschieden, und so wurde ihm wohl das erste Requiem von Robert gesungen. Dies sowie die Komposition seiner Lieder brachte eine eigne wehmütig Stimmung in alle'].

[70] The immanence of the Romantic in music is exemplified in one of Jean Paul's passages in the *Vorschule der Ästhetik*, JP IX, p. 88: 'Es ist noch ähnlicher als ein Gleichnis, wenn man das Romantische das wogende Ansummen einer Saite oder Glocke nennt, in welchem die Tonwoge wie in immer fernerer Weiten verschwimmt und endlich sich verliert in uns selber und, obwohl außen schon still, noch immer lautet [It is even more similar than a simile if one calls the Romantic the undulating singing of a string or bell in which the wave of the tone appears to blur in ever more remote distances, and which eventually loses itself in ourselves where, although externally already silent, it still resounds].

Ex. 2   Closing bars of 'Ich hab' im Traum geweinet' (Op. 48, no. 13) and opening bars
of 'Der schwere Abend' (Op. 90, no. 6)

Ex. 3   'Ich hab' im Traum geweinet' (Op. 48, no. 13), bb. 3–5

Ex. 4 (a) 'Ich hab' im Traum geweinet' (Op. 48, no. 13), bb. 26–27;
(b) and closing bars

The subliminal longing for the Other, the 'du' in the *Dichterliebe*-dream, continues in 'Der schwere Abend' as the same chords echo these same words at its beginning. Perhaps the last whisper of Heine's words through Schumann's hands, those closing two chords of 'Ich hab' im Traum geweinet', already echo the harmonically heightened and ritardando-lingering 'du *wärst*' as sung in b. 27, the vain hope for this Other to exist. It is this longing, as Romantic *Sehnsucht*, that carries over into the Lenau song (see Ex. 4).

Giving this last point some detailed thought, note that the vocal phrase on 'träumte, du wärst mir noch gut' (bb. 27–28) differs distinctly from the two parallel situations in the *Dichterliebe* song, where each time, the voice descends stepwise, on 'träumte, du lägest im Grab' (bb. 4–6), and on 'träumt', du verliessest mich' (bb. 15–17). In contrast to these first two instances (which, in practice, resemble a strophic treatment), the words 'wärst mir noch gut' (bb. 26–28) diverge from the pattern of stepwise descent. Instead, the voice moves upward on the pivotal word 'wärst', held back in tempo by the ritardando as well as underscored by the crescendo, reaching its peak at the moment of 'wärst'. The shift of tone that we observed in b. 22 onwards, as expressed by the piano's sudden change of diction, now happens in the voice.

Not only the topical chords of the opening of 'Der schwere Abend', but also the characteristic duplets of the voice take us back to *Dichterliebe*. Rhythmically so akin

Ex. 5   'Der schwere Abend' (Op. 90, no. 6), opening vocal line

Die   dunk - len Wol - ken hin -   gen

to the vocal opening of 'Ich hab' im Traum geweinet', the distinct 'Traum'-motive
is instantly present (Ex. 5).

Thus within the first few moments of 'Der schwere Abend', Schumann has provided a link to one of the most pregnant songs of *Dichterliebe*. By sheer likeness of
musical atmosphere (soft chords, E♭ minor, the motive, no voice), Schumann makes
us revisit the past.

On the whole, the formal outline of 'Der schwere Abend' is very similar to
'Ich hab' im Traum geweinet'. It is tri-partite in structure (part I: bb. 1–19; part II:
bb. 19–39; part III: bb. 40–59; postlude: bb. 60–67) and the $\frac{3}{4}$ time recasts the iambic
meter. The dynamics resemble those of the earlier song, although a sudden *forte* at its
end (bb. 60–67) trumps the earlier song in vigour and magnitude: the octaves in the
left hand descend into the lowest register of the keyboard, definite pitches become
indiscernible, creating – together with the full chords in the right hand – a density
of sound and sonority that is more of an abyss than we ever perceived in 'Ich hab
im Traum geweinet'. At the pivotal word 'Tod' (b. 59), right and left hands move
apart (bb. 59–65; as the dynamics rise (bb. 62–64)) while 'Tod' itself is sung and
accompanied *piano*. The song ends, like 'Ich hab' im Traum geweinet', *pianissimo*,
prolonged by a fermata, but this time fully resolved on an E♭ minor chord in root
position (Ex. 6).

The ending of 'Der schwere Abend' thus exhibits a more driven mood. An
impatience seems to animate this piece, perceptible in the unprepared occurrence
of the *sforzato*-outburst in bb. 8–9. It obviously derives from the equally unexpected
and sudden *sforzato* in bb. 32–33 of the *Dichterliebe* song. In 'Der schwere Abend'
however, this striking moment seems aggravated, permeating the song with this
alarming signal of disquiet from an earlier stage (Ex. 7).

Yet another aspect speaks for an 'intensified state of the mind' in the Lenau song
compared with 'Ich hab' im Traum geweinet'. I have already mentioned, with regard
to this song's sense of a Romantic *Sehnsucht* for someone to exist,[71] the marked
difference in musical setting of the word 'wärst' (b. 27). The following words 'noch
gut' (still kind), marking the Heinean shift of tone, have been set to a rising fourth.
This interval is transferred to the Lenau song (bb. 2–3) for 'Die dunklen' (the dark)
as well as expanded in bb. 6–7 into a rising sixth leap for a word indicating this
motion's very opposite, namely 'herab' (downward) (Ex. 8).

In comparison with the parallel moment in 'Ich hab' im Traum geweinet',
the determination with which Schumann further inverts what was once the
characteristic move of a fourth upwards on Heine's pivotal word 'gut' is truly

---

[71] See pp. 153–154, above.

Ex. 6 'Der schwere Abend' (Op. 90, no. 6), closing vocal line and postlude

remarkable. It appears in 'Der schwere Abend' at its beginning. The idea behind this transferred metaphor may derive from what Schumann perceived in Heine's text: a juxtaposition and opposition of word ('gut') and meaning (melancholy). In other words, whilst one essential characteristic of Heine's convoluted poetic style, namely the negation of literal meaning by way of contextual contrast – 'gut' within a consistently melancholic cast – is not part of Lenau's style, the content, or *core*, of these two poems is perceived by Schumann as similar. What lies beneath Heine's poem of 'Traum' and 'Tränen' is spelled out unambiguously by Lenau: melancholy.

Die *dunklen Wolken* hingen	The *dark clouds* hung
herab so *bang* und *schwer,*	so *oppressively* and *heavy*;
wir beide *traurig* gingen	we were walking *sadly*
im Garten hin und her.	in the garden together.
So heiß und *stumm,* so *trübe*	So sultry and *silent,* so *overcast*
und *sternlos war die Nacht,*	and *starless was the night,*
so ganz wie unsre Liebe	so like our love,
zu *Tränen* nur gemacht.	fit only for *tears.*

Ex. 7 (a) 'Ich hab' im Traum geweinet' (Op. 48, no. 13), bb. 32–33;
(b) 'Der schwere Abend' (Op. 90, no. 6), bb. 8–9; (c) 'Der schwere Abend'
(Op. 90, no. 6), bb. 28–29

Ex. 8 (a) 'Ich hab' im Traum geweinet' (Op. 48, no. 13), vocal line,
bb. 27–28; (b) 'Der schwere Abend' (Op. 90, no. 6), opening vocal line

(a)

träum - te, du wärst mir noch gut

(b)

Die dunk- len Wol -ken hin - gen her - ab so bang und schwer.

Und als ich mußte scheiden,	And when I had to go
und gute Nacht dir bot,	and bade you goodnight
wünscht' ich bekümmert beiden	I found it in my anguished heart
im Herzen uns den *Tod*.	to wish us both *dead*.[72]

Both of Schumann's settings reflect the late Romantic attitude of *Weltschmerz*,
latent in Heine but fully idiosyncratic in Lenau. The vocabulary of this particular poem by Lenau ('traurig', 'stumm', 'trübe', 'sternlos', 'Tränen', 'bekümmert',
'Tod')[73] exposes the reader to a thoroughly dark emotional cast, as the atmosphere
is literally 'overcast' by 'Dark clouds hung / oppressively and heavy' ('Die dunklen
Wolken hingen / herab so bang und schwer'). The state of dreams in the *Dichterliebe*
song becomes a 'starless night' ('sternlos war die Nacht') and its central motive of
tears recurs as 'just like our love / fit only for tears' ('so ganz wie unsre Liebe / zu
Tränen nur gemacht').

What motives prompted Schumann to cast a retrospective glance at *Dichterliebe* in
this way? In the first instance, his use of strikingly similar music for two different
poetic texts gives rise to the question of musical metaphor, an intricate aspect of
Schumann's musical language which I shall explore in more detail with regard to
another similarly metaphorical trait throughout *Dichterliebe*, the diminished-seventh
chord.[74] Ultimately, however, the idea of restating musical material in different
poetic contexts strikes one as a *critical* act on Schumann's part. The ways in which
Schumann echoes and then diverges from his earlier material indicates the nature of
his later reading of an earlier song and poem. But the urge to relive, by resuming as
well as revising, his musical material may also derive from the desire to appraise its
aesthetic success, for the later song seems to depend on everything that Schumann
achieved with the earlier – to remember it, just as its opening repeats the close of the
earlier song. Thus, 'Der schwere Abend' seems to continue, amplify and enhance

---

[72] Translation from Sams (1993), p. 255. The emphasis in both the German original and the translation is mine.
[73] 'sad', 'mute', 'cloudy/gloomy', 'starless', 'tears', 'worried', 'death'.   [74] See pp. 177–208, below.

the *Dichterliebe* song in the sense of Schumann's belief that 'The future must be the higher echo of the past'.[75]

Schumann's critical re-reading also reflects his 'poetic consciousness'. We might surmise that upon reading the Lenau poem, Schumann was reminded of the sentiment, the 'mood' or 'state of mind' Heine's poem had generated years earlier. In this way, Schumann links the two compositions, and almost involuntarily so, for he seemed to have been compelled to set the Lenau poem within the compositional terms of the Heine song. In perceiving the mood of the Lenau poem, Schumann instinctively knew the specific gestural direction in which to take the poem, and himself, musically. Thus, the two songs interact and reflect upon each other, but with the difference – an added gestural element – that through its postlude the Lenau poem/song spells out in harsher words the feeling of forlornness which was already immanent in the Heine poem/song.

In Heine's poem, the woman is indeed the poet's *imago*, an unconscious prototype, a lingering, yet effusive, at times maternal, presence which Schumann evokes and invokes through the voice: a calm and quiet (*leise*), almost static, lament of Heine's Holy Mother or the Romantics' Blue Flower. The piano, that is the poet's, thus Schumann's, genuine voice, 'speaks only sometimes, haltingly, like in a dream'.[76] It breaks through, however, and unites with the voice in a dramatic moment (bb. 29–33) as the drama reveals itself: despite the security encapsulated in the voice, unity will not and cannot happen. After the phantom of fullness (the voice) has seized not only our attention, but more importantly the poet's/piano's attention throughout the song, and to the point of comatose unconsciousness, its hollowness is suspected (the subjunctive of 'du wärst mir noch gut' has been pointed out). The belief and hope in unity is shattered, and the final awakening is an awakening into solitude. Its sign is a spasm of tears and a culmination of clusters (bb. 29–33).

With this deliberate arrangement of musical material, Schumann re-evaluates the emotional origins of a musical idea that was initially inspired (*angeregt*) by a Heine poem, and which he then transferred on to Lenau's words. In this respect, time and occasion raise a number of questions. Why did Schumann return to 'Ich hab' im Traum geweinet', part of his most profound work *Dichterliebe*, precisely at this point in time? One answer may be proposed: to quote from *Dichterliebe* with such faithfulness shows Schumann drawing *himself* back to a biographical context that was emotionally similar to the one he found himself in again in 1850. The circumstances in Leipzig had been exceptionally unstable. But the year 1840, when a long period of uncertainty concerning private and professional developments came to what seemed like a 'solution',[77] also meant a year of frantic production.

---

[75] *TB* I, p. 304 [Die Zukunft soll das höhere Echo der Vergangenheit sein].

[76] *TB* I, p. 44 [das Herz spricht nur manchmal wie gebrochen im Traume].

[77] Schumann speaks of 1839 as the 'Prüfungsjahr' (letter to Clara on 30 December 1839; see *Briefe einer Liebe*, p. 244): the acrimony between Schumann and Friedrich Wieck over Schumann's wish to marry Clara had come to a head in 1839 when Schumann referred the matter to the courts. It was legally resolved in August 1840.

His move into the security of marriage may have originated in Schumann's awareness of his own disintegrative tendencies, and feelings of anxiety that he had previously recognized: 'A fixed idea to go insane had seized me'.[78] Whilst he was seized – 'the much fixated Schumann'[79] – the urge to throw himself matched his very ability to do so in music. The fragmented body – 'intoxicated, distracted, and at the same time ardent' as Barthes senses[80] – was able to manifest itself, or momentarily construct itself, in producing fragmentary characters (Florestan, Eusebius and many others) and small forms: 'I am totally enthusiastic about all these characters whom I should now cast in music'[81] and 'you will be amazed at what I have accomplished during this time – *small* things for the piano'.[82] This process was partly impulsive:

I: everything comes just by itself. The human being has an abhorrence of intention. In general many ideas about the feeling of reflection; reflection of feeling; *consciousness of pleasure*; objectivity and the transition to subjectivity; self-observation, strokes of genius and the zest of nature freed; first life etc.[83]

Schumann was indeed able to assert himself by following the 'flow' and 'charm of imagination [*Fantasie*]',[84] the 'imagination which speaks more truthfully and freely when it derives from the midst of life'.[85] *Fantasieren* – to recall Barthes – is 'a pure *wandering*'.[86] Hence Schumann's fragments: a form that is 'even tangibly revealed at the organic level, in the lines of "fragilization" that define the anatomy of phantasy, as exhibited in the schizoid and spasmodic symptoms of hysteria'.[87]

The *Fantasie* of Schumann as a wanderer came to an end in 1840 with the beginning of a more structured, socially more secure, existence. It seems as if this spurred one last spell of genius, when Clara was away for most of the year and a few hundred songs emerged as if there were to be no second chance. Then followed years of attempts to systemize, coordinate and discipline what was once boundless energy, when Schumann tried to master the accepted Classical forms: first symphony,[88] then

---

[78] *TB* I (1833), p. 419 [Die fixe Idee wahnsinnig zu werden hatte mich gepakt].

[79] *TB* I (1829), p. 221 [– der viel fixierte Schumann –] as Schumann recounts (and keeps returning to throughout his diaries) in the midst of other reflections.

[80] Barthes (1985d), p. 300.

[81] *Briefe einer Liebe* (letter to Clara of May 1840), p. 276 [Ganz begeistert bin ich von allen den Gestalten, die ich nun in Musik gießen soll].

[82] *Briefe einer Liebe* (letter to Clara of February 1840), p. 251 [Du wirst Dich wundern, was ich alles gemacht habe – *kleine* Klaviersachen]. Emphasis original.

[83] *TB* I, p. 329 [Ich: nur Alles von selbst; der Mensch hat eine Abscheu vor der Absicht. Ueberhaupt viel Ideen über Empfindung der Reflexion, Reflexion der Empfindung, *Bewußtsein des Genußes*, Objectivität u. Uebergang zur Subjectivität, Selbstbelauschung, Geniusblitze u. Schwung der freien Natur, erstes Leben pp]. Emphasis original.

[84] *TB* I, p. 363 [Fluß und Reiz der Fantasie].

[85] *TB* I, p. 417 [Um wie viel reicher spricht die Fantasie, wenn sie mitten aus dem Leben kommt! . . . der Reiz der Fantasie].

[86] Barthes (1985b), p. 291. Emphasis original.

[87] Lacan (1966), p. 5. That my comments here are not meant as a clinical interpretation should be obvious.

[88] Within days of the wedding, Schumann began his first symphony. In December 1839, after listening to Schubert's Ninth Symphony in C major, he wrote to Clara: 'and such instrumentation despite Beethoven – and such length, such heavenly length like a novel in four volumes, longer than the ninth symphony. I was totally happy and wished

string quartet, symphony again, sonata form, and opera (and the occasional return to the small form). With this, Schumann left, in the full sense of the word, his medium, the piano. 'Fantasizing on the piano' was soliloquy in dialogue form – the voices of characters – but this kind of speaking was abandoned for the sake of larger forms. The productive fit of 1840 thus signals Schumann's sensing his last chance.

Let us make an essential distinction. 1840 was the year of songs, not of character fragments for the piano. The question here is one of a change of musical genre, and as such becomes a purely technical one. The human voice has been introduced into Schumann's fantasizing processes, a real voice of warmth and continuity which is so characteristic of Schumann's vocal melody. On a vertical level, the dialogical nature of Schumann's piano pieces (a series or ensemble of 'characters' or 'states of the soul') is maintained in the song collections and cycles. Horizontally, however, the musical texture becomes more complex with a new voice entering Schumann's phantasy: the voice of the Other as a source of solace with which the voice of the piano interacts. The human voice here means rather subjectified stability, while the piano remains 'authentic Schumann': affective, solitary, subtly or coarsely disruptive. Schumann comments. The Romantic scenario, the desire for the Other, is what can be observed here: 'The Eichendorff-cycle is probably my absolutely most Romantic and there is much of you in it' writes Schumann to Clara in May 1840. And indeed there was, given that, in 1840, Schumann lived in constant desire for her return.[89] The amazing thrust of the year of songs results from a sense of longing which Schumann could only counteract by a constant invocation of the beloved: 'Again I have composed so much that I sometimes have a feeling of great unease. Yet, I cannot do otherwise; I want to sing myself to death like a nightingale.'[90] In this sense, 1840 had to be the year of songs.[91]

As regards 1850, the Dresden years (1845–50) were, apart from the 1848 Revolution and Dresden's May uprising in 1849, marked by the Schumanns' isolation in a largely conservative environment. The cold reception of Schumann's opera *Genoveva* in the summer of 1850 prompted the decision to leave Dresden for Düsseldorf in the hope of a better artistic climate. The emphasis on melancholy in the Lenau settings seems to derive from a sense of loss that the years in Dresden had come to represent. Finally, as Schumann wrote Op. 90 in memory of one of his most highly valued poets, the song 'Der schwere Abend' links Lenau compositionally to Heinrich Heine, who had already, in 1838, appeared in connection with Lenau.

---

nothing more than that you were my wife and I too could write such symphonies' [und diese Instrumentation trotz Beethoven – und diese Länge, diese himmlische Länge wie ein einziger Roman in vier Bänden, länger als die neunte Sinfonie. Ich war ganz glücklich und wünschte nichts, als Du wärest meine Frau und ich könnte auch solche Sinfonien schreiben].

[89] See Schumann's letters to Clara during 1840 in *Briefe einer Liebe*, pp. 245–281.

[90] *Briefe einer Liebe* (letter to Clara, 15 May 1840) p. 277 [– – – Ich habe wieder so viel komponiert, daß mir's manchmal ganz unheimlich vorkommt. Ach, ich kann nicht anders, ich möcht mich totsingen wie eine Nachtigall].

[91] In addressing the undeniably intriguing question of the 'Liederjahr', Feldmann (1952) and Turchin (1981) in particular, as well as the biographical literature as a whole (see the Bibliography), have taken an altogether different approach to that proposed here.

Schumann read and excerpted epigraphs from both Lenau's and Heine's poems on the same day,[92] and had inserted their poems as epigraphs in the *NZfM*.[93] Thus, both Heine and Lenau were among the most important writers in Schumann's campaign for a 'new poetic age'. Lenau's death in 1850 coincided with what Schumann slowly came to realize: that his early aesthetic ambitions, so forcefully proclaimed in the 1830s, had not led to the kind of public acclaim he had perhaps envisioned for himself. Put sympathetically, Op. 90 carries the tone of nostalgia – is imbued with sounds of a better past which Schumann tried to re-evoke. Put drastically, the Lenau song demonstrates a sense of panic.

One more point must be made: musically, Schumann fixed twice on a particular 'poetic mood' and character. In this regard, it should be noted that, in comparison with all other poems in the *Lyrisches Intermezzo*, Heine's 'Ich hab' im Traum geweinet' is an exception. It exhibits an 'extraordinary state of the mind'. Schumann seems to have realized this. His setting, denying as it does a continuous flow of melody and harmonic support, seems less 'natural', or idiosyncratically 'song-like', than the other songs in *Dichterliebe*. He invested his powers of imagination in creating a song that, on some level, no longer belongs to the genre. Indeed, the lament characterizing this setting is so carefully worked out that it gives a sense of extreme artificiality.

In view of the similarity of these two songs, the term 'paraphrase' seems justified.[94] What has not been spelled out here – the obvious notion of 'intertextuality' – can now be seen in the light of Early Romantic theory: 'allusion' and 'evocation' is part of the concept of reflection, which emphasizes and ennobles subjectivity, and the centrality of the self. Because an original idea, or 'state of the soul', has been mirrored and transferred into a new context, inner discourse with this idea has been made infinite. Meaning within the *discours d'amour* of *Dichterliebe* is hence overlaid with meaning from the Lenau song, and the poetic present moves between these realms.

(II) *SEHNEN UND VERLANGEN* FULFILLED IN A ROMANTIC FRAGMENT

> . . . *das 'Sehnen' von Heine, für dessen tief wunden Schmerz die Musik noch ganz andere Zeichen besitzt, –*

> [. . . the 'Sehnen' of Heine, for whose deeply wounded pain music still possesses very different signs indeed, –].   Schumann in 1837 GS II, p. 140

If there is one song in *Dichterliebe* that epitomizes the idea of the Romantic fragment, then it is 'Im wunderschönen Monat Mai'. One aim of the following analysis is to show the ways in which Schumann realized the formal characteristics of the

---

[92] *TB* II, p. 78.   [93] *NZfM* 10 (1839).

[94] There are very few examples of Schumann returning to important song compositions in his later years. One example is 'Im Walde' (Op. 39/11), with its striking shift from fanfare-like optimism to unadorned lyricism on the last line 'Und mich schaudert's im Herzensgrunde', which was set for choir in 1849 (Op. 75).

fragment. Another aim is to clarify and elaborate further the theoretical concept of the Romantic fragment by way of introducing some viewpoints by the contemporary French writer Maurice Blanchot, who has offered succinct insights into the idea of the fragment as a modern form of writing and thinking.

This discussion of Song 1 as a fragment involves viewing the Romantic fragment from two different historical perspectives, whose focus, however, remains intra-theoretical. First, the discussion returns to those characteristics of the fragment as laid out in Part I on the basis of texts by Novalis and Friedrich Schlegel. As a name for an abstraction, and conceptually located at the centre of the Early Romantics' theory, the fragment may be said to elucidate that theory from the inside. In other words, if, as Benjamin claimed, 'the Romantic theory of the art work is the theory of its form',[95] then the fragment may indeed be seen to contain the essence of that theory. To what extent is this valid in the case of Schumann's 'Im wunderschönen Monat Mai'? The second perspective reflects on the fragment from a historical distance. The intention is not only to enhance and clarify the definition of the concept, but also to draw attention to the noteworthy fact that there are strong resonances of Early Romantic thought to be perceived in recent thinking. Such contemporary engagement with a past topos of thought is testimony to the viability of the Early Romantics' aesthetic across a historical field displaying major ideological deviations. Not only, however, does the Early Romantic conception of fragmentary writing challenge the Classical ideal of structurally balanced works, it also undermines the commonplace truth applied to Romantic works as structurally ambiguous, yet eventually composite – that is, as longing-and-achieving organisms. There is a caesura between the early and the later forms of Romanticism, and the line of continuity breaks off only to be taken up again in the later twentieth century. Although the focus of this enquiry is to show how these literary and philosophical explications pertain to music, and to the song 'Im wunderschönen Monat Mai' in particular, my attempt is not to reduce Schumann's song to a network of related themes and ideas. Rather the opposite: it is to test one core concept of Early Romantic literary theory against the famously open structures of a canonical piece of Romantic music.

Two musicological studies have taken up Romantic literary theory and the form of the Romantic fragment with the aim of expanding explicatory strategies towards nineteenth-century music.[96] Just as Daverio proposes to discuss as 'the fundamental form of literary Romanticism, the system of fragments' by asserting that 'music critic-ism need only accept the simple fact that the fragment, as constructive mode and artis-tic phenomenon, was fundamental to the whole Romantic worldview', so Rosen hopes 'to give an account of the place of [Romantic] music within two important lit-erary traditions', one of which is 'the fragment as an artistic form'.[97] The titles of these studies, *Nineteenth-century Music and the German Romantic Ideology* by Daverio and *The Romantic Generation* by Rosen, indicate the wide range of Romantic composers under consideration. Yet, both writers find the fragment concept to be most successfully applied in the case of Schumann, who is presented as the main exponent of the form.

---

[95] Benjamin (1973), p. 67.   [96] Daverio (1993) and Rosen (1995).
[97] Daverio (1993), pp. 15 and 53, and Rosen (1995), p. x.

3 *Im wunderschönen Monat Mai* Op. 48, no. 1

Dichterliebe

(Heine)

Im wunderschönen Monat Mai

Robert Schumann (1810-1856)
Opus 48
Herausgegeben von H. J. Köhler

3   (cont.)

Ex. 9 'Im wunderschönen Monat Mai' (Op. 48, no. 1), succession of harmonies

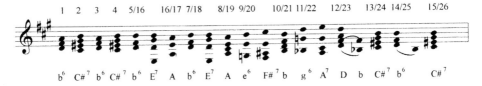

Methodologically, there is scope for adding further precision to the concept of the fragment.[98] Since Rosen's treatment of the subject is closely related to a discussion of the first song of *Dichterliebe*, which opens his extensive chapter entitled 'Fragments',[99] a few remarks may be offered here in order to achieve greater clarity of definition.

There are many invaluable observations throughout Rosen's analysis of what he enthusiastically calls 'a brilliant and famous example of the open form which was one of the ideals of the period'.[100] Whereas there can be little doubt that this song, due to its formal and harmonic peculiarity, is also the most frequently discussed in the critical literature on *Dichterliebe*,[101] Rosen's renewed interest in the light of his innovative theoretical aim is justified and indeed to be welcomed.

In order to follow the analytical discussion more easily, Example 9 simply states the underlying harmonies as they occur in Song 1, without suggesting their functions in relation to each other.

Rosen's central thesis about Song 1 – 'it is a perfect Romantic fragment'[102] – rests on two main observations. First, he notes that 'the [piano] introduction returns not only before the second stanza but at the end as well'. Second, he observes that the song 'ends unresolved on a dissonance'. He then claims that this 'last chord . . . is the dominant seventh of F♯ minor'.[103] Based on his first two observations, and explaining that 'the dominant-seventh chord is only the apparent close of a form that has no end, of a *da capo senza fine*', Rosen suggests that 'the form is circular'. Although affirming that the song's tonic is F♯ minor, Rosen qualifies his interpretation by remarking that whilst 'insisting upon the implicit resolution', he does 'not want to minimize the magical effect of the final chord which suspends motion without completing it'. Finally he concludes that 'the form is closed on itself, although open in all imaginable realizations'.[104]

---

[98] In order specifically to elucidate 'Schumann and the System of Musical Fragments', Daverio suggests 'five categories' – 'quotation (both literal and figurative)', '*Kater Murr* technique', '*Selbstvernichtung* as an ordering principle', '[Schumann's] refiguring of Jean-Paulian *Humor*', and 'Schlegel's *Witz*' – 'to provide us with a point of entry into the workings of the musical fragment system'. See Daverio (1993), pp. 58–86 (here 58–59).

[99] Rosen (1995), pp. 41–115.   [100] Rosen (1995), p. 41.

[101] See Benary (1967), pp. 21–29; Komar (1971), pp. 66–70; Neumeyer (1982), pp. 94–105; Agawu (1984), pp. 167–170; Pousseur (1993), pp. 12–19.

[102] Rosen (1995), p. 48.

[103] Rosen (1995), p. 41. Both Neumeyer (1982, p. 95) and Agawu (1984, p. 168) agree on the dominant function of the C♯[7] chord.

[104] Rosen (1995), p. 44.

Unlike Komar, whose attitude ('I shall assume A major as tonic') has the undeniable advantage of allowing for the discovery of a 'large-scale harmonic progression of Song 1, A–D–C♯', which then leads to his construction of a 'typical *Ursatz* in A major',[105] and unlike Pousseur, whose preference for F♯ as the tonic results from retrospectively identifying a iv⁶ – V⁷ progression in F♯ in bb. 1–2 whose resolution to F♯ never actually materializes,[106] Rosen does not engage further in the 'largely misguided... controversy about the real key of the song'. He claims 'it should also be obvious that the contrast of F♯ minor and A major is only a surface opposition'. Once he continues, however, that 'Schumann treats the relative minor here and elsewhere as a variant form of the tonic, using it rather for a change of mode and not of tonality',[107] the rationale underlying Rosen's stance becomes clear. He is thinking of the sonata form from 1810 onwards and, more specifically perhaps, the finale of Schumann's F♯ minor Sonata Op. 11. There indeed, as Rosen has convincingly shown elsewhere, Schumann established a tonally ambiguous situation by replacing the Classical sonata form model of tonal hierarchy with an F♯ minor – A major equivalence.[108] With the teleological structure of the sonata firmly in mind, Rosen concludes that 'without for a moment challenging the system of tonality, Schumann here stands basic tonal structure on its head', for Schumann's song 'starts with a traditionally unstable chord, moves to a point of rest, a stable cadence [A major], and returns to the unstable chord *as its goal*'.[109] Hence, the dominant seventh of F♯ minor 'becomes the stable pivot around which everything turns'.[110] These conditions, a 'pivot' or focal point, and 'that the return be identical with the opening so that the form is infinitely repeatable' are, as Rosen states, 'crucial for the conception'. As we shall see, these conditions are integral to Rosen's theoretical understanding of the Romantic fragment in the light of the sonata-allegro form.

But considering once more the tonal events of Song 1 as they present themselves (see Ex. 9 above), there is indeed reason to engage with the question of the 'real key', or rather with what it may mean to be in a key at all. The first arpeggio – apart from what Pousseur pertinently calls a 'literally Webernian moment' with the C♯/D constellation that opens the piece[111] – cannot truly be burdened with any functionality as it stands. Here, the argument for F♯ minor only holds if one accepts the retrospective interpretation of the first arpeggio (b. 1) as IV⁶ in the light of the arpeggio in b. 2 on C♯ as V⁷ (with E♯ as 3 and B as 7), and if one further accepts that the positive absence of an F♯ chord throughout the song does not challenge its absolute status as tonic. The argument for A major works best if we look ahead to Song 2 where the A-major opening chord appears to resolve the tension of C♯⁷ at the end of Song 1 via reference to its sections in A major (bb. 5–8 and 16–19). That Schenker's graph of Song 1 should have remained incomplete after b. 8

---

[105] Komar (1971), pp. 67–69.   [106] Pousseur (1993), p. 13.

[107] Rosen (1995), p. 47.   [108] Rosen (1988), pp. 369–388.

[109] Rosen (1995), pp. 47–48. My emphasis.   [110] Rosen (1995), p. 47.

[111] Pousseur (1993), p. 12. Although this is a fitting way of describing the opening events of Song 1, Pousseur is contentious in his proposing that *Dichterliebe* constitutes a proto-serial work. See my summarizing account of Pousseur's approach on pp. 115–116.

(whilst nonetheless defining A as the fundamental tonal reference) indicates, however, how much such analysis relies on the idea of prolongation, and how difficult, indeed impossible, matters become when trying to view Song 1 in its own right.[112] But even the harmonically more defined vocal passage, clearly cadencing in A (bb. 6 and 8), does not achieve tonal authority. It is introduced in the place of an expected F♯ with b. 5^1 being reinterpreted as a ii of A.[113] This procedure not only destabilizes the F♯ tonality assumed to be underlying the previous four bars; it also projects how A major will undergo destabilization itself, indeed twice in succession: again via reinterpretation, bb. 9–10 and 11–12 move first to B minor and then to D major. Thus, A major is never unequivocally affirmed.

Such formation of only momentary tonal centres as a result of a continuous process of 'reinterpretation' is precisely what denies 'Im wunderschönen Monat Mai' the opportunity to be grounded in any one tonality. Instead, the song briefly establishes three tonal areas – A major, B minor and D major – and even those attain only cursory stability, as we have seen. Furthermore, even if we do recognize F♯ as a suspended reality, the apparent shift from F♯ minor to A major may, together with the corresponding shift of B minor to D major (bb. 10–12), be an allusion to a cyclic pattern that could in principle be prolonged (e.g., E minor to G major; A minor to C major etc.). Yet there is no reason to think of the song's opening phrase as the logically necessary first phrase in such a series of fourths. In this sense, Song 1 is not constructed around a centre. It has no tonal ground. Instead, the very absence of tonal definition constitutes an ever-present gap within the song.

This sonorous 'gap' remains a constant – a silent exaggeration of the poem's theme. For 'Sehnen und Verlangen' is all that concerns Heine's poem, a poem that, in its simplicity and imagery, draws on a medieval prototype.[114]

---

[112] Schenker (1979), Figure 110c. Schenker's graph is part of a section about incomplete manifestations of the *Ursatz*. See also his analysis of Chopin's Op. 28, no. 2 in the same context. Hence, the early harmonic events in the first song of *Dichterliebe* are interpreted retrospectively in the light of the two A-major cadences in bb. 5–8. Cf. here Neumeyer (1982), pp. 103–104: 'Even if the harmonic-contrapuntal structure is only a middle-ground feature in the song pair, bias towards one key orientation – f♯ or A – must still enter. I have favored f♯ somewhat (through its dominant, of course), because I find that treating the tonal emphasis of the piano prelude and postlude frame as more significant than the internal move to A is more satisfying than the reverse, which would make the close simply gratuitous – or worse, not just 'open', but inexplicable. Still, if obliged to do so, I would think of the first song, taken by itself, as both f♯ and A – an indefinite harmonic relation of the third.' As Neumeyer explains on p. 104, n. 28, the argument is, as in Rosen, the mingling of parallel major and minor modes by nineteenth-century composers, as well as the mingling of 'relative modes, as Schumann has done here'. Since Neumeyer intends to demonstrate that the first two *Dichterliebe* songs are a '1/2 song pair' (p. 94, n. 13), he adds in parenthesis: 'It has, however, been the argument here that the first song should not be taken by itself'. In contrast to the unanimous view that Songs 1 and 2 form a unity, Schumann's letter to the publishers Breitkopf & Härtel on 6 August 1843 implies, however, the autonomy of each song: 'It is a cycle of 20 songs, which form a whole, but each of which is also self-contained' [Es ist ein Zyklus von 20 Liedern, die ein Ganzes, aber auch einzeln für sich ein Abgeschlossenes bilden]. See the full quotation of this letter and discussion on pp. 117–120.

[113] Rosen (1995, p. 47) admits that 'the A major that enters with Heine's poetry is, in fact, a surprise'. Yet, he continues 'line 3 of the stanza immediately initiates a turning back towards F♯ minor, a movement that is never completed'.

[114] See Grappin's detailed commentary (*DHA* I/2, pp. 773–775) regarding the 'tradition of folk-literary analogy' within which Heine's 'Im wunderschönen Monat Mai' is located.

Im wunderschönen Monat Mai,	In the lovely month of May,
Als alle Knospen sprangen,	When all the buds were bursting,
Da ist in meinem Herzen	Then in my heart
Die Liebe aufgegangen.	love broke forth.
Im wunderschönen Monat Mai,	In the lovely month of May,
Als alle Vögel sangen,	When all birds were singing,
Da hab' ich ihr gestanden	Then I confessed to her
Mein Sehnen und Verlangen.	My longing and desire.

Such invocation of the eternal topos of the month of May as love's beginning, complete with flowers and singing birds, serves well at the outset of the *Lyrisches Intermezzo*. Almost ostentatious in its archetypical representation and unassuming naiveté, it is that hymn which Heine hums, subliminally, throughout the cycle – and whose implosion into death and pain reaches its height in 'Die alten, bösen Lieder'. 'Im wunderschönen Monat Mai' thus conjures up *the* Romantic dream, a paradisia-cal situation distant in time and place, with 'Sehnen' named as Romanticism's ruling sentiment. And in this, the poem is unproblematic. Heine's optimistic, indeed trust-ing, tone – deceptively – inaugurates a lyrical cycle whose traumatic images are yet to come. Hence, there is nowhere a dramatic reversal (*Stimmungsbruch*) in these first few lines,[115] and nothing, neither 'Liebe' nor 'Sehnen und Verlangen', can be truly second-guessed. In a deliberately formulaic way, Heine simply names the Romantic state of affairs. That 'Sehnen und Verlangen' may also be an ongoing affair, structured like a gap or lack, is nonetheless semantically explicit.

Apart from its lack of a tonal centre, Song 1 also shows a gap in continuity. Pousseur's observation of a one-bar elision (*suppression*) each time the piano part recurs (bb. 12 and 23) is particularly valuable. Having shown the induced acceleration of the harmonic rhythm for A major in b. 6, Pousseur recognizes bb. 11–12 as being modelled on this earlier chordal sequence (V^7–I) in bb. 5–6. It results in the elision in b. 12, where D major directly moves into B minor, leading back to the arpeggio in b. 2.[116] Ultimately this means, however, that, just as a grounding of A major has previously been interrupted by tonal reinterpretation, the possible continuation of a pattern briefly naming yet further tonal areas is interrupted. Since the song ends at this moment on C$\sharp^7$, however, this end does not represent a 'goal'.[117] It is the opening for a potential continuation in any tonal direction, and indeterminably so.[118]

The song's structure is thus self-involved. It does not await a solution from outside and 'Schluß' (end) is indeed what Schumann added in the vocal sketch above the

---

[115] Cf. Agawu (1984) whose general concern for Heine's *Stimmungsbruch*, occurring 'typically at the end of a poem', leads in the case of 'Im wunderschönen Monat Mai' to a somewhat over-taxed interpretation: 'there is a reversal occurring at the end of the second quatrain with the introduction of a disturbing and highly implicative sentiment in the two words "Sehnen" and "Verlangen". We now know that all is not well in this "lovely month of May". The buds may be bursting forth, and the birds may be singing, but for the protagonist there is a growing sense of longing and desire.' See Agawu (1984), pp. 160 and 167.

[116] Pousseur (1993), pp. 15–17.   [117] Rosen (1995), p. 48.

[118] Komar (1971, p. 77), with his organicist perspective standing in contrast to my argument, suggests that 'the overall form of *Dichterliebe* can be viewed as an outgrowth of the initial tonal events in the cycle'.

final C♯^{7} arpeggio, before the fermata.[119] This inscription may refer to two things at
once. On the one hand, it confirms what from a Classical viewpoint the score seems
to deny – that the song truly ends here, on an unresolved C♯^{7} (see Ex. 10). In this
sense, Song 1 is 'self-contained' as Schumann indicated, by implication, in his letter
to the publisher Breitkopf & Härtel in August 1843.[120] On the other hand, it may
refer to the cycle's last song, whose postlude notoriously shifts to an abrupt D♭ major.
Originally, Schumann wrote out this postlude, like the song proper, in C♯ minor.
But the remark he made in the margin of the sketch reads like an afterthought
at the sight of the last chord's bearing such a resemblance to the first song's final
chord. To himself he suggests: '? NB: Here it is better to put accidentals for D♭
major'.[121]

    This, of course, reopens the question of cyclicity in *Dichterliebe*, to which more
consideration will be given in my fourth analytical section, on the last postlude.[122]

    So far, one notes that Song 1 refrains from elaborating on its tonal origin, since
its brief tonal moments elude the fixture of stable functions. This is why the song
that follows is of so little concern for Song 1. Instead, the instant and unambiguous
statement of A major in Song 2, repeatedly confirmed by the cadencing figure in
the piano, together with a fairly dense, certainly not arpeggiated, chordal texture
and the perfect alignment of voice and piano for the greater part of that song, marks
it as different. It sets it off from 'Im wunderschönen Monat Mai'. Indeed, the final
arpeggio of Song 1 (a changed version of its model in bb. 2, 4, 13, 14 and 15) lacks
a connecting tone since E♯^{2} is not cancelled by the A-major chord at the beginning
of Song 2. This makes the pause between the two songs all the more important,
because Song 1 does not anticipate an A-major resolution, but remains revolving
around an esoteric centre. And even if one were to view the solo piano sections
as having an F♯ tonal centre, and the sections for piano and voice as being in A,
there is still no tonal framework within the song which would suggest that these
keys are related 'variant forms' of a single tonic.[123] Song 1 thus bears within itself

---

[119] Hallmark (1979), pp. 34–35.   [120] See above, note 181.

[121] Quoted in Hallmark (1979, p. 110) whose translation of '?NB: Hier ist besser Des Dur vorzuzeichnen' as
    '? NB: D♭ major is preferable here' does not make clear that a visual effect of different notation is at issue here.

[122] See pp. 208–221, below.

[123] On the basis of this and his assertion that Song 2 'has even less of a beginning or an end than the first song',
    Rosen (1995, pp. 51–55) eventually turns to the concept of 'performance' in order to further advance his
    Classicist idea that the Romantic fragment ought to attain completion through adjacent entities. However,
    what his interpretation brings to light are, on the contrary, precisely those characteristics that indeed distinguish
    at least Song 1 as a Romantic fragment. Songs 1 and 2 are called 'puzzling and even inexplicable' if not seen as a
    whole. Song 2, Rosen explains, 'is complete and perfectly shaped, but without a satisfactory beginning or end.
    Its opening makes independent sense on paper, but in performance it seems above all to prolong the first song,
    'Im wunderschönen Monat Mai' – not merely to complement it, and fit with it the way the Adagio of a sonata or
    symphony is related to the opening movement. The harmonic sense of the first bar of the second song depends
    absolutely on the previous song. ... "Aus meinen Tränen", like "Im wunderschönen Monat Mai", is both an
    independent form and nonsense if executed on its own – not merely poorer in meaning and disappointing in
    effect, but puzzling and even inexplicable.' Here again, attention should be drawn to Schumann's letter of 1843
    stating that *Dichterliebe* is 'a cycle of 20 songs, which form a whole, but each of which is also self-contained'.
    See n. 181, above.

Ex. 10 'Im wunderschönen Monat Mai' (Op. 48, no. 1), last bar; 'Die alten, bösen
Lieder' (Op. 48, no. 16), last bar of the manuscript version as transcribed by Hallmark
(1979, p. 111); and last bar of the published version

'that which is yet to be revealed'.[124] Anticipation is the general gesture by which
Song 1 is characterized, the defining gesture of a piece that reaches out ever further
beyond itself. In this sense, Song 1 is not connected to Song 2, and thus does not
support a totalizing argument. It nonetheless is part of a new kind of totality in its
negative contribution to, or opposition to, the adjacent song, as well as those to
come.

Tonally, Song 1 does not obey what Novalis called *One Principle*,[125] but is part
of a constellation of individual positions within the fragment world of *Dichterliebe*.
Blanchot's description of the nature of fragmentary writing captures well the atmosphere of 'Im wunderschönen Monat Mai':

The sheer suspense which without restraint breaks the seal of unity by, precisely, not breaking
it, but by leaving it aside without this abandon's ever being able to be known. It is thus,
inasmuch as it separates itself from the manifest, that fragmentary writing does not belong to

---

[124] Novalis as quoted in Frank (1989), p. 278.
[125] NO II, p. 269, no. 566. See the complete quotation on p. 4.

the One. And thus, again, it denounces thought as experience (in whatever sense this word be taken), no less than thought as the realization of the whole.[126]

Song 1 is Blanchot's 'sheer suspense' – even on a local scale, for suspensions and appoggiaturas amount to the very signature of the song.[127] But it is the overall poetic process of the song that is able to 'break the seal of unity by . . . leaving it aside without this abandon's ever being able to be known', for there exists no frame of reference which would so much as give the song directives and lead it to a tonal centre and primary origin. Only through its very withdrawal does a centre make itself felt, but it remains undefined, and hence unknown. Because of this lack of reason and objective, Song 1 is an inscription of 'Sehnen und Verlangen' in structural terms.

And the significance Schumann ascribed to the concept of 'Sehnen' is inserted into a poetic process of motivic intensification. Exposed by the piano (b. 1), then transferred to the voice (b. 5), the C♯ – B motive also leads us to see that the piano and the voice each follow different concerns. Whilst they both share the lack of tonal definition, there is still the piano's tendency to cadential incompletion versus the voice's tendency to cadential completion. This, however, does not simply underscore an A-major primacy. It rather compels one to recognize a field of tonal values that includes both B minor and D major. For the voice moves on to these two regions (bb. 9–12), where they are anchored in a cadential progression that is as clear as the earlier progression for A major in bb. 5–8 (IV–V–I). Hence, on a first level of differentiation, the vocal part is harmonically more fixed than the purely instrumental part. On a second level, the motive C♯ – B then further emphasizes the song's musico–poetic dynamics. As shown in Example 11, this process involves moving from the absence of words (*a*), to stating the poem's topical lines (*b*), to elaborating on the poem's emotive words through chromatic intensification (*c*).

Although Rosen champions an altogether different cause, his detailed analysis of the piano and the voice forming an 'unbroken line', due to the continuous development of a single motive, leads him to make a fine observation. At the moment when the sung G♮ prepares a G♯ clash with the piano after 'aufgegangen' and 'Verlangen' (bb. 12 and 23), 'we might consider the voice and piano to have split apart' although 'the melodic line remains essentially unbroken'.[128] This is indeed so, but it shows once more how much weight is being attributed in this passage to B minor and D major. It leads up to emotional intensification and culminates in the 'dramatic moment' of splitting within the song. It is, however, arguable whether the song should be considered as 'infinitely repeatable' like 'an emblem . . . of

[126] Blanchot (1995), p. 61.
[127] According to Hallmark (1979, p. 35) Schumann enhanced the conception of suspending resolution, for 'the opening C sharp is not the only suspension/appoggiatura missing in the earlier version of this song, which in its final state is full of them'.
[128] Rosen (1995), pp. 45–46.

Ex. 11   (a) 'Im wunderschönen Monat Mai' (Op. 48, no. 1),
motive in bb. 1–2 and 3–4 as well as in 14–15 and 25–26; (b) motive
in bb. 4–6 as well as 15–17; (c) motive in bb. 9²–12 as well as 20²–23

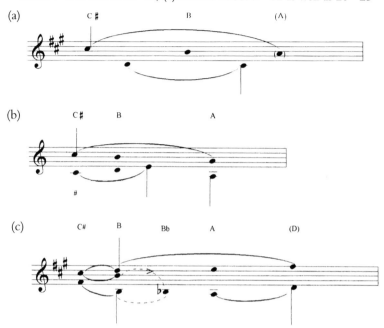

longing eternally renewed',[129] for the final C♯⁷ arpeggio following the second split
on 'Verlangen' makes this impossible. It is a modified version of the introductory
one in b. 2 and adds only the B in the bass compared with b. 1. This subtle but
indicative procedure thus denies (as had happened earlier in bb. 12–14) the song
a return to its beginning. 'Sehnen und Verlangen' does not go around in circles,
returning to where it started, for it is not 'self-centred', nor is it focused. It is
only fulfilled by leaning forwards, endlessly, into the unknown. *Longing-without-
achieving*.

Let us note then that Rosen's preference for an A major/F♯ minor focus, and its
C♯⁷ distraction, remains within the Classical orbit. The teleological model has simply
been inverted through replacing the conventional sonata procedure of 'stability–
instability–stability' with one representing 'instability–stability–instability'. The key
of A major is, however, not to be experienced as a point of stability because of
the patterning process explained above, and because of its rather hastened cadential
progression. This constitutes an obstacle even to the inverse teleological model that
Rosen proposes.

Yet the argument may well be made that the key signature must imply a tonal
centre of either F♯ minor or A major, or even both (see Neumeyer and Rosen).
Here, it needs to be emphasized once more that neither of these tonal fields is clearly

[129] Rosen (1995), pp. 48 and 41.

defined in the execution of the composition. Hence, although Schumann supplies a key signature in accordance with the conventions of the time, he is nonetheless working at the margins of these conventions.[130]

Although it is clear that the motivating force behind Rosen's argument is a search for unity, it may be useful to follow Rosen's commentary further in order to identify the sources of his views, noted above, about the form of the Romantic fragment. Initially, he correctly relates the historical context of the fragment as having 'come into being with the Early Romantic movement in Germany' and with Friedrich Schlegel as its originator.[131] Yet his principal example, taken from the *Athenaeum*, turns out to be a somewhat unhappy choice. As one can see from Rosen's comment, it serves his organicist orientation:

> A fragment should be like a little work of art, complete in itself and separated from the rest of the universe like a hedgehog.[132]

> The hedgehog (unlike the porcupine, which shoots its quills) is an amiable creature which rolls itself into a ball when alarmed. Its form is well defined and yet blurred at the edges. This spherical shape, organic and ideally geometrical, suited Romantic thought: above all, the image projects beyond itself in a provocative way. The Romantic Fragment draws blood only from those critics who handle it unthinkingly. Like its definition, the Romantic Fragment is complete (this oxymoron was intended to disturb, as the hedgehog's quills make its enemies uncomfortable): separate from the rest of the universe, the Fragment nevertheless suggests distant perspectives. Its separation, indeed, is aggressive: it projects into the universe precisely by the way it cuts itself off.[133]

One can invoke Blanchot to give an alternative to Rosen's perspective on this same *Athenaeum* fragment. Since Blanchot so brilliantly rectifies the Early Romantic position vis-à-vis Friedrich Schlegel's infamous hedgehog-fragment, his commentary is worth quoting in full:

> In truth, and particularly in the case of Fr. Schlegel, the fragment often appears a means for complacently giving oneself over to oneself rather than an attempt to develop a more rigorous mode of writing. To write fragmentarily then simply means to accept one's own disorder, to close up upon one's own self in satisfied isolation, and to thereby refuse the opening which the fragmentary exigency represents; this exigency does not exclude, but goes beyond totality. When, with great frankness, he writes: '*I can give for my personality no other pattern than that of a system of fragments, because I myself am something of this genre; no style is as natural to me and as easy as the fragmentary one*', he announces that his discourse will not be a dis-course, but the reflection of his own discordance. Likewise when he notes: 'A fragment must be

---

[130] This issue of the status of key signatures became more acute in the later half of the nineteenth century and most strikingly so in early twentieth-century Second Viennese music. See Ayrey (1982), pp. 192 and 201, n. 15.

[131] Rosen (1995), p. 48.

[132] *Athenaeum*, p. 137 [Ein Fragment muß gleich einem kleinen Kunstwerke von der umgebenden Welt ganz abgesondert und in sich selbst vollendet sein wie ein Igel]. The translation given above follows Rosen since it is part of the whole passage as quoted, which, however, differs insignificantly from the translation offered below in the context of Blanchot's commentary on this same *Athenaeum* fragment.

[133] Rosen (1995), pp. 48–49.

like a little work of art, entirely separated from the world surrounding it, and complete in itself like a hedgehog', he leads the fragment back to the aphorism, that is to say, back to the closure of a perfect sentence. This is perhaps an inevitable distortion, leading to: (1) viewing the fragment as a concentrated text that has its centre within itself and not in the surrounding field which it [the fragment] constitutes together with the *other* fragments; (2) neglecting the interval (anticipation and pause) that separates the fragments and makes of this separation the rhythmic principle of the work's structure; (3) forgetting that this manner of writing does not tend to make an overview of the whole more difficult or the relations of unity more lax, but rather to render possible new relations which exclude themselves from unity, as they exceed the whole. Naturally, this 'omission' is not to be explained by the simple failings of personalities that are too subjective or too impatient for the absolute. It is also, and more decisively, to be explained (at least in the original sense of this verb) by the orientation of history, which, become revolutionary, places at the forefront of its action the work in the view towards the whole, and the dialectical search for unity.[134]

As Blanchot retraces the misconceptions emanating from the hedgehog-fragment to the 'aphorism', 'closure of a perfect sentence' and the 'concentrated text', Rosen thrives on the 'well defined', 'organic', 'ideally geometrical' and 'complete'. Diverging from the accepted notion of the fragment system, Rosen now presents the fragment as the fitting part of a jigsaw, 'blurred at the edges' and thereby complementary. Rosen's engagement with Early Romantic literary theory through isolating this one *Athenaeum* fragment, as well as taking note of Friedrich Schlegel's fascination with the French maxim,[135] leads him to extend his remarks in some conceptually less accurate ways:

The literary form is generally aphoristic, and derives ultimately from the French maxims of the seventeenth century, perfected by La Rochefoucauld and La Bruyère. The most direct source, however, was the late eighteenth-century polemicist Chamfort, whose *Maxims and Characters* showed that the form could be given a more provocative and cynical twist. . . . The classical aphorism not only expressed its thought with precision; it also narrowed the sense of the words, focused on their meaning. La Rochefoucauld was a master in this kind of focus.[136]

Rosen's association of the Romantic fragment with the aphorism and the concept of the maxim as developed in seventeenth-century France is symptomatic of a wish to construct an unbroken line of continuity between earlier and later literary forms of expression. It also assumes a kind of ideological continuity in which progress is merely a question of degree, and not one of principle. But the differential that separates the fragment from the maxim, or from the aphorism for that matter, is precisely that the Classical focus (the Absolute) has drifted out of view. As one of several segments in an ensemble of fragments, the ensemble's anticipated centre still lies outside itself. As 'part of an extensive series',[137] a 'series of thoughts',[138] the fragment neither is, nor contributes to, a Master thought. The fragment is neither a 'closed sentence', nor does it, together with all other fragments, form a syntagmatic

---

[134] Blanchot (1969), p. 527. Emphases original.   [135] Cf. Behler (1993), pp. 150–153.
[136] Rosen (1995), pp. 48–49.   [137] *KFSA* I, p. 472 [Glied einer großen Reihe].
[138] *Athenaeum*, p. 199 [Ideenreihe].

whole. Rosen's analogy with the aphorism and maxim does not help to elucidate the matter – except by antiphrasis: the aphorism as a concise statement of principle, and the maxim as an axiomatic statement, 'a conclusion upon observation of matters of fact',[139] are both alien to the concept of the Romantic fragment.

Rosen's discussion eventually becomes unfocused. His view that with the fragment-turned-maxim 'we move toward a kernel of meaning: the force is centripetal' or that 'the direction is centrifugal', as well as his argument that 'the Romantic Fragment, imperfect and yet complete, was typical of the age in its effort to have its cake and eat it too'[140] are somewhat puzzling. Real inconsistency, however, begins to assert itself once we learn that 'this expansive movement [of the maxim] attains its greatest power with the Romantic Fragment, *and it entailed a renunciation of classical focus*'.[141]

It is perhaps not surprising that Rosen's case proves hard for him to sustain with complete consistency, and he faces considerable difficulty in accommodating all these conflicting conceptions to Schumann's song. For example, he seems to undermine his own Classical premises by invoking the more adequate concept of tonal oscillation: 'The structure is finished in conception, although both beginning and end are open in sound. The closure is defined not by the points of rest [A major] but by a *potentially infinite oscillation*.'[142] And as if paraphrasing a fairly accurate description of the Romantic fragment, Rosen finally suggests:

The Romantic Fragment is, therefore, a closed structure, but its closure is a formality: it may be separated from the rest of the universe, but it implies the existence of what is outside itself not by reference but by its instability. The form is not fixed but is torn apart or exploded by paradox, by ambiguity, just as the opening song of *Dichterliebe* is a closed, circular form in which beginning and end are unstable – implying a past before the song begins and a future after its final chord.[143]

The thought that there may be a beginning prior to the first song proper in *Dichterliebe* is an inspiring one. It echoes Novalis, who meditates:

Every real beginning is a *2nd moment*. Everything that is there, that appears, is and appears only under *one precondition* – its individual root, its *absolute Self* precedes it – must at least be thought *before* it. I must, for *everything*, pre-meditate [something] absolute set before it – pre-posit – perhaps *post-meditate, post-posit* as well?[144]

With greatest emphasis on the kind of systematic tonal deterritorialization characterizing 'Im wunderschönen Monat Mai', the song may well be seen as a '2nd moment'. In this sense, it would follow something that pre-exists, something prior the 'real' beginning of *Dichterliebe*. And such a Song no. 0 would then perhaps

---

[139] Coleridge's definition of the maxim as provided in the *OED*.

[140] Rosen (1995), pp. 49–50.   [141] Rosen (1995), pp. 49–50. My emphasis.

[142] Rosen (1995), p. 48. My emphasis.   [143] Rosen (1995), p. 51.

[144] Novalis as quoted in Frank, p. 274 [Aller wirckliche Anfang ist ein *2ter Moment*. Alles was da ist, erscheint, ist und erscheint nur unter *einer Voraussetzung* – Sein individueller Grund, sein *absolutes Selbst* geht ihm voraus – muß wenigstens *vor* ihm gedacht werden. Ich muß *allem* etwas absolutes *Voraus*denken – voraussetzen – Nicht auch *Nach*denken, *Nachsetzen?*]. Emphasis original.

have an *absolute* centre, would represent the *total tonic*; but then again, it probably wouldn't, for the 'series of thoughts' would rather regress infinitely, to Song no. − 1, Song no. − 2 etc. − never finding its real beginning. 'Fragmentary writing is risk' as Blanchot says, 'risk itself. . . . Thus, if it claims that its time comes only when the whole − at least ideally − is realized, this is because that time is never sure, but is the absence of time, absence in a nonnegative sense, time anterior to all past-tense, as well as posterior to every possibility yet to come.'[145]

And Blanchot writes further:

Fragments are written as unfinished separations. Their incompletion, their insufficiency, the disappointment at work in them, is their aimless drift, the indication that, neither unifiable nor consistent, they accommodate a certain array of marks − the marks with which thought (in decline and declining itself) represents the furtive groupings that fictively open and close the absence of totality. Not that thought ever stops, definitively fascinated, at the absence; always it is carried on, by the watch, the ever-uninterrupted wake. Whence the impossibility of saying there is an interval. For fragments, destined partly to the blank that separates them, find in this gap not what ends them, but what prolongs them, or what makes them await their prolongation − what has already prolonged them, causing them to persist on account of their incompletion.[146]

'Aimless drift' and 'ever-uninterrupted wake' − this is the sort of gesture compositionally realized through the 'incompletion' of 'Im wunderschönen Monat Mai' in order to capture the movements of a Romantic hero's 'Sehnen und Verlangen', as if to follow Novalis' recommendation: 'If the character of a given problem is that of indissolubility, then we solve it if we represent its indissolubility'.[147]

As a matter of common sense, Song 1 *is*, of course, Song 1. However, to quote *King Lear*, 'nothing can come of nothing'.[148] The very existence of Song 1 presupposes an artistic matrix prior to its own existence, and out of which it has arisen.

(III) ROMANTIC REFLECTION ON A TONAL METAPHOR FOR THE AMOROUS: THE DIMINISHED-SEVENTH CHORD IN *DICHTERLIEBE*

Und was ist denn unser Leben auch weiter als ein zweifelvoller septimenaccord, der nur unerfüllte Wünsche u. ungestillte Hoffnungen in sich führt.

[And what more is our life than a seventh-chord full of doubts which contains nothing but unfulfilled desires and unsatisfied hopes].   Schumann in 1828 *TB* I, p. 138

The semiological aspect of the Early Romantics' theory lies within their central thesis to 'represent the Unrepresentable'.[149] They thus abandoned an absolutist position

---

[145] Blanchot (1995), p. 60.   [146] Blanchot (1995), p. 58.

[147] NO III, p. 376, no. 612 [Wenn der Character eines gegebenen Problem Unauflöslichkeit ist, so lösen wir dasselbe, wenn wir seine Unauflöslichkeit darstellen].

[148] Act I, scene 2.

[149] Novalis' programmatic dictum epitomizing the Romantics' aims. See NO III, p. 685, no. 671 [Das Undarstellbare darstellen].

towards signification: meaning exists on another level – beneath the surface, subcutaneously. Such meaning is not actively hidden, however. Rather, meaning does not make expansive gestures, is not ostentatious. It is also, to make a dialectical point, the tissue of dreams and their images: unconscious language.

Such *signifiance*[150] may be perceived in *Dichterliebe*. As the work remains outside signification through the opacity of Schumann's poetic language, it contains 'constellations of a subterranean firmament' – Jean Paul's description of poetic language in the *Vorschule der Ästhetik*.[151] Friedrich Schlegel speaks in similar terms of 'peculiar combinations' and 'surprising turns and configurations which reach out ever further beyond themselves'.[152] Thus both writers are referring to the metaphorical content of poetic language. In accordance with Jean Paul, who proposed that metaphors precede denotative expression in linguistic formation, the term 'metaphor' will be used here in order to refer to a tonal formation in *Dichterliebe* which crystallizes into an image of this song cycle's very theme: A Poet's Love. The diminished-seventh chord, denoting Schumann's involvement with this Romantic theme, also mirrors in its density and ambiguity the overall harmonic procedures employed in *Dichterliebe*. Whilst diminished-seventh chords of course occur at numerous points during *Dichterliebe*, attention will be drawn to the special status of one of the three possible transpositions: 2, 5, 8, 11 (spelled variously as D–F–G♯–B; D–F–A♭–C♭; or D–F–A♭–B).[153] In this particular combination, the diminished-seventh chord becomes a sonorous sign, surpassing at certain significant moments in *Dichterliebe* its traditional function as a passing chord. No longer transitional and promoting movement, it induces instead a sense of stasis, of rupture, or of concentrated inwardness. At these moments, when its effect is essentially one of defamiliarization, the chord assumes the status of a metaphor – a symbolic figure in *Dichterliebe* which produces the cycle's 'effect of reality'.[154] And to concur with Jean Paul, it is 'the earlier word' which emerges when 'the I and the World fuse' – as happens when Schumann fantasizes.[155] *Dichterliebe* revolves around the Romantic fantasy of the amorous state in all its ambiguity, and thus has neither plot nor narrative. Rather, it holds within itself all shades of possible meaning. Hence, if *Dichterliebe* can be said to have a core – a place where sense is most memorably inscribed – then that core

---

[150] Barthes (1985a), p. 270.

[151] JP IX, p. 58 [Sternbilder eines unterirdischen Himmels].   [152] *KFSA* III, p. 51.

[153] Where C = 0, C♯/D♭ = 1 etc. The economy with which Schumann uses higher dissonance chords in *Dichterliebe* turns the occurrence of a diminished-seventh chord into a striking musical event. What I am proposing in the following analysis is that the 2, 5, 8, 11 diminished-seventh chord has a pitch-specific function in the cycle which metaphorically also carries very specific poetic implications. Of course, there can be no invariance without variance, and Schumann has indeed used the two other transpositions of this chord at important points in *Dichterliebe* in order to create a special effect (see Song 2, b. 10, at 'Kindchen', for example). This means that the pitch-specific 2, 5, 8, 11 diminished-seventh chord used at nodal poetic points is in fact woven into a greater compositional web of musico-poetic *signifiance*. In order also to account for these other diminished-seventh chords and their meaning, a more extended analysis would be necessary, which is, however, beyond the scope of this study.

[154] See Barthes (1968), pp. 84–89, on details which quite conspicuously do not advance a plot but which attain over the course of a work a level of symbolic meaning that produces 'l'effet de réel'.

[155] Schumann's *Fantasieren* is discussed on pp. 114 and 160.

lies perhaps in the striking sound of the diminished-seventh chord as it traverses this work, keeping its very meaning in constant flux.

In the following analysis of Songs 4, 4a, 12 and 16, I shall trace the diminished-seventh chord as it lights up like a striking sound-gesture in *Dichterliebe*. A type of poetic logic can then be discovered, for it functions like a figure of musical speech which consistently occurs when imaginary love is named. Projected into a crucial role within the flow of a few significant songs, this chord, essentially disruptive in its force, is transported to the fore. With this capacity to bring the flow of the music to a halt, it becomes the agent of those ambiguous relations that signal the amorous state. This is the very nature of the metaphor in the Romantic as well as modern sense which Jean Paul describes as:

a synonym of body and mind. As there was in writing hieroglyphics before alphabetic script, so in speech the metaphor – to the extent that it denotes relations and not objects – was the earlier word.[156]

The poems Schumann selected for *Dichterliebe* map out an archetypical scenario, using metaphorical language and imagery well within the conventions of Romantic folk poetry. In his choice of poems Schumann focused on the naive and emotive and sought out those poetic images which carry semantic potential germane to true Romantic poetry. In Heine too, despite his active denial of Romantic sense, a core can be perceived. But the 'little theme' which Heine claimed permeates the *Lyrisches Intermezzo* is not to be located in a single poem, as most musicological commentators have implied when speaking about Heine's poems in terms of the Goethean model of the *Erlebnisgedicht*.[157] Rather 'the little theme' is continuous, like the flux of mental images. In the course of the *Lyrisches Intermezzo*, Heine locks on to the *imago* of a woman and the theme of oxymoronic love throughout the cycle with extraordinary tenacity and pathos. If this theme becomes in *Dichterliebe* the sign of desire's Janus face – drawing together the oppositions of presence and absence, bliss and pain, life and death – it shows Schumann as the discoverer and restorer of lost orders of meaning. For in Heine's poems these opposites are deployed with a sharpness and inexorability that relegates the theme itself to the sphere of empty nothingness: love and death, or light and darkness, cancel each other out into a white-walled world of semantic equality, for the senses are anaesthetized by the plethora of oppositions and contradictions. Everything and nothing makes sense, and the moment of the *Stimmungsbruch* fully achieves the levelling out of either

---

[156] JP IX, p. 184 [Synonyme des Leibes und des Geistes. Wie im Schreiben Bilderschrift früher war als Buchstabenschrift, so war im Sprechen die Metapher, insofern sie Verhältnisse und nicht Gegenstände bezeichnet, das frühere Wort].

[157] There is on the whole in the literature on *Dichterliebe* a notable lack of awareness of the nature of Heine's poems, and, except for Hallmark, little effort has been made to refer to these poems in detail. The intricacy of the structural as well as the semantic relationship between Heine's poems and Schumann's settings in *Dichterliebe* has thus remained unclear. See, for example, Benary (1967), Gerstmeier (1982), Haesler (1982 and 1987), Hallmark (1979), Komar (1971), Neumeyer (1982), Pousseur (1993), Sams (1993). See Part II for an extensive discussion of the refusal of Heine to write in the style of the *Erlebnisgedicht*. For further references regarding Heine and the structure of the *Lyrisches Intermezzo* throughout the analysis, see Part II.

stance. In this respect, one notes the fate of a selected few Romantic images. Each one carries a wealth of associations and sentiments; and yet, through their constant use and misuse, these images are – even during the course of a single poem – stripped of their original symbolic potential. Heine's *Stimmungsbruch*, always the moment of reversal, breaks with too much power for these symbols not to be hollowed out. Such rhetoric also relies on an extremely economical display of borrowed Romantic images which, in each poem as well as in the whole cycle, are on their way to becoming non-images. The lyricism of the *Lyrisches Intermezzo* thus amounts to a profusion of words versus a poverty of symbolic sense – a stylistic achievement from which emerges the gesture of pain in its purest state: paralysis in the midst of tension.

Dichterliebe has more cathartic potential. Its structure, so unlike Heine's sophisticated 'art of arrangement' in which the idea of an end dominates each poem as well as the whole poetic cycle, is itself a metaphor. With the Romantic form of the fragment, the view into the Beyond is laid open, and reflection takes us in the direction of another world. Heine's rigid 'mask of irony'[158] is thus removed, for opposites are synthesized into a gesture of ambiguity. The diminished-seventh chord as used by Schumann achieves this effect in *Dichterliebe*, for he does not, in following Jean Paul, focus on objects, but instead on relations, relations that he renders ambiguous. The following analysis contends that a musical detail such as this particular diminished-seventh chord may be viewed as the centre of Romantic reflection within *Dichterliebe*.

The question of musical metaphor has been mentioned briefly in the light of Schumann's reworking of 'Ich hab' im Traum geweinet' in the late song 'Der schwere Abend'.[159] Both thematic identity and the rare key of Eb minor carry over a certain darker tone and sentiment from the earlier song to the later one. The resemblance is, as has been emphasized, indirect rather than direct however, for the differences to be perceived in the later song imbue it with a quality that did not exist in the earlier one.

A similar situation occurs within *Dichterliebe* as regards this diminished-seventh chord. It appears notably at moments of intensity which are, to use Schumann's phrase, connected by the 'silver-thread of imagination'.[160] Most memorably, and for the first time, this chord emerges in the fourth song, 'Wenn ich in deine Augen seh' – a point of reflection which resumes trans-structurally the sense of a never-ending openness chosen for the 'Sehnen und Verlangen' in the first song, as we have seen. Let us clarify this connection between Songs 1 and 4: the first song's 'never-ending openness' results from the absence of an explicitly stated tonic, and from Schumann's dwelling on a dominant-seventh chord on C♯, with which the song ends, unresolved. Another means of signifying a 'never-ending openness' is exhibited by Schumann's use of the diminished-seventh chord in Song 4. Since this is a sonority that can be made to function in any of the twenty-four keys, it is imbued with an unsurpassed

---

[158] *GS* I, p. 144. See the Schumann quotation serving as the epigraph of this Part.
[159] See p. 158.   [160] *GS* I, p. 33 [Silberfaden der Phantasie].

multiplicity of meaning. The connection between Songs 1 and 4 is 'trans-structural' because the means by which Schumann establishes the atmosphere of openness are structurally different in each case: the first song is open in a large-scale sense, whilst the diminished-seventh chord in the fourth song induces openness on a smaller, more local scale.

As regards this transposition of atmosphere from Song 1 to Song 4, note Schumann's tempo indications: from the *Langsam, zart* of the first song, *Langsam* is retained in the fourth, whilst the *Nicht schnell* of Song 2 and the *Munter* of Song 3 indicate an altogether different pace. Both the intervening songs pass by like fleeting images, Song 3 even more so than Song 2.[161] Songs 2, 3 and 5 thus contrast with the two *langsam*-planes of Songs 1 and 4. With such inscription of atmosphere, similar but not identical, references are made across and beyond the certainties of the purely musical text. Thus a common space is constituted not only through key relations – the progression of fifths from A major/F♯ minor (Song 1) to A (Song 2), D (Song 3) and G (Song 4) – but also through a reverberation in time. The reappearance of *langsam*, indicating the merging of a specific atmospheric plane, will be noted again in Songs 4a, 12 and 16 of *Dichterliebe*, as we pursue the diminished-seventh chord whenever it is exposed.

Song 4

Wenn ich in deine Augen seh',	When I look into your eyes,
So schwindet all mein Leid und Weh;	All my suffering and pain disappear;
Doch wenn ich küsse deinen Mund,	But when I kiss your mouth,
So werd' ich ganz und gar gesund.	Then I regain my health totally.
Wenn ich mich lehn' an deine Brust,	When I lean upon your breast,
Kommt's über mich wie Himmelslust;	There comes over me a feeling of heavenly passion;
Doch wenn du sprichst: Ich liebe dich,	But when you say: I love you,
So muß ich weinen bitterlich.	Then I must weep bitterly.

The poem 'Wenn ich in deine Augen seh'' traverses the stages of desire: the poet gazes into the beloved's eyes and all his agony disappears. The kiss brings him back to health. To lean on her breast overwhelms him with passion. Since we are, when speaking of the beloved in Heine's poems, always speaking of an *imago*, this drive towards the woman describes what is always perceived as having a healing effect: to see one's double and to get closer and closer towards it. The Romantically erotic nuance of 'heavenly passion' (*Himmelslust*) indicates the last stage *before* Heine's *imago* lures the poet into actual identification. When the silent spell of gazing into the *imago*'s eyes and moving towards the still statue is broken by the beloved speaking

---

[161] Most performances of Songs 2, 3 and 5 take less than a minute. See Dietrich Fischer-Dieskau's interpretations with Vladimir Horowitz (1976 for Sony, no. SM2K 46743), Christoph Eschenbach (1979 for Deutsche Grammophon, no. POCG–9004/6), and Alfred Brendel (1986 for Philips, no. 416352–2). The same is true for Olaf Bär and Geoffrey Parsons (1985 for EMI, no. 7 47397 2), Eberhard Wächter and Alfred Brendel (1962 for Decca, no. 425 949–2), and (except for Song 5 at 1 min. 5 secs) Lotte Lehmann and Bruno Walter (1942 for CBS, no. 44840).

4   *Wenn ich in deine Augen seh'* Op. 48, no. 4

Wenn ich in deine Augen seh'

the ultimate words of fulfilment ('Ich liebe dich'), the process comes to a halt. The experience of abundance and exuberance shifts to its opposite and the poet 'must weep bitterly' ('So muß ich weinen bitterlich'). His reaction indicates the realization that he does not know whether an 'Ich liebe dich' could possibly exist at all. And more importantly, whether he could ever receive it within himself. Notably, there is no sense of danger associated with looking at and moving closer towards the *imago* that could explain the poet's withdrawal as the fear of becoming engulfed by it; rather,

4   (*cont.*)

the tears imply the poet's inability to give himself over to his *imago*. Stylistically, the appearance of a speaking voice in the poetic scene not only marks the *Stimmungsbruch*; it also is the typical signal marking the moment of waking from dreams – Heine's constant gesture of 'Aufwachen' permeating his entire work, poetry and prose alike.[162]

Structurally, the point of reversal, which takes place in the last line of the poem, is shifted forward in Schumann's song. Therefore, Heine's gesture does not coincide with Schumann's; instead, in ascribing significance to what takes place before the *Stimmungsbruch*, the whole working of Heine's poem is transformed: 'meaning' is inscribed before the literal fact, and 'Ich liebe dich' assumes the central place in Schumann's song.[163] What may be called a 'thematic' gesture, 'Ich liebe dich' (bb. 13–14), rises above all other musical events in this song – indeed, it stands out in the whole of *Dichterliebe*. However, the diminished-seventh harmony on 'doch wenn du *sprichst*:' (b. 13) prepares for the moment of intimation: slowly (ritardando) and in falling motion the chord evolves out of a $VI^{3-\sharp3}$ progression (bb. 12–13)[164] within the span of the $G\sharp^2$–$G\sharp^1$ octave (b. 13). The hands are closely intertwined. The diminished-seventh chord in b. 13 is literally the moment of elevation, for G (repeated throughout b. 12) is raised to $G\sharp$ on all levels as voice and piano move up a semitone in parallel motion. Although the voice has been doubled before, in b. 13 it is reinforced by an additional octave. Let us also note in bb. 12–14 the E^1–D^1–C^1 descent in the bass: the descent to D^1 yields a tritone against $G\sharp$. Hence, 'elevation' is achieved here not only spatially, but also on the level of dissonance (see Ex. 12).

---

[162] This idiosyncratic gesture of 'waking from dreams into reality' has on occasion been underestimated. See for example the interpretation by Richard Kramer (1994) who suggests that 'Romantic poetry tells us often enough of erotic adventure' (p. 10) and assuming that Heine's poetry belonged to this tradition sees in Heine's poems the expression of 'consummation'. 'Tears' are then 'the mysterious elixir of the act'. In asserting that 'that literal act strains a conventional metaphor', Kramer explains: 'On tears as a symbol for the love act, see . . . (Heine, again) two songs from Schumann's *Dichterliebe*: "Aus meinen Tränen sprießen / Viel blühende Blumen hervor" (the fertility of tears) and, most evocatively, in the fourth song, "Doch wenn du sprichst: Ich liebe dich / so muß ich weinen bitterlich". Two songs later, in the unexpurgated version, Heine reads "Lehn' deine Wang' an meine Wang, /dann fließen die Tränen zusammen". The metaphor is pursued with gusto elsewhere in *Die Heimkehr*. in no. 19, "Wo einst ihre Tränen gefallen, / sind Schlangen hervorgekrochen"; and in no. 27, "Was will die einsame Träne?"' (p. 127 and p. 127, n. 5). The meaning of 'tears' in poetry as a literary motif can, however, be multiple. See for example Lurker (1991), pp. 764–765.

[163] Hallmark (1979, p. 48) offers a different interpretation, suggesting that 'his [Schumann's] music therefore surprises us before it should; it anticipates the poem's reversal rather than underlining it'.

[164] See Heinrich Schenker's eloquent graph of 'Wenn ich in deine Augen seh" (Op. 48, no. 4) in *Free Composition* (1979), supplement, Fig. 152¹.

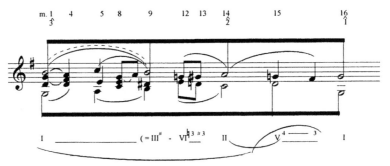

Ex. 12   'Wenn ich in deine Augen seh" (Op. 48, no. 4)
bb. 12–17

Obviously, the singular prominence and impact with which Schumann projects the diminished-seventh chord owes much to the repetition of the E-minor chord in the preceding bar (b. 12) from which it emerges. While this rhythmic and interval-lic structure of b. 12 has been established as the song's nucleus from the very start (bb. 1–2), and although this motive has been transformed constantly up to this point through intricate interaction between voice and piano (bb. 1–11), its unison presen-tation at the words 'doch wenn du' (b. 12), just before 'sprichst', is certainly new. Earlier, the piano either followed the voice (b. 2) or preceded it (b. 4) in the statement of the motive. Thus, the repeated E-minor chords before 'sprichst' (b. 12) with their new-found congruence between voice and piano convey a sense of 'expectation'.

The diminished-seventh chord before 'Ich liebe dich' is the structurally crucial aspect of 'Wenn ich in deine Augen seh", leading as it does to the striking suspension on 'liebe' (b. 14).[165] Let us note here the movement of the voice: a third-step up followed by a whole-step down. This lyrical detail will reappear conspicuously three times at a later stage in *Dichterliebe*.

In bb. 13–14, that is from 'sprichst' through 'dich', the song conveys a sense of stasis: for a moment, nothing moves as the diminished-seventh chord spreads its veil

---

[165] Pousseur (1993, p. 50) characterizes this diminished-seventh chord as 'particularly insistent'.

over 'sprichst' in order to come to a halt on 'liebe dich', again constrained in terms of time and tempo by a ritardando.[166] Motion resumes again all the more perceptibly at 'so muß ich weinen bitterlich' (bb. 14–16) which the piano continues to 'sing' three times, decreasing in tempo (ritardando in bb. 17 and 19) and dynamics (*p* in b. 16 and *pp* in b. 18). The ambiguity created by the diminished-seventh chord is resolved locally on 'dich'; however, this resolution is only tentative, as the A-minor sonority (on the second beat of b. 14) functions as ii^6 of G and is hence tonally distant from the home key. The real resolution is the ensuing V^7–I progression (bb. 15–16) on 'bitterlich'.

The contrast between the setting of 'liebe' and 'bitterlich' deserves further comment. The motive B–A–G, which occurs twice in bb. 9–10^{1}and 11–12^1, is a salient constituent of both the vocal line and the overall structure of this song. In b. 14 on 'liebe' the B, previously harmonized by a consonance, becomes a dissonant suspension after the disintegration caused by the diminished-seventh chord. Triadic support for the B is then re-established for the final occurrence of this B–A–G motive in b. 15 on 'bitterlich', where it forms part of the cadential V^7–I progression.

Evidently, Schumann does not offer what one might expect of a song composed according to the principle of 'word-painting'. But the disappointment some have felt at 'the lack of any musical equivalent for a rather obvious verbal point'[167] surely originates in these commentators having a preconceived idea of the poem's meaning, as well as in insisting on being presented with a literal musical translation. Indeed, if it is asserted that 'Heine means that "Ich liebe dich" was a lie', Schumann must appear as having failed with this song: 'Schumann is innocent of innuendo. His music's meaning is not even discontent, let alone distress.'[168] As Hallmark has noted, however, Schumann was well aware of the significance of the poem's closing lines.[169] In a review of W. Taubert's *An die Geliebte. Acht Minnelieder für das Pianoforte* Op. 16, a collection of melodious piano pieces with epigraphs ascribed to various poets,[170] Schumann comments on the fact that Taubert makes no attempt to account for the poem's *Stimmungsbruch* compositionally:

To me the most beautiful and soulful is the one which is also the simplest: 'Wenn ich mich lehn' an deine Brust, kommt's über mich wie Himmelslust.' A musical translation of the ending of the same Heine poem, 'Doch wenn du sagst [*sic*]: ich liebe dich, so muß ich weinen bitterlich', the composer should have put aside for the future.[171]

---

[166] Cf. an evocative description of the passage by a performer: 'Time seems to stand still, so lovingly is the moment prolonged. The falling quavers in the pianoforte move reluctantly to "ich liebe dich" which is breathed upon the air.' Moore (1981), p. 6.

[167] Sams (1993), p. 111.

[168] Sams (1993), p. 111. Cf. also Moore's view that 'Heine's piteous "so muß ich weinen bitterlich" is not underlined by Schumann, in fact it is almost thrown away. . . . In effect, the message is "I weep bitterly because you are not to be trusted".' See Moore (1981), p. 6.

[169] Hallmark (1979), p. 48.   [170] See the earlier discussion of this review on p. 57.

[171] GS I, p. 169 [Als schönstes, innigstes gilt mir das, was auch das leichteste ist: 'Wenn ich mich lehn' an deine Brust, kommt's über mich wie Himmelslust.' Eine musikalische Uebersetzung des Schlusses desselben Heineschen

If Heine's poem is reduced to a mere narrative scene, the question as to the speaker's identity is bound to find a somewhat simplistic answer. By agreeing with Sams in principle, Hallmark's suggestion calls for a perspective which ultimately proliferates into three directions: is *Heine* speaking *about* 'the inadequacy of the *woman* to take language seriously, to mean what she says, to have any meaning other than a superficial, soul-less one'[172] – a situation which *Schumann* is then expected to re-enact? A different sense of the shift of tone in the last line emerges, however, if the woman is perceived as the poet's *imago*, and the speaking voice as imaginary, imaginary to the extent that the 'Ich liebe dich' is internalized and part of an inner, and the poet's, discourse. The aspect of projective identification is here more prominent than elsewhere in the *Lyrisches Intermezzo*, for it is the only instance in all of the sixty-five poems where the *imago* is given direct speech. If this invokes her presence more intensely, exceeding in its absorbing power both gaze (line 1) and touch (lines 3 and 5), then the speaking voice, articulating the phantasmal bond ('Ich liebe dich') resides once more within the poet. As Heine advances from the language of the eyes (*Augensprache*) to the speaking subject, the *imago* recedes from outward poetic scene towards the heart of poetic speech itself – a 'you' who lies within.

As exalted as the 'Ich liebe dich' may be in Schumann's song, let us note that the phrase is linked with the final word 'bitterlich'. By way of the ritardando in b. 14, the motive for 'liebe' is prolonged in metrical time. While the first syllable is integral to the suspension, the second departs from it, anticipating the piano's descent to ii^6, thereby increasing the tension between voice and piano. Likewise, the emphasis on 'bit-terlich' in b. 15 also focuses on the first syllable and the small motivic gesture equals in relative duration the earlier one (the note values are augmented). Note also that the B on '*lie*-be' in b. 13 is part of a 7–6 suspension, whereas the B on '*bitter*lich' in b. 15 is part of a V^{13}–I suspension (see Ex. 13). In neither case is B a harmony note. To differentiate further however: although the status of the B is an important one throughout this song, its most dissonant harmonization occurs on 'liebe'.

It is now the piano which precedes the voice in resolving harmonic tension. In this complex of counter-reflection, the words 'liebe' and 'bitterlich' are linked and merge through their similarity as regards rhythmic setting as well as phonetic emphasis on the 'i'-sound (b*i*tterlich/l*ie*be). Harmonically, however, the two words are linked only as a difference, as has been emphasized above. Thus semantically linked, neither 'liebe' nor 'bitterlich' escapes the connotations of the other. The song maintains this level of multivalency beyond this passage until its end: as the piano thrice confirms by way of rhythmic and melodic recall the last vocal phrase (bb. 16–17, 18–19 and 20–21), perhaps not only the 'so muß ich weinen bitterlich', but also the 'doch wenn du sprichst: Ich liebe dich' is here reinvoked simultaneously. As the piano descends

Gedichtes: 'Doch wenn du sagst: ich liebe dich, so muß ich weinen bitterlich', möge sich der Componist für die Zukunft zurückgelegt haben].

[172] Although objecting to Sams's earlier judgement as well, Hallmark (1979, p. 185, n. 23) nonetheless retains the view of the descriptive nature of Heine's poetry.

Ex. 13   'Wenn ich in deine Augen seh' (Op. 48, no. 4) closing bars

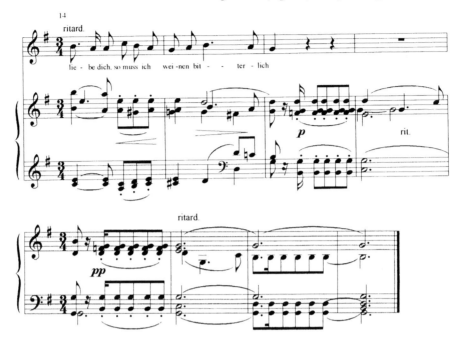

into a lower register, the music is perpetually gaining ground. After the repeated third degree of G major (in the bass in b. 18 and the lower part of the right hand in b. 20), tonal equilibrium is finally regained through the G in the tenor (b. 21), structurally leading back to the song's opening register (see Ex. 14).

And through this device, the polysemous sense with which the postlude is imbued enters the entire song in retrospect, for the piano alone speaks the last, as well as the very first, word. That the postlude's words do indeed traverse the entire song can be perceived by following the development of its most distinctive characteristic: motivic repetition. After all, the subtle interplay between voice and piano that unfolds initially (bb. 1–11) leads to the apex of accumulation on 'doch wenn du sprichst' (bb. 12–13). This motive then unfolds anew, as the 'voice of the piano', as suggested above. This procedure makes it one of the most remarkable postludes in *Dichterliebe*. Through repetition, Schumann indicates what is essential in the poem: the changing inflection of Heine's 'liebe', modulated through the final word 'bitterlich'. If the diminished-seventh chord on 'sprichst' emerges already as an ambiguous space, polyvalence is further ensured by Schumann for both the last and penultimate line of the poem as one crosses over into the other (Ex. 14). Ultimately then, the very absence of words in the piano postlude makes it possible to designate this merging of semantic fields. Schumann does not embellish or develop, let alone alter this his final, oxymoronic statement, and by carving it deeper and deeper into the song's surface, this statement is made forever irreducible by its own strength.

Ex. 14 'Wenn ich in deine Augen
seh'' (Op. 48, no. 4) closing and opening
bars

Song 4a

This oxymoronic atmosphere carries over into Song 4a, 'Dein Angesicht, so lieb
und schön'. Significantly, the slow motion of Song 4 is retained through Schumann's
tempo indication *langsam*.

Dynamically resuming the quiet ending of the previous song, the tonal connection
between the two songs is relatively close: set in E♭ major, Song 4a continues in the
major mode and prolongs the tonic note G of Song 4 as its mediant. Neither the B♭, as
Hallmark notes, nor the E♭ fits into the G-major harmony of the preceding song.[173]
Analysis focusing on harmonic functionality has therefore disregarded Song 4a from
further consideration, accommodating only what is more overtly compatible with its
totalizing theory of *Dichterliebe*.[174] In such analysis, which thus denies itself *a priori* the
discovery of musical features outside the limits of organic growth, some significant
structural patterns could not have been observed. For example, *beneath* the level of
harmonic logic, another, more enunciative kind of correspondence between Songs 4
and 4a lights up as a gesture of momentary reflection: the diminished-seventh chord

[173] Hallmark (1979), p. 143.

[174] See Komar's Schenkerian study in particular, in which he presents 'an overall compositional plan according
to which the sixteen songs of *Dichterliebe* are interdependent "movements" governed by a single key'. Komar
(1971), pp. 63–94 (here 66).

5   *Dein Angesicht* Op. 48, no. 4a

Dein Angesicht.

(Heine.)

5   *(cont.)*

in bb. 11–12 is more than a matter of coincidence. Sliding into the gentle flow of 'slow semiquavers', 'tranquil' bass notes and the generally 'warmer pulse'[175] of this most Schubertian and most paradigmatically Romantic song in *Dichterliebe*, the disruption this chord causes goes to the song's very core. At the same time, it *is* this song's very core, for it denotes those relations that constitute the logic of Heine's poem.

Dein Angesicht, so lieb und schön,	Your face, so sweet and beautiful,
Das hab' ich jüngst im Traum geseh'n.	I have seen it in a dream most recently.
Es ist so mild und engelgleich,	It is so gentle and angelic,
Und doch so bleich, so schmerzenbleich.	And yet so pale, so pale with pain.
Und nur die Lippen, die sind roth;	And only the lips, they are red;
Bald aber küßt sie bleich der Tod,	But soon death kisses them pale,
Erlöschen wird das Himmelslicht,	Extinguished will be the celestial light,
Das aus den frommen Augen bricht.	Which breaks forth from the pious eyes.

The very first words, 'Dein Angesicht', at once indicate the unchanged state of the poet's gaze. In exact keeping with the formal pattern of the previous poem, 'Wenn ich in deine Augen seh'', this poem has two stanzas, is in iambic metre and follows the simple, folk-lyrical scheme of an alternate rhyme. Also consonant with the earlier poem is the semantic field that reappears with 'Angesicht'. It conjures up the eyes of the beloved to which the poem indeed returns in the last line ('frommen Augen'). Thus embracing the visual radius of the earlier poem, 'Und nur die Lippen, die sind roth' (line 5) reinvokes 'Doch wenn ich küsse deinen Mund' (line 3 of 'Wenn ich in deine Augen seh''). But whereas the reference to the beloved's lips had originally been integrated into the symbolic order of the poet's increasing desire, it now draws the red line of a Heinean cut: after describing the beloved as 'sweet', 'beautiful' (line 1), 'gentle' and 'angelic' (line 3), no less than 'pale' and 'pale with pain' (line 4) – a typical example of Heine's invocation of the marble statue of the Virgin Mary, as well as more specifically an allusion to the Madonna-image in poem 11, as has been noted[176] – 'red' breaks through and disturbs the studied collection of mellow qualifiers denoting pious devotion.

No doubt, one could also locate the *Stimmungsbruch* in line 4, where 'bleich' and 'schmerzenbleich' unexpectedly challenge the luminous grace and beneficence of the beloved. The 'doch' most certainly supports such a reading. In a poem where concepts trigger colours, the collision between 'engelgleich' (line 3) and 'schmerzenbleich' (line 4) becomes then the first sign of what is to follow: 'red' as in lips and erotic kisses meets with 'death' that renders all 'pale' (lines 5–6). Such cancellation as a result of extreme opposition is followed through with exactitude, between the lines when the rhyme suggests semantic similitude ('roth'/'Tod'; '[Augen]-licht'/'bricht' in lines 5–6 and 7–8), and across a poetic web at whose centre lies the idea of extinction itself: 'Erlöschen' versus 'Himmelslicht' (line 7), and the literal breaking of the heavenly light in the beloved's eyes as suggested in line 8 ('Das aus den frommen Augen bricht'). Its most drastic expression is in line 6, a convoluted metaphorical block that merges red, white and black at once:

[175] Sams (1993), p. 124.   [176] See Grappin's commentary in *DHA* I/2, p. 780.

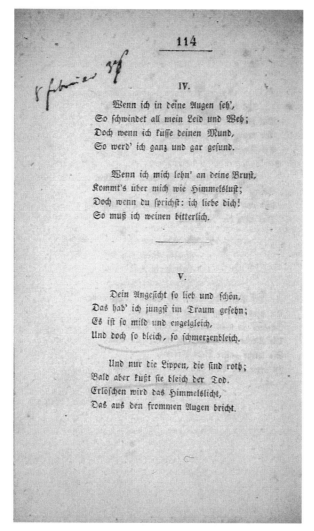

Fig. 4. Page 114 of Schumann's personal copy of the
first edition of Heinrich Heine's *Buch der Lieder*
showing the poem 'Wenn ich in deine Augen seh"
with (presumably) Schumann's underlining.

'Bald aber küßt sie bleich der Tod'. Consummation indeed, and precisely the kind
that leaves no trace. To 'kiss pale' blankets all senses, as the adverbial construction
bespeaks the modality of a white-walled void. The *imago* disappears.

MS 83.5037, Schumann's personal copy of Heine's *Buch der Lieder*, shows that
line 4, 'Und doch so bleich, so schmerzenbleich' had indeed been underlined
(see Fig. 4).

As an indication of the composer's reading of Heine's poem, the notion of morbidity and first mention of pain obviously caught his attention. Seen in conjunction

Ex. 15   'Dein Angesicht' (Op. 48, no. 4a) bb. 7–11

with Hallmark's careful examination of the sketch for this song, it is interesting to learn that Schumann took great care in adding syncopations at 'und doch so bleich, so schmerzenbleich' (bb. 7–9) in his emendations.[177] Voice and piano, truly complementary from the beginning, unhinge at this point for the first time. The little melismatic figure on 'schmerzenbleich', also added in the revision, and high-lighted by a ritardando (b. 9), is in this context of further interest. Its function is to re-establish the perfect interlocking between voice and piano. With apparent innocence, 'schmerzenbleich' crowns the first stanza as a conventional vocal closing figure, entirely on a par with the equally conventional IV–V–I motion in the key of G in the piano, even if the modal inflection B♭ to B♮ (beats 2 and 3) reinforces the significance of 'schmerzenbleich' (Ex. 15).

No simpler solution could have been found to affirm G major for the second stanza's beginning than by establishing a bass pendulum going back and forth between V and I, completing the harmony in the right hand, and fixing the voice on top. But this procedure to ensure utmost tonal stability is precisely what enables the diminished-seventh chord to break through to the surface with such alienating force. The basic tonal structure is shaken up and disintegrates into a single gesture of

[177] Hallmark (1979), pp. 51–52.

Ex. 16 'Dein Angesicht' (Op. 48, no. 4a) bb. 11–13

sonorous rupture. The material investment in this passage should not be underestimated. It involves an extreme exploitation of the low register as, once propelled into motion by the accent on F♮ (b. 11), syncopated bass octaves keep descending chromatically into unanticipated depths. Unusual, to say the least, especially when considering the ceaseless vocal stream of C♭s on 'bald aber küßt sie bleich' holding against it (Ex. 16).

As far as the keyboard is concerned, this procedure pushes things to the limit, from a structural as well as a practical point of view. Structurally, the achievement of this passage (bb. 11–13) is two-fold. First, the diminished-seventh chord is drawn out considerably with the right-hand figure on D^1, Cb^1 and Ab^1 remaining the same despite the bass's stepwise descent. Schumann thus capitalizes on its initial impact, and by dwelling on it, asserts its significance as something more than a passing chord. It is a separate space that has been inserted between two tonally well-defined fields: G major in bb. 9–11 and G♭ major in bb. 14–18. Second, the achievement of this passage rests in creating a degree of delineation between voice and piano that grants both the status of autonomy. Whilst the voice remains in its designated mode, retaining rhythmic pattern as well as pitch (enharmonically changed from $B\natural^1$ to Cb^1) from previous bars (10–11), the piano pulls away from the whole idea of close accompaniment and, with the off-beat presentation of the diminished-seventh chord, claims a stance adverse to the voice, as every articulation of the syncopated bass scheme manifests anew a fundamental difference. Only the voice is, it seems, oblivious to the text; the piano rather faithfully reflects the poetic signal – a sudden, extended and reverberating reaction to 'red'.

But beyond these procedures taking place within Song 4a itself, Schumann achieves a further goal. By means of his effort to reach G major in bb. 10–11 in a song written in E♭, and by way of his fixing into this harmonic field the previously mentioned vocal line B–A–G, this passage bears the *signum* of Song 4. Once more the aim is to introduce and establish B as a harmony note, as part of an unchallenged B–A–G motive within the purity of G major; just as in Song 4 (bb. 9–10 and 11–12), the motive appears twice in Song 4a, this time condensed within two bars (10–11). Then occurs the diminished-seventh chord (end of b. 11), the piano's gesture marking the *Stimmungsbruch*, after which the B♮ in the voice turns into a C♭ through enharmonic change (b. 12); and just as the diminished-seventh chord in Song 4 had caused the B to turn under its veil into a dissonance, the same procedure is undertaken in Song 4a when the B is drawn into the diminished-seventh chord's disruption and then continued as a stream of C♭s (bb. 12–13). Schumann insists on this pitch, as he did before in Song 4 (b. 14) with the suspension on B held over a ritardando, and after more than one bar of equally suspended harmonic release, the high point of tension is reached at 'Tod' – recalling and reflecting upon the moment of 'liebe' with remarkable structural fidelity (Ex. 17).

Returning to Song 4a, Schumann's word setting begins to exceed all conventional logic: with 'Tod' and 'Erlöschen' this song is to see its most intense moment of lyrical beauty. Through a V^7–I operation into the key of G♭, the harmonic structure is lifted as part of an overall registral shift in which the melisma on 'Tod' (b. 13) is simultaneously both goal and turning point. Mindful of the fact that the articulation of this word recalls the expressive means used for 'Ich liebe dich' in the previous song (a third-step up followed by a whole-step down, including the ritardando to heighten the effect), 'Tod' releases into 'erlöschen' by way of a tonicizing, highly expressive arpeggio in the new key of G♭ in b. 14 (see Ex. 18).

With this, the song reaches its dramatic climax. As an elaborate attempt to infuse the future vision of the beloved's death with a degree of exaltation that confirms rather than denies the lethal wish, Schumann renders Heine's undoing of the loved one as one of the extreme forms of amorous attachment: to inflict upon the Other that death-bearing pain which reigns in equal measure within the walls of a hollow Self – a void too great and petrified as not to have to swallow up the light that challenged such guarded darkness. To be sure, the 'heavenly light' is desired and seen, but also seen as not to be had, and thus desired not to be there; hence the breaking, blinding and extinction (lines 6–8). Schumann captures this other side of intense desire by making it the lyrical high-point of his song. For the moment of fulfilment ('Erlöschen wird das Himmelslicht, / das aus den frommen Augen bricht') is only a heightened version of the primary sensation of glowing admiration with which the song had taken its course. In memory of the radiant image ('Dein Angesicht, so lieb und schön, / das hab' ich jüngst im Traum geseh'n'; bb. 1–5), and indicatively stepping into a supported falsetto,[178] the voice soars up and resumes on a transposed level the melodic material of its beginning (bb. 14–15). Both truth and falseness are enshrined in the voice here, for, in the melody, it fains continued, even increased admiration, while, in the text, it articulates those words that name the destruction. That the highpoint is precisely here and at no other moment in the song is also signified by the piano's doubling of the vocal line. This begins at 'Tod', where the intensifying layer is inserted in order to strengthen the lyrical

---

[178] Cf. here Dietrich Fischer-Dieskau's interpretation together with Christoph Eschenbach (1979 for Deutsche Grammophon, no. POCG–9004/6).

Ex. 17 'Wenn ich in deine Augen seh" (Op. 48, no. 4) bb. 9–14 compared with 'Dein Angesicht' (Op. 48, no. 4a) bb. 10–13

melisma (b. 13), and continues throughout 'erlöschen wird das Himmelslicht, / das aus den frommen Augen bricht' (bb. 14–17). In fact, this doubling layer completes the steps of the original melody (bb. 1–4) wherever the voice diverts from it (Ex. 18).

Harmonically, the tendency here is to lead back from G♭ to the home key of E♭ (bb. 14–16 as I–IV–V) in order to pave the way for Schumann's return to the first stanza, but a deceptive cadence in b. 17 defers the process so as to complete

Ex. 18   'Dein Angesicht' (Op. 48, no. 4a) bb. 13–19

the necessary four-bar phrase structure. Further, the actual return to E♭ (b. 18) is weakened by the bass arriving on the third degree rather than the root.

But this subtle avoidance of a clear return to the expected tonic (on the main beat of b. 18) foreshadows what is to develop into a continued expression of deferring final certainty. Potentially representing the closing part of a song designed in a seemingly simple ternary form (ABA'), bb. 18–26 do not, however, preserve the identity of the original material of part A (bb. 2–9) beyond the near-literal restatement of the first four bars ('Dein Angesicht, so lieb und schön') – nor could they. For what has indignantly been called a 'wholesale repetition of the first stanza, . . . the largest textual distortion in the cycle'[179] is in truth an intricate re-reading of the poem's first four lines. It also reassesses the song's own original interpretation of these same lines in the light of those musico-poetic events which have taken place in part B (bb. 14–17). Schumann thereby challenges the message of extinction on which the resolution of Heine's poem structurally and semantically relies. In contrast to the original Heine poem, Schumann's song creates the following situation:

---

[179] Hallmark (1979), pp. 51–52.

Dein Angesicht, so lieb und schön,	You face, so sweet and beautiful,
Das hab' ich jüngst im Traum geseh'n.	I have seen it in a dream most recently.
Es ist so mild und engelgleich,	It is so gentle and angelic,
Und doch so bleich, so schmerzenbleich.	And yet so pale, so pale with pain.
Und nur die Lippen, die sind roth;	And only the lips, they are red;
Bald aber küßt sie bleich der Tod,	But soon death kisses them pale,
Erlöschen wird das Himmelslicht,	Extinguished will be the celestial light,
Das aus den frommen Augen bricht.	Which breaks forth from the pious eyes.
Dein Angesicht, so lieb und schön,	You face, so sweet and beautiful,
Das hab' ich jüngst im Traum geseh'n.	I have seen it in a dream most recently.
Es ist so mild und engelgleich,	It is so gentle and angelic,
Und doch so bleich, so schmerzenbleich.	And yet so pale, so pale with pain.

After reinvoking the poet's entranced gaze into the beloved's face (bb. 18–21), Schumann states what he deems to be lying at a deeper level of Heine's poem in the last compositional analysis. To begin with, the second phrase (bb. 22–23, 'es ist so mild und engelgleich') bears the sub-text of bb. 11–12 with syncopations for the descending chromatic bass (bb. 21–22). And those words that Schumann had underlined ('und doch so bleich, so schmerzenbleich') are now to be given their final connotation. The voice, supported by a full triad in the piano, enunciates the falling pitches of a half-diminished-seventh chord (F–Ab–Cb–Eb in b. 24; the D is raised a semitone to Eb), a gesture that recalls the 'sprichst' in Song 4 (b. 12). When finally reaching the tonic note, the closing figure in the voice on 'schmerzenbleich' (bb. 25–26) can then be recognized as the inversion of the lyrical expression on 'Ich liebe dich' in Song 4; it had already reappeared in Song 4a on 'Tod' (b. 13) (Ex. 19).

The *Stimmungsbruch* 'und doch so bleich, so schmerzenbleich' has thus been validated, and in closing the song on what is, for the poem, the symptomatic statement of ambiguous admiration, Schumann recovers and asserts this emotional middle ground as the genuine sign of the amorous – the cutting edge of all desire. To this, crisis itself, value is granted, above and beyond its destructive reverse. Hence, Schumann restores in Heine what is otherwise crushed motionless between the pressure of extremes, between admission and denial, love and death, or brightness and eclipse.

Song 12

In Song 12, 'Am leuchtenden Sommermorgen' in Bb major, the diminished-seventh chord comes to convey not a sense of stasis (as in Song 4) or of rupture (as in Song 4a), but one of concentrated inwardness.

As the only simultaneously struck chord in a song entirely based on the dispersion of harmonic planes through arpeggiation, it appears in b. 24 after the first half of the piano postlude, emphasized by a '<>' marking. Schumann's two tempo indications –

Ex. 19 'Dein Angesicht' (Op. 48, no. 4a) bb. 23–25

Ziemlich langsam for most of the setting and *langsamer* for the last couplet and the postlude (at b. 17) – function as cross-references connecting this song with Songs 4 and 4a.[180] Unlike in the earlier songs, however, here the diminished-seventh chord is no longer directly bound up with the poetic text. In order to explore the musico-poetic relevance of its occurrence in the 'wordless' postlude, a brief examination of its structural context within the song is necessary. The question is essentially: why is there a diminished-seventh chord at all, and why is it deployed in such a contracted form?

The whole structure and development of Song 12 hinges on the German-sixth chord with which, strangely, the song opens. Three times (in bb. 1, 6 and 11) this chord appears like a fissure, introducing each of the poem's first three couplets. To ground the German-sixth chord, Schumann resolves it each time with the cadential progression V–I in B♭ major. He thereby establishes a formal pattern. Heine's poem consists, however, of four couplets, and it is the last two lines for which Schumann reserves a different solution.

---

[180] Although Song 10 is also marked *Langsam* and bears some superficial resemblance to Song 12 in terms of texture, the minor mode and musical material, it contains no complete 2, 5, 8, 11 diminished-seventh chord (cf. b. 26) and does not appear to belong to the network of trans-structural relationships under discussion here.

6   *Am leuchtenden Sommermorgen* Op. 48, no. 12

Am leuchtenden Sommermorgen

6   (*cont.*)

Am leuchtenden Sommermorgen	In the bright summer morning
Geh' ich im Garten herum.	I walk around the garden.
Es flüstern und sprechen die Blumen,	The flowers are whispering and talking,
Ich aber wandle stumm.	But I wander around silently.
Es flüstern und sprechen die Blumen	The flowers are whispering and talking
Und schau'n mitleidig mich an:	And are looking compassionately at me:
Sei unsrer Schwester nicht böse,	Don't be angry with our sister,
Du trauriger blasser Mann.[181]	You sad, pale man.

'A "bright summer morning" is for Heine an extremely rare chord', writes Grappin in his editorial commentary, 'and usually brings on the contrary the end of dreams and visions of happiness'.[182] One other poem in the *Lyrisches Intermezzo*, as well as in *Dichterliebe*, begins with the notion of a marvellous natural set-up: 'Im wunderschönen Monat Mai'. And as if Schumann felt compelled to lean backwards to the beginning of his cycle (*Ziemlich langsam*) at this mid-point, the gesture of the bass moving down a semitone to resolve the dissonant harmony reappears in Song 12 (Ex. 20).[183]

As in the first song, the beloved is absent in Song 12. Rather like an abstract emotional entity lingering on the poet's mind, she can no longer be described, envisioned or named. It is thus that the poet is thrown back on to himself, to see within himself a subterranean reality, the Romantically heightened imagery of a magical garden with speaking flowers through whom he addresses himself in perfect solitude ('Du trauriger, blasser Mann'). Heine's poem is soliloquy *per se*, and with the double-reference 'es flüstern und sprechen die Blumen' (lines 3 and 5) Heine thematizes and centralizes what was earlier referred to as the Romantic idea of 'a language of the soul'.[184]

In the song, Schumann instantly infuses the line 'Es flüstern und sprechen die Blumen' with the deeper quality of a 'language of the soul': although introducing the phrase according to the pattern with the German-sixth chord followed by V–I in B♭ major (bb. 6–8[1] on 'es flüstern und'), the second arpeggio (b. 8[2] on 'sprechen') is enharmonically reinterpreted as the dominant of B with F♯ in the bass and the B♭ changed to an A♯. This opens up a new harmonic dimension for the word 'Blumen' (b. 9). On the one hand, the voice noticeably dwells on this word with each syllable sung on the longest consistent note values in the song. On the other hand, the voice has, curiously, not been enharmonically notated[185] – a question to which the song itself will give an answer, albeit very late on.

---

[181] In the 1827 edition of Heine's *Buch der Lieder* containing this poem, no exclamation mark follows the last word 'Mann'. Since Schumann used this edition (see the discussion on pp. 127–130), the poem is here reproduced without the exclamation mark. This is in contrast to the current editions of *Dichterliebe*, for example Komar (1971) and Köhler (1986).

[182] *DHA* I/2, p. 831.

[183] Pousseur (1993, p. 120) also notes this reminiscence of the first song, although without reference to the poetic connection.

[184] See p. 138.

[185] Cf. here Hallmark's interesting observation that 'in the draft Schumann notated the chord which is to cadence to B major (m. 9) as a G♭⁷ chord. In the final version he notated [it] enharmonically as an F♯⁷ chord to distinguish it functionally from the G♭ harmonies. One wonders why he did not also notate the vocal line enharmonically at that point.' See Hallmark (1979), p. 88.

Ex. 20 'Im wunderschönen Monat Mai' (Op. 48, no. 1) and 'Am leuchtenden
              Sommermorgen' (Op. 48, no. 12), opening bars

Having arrived at B⁷ (b. 9), a possible harmonic progression back to B♭ would be an elaboration of a rising 7–10 linear intervallic pattern: B^7–E^7–C^7–F^7. The connecting E^7 has, however, been omitted, as a result of which a sense of rupture is induced at 'ich aber wandle stumm' (bb. 10–11). The phrase closes nonetheless neatly in B♭ major, and the first couplet of the second stanza is introduced according to the established formal pattern (bb. 11–16¹). But this time the expected German-sixth chord does not follow the initial closed phrase; instead, a foreign harmony is constructed on a passing note A♭ (b. 16²), which is strengthened by another F♯ passing note in the voice above the bass functioning as a leading tone, thereby making possible the tonicization of G major (b. 17). Into this pure region of G major, the inner voice of the poet enters to speak in the miraculously modulated, slower (*langsamer*) mode of non-discursive soliloquy: to say that 'she', the 'sister' of the floral kind, is the most beautiful of all ('she' therefore has to be absent), and that 'he' (note yet another signifier for the psychomotoric retardation, b. 19) is of a different kind. G minor denotes this polar difference, with an accented B♭ for 'sad', and with the fissure of the German-sixth sound on 'pale' – except that it is no longer a fissure: this time the German sixth is heard as a passing chord, for it is integrated into a descending

Ex. 21 'Am leuchtenden Sommermorgen' (Op. 48, no. 12), harmonic synthesis

chromatic bass line (G–G♭–F), is integrated into the poetic logic, and is filled up with that sense which Schumann had suspended all along. It is this procedure that necessitates the afterthought, following the pattern that 'makes' this song (German sixth going to F to resolve on B), and to break the downfall of a desiring, unresolved 'I' (b. 20[1]). Yet, even this remains harmonically unresolved, despite (and also because of) the expected move to F, for the vocal part ends on C as part of the dominant harmony. The piano thus has to complete the voice and reach B♭. But why, it must be asked, is this final return to the tonic such a long process, thereby becoming one of the longest postludes in *Dichterliebe*? The answer rests in Schumann's involvement with the text: with the bass pedal on F in b. 20[1], the upper register of 'the language of the soul' is summoned up a second time, to continue from the heights of the F♯[3] arpeggio in b. 9[1] with one on G[3] (b. 20[1]), and to elaborate from here for the next two bars (21–22). This ensuing stepwise falling motion of top notes (G[3]–E♭[2]–F[3]–D[2]–E♭[3]) is then reversed upwards with the arrival on C[2] in b. 23. From this C[2] onwards, essentially the vocal C[2] of b. 20, and with a notable condensation of texture, Schumann returns to the main body of the song and its semantic centre, for all of bb. 24–30 represent the harmonic essence of bb. 8–13 ('Es flüstern und sprechen die Blumen, / Ich aber wandle stumm'), as a harmonic summary easily shows (see Ex. 21).

And here, in this act of musically poeticizing Heine's poem, Schumann's earlier invocation of 'Blumen' (b. 9) crystallizes into a single gesture of concentrated inwardness: the diminished-seventh chord. It is now highly contracted, which could only be achieved by two A♭ pitches that have been added outside any voice-leading procedures (b. 24^2). What is truly remarkable about the way in which the diminished-seventh chord enters here, is the bass going from G♭ to F, for this mirrors the procedure in bb. 19–20 with the extraordinary exposed parallel fifths between the voice and the piano. Achieved outside the conventions of traditional voice-leading procedures, Schumann hence draws attention to the words 'trauriger, blasser Mann' with this 'open sound'. As the diminished-seventh chord in b. 24 contains the identical bass motion, a transference of meaning from the spoken to the unspoken is ensured. Yet, in the second instance, the bass moving from G♭ to F forms part of a progression that ultimately leads to a more conventional resolution of the German-sixth chord in b. 27. Silently withdrawing into himself, Schumann realizes compositionally what he once stated to be the principle underlying the 'language of the soul':

When man wants to say Something that he cannot say, he turns to the language of music or to that of the flowers – because the world of the flowers is as sacred as the world of music, and at moments of pain or of joy man prefers to turn to music or to nature, and both are guarantors of one deity and one endlessness.[186]

Once this 'surprising turn, reaching out ever further beyond itself' (Schlegel) has been taken, once Schumann's text has turned back on to itself, to come to rest at the core of its desire, at the core of a 'solitary Romantic soul', the third attempt at closing the song from C^2 (b. 25) to B♭ becomes natural: even the last resolution of the German-sixth chord is now a smoother, in fact a 'corrected', V of V–V progression.

Finally, let us note that this inward discourse of a 'solitary Romantic' as signified through the musical events in b. 9 on 'Blumen' is further indicated in Schumann's seemingly awkward notational practice in bb. 8–10. The use of the enharmonic pitches B♭–C♭–D♭ in the voice on the words 'flüstern und sprechen die Blumen', despite the piano's shift to sharps, suggests a direct connection with the B♭–C♭–D♭ linear motion in the voice in bb. 19–20 on 'trauriger, blasser Mann'. As this is preceded by the pure region of G (bb. 17–18) in which the beloved is named ('sei unsrer Schwester'), one also notes a possible musico-poetic cross-reference to Songs 4 and 4a insofar as the vocal pitch of B^1 is retained in Song 4 in bb. 1–2 for 'Wenn ich in deine Augen seh'', and in Song 4a in bb. 9–10 on 'Und deine Lippen, die sind roth'.

Song 16

Once more, the diminished-seventh chord lights up in *Dichterliebe*. This is in Song 16 in bb. 44–45; during the long soliloquy of the piano's postlude, the Andante espressivo, in b. 54; and over and over again with the B lowered to B♭ as V of ii in bb. 61–64 (see Ex. 22).

---

[186] *TB* I, p. 101 [Wenn der Mensch Etwas sagen will, was er nicht kann, so nimmt er die Sprache der Töne oder die der Blumen – denn die Blumenwelt ist ja so heilig als die Tonwelt u. in Schmerzen oder in der Freude geht der Mensch am liebsten an die Saiten oder in die Natur, u. beyde sind ja Bürgen einer Gottheit u. einer Unendlichkeit].

Ex. 22 'Die alten, bösen Lieder' (Op. 48, no. 16), the diminished-seventh chord
in bb. 44–45, 54 and 61–64

Notoriously, the postlude recalls material from Song 12 (bb. 23 ff.), and with it, the diminished-seventh chord. For Schumann, when writing the score, a great enharmonic shift (bb. 52–53) has to happen first, before Song 12 as well as some other songs can come into view in his ironic glance back. The pages and images of *Dichterliebe* are unfolding anew, with words from the spoken and from the unspoken, and in this 'wordless' *Representation of the Unrepresentable*, the diminished-seventh chord as a metaphor of the amorous becomes at last indeterminable. Ingrained in the meanderings of retrospective thought, it turns into knots along the 'silver thread of imagination', and Schumann's last postlude into faltering speech. The following discussion of the last postlude will explore this process in the light of the structurally sovereign capacity of Romantic irony. In that specific conceptual context, the diminished-seventh chord will have become an elliptical word, a mere *simulacrum* of those relations it so eloquently designated in Songs 4, 4a and 12. But so far, this much can still be said: that this chord is a sonority in *Dichterliebe* that speaks when words become deficient in naming desire's alienating, disintegrating force. This sonority is not often exposed in *Dichterliebe*, and it is thanks to this frugality that it means something.

(IV) THE IRONIC GLANCE BACK: THE LAST POSTLUDE

The question of finality arises in *Dichterliebe*, not primarily with its last song, but rather with its final postlude. Although the powerful effect of the song proper can be compared with that of 'Die alten, bösen Lieder' as the closing poem of Heine's *Lyrisches Intermezzo*, the piano epilogue exceeds the significance of the preceding musical material by virtue of its lasting impact. Visually cut off from the song by a double bar, a new time signature, the enharmonic notation changing C♯ into D♭ and minor into major, and the Andante espressivo indication, this final postlude is connected to the song only by contrast.[187] And just as Song 1, with its harmonically ambiguous piano-solo sections, raises the question of the cycle's 'beginning', the piano postlude has the last word as regards the cycle's 'end'. Those two positions are obviously the vital structural pillars of any piece of music and here of a form that has often been claimed to represent a rounded whole. Doubtless, this is also the main opportunity to enquire about how Schumann evaluated Heine's final statement. What is Schumann's compositional solution for Heine's closing poem beyond the actual setting of the text, and how does he make his own final statement? – if finality there is.

The compositional procedures characterizing 'Die alten, bösen Lieder' have been well described in the critical literature.[188] My main concern in the following analysis is therefore to elaborate on the connotations of some of its most striking features, and to comment on the postlude in terms of Romantic irony. Before attaining the sublimely unrepresentational heights of irony ending *Dichterliebe*, where Schumann's poetic language once more reflects upon itself, let us trace those musico-poetic

---

[187] Pousseur (1993, p. 164) aptly describes the postlude as a 'completely autonomous construction'.
[188] See in particular Komar (1971), pp. 91–93, and Pousseur (1993), pp. 159–164.

points which are still directly tied to Heine's text. MS 83.5037 (see Fig. 5) shows that Schumann underlined what could then be structurally emphasized in the setting.

Die alten, bösen Lieder,	The old, evil Lieder,
Die Träume bös und arg,	The dreams, evil and terrible,
Die laßt und jetzt begraben,	Let us bury them now,
Holt einen großen Sarg.	Fetch a great big coffin.
Hinein leg ich gar manches,	Therein I put many a thing,
Doch sag ich noch nicht was;	But I do not yet say what;
Der Sarg muß sein noch größer	The coffin must be greater even
Wie's Heidelberger Faß.	Than the Heidelberg Cask.
Und holt eine Totenbare,	And fetch a bier,
Von Brettern fest und dick;	Of boards strong and thick;
Auch muß sie sein noch länger	It must also be longer
Als wie zu Mainz die Brück.	Than the bridge at Mainz.
Und holt mir auch zwölf Riesen,	And fetch me also twelve giants,
Die müssen noch stärker sein	They must be even stronger
Als wie der heilige Christoph	Than the holy Christopher
Im Dom zu Köln am Rhein.	In the Cathedral at Cologne on the Rhine.
Die sollen den Sarg forttragen,	They should carry away the coffin,
Und senken ins Meer hinab,	And lower it into the sea,
Denn solchem großen Sarge	For such a mighty coffin
Gebührt ein großes Grab.	Deserves a mighty grave.
Wißt ihr, warum der Sarg wohl	Do you know why it is that the coffin
So groß und schwer mag sein?	Must be so mighty and heavy?
Ich senkt' auch meine Liebe	I've also buried in it my love
Und meinen Schmerz hinein!	And my agony!

With the massive C♯ opening gesture, strength has been gathered for a constricted, essentially Baroque, compositional delivery of Heine's rather manic exit out of his poisoned poetic cycle.[189] This opening gesture reappears with modifications in bb. 35^1–37 ('Die sollen den Sarg forttragen'), whereafter 'Senken in's Meer hinab' (a retrograde of bb. 11–15 and underlined by Schumann) produces that greatly 'deceptive' sound (b. 39) which summarizes Heine's hyperbolic speech about burying his songs. This sonority is indeed, as Pousseur has noted, unmatched in its dramatic impact since the 'Ich liebe dich' in Song 4.[190] With the following two lines, 'Denn solchem großen Sarge / Gebührt ein großes Grab' (lines 19–20 underlined by Schumann), the musical action is finally contained in heavy, accented chords (bb. 40–43). As if to symbolically indicate an abyss, a dense diminished-seventh chord, emphasized by a *sforzato* and prolonged by a fermata (b. 39), precedes the

---

[189] Cf. the beginning of poem LI: 'Vergiftet sind meine Lieder; – / Wie könnt es anders sein?' [Poisoned are my Lieder; – / How could it be otherwise?].

[190] Pousseur (1993), p. 161. Note also that this 'pathetic diminished-seventh chord' (Pousseur) is the same variant which Schumann used in Song 2, b. 10.

7   *Die alten, bösen Lieder* Op. 48, no. 16

Die alten, bösen Lieder

7   (cont.)

7 (*cont.*)

senkt' auch meine   Lie _ be und   mei _ nen Schmerz hin _ ein!

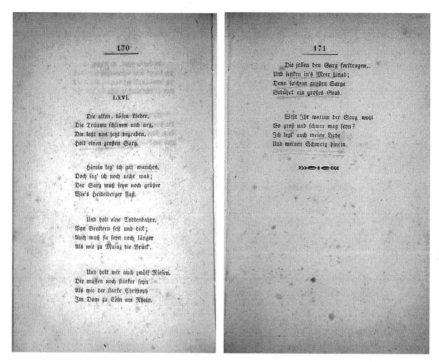

Fig. 5. Pages 170 and 171 of Schumann's personal copy of the first edition of Heinrich Heine's *Buch der Lieder* showing the poem 'Die alten, bösen Lieder' with (presumably) Schumann's underlining.

'denn'. The following four bars eventually lead to a last bass octave on C♯ at 'Grab' (b. 43) which takes the music down to one of the lowest pitch levels in the whole of *Dichterliebe*. The series of syncopations, in conjunction with a decrescendo, first on C♯, then within the dense texture developing around various inversions of the now-familiar diminished-seventh chord (bb. 43–44), gradually builds up tension to arrive at a quiet breaking point: the 'Ich' in b. 47, highlighted by a portamento, is the last 'dramatic moment' in this long drawn-out passage where voice and piano have most notably become texturally unhinged.

Following up more closely the tonal surroundings of this cardinal poetic moment in Song 16 and its postlude sheds further light on the cyclic nature of *Dichterliebe*. It is clear that bb. 41–43 advance the conclusive cadence in C♯ minor by a i^6–$ii^{6/5}$–V^7–[i] progression. However, bb. 44–47 convert the unison on C♯ into a dominant seventh on C♯, which destabilizes the previous cadence, but which also resembles the close of Song 1. There then unfolds a progression asserting C♯ as the tonal centre once more, a progression which could conceivably have also provided a resolution for Song 1 – to recall an archetypical invocation of 'mein Sehnen und Verlangen', and now to call it by the name of experience contained in the words 'meine Liebe und meinen Schmerz'. Initially suggesting a cycle of fifths (A^7–D–G♯^{7}–C♯), the deceptive cadence to VI of C♯ in b. 50 is followed by ii$^{6/5}$–V of C♯ minor, only to be disrupted, in the written score, by the visually striking shift to D♭. Let us note, then, that after the apparent C♯ stability of the cadence at b. 43, the C♯^{7} chord opens up the song's structure once more. It denies C♯ a definitive role as a pitch centre. Overall, this procedure reminds one of the open harmonic scheme explored by Schumann in his enigmatic and strangely Baroque song 'Auf einer Burg' (Op. 39/7) from *Liederkreis*. The main issue in Song 16 is, however, that the events taking place between bb. 44 and 52 initiate a fracture between the earlier stable C♯ and the D♭ of the postlude.

Henceforth, through a quotation from the postlude of Song 12, the weight is lifted. In terms of dramatic development, Schumann's emphasis on 'groß' and 'schwer' in the manuscript represented by an ascent of a fifth in b. 46 is followed by an ascending registral transfer of an octave in b. 47. The grave thus only brightens in the light of the poet's ultimate submission to both his love and his own agony ('Ich senkt' auch meine Liebe / und meinen Schmerz hinein!'). And for this moment of amatory incandescence, Schumann reserves a slow (Adagio) and hymnic incantation that celebrates once more a lyrical detail that has lit up three times before: a third-step up followed by a whole-step down, unfailingly on 'Liebe' (bb. 48^2–49), is here again a figure of poetic speech. Exposed in Song 4 at 'Ich liebe dich', it returned in Song 4a when semantically equated with 'Tod',[191] and again, as the unspoken 'forgotten word' with which the piano ends Song 14 after 'Und's Wort hab' ich vergessen'.[192] 'Schmerz', as the reverse side of desire's Janus face, hence receives the retrograde of this motive (bb. 50-51),[193] and, 'underlined' by low-register octaves, it may be seen as an insertion of Schumann's marking (note the underlining) from the manuscript into the score. 'Liebe' and 'Schmerz' thus bound up with each other, named in one breath and sung on one motive, have become synonymous and are jointly drawn into the grave. Yet, as mentioned above, 'meinen Schmerz' enters into a deceptive cadence – the first of a series of moments devised to delay the arrival of the tonic.

The tide then turns. But across the threshold Schumann has intercalated once more the 'forgotten word', or at least its first two signifying notes (bb. 52–53, see Ex. 25 below).[194] For if the poet's drowning of his songs means also to abandon his voice, then the loss for words can only be sublimated through gestures solely remembered by the piano. So it is that the postlude of the twelfth song begins to speak, transposed, in place of the Other, and *for* the poet's psyche, to commune with himself in the 'language of soul' (bb. 53–58).[195] This is not, however, in the spirit of 'reconciliation'[196] – with whom? a shadow? – nor in the spirit of recovery, for memory does not mean salvation here. To reinvoke the 'sad, pale man', choked with solitude and withdrawn into some inward realm where only flowers whisper and speak,[197] is not an image that lifts the spirit.

---

[191] See discussion on pp. 181–199 on Schumann's re-evaluation of the Heinean love/death dichotomy in Song 4a.
[192] See Pousseur (1993), pp. 141 and 163.   [193] Cf. Pousseur (1993), p. 163.   [194] See Pousseur (1993), p. 166.
[195] See discussion of Song 12 on pp. 200–206.   [196] Sams (1993), p. 123.
[197] As a literal, although transposed, quotation from Song 12, b. 54 contains *the* diminished-seventh chord.

Ex. 23   'Dein Angesicht' (Op. 48, no. 4a) bb. 15–18 and postlude of 'Die alten,
bösen Lieder' (Op. 48, no. 16), bb. 61–63

But Song 12 is not the only fragment from the faded music of *Dichterliebe* that suddenly enters the piano postlude. Song 4a, 'Dein Angesicht', is also commemorated
(see Ex. 23).

As one of the most intense invocations of the Other in perhaps the only paradigmatically Romantic song in the cycle, the quotation is more concealed than that
from Song 12. However, the fact that 'Dein Angesicht' became part of the last song's
postlude gives good reason to reconsider the assumption that Song 4a should be excluded from the cycle.[198] Its presence in the last postlude may have been recognized
earlier if Song 4a had been included in the published version.

With the mention of these two 'old' songs, Schumann recalls, as well as renounces,
their original meaning; for they draw into the last song's postlude a semantic property
which belongs to different, and former, atmospheres. Yet, even in their contradictory
nature – Song 12 as an image of a Romantic's lost voice versus Song 4a as a paradigm
of the Romantic's Lied – the two fragments form a small 'series of thoughts'.[199] They

[198] See Komar (1971, p. 6, n. 9), who is 'only interested in describing Schumann's cycle in its final form' and whose
'references to *Dichterliebe* thus omit Songs 4a, 4b, 12a, 12b from consideration'; See also Hallmark (1979), pp. 125
and 143–145; Sams (1993, p. 125) explains the omission of 'Dein Angesicht' by saying that the song's words 'no
doubt . . . seemed too ominous for a wedding year'. Pousseur (1993, p. 177) considers the omission as a sign of
Schumann's intention to purify the narrative and formal structure of the cycle. See, in contrast, my argument
advanced on pp. 116–122 of this Part. The intention to include the four songs is also confirmed by a number
of letters by Schumann in which he consistently expressed his wish to see all twenty songs published.

[199] *Athenaeum*, p. 199 [Ideenreihe].

make up a dreamlike '*ensemble*' in which 'wondrous incidents' are connected 'without coherence', as Novalis put it.[200] And hence, there also develops a small dialogue, for Schumann returns here, more than anywhere else in *Dichterliebe*, to the atmosphere of a pure 'musical fantasy',[201] as he lets these two songs speak again through 'his' medium, the piano. With the more abstract means of 'absolute' music, the two songs' singers, like two different characters, encounter each other in the postlude. They also, however, contradict each other.

Thus, Schumann set two extreme positions from *Dichterliebe* side by side, a procedure which ultimately creates a floating meaning: on the one hand there is negation (Song 12), on the other there is affirmation (Song 4a), and yet these two positions neither complement nor erase each other, but rather follow the Early Romantic logic of a '*progressive dialectic*'.[202] Each one merely a piece broken off from an originally whole song, in succession they represent only moments in time, as if to say, with Tieck, 'the poet always forgets what he has said a moment earlier'.[203] And it is intriguing to observe the reverse order in which the two songs appear in this last postlude, as well as important to remember that Song 4a has achieved most memorably and demonstratively in *Dichterliebe* an Early Romantic reading of Heine's poem which exhibited a truly generous and thus deeper understanding of the emotional dynamics involved. Conceptually, however, such diametric opposition as occurs here in the last postlude between the quotations from Songs 12 and 4a is precisely what Romantic irony allows for: the coexistence of contradictory statements arising from the Early Romantic's '*fragmentary consciousness*'.[204] By way of positing one fragment against another, the Romantics' innermost nature, '*pluralism*',[205] is thus given a 'formal' expression. With this procedure, the artist is also able to 'represent the Unrepresentable',[206] since the formal as well as semantic limit of one fragment is successively superseded by the next fragment's beginning.[207] This involves the alternation between one constructive thought (say Song 12) followed by its destruction through the construction of another, new and different thought (say Song 4a); in other words, the 'constant alternation between self-creation and self-annihilation' that defines Romantic irony.[208] This generates an 'eternal agility'[209] of meaning that ironizes the idea of an ever-coherently representable whole and proposes instead 'glimpses into the infinite'[210] to which there is no end. In the last postlude, the flux of opposite 'states of the soul'[211] (Schumann's phrase) is rapid, as we have seen, and

---

[200] NO III, p. 454 [Wie ein Traumbild – ohne Zusammenhang – Ein *Ensemble* wunderbarer Dinge und Begebenheiten]. Emphasis original.

[201] NO III, p. 454 [*musikalische Phantasie*]. Emphasis original.

[202] *KFSA* XVIII, p. 83, no. 646 [progressive *Dialektik*]. Emphasis original.

[203] Tieck in his novel *Phantasus* as quoted in Frank (1989), p. 377 [Der Dichter vergißt immer selbst, was er den Augenblick vorher gesagt hat].

[204] *KFSA* XII, p. 393 [*fragmentarisches Bewußtsein*]. Emphasis original.

[205] NO III, p. 571, no. 107 [*Pluralism* [sic] ist unser innerstes Wesen]. Emphasis original.

[206] NO III, p. 685, no. 671 [Das Undarstellbare darstellen].   [207] See Frank (1989), p. 302.

[208] *KFSA* II, pp. 172–173 [steten Wechsel von Selbstschöpfung und Selbstvernichtung]. See the discussion of the concept of Romantic irony in Part I, pp. 33–39.

[209] *KFSA* II, p. 263 as quoted in Behler (1993), p. 151.

[210] *KFSA* II, p. 200, no. 220 [échappées de vue ins Unendliche].   [211] Kreisig *GS* I, p. 343 [Seelenzustände].

it is by virtue of such mobile semantic shifts that Romantic irony can manifest itself. Mind and judgement then 'surrender to illusion'.[212] As the young Tieck writes:

This is part of the incomprehensibly rapid agility of imagination, which is able to tie to one and the same object, [and] within two successive moments, [some] entirely different ideas, and [it can] now produce laughter, and immediately thereafter produce horror.[213]

The notion of 'moments' coming and going along the endless stream of time is indeed central to the idea of Romantic irony. 'Time', as Frank notes, 'is the perfect scheme of irony' because 'no moment in time can be proposed as the last one, as the closure of the chain [of moments]'.[214] Accordingly, music, 'in an eminent sense a temporal art form', can represent most successfully the fading away of that which has previously been said.[215] Without assigning the superior place of meaning either to Song 12 or to Song 4a, Schumann denies his listeners the opportunity to fix their attention on a single mood; instead, certain moments from *Dichterliebe* have been chosen like 'rare states of the soul'[216] to form an 'antisynthetical synthesis'.[217]

But in between these two positions of Songs 12 and 4a, Schumann has inserted yet another, third, allusion, which derives from an even more rarefied atmosphere. As Pousseur brilliantly suggested,[218] b. 59 recalls *Der Dichter spricht*, the concluding piece of *Kinderszenen* (see Ex. 24).

This is a return to the realm of solitary piano music, in which there is no human voice of the Other. Again, in the spirit of Friedrich Schlegel's thesis of 'self-creation' (*Selbstschöpfung*) and 'self-annihilation' (*Selbstvernichtung*),[219] three fragments of absolute music amount to a moment of poetic reflection in their ironic interplay of productive action and destructive reaction – a moment of transcendence which, however, does not claim to reveal an absolute truth. Each one of the three musical references represents one way of looking at things, so to speak, and none can claim the superior status of semantic significance. No doubt, these quotations are different in kind, the one from Song 12 being direct, the one from Song 4a being a pitch-specific allusion, and the one from 'Der Dichter spricht' being a more gestural allusion. This difference of quality and range of quotation does not suggest an organicist interpretation, however; nor could it, for it would be difficult to clearly define the hierarchical status of either quotation. As I shall explain in more detail below, the procedure used by Schumann can more satisfactorily be described as involving the concept of Romantic irony.

Metaphorically speaking neither Master nor Slave, these three moments of thought are involved in a dialectic or, better, triathletic struggle for the naming and claiming

---

[212] Tieck as quoted by Frank (1989), p. 373 [in die Illusion sich ergibt].

[213] Tieck as quoted by Frank (1989), pp. 373–374 [Es gehört dies zur unbegreiflich schnellen Beweglichkeit der Imagination, die in zwei aufeinanderfolgenden Momenten ganz verschiedene Ideen an einen und denselben Gegenstand knüpfen, und jetzt Lachen, und gleich darauf Entsetzen erregen kann].

[214] Frank (1989), p. 310 [die Zeit [ist] das vollkommene Schema der Ironie. . . . Nie kann ein Moment der Zeit als letzter, als Abschluß der Kette vorgestellt werden].

[215] See Frank (1989), p. 369.   [216] Schumann in Kreisig GS I, p. 343 [seltene Seelenzustände].

[217] KFSA XVIII, p. 82, no. 637 [antisynthetische Synthesis].   [218] Pousseur (1993), p. 167.

[219] KFSA II, pp. 149, 151, 172 and 217.

Ex. 24   The postlude of 'Die alten, bösen Lieder' (Op. 48, no. 16), bb. 59–60, recalling
'Der Dichter spricht' (Op. 15, no. 13), bb. 16–17

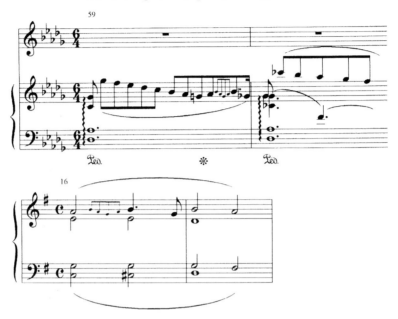

of truth which only Romantic irony can expose as a futile activity.[220] However,
through quoting from a piece entitled *Der Dichter spricht*, it is as if Schumann reflected
retrospectively upon the whole poetic enterprise of *Dichterliebe*. Perhaps it is a hint
that its main issue is indeed less to do with a narrative, or a story, but rather more
with musico-poetic reflections upon the idea of poetic composition itself. At issue is
then, in Blanchot's words, 'the heart of poetry, which is knowledge itself; its essence
is to be both a quest and a quest for itself'.[221]

Here in the postlude, *Dichterliebe* truly opens up to the dialogical nature of
fragmentary piano music, hence demonstrating with particular directness how
Schumann combines and separates two modes of speech: one in which a voice
is invoked to which the piano reacts, another in which instrumental music interacts and reflects upon itself across a number of differing semantic fields. Throughout
Dichterliebe, Schumann has explored his contrasting dispositions towards Heine's 'little
theme' without aiming to draw a thread of narrative or psychological logic through
this cycle. But in the last postlude, the sense of a lack of this kind of continuity is
heightened, for the semantic ambiguity arising from the ensemble of three unconnected 'ideas' or 'thoughts' fragments the illusion of a coherent text more than ever
before. The last postlude is hence the musical expression of a mode of thought and
a mode of diction that is intrinsically polymorphous, polyvalent and fractional. This

---

[220] See my corresponding description of Romantic irony in Part I, pp. 33–39.

[221] Blanchot (1969), p. 518 [c'est le cœur de la poésie qui est savoir, c'est son essence d'être recherche et recherche
d'elle-même]. See the discussion of Blanchot's statement in context with the idea of Early Romantic poetry
and Schumann's mode of composition on p. 113.

endows the cycle with an air of coincidence and non–decidability akin to an infinite conversation, or the endless text. The whole cycle, but the last postlude most perceptibly, follows the Early Romantic poetic process as described by Friedrich Schlegel:

The thread of thought moves imperceptibly forward in constant interconnection until the surprised spectator, after the thread abruptly breaks off or dissolves in itself, suddenly finds himself confronted with a goal he had not at all expected: before him an unlimited, wide view, but upon looking back at the path he has traversed and the spiral of conversation distinctly before him, he realizes that this was only a fragment of an infinite cycle.[222]

In this process of self–reflection, Schumann eventually distances himself from his work, refusing to make a final statement, and arousing instead a 'feeling of indissoluble antagonism between the absolute and the relative' by means of Romantic irony – 'the freest of all licenses, for by its means one transcends oneself':[223]

The novel is about life – represents *life*... The novel as such does not contain a particular result – it is not an image and a fact of a *sentence*. It is a vivid realization – the realization of an idea. But an idea cannot be captured in one sentence. An idea is an *infinite series* of sentences – an *irrational quantity* – unpositable... incommensurable.[224]

Having created a '*second* world in the world around us'[225] through casting into sound the images of one idea, the constant flux of contradictions eventually ceases to flow. The famous last few bars (63–66),[226] unable to ground themselves in a harmonic environment that would indicate a confident retreat to a more stable semantic territory, are pure elaboration, filigreed poetic *texture*, around the whole idea of attempting, but failing, to end the cycle. Having intensified the process begun in b. 61 by attaining with the Gb^3 in b. 64 the highest pitch register since the G^3 in b. 20 of Song 12,[227] Schumann enters two last diminished–seventh chords in b. 64 (inversions of the 'central' one for 'Ich liebe dich' alluded to five times on the first and third beats of bb. 61–63 with a lowered B) on a ritardando that is structurally prolonged three times by a dominant thirteenth (bb. 65–66) – the affirmation of a kind of solution first found for 'bitterlich' in Song 4, b. 15.[228] Here we have, then, the apposition of extreme chromaticism and diatonicism, for the diminished–seventh chord is the 'narrowest' possible triadic chord denoting the gesture of a 'concentrated inwardness',[229] as opposed to the dominant thirteenth as the 'widest', and highest possible diatonic dissonance. The last words sung before the postlude,

---

[222] One of Friedrich Schlegel's description of poetry. See *KFSA* III, p. 50. Trans. Behler (1993), p. 141.

[223] *KFSA* II, p. 160 as quoted in Behler (1993), p. 149.

[224] Novalis as quoted in Frank (1989), p. 284 [Der Roman handelt vom Leben – stellt *Leben* dar . . . Der Roman als solcher enthält kein bestimmtes Resultat – er ist nicht Bild und Factum eines *Satzes*. Er ist anschauliche Ausführung – Realisirung einer Idee. Aber eine Idee läßt sich nicht in einem Satz fassen. Eine Idee ist *eine unendliche Reihe* von Sätzen – eine *irrationale Größe* – unsetzbar. . . inkommensurabel]. Emphasis original.

[225] JP IX, p. 30 [Die Poesie ist die einzige *zweite* Welt in der hiesigen]. Emphasis original.

[226] Described best by Pousseur (1993), pp. 169–172.

[227] See p. 204 for my discussion of the G^3 in b. 20 of Song 12 in connection with it being a prolongation of the second F♯s in b. 9 on the second syllable of 'Blumen'.

[228] See my discussion of Song 4 on pp. 181–189, above.

[229] See my discussion of the diminished–seventh chord as connoting what I called 'concentrated inwardness' on p. 178, above.

Ex. 25   The postlude of 'Die alten, bösen Lieder' (Op. 48, no. 16), bb. 52–53
and last bar recalling the motif of the 'forgotten word' with which closes
'Allnächtlich im Traume' (Op. 48, no. 14)

'meine Liebe und meinen Schmerz', can thus be related, perhaps, to the diminished-seventh chord as a tonal metaphor for the amorous ('Liebe'),[230] giving way to the dominant thirteenth as what could then be called a gesture of 'widening agony' ('Schmerz') which was first indicated when repeated three times in connection with the word 'bitterlich' ending Song 4. However, what does it *mean*? 'It must mean something, mustn't it?' I hear some readers ask. What is the precise logical relation between these two opposite gestures beyond what this relation openly indicates – the naming of two contrasting sensations, 'Liebe' versus 'Schmerz' (Song 16) or 'Ich liebe dich' versus 'muß ich weinen bitterlich' (Song 4)?

Perhaps we can leave this unanswerable question, and say instead that by reading 'Allnächtlich im Traume' in an Early Romantic mode, 'Liebe' and 'Schmerz' here crystallize into Heine's 'leises Wort', which, growing into a bouquet of exegetical cypresses ('Strauß von Zypressen') always, however, disappears: 'Der Strauß ist fort. Und's Wort hab' ich vergessen'. Thus, in Song 16, the agile mind of a Romantic, having overexerted itself, finally comes to a rest by naming, mysteriously, the last element of the 'forgotten word' (Ex. 25).[231]

The sense of apathy in the last few bars (63–67) of *Dichterliebe* is undeniable. The listener's 'real judgement' has, in Tieck's words, been 'lulled to sleep' by the 'extremely swift shift and multitude of representations' so as not to let 'the viewer [listener/reader] be able to fix his attention on one object firmly and lastingly'.[232] At the same time, however, there is also a wonderful, indeed wondrous, sense of lightness permeating the whole postlude since Schumann began to fantasize in the freest possible manner here. And this lightness is the very *signum* of Romantic irony as it arises once the weight of love and agony has been lifted. The stream of thought simply keeps flowing, not knowing where it comes from nor whereto it goes. 'Floating'

---

[230] See again pp. 177–208 above, entitled.

[231] Pousseur (1993), p. 166.

[232] Tieck's description of the poetic procedure characterizing Early Romantic poetry, and irony in particular as quoted in Frank (1989), p. 381 [den richtigen Verstand einschläftern . . . durch eine extrem rasche Abfolge und Mannigfaltigkeit der Darstellungen . . . daß der Zuschauer nie auf irgend einen Gegenstand einen festen Blick heftet].

is the *terminus technicus* for the workings of Romantic irony in order to describe the nature of a procedure that abandons the search for an absolute truth.[233] Instead of this absolute truth, Romantic irony rises from the ashes of the burned fields of signification left behind by the combat between the Master and the Slave, and floats above all with an irresistible lightness, a lightness which we admire for its sublimely sovereign detachment and for its utter grace. The *Fragmentation of Desire* has here reached its highest point, as vent has been given to the endless interplay of statement and counter-statement, primary and secondary thought, aligned and knotted ideas, and the presence of what has been said is as significant as the pressing force of what remains unsaid. In *Dichterliebe*, all has been said, it seems. Yet, nothing lasts for more than a moment as it is held in the abeyance of Schumann's *nous poietikos*.

[233] See Frank (1989), pp. 380–387.

CONCLUSION

As I conclude my study on structural fragmentation and retrace the tracks of thought that guided this journey through Schumann's *Dichterliebe*, I shall avoid the air of an ironic glance back. I started out to explore analytically the poetics of this intricate ensemble of songs by proposing Early Romantic literary procedures as a mode of writing and experience aesthetically akin to Schumann's own mode of composition. In order to indicate the element of disintegration and decomposition characterizing the aesthetic theory developed by Novalis and Friedrich Schlegel, Part I outlined their core categories – the Romantic fragment, Romantic irony, and reflection – as Forms of Difference.

My central concern, therefore, has been to show how these Early Romantic forms (fragment, irony, and reflection) assumed an artistic role in achieving for music a paradoxical 'expression' of the inexpressible able to 'represent the Unrepresentable'.[1] A second, inevitable concern of mine has been, in consequence, to explore the Romantically redefined relationship between language and music. To this end, Part II's literary-critical expedition into Heine's subversive post-Romantic land of hope and disenchantment led me to perceive in the *Lyrisches Intermezzo* the phenomenon of the *Stimmungsbruch* ('cut' or 'dramatic reversal') as an affect paroxysmally breaking through in the one who, struck by Medusa's glance as it were, laboured with a petrified wrath to turn it into glory. Rejecting Romantic Germany and rejected by it, yet born prisoner to the law of social approval and public success, the language of Heine's early poems betrays 'the excessive mimetic zeal of the person who is excluded'.[2] Upon re-reading Adorno's astute five-page analysis of Heine's poetry as 'an attempt to draw estrangement itself into the sphere of intimate experience',[3] the truism of its eternal topos of 'unrequited love' has then been shown to centre around a very specific, yet rather universal, obsession. Like an ever-present shadow darkening the poet's soul, the *imago* of a woman shimmers forth in all his poems. Essentially due to his pervasive mistrust, Heine's destruction of the *imago* is then, however, a stylistically constant muse to a poet disillusioned with himself. Forever deprived of the solace of an imagined 'heavenly' Madonna in replacement for

---

[1] Novalis' programmatic dictum epitomizing the Early Romantic position. See NO III, p. 685, no. 671 [Das Undarstellbare darstellen].
[2] Adorno (1968), p. 83. [3] Adorno (1968), p. 85.

'the worldly',[4] Heine's poetic visions lack an Idealist spirit, and instead weave their spells around a suffocated heart. At issue is here too, to invoke Blanchot, the heart of poetry. But this poetry's heart lies outside the very mother tongue from which its vocabulary has been drawn: 'Everything German disgusts me; . . . The German language splits my ears', the young Heine once confessed.[5] Hence the travesty of the German folk-song through his 'little malicious songs'[6] – unmelodious, bilious, bizarre – which bear his particular Signature of Modernity.

To draw Heine the satirist into the sphere of immediacy identified with the German Romantic Lied is testimony to a kind of conviction that sees value behind the petrified mask. Indeed, Heine's overt shifting between the sentimental and the cynical, notwithstanding the occasional pretence of simplicity, may in fact be truly elusive. For these sarcastic gestures of always remaining down-to-earth are, after all, an efficient strategy to keep the private out of public sight. One might have thought, though, that within Schumann's own creative world a more congenial, less protective poet would have been more suited to the genre, as perhaps the Eichendorff Lieder suggest. Yet, in Schumann's choice and treatment of the poems from the *Lyrisches Intermezzo*, the tones of vulnerability and ambiguity lying beneath the alienating linguistic surface have been contained, if not heightened, precisely because Schumann allowed himself not to be assertive and final about their meaning.

Of course *Dichterliebe* is more than an attempt to 'interpret' Heine's poems, even apart from Schumann's emancipation from older models of song writing towards becoming the 'second poet' of these poems. The cycle shows at once an involvement with Early Romantic aesthetic thought and its intensification through procedures made possible by the very means of music. If the philosophers themselves had confessed 'Where philosophy ends, *poiesis* must begin',[7] then Schumann succeeded in introducing into music the Early Romantic idea of 'discourse' in what are in a literal sense 'character pieces' for the piano. But this idea of an ongoing dialogue within the Romantic Solitary, whose Schlegelian 'I finds itself split and divided'[8] and who seeks to 'identify the low Self with a better Self',[9] has found its ultimate realization in Schumann's song composition. Here is rendered audible the Romantic's desire that the Other, on the higher level of a human voice, enter into an intimate *discours d'amour* with the piano. With words speaking more often than not of the impossibility of fulfilment in love, Song 13 is perhaps the most powerful example in *Dichterliebe* conveying the sense of disintegration by its dramatization of the beloved's absence.

---

[4] See discussion of this issue in Part II, pp. 000–00, where Heine's letter (*HSA* XX, p. 22), here alluded to, has been fully quoted.

[5] *HSA* XX, p. 50 (Letter to his friend Sethe of 14 April 1822); [Alles was deutsch ist, ist mir zuwider; . . . Die deutsche Sprache zerreißt meine Ohren].

[6] *HSA* XX, p. 61 [kleine maliziöse Lieder].

[7] *KFSA*, p. 261, no. 48 [Wo die Philosophie aufhört, muß die Poesie anfangen]. For the term 'Poetry' as in *poiesis*, see the Introduction to Part I.

[8] *KFSA* XII, p. 381 [Das . . . Ich findet sich selbst gespalten und getrennt].

[9] Novalis as quoted in Frank (1989), pp. 272–273 [Das niedre Selbst wird mit einem bessern Selbst . . . identificirt]. See the Introduction., p. 27.

Drawn back into it a decade later, the Lenau song Op. 90/6 is a paraphrase so acute that it forms a critique as well as an anxious hyperbole of the earlier poetic sentiment, not without Schumann thereby risking pathos. The interlocking of present and past devolves here upon a Romantic dialectic of 'poetic time', a dialectic doubtlessly turning against the hope of memory-as-salvation.

'Sehnen und Verlangen' as a sentiment paramount to Romanticism has been seized structurally in its purest manifestation – through lack itself – in the first song of *Dichterliebe*. Without a tonal centre and by forgoing formal closure, it widens the 'wounded agony' sensed in Heine's 'Sehnen'[10] by virtue of its fragmentary form. Since 'the outside towards which it falls is not its edge',[11] Song 1 does not, as has been assumed in previous studies, provide a stable basis on which all other songs can rely, nor is it forcibly connected to Song 2. Instead, it opens up the structure of *Dichterliebe* into a constellation of phantasmal dialogues.

Across the subdued harmonic landscape of *Dichterliebe*, the rare exposure of a higher dissonance chord such as the diminished seventh on 'sprichst' prior to 'Ich liebe dich' in Song 4 is that sonority of Otherness that carries within it both distance and immediacy, for it is arresting in that it is alienating. Neither grounded nor lasting whenever it occurs (Songs 4a, 12 and 16) it transports *Dichterliebe* to reach those phosphoric moments of ascendancy or abyss that must be called either a nothing or a beyond. *Dichterliebe* in its passage through this sonority has not sought to solidify its meaning, but has at these moments of rupture and stillness manifested a time when the Janus face dissolves, when the mask is lowered to reveal a true face. Schumann shows here a kind of Mastery that neither submits to nor subjugates what it values most within the poetics of *Dichterliebe*.

Such sovereignty always unfolds on a different plane of signification, above the logic of continuity and coherence, in other words, behind the scenes and across the drama of Schumann's *fragments d'un discours d'amoureux*. In this way, the last postlude exerts an intensity that transcends the events accumulated over the course of *Dichterliebe*. With the fading away of the voice of the Other, which had for once been entirely outspoken, Schumann is able to fantasize in the void. Rhapsodically quoting and evoking moments of a past that is to decompose itself, the poet speaks with the voice of detachment, with the fractional diction of Romantic irony. Unlike Heine, who on closing the covers of the *Lyrisches Intermezzo* consigns it to an irrevocable darkness of disconsolation, Schumann renders the end with a lightness of tone that nominates *Dichterliebe* for a cathartic eternal return.

Over the course of its complicated publication history, *Dichterliebe* has already been decomposed in a material sense, when, in 1844, four songs were deleted from the original conception of 1840. The evidence brought together in this study suggests, however, that there is sufficient reason to consider the conception as valid. Numerous

---

[10] See Schumann's remark of 1835 in *GS* II, p. 140: 'the "Sehnen" of Heine, for whose deeply wounded pain music still possesses very different signs indeed, – ' [das 'Sehnen' von Heine, für dessen tief wunden Schmerz die Musik noch ganz andere Zeichen besitzt, –].

[11] Blanchot (1995), p. 46.

statements made by the composer between 1840 and 1843 in his correspondence with the publishers indicate his wish to see *Dichterliebe* published as consisting of twenty songs. Of significance here is also Schumann's assertion that 'it is a cycle of twenty songs, which form a whole, but each of which is also self-contained',[12] as well as the various terms he used as genre descriptions. In addition to the structural characteristics which the analytical discussion has hoped to demonstrate, it may ultimately be contended that *Dichterliebe* points to a compositional conception that not only tolerates, but elevates, the notion of the Romantic fragment system to the extent that its 'integrity' is not in jeopardy, even if parts of its text are missing.

In this study I hope, by way of interpreting a few selected songs from *Dichterliebe*, to have offered representative examples which demonstrate what may ambitiously be called a transposition into sound of theoretical speculations which found their highest expression with Friedrich Schlegel and Novalis. In this aim, the conflation of various techniques of analysis, including those generally excluded from the musicological domain, has been seen as a real advantage. In the concern with structure, with the structure of desire that distinguishes Schumann's musical language, the lessons taught by more recent French thinkers have contributed to greater conceptional clarity. Such influence must not be at the cost of 'authenticity'. Rather, the attempt to be true to a theory, and to proceed in accordance with certain original texts, means also, in this case, the acknowledgement that the substance of Early Romantic thought has found a response in contemporary critical thought.

[12] See the full discussion in the Introduction to Part III.

BIBLIOGRAPHY

Abbate, Carolyn, 1991 *Unsung Voices: Opera and Musical Narrative in the Nineteenth Century* (Princeton: Princeton University Press).

Abraham, Gerald, 1980 'Robert (Alexander) Schumann' (text), *The New Grove Dictionary of Music and Musicians*, ed. Stanley Sadie, 20 vols. (London: Macmillan), XVI, 831–854.

Adorno, Theodor Wiesengrund, 1928 'Situation des Liedes', *Gesammelte Schriften*, ed. Rolf Tiedemann, 20 vols. (Frankfurt am Main: Suhrkamp, 1970–86), xviii: *Musikalische Schriften* V, 345–353.

1934 'Brahms aktuel', *Gesammelte Schriften*, ed. Rolf Tiedemann, 20 vols. (Frankfurt am Main: Suhrkamp, 1970–86), xviii: *Musikalische Schriften* V, 200–203.

1949 'Toward a Reappraisal of Heine', *Gesammelte Schriften*, ed. Rolf Tiedemann, 20 vols. (Frankfurt am Main: Suhrkamp, 1970–86), xx/1: *Vermischte Schriften* I, 441–452.

1968/91a 'Die Wunde Heine, sowie Reden über Lyrik und Gesellschaft', *Noten zur Literatur I* (Frankfurt am Main: Suhrkamp). Also available as 'Heine the Wound', *Notes to Literature*, ed. Rolf Tiedemann, trans. Shierry Weber Nicholsen, 3 vols. (New York: Columbia University Press, 1991–92), I, 80–85.

1969 'Zum Problem der musikalischen Analyse' [lecture given at the Hochschule für Musik und Darstellende Kunst, Frankfurt am Main in 1969; tape recording of a lecture held at the Library of the Hochschule, and as yet unpublished in German]. Trans. Max Paddison as 'On the Problem of Musical Analysis', *Music Analysis*, 1:2 (July 1982), 169–187.

1978 'Fragment über Musik und Sprache', *Gesammelte Schriften*, ed. Rolf Tiedemann, 20 vols. (Frankfurt am Main: Suhrkamp, 1970–86), XVI: *Musikalische Schriften* I–III; I: *Quasi una fantasia*, 251–256.

1974/91b 'Zum Gedächtnis Eichendorffs – Coda: Schumanns Lieder', *Gesammelte Schriften*, ed. Rolf Tiedemann, 20 vols. (Frankfurt am Main: Suhrkamp, 1970–86), XI: *Noten zur Literatur*, 69–74. Also available as 'In Memory of Eichendorff', *Notes to Literature*, ed. Rolf Tiedemann, trans. Shierry Weber Nicholsen, 3 vols. (New York: Columbia University Press, 1991–92), I, 55–79.

1993 *Ästhetische Theorie*, ed. Gretel Adorno and Rolf Tiedemann, 13th edn (Frankfurt am Main: Suhrkamp). Also available as *Aesthetic Theory*, ed. Gretel Adorno and Rolf Tiedemann, trans. C. Lenhardt (London: Routledge & Kegan Paul, 1984).

Agawu, Kofi V., 1984 'Structural "Highpoints" in Schumann's *Dichterliebe*', *Music Analysis*, 3:2, 159–180.

1994 'Ambiguity in Tonal Music: a Preliminary Study', *Theory, Analysis and Meaning in Music*, ed. Anthony Pople (Cambridge: Cambridge University Press), 86–107.

1996 'The Narrative Impulse in the Second Nachtmusik from Mahler's Seventh Symphony', *Analytical Strategies and Musical Interpretation: Essays on Nineteenth- and Twentieth-Century Music* ed. Craig Ayrey and Mark Everist (New York: Cambridge University Press), 226–241.

Allemann, Beda, 1969 *Ironie und Dichtung*, 2nd edn (Pfullingen: Neske).

Altenhofer, Norbert, 1979 'Chiffre, Hieroglyphe, Palimpsest: Vorformen tiefenhermeneutis-cher und intertextueller Interpretation im Werk Heines', *Texthermeneutik: Aktualität: Geschichte: Kritik*, ed. Ulrich Nassen (Paderborn: Schöningh), 149–193.

1982 'Ästhetik und Arrangements: Zu Heines "Buch der Lieder"', *Text und Kritik: Heinrich Heine*, 18/19, 16–32.

1987 'Nachwort' for Heinrich Heine, *Die Romantische Schule* (Frankfurt am Main: Insel), 221–236.

1993 *Die verlorene Augensprache: Über Heinrich Heine*, ed. Volker Bohn (Frankfurt am Main: Insel).

Altenhofer, Norbert, and R., eds., 1971 'Anordnung' and 'Zyklus', *Heinrich Heine*, 3 vols., Dichter über ihre Dichtungen 8 (Munich: Heimeran), III, 459 and 516.

Altmann-Berlin, Wilhelm, 1923 'Bisher unveröffentliche Briefe Robert Schumanns', *Die Musik*, 15 (1923), 865–869.

Arnim, Achim von, and Brentano, Clemens, 1987 'Von Volksliedern', *Des Knaben Wunderhorn: Kritische Ausgabe*, ed. Heinz Rölleke (Stuttgart: Reclam), 379–414.

Atkins, Stuart, ed., 1973 *Heine Werke I: Buch der Lieder: Studienausgabe*, 2 vols. (Munich: Beck).

Ayrey, Craig, 1982 'Berg's "Scheideweg": Analytical Issues in Op. 2/ii', *Music Analysis*, 1:2 (July), 89–202.

Barilier, Etienne, 2000 'Poésie et musique: IV: Heine-Schumann, Dichterliebe', *Revue musicale de Suisse romande*, 53: 4, 31–50.

Barthes, Roland, 1968 'L'effet de réel', *Communications*, 11, 84–89.

1975 *Roland Barthes sur Roland Barthes* (Paris: Editions du Seuil).

1977a *L'empire des signes* (Geneva: Editions d'Art Albert Skira).

1977b *Fragments d'un discours amoureux* (Paris: Editions du Seuil).

1985a 'le grain de la voix', *musique en jeu*, 9 (1972), 57–63. Also avaliable as 'The Grain of the Voice', *The Responsibility of Forms: Critical Essays on Music, Art, and Representation*, trans. Richard Howard (New York: Hill and Wang), 267–277.

1985b 'The Romantic Song', *The Responsibility of Forms: Critical Essays on Music, Art, and Representation*, trans. Richard Howard (New York: Hill and Wang), 287–296.

1985c 'Loving Schumann', *The Responsibility of Forms: Critical Essays on Music, Art, and Representation*, trans. Richard Howard (New York: Hill and Wang), 293–298.

1985d 'Rasch', *The Responsibility of Forms: Critical Essays on Music, Art, and Representation*, trans. Richard Howard (New York: Hill and Wang), 299–312.

1995 'Piano-souvenir', *Œuvres complètes*, ed. Eric Marty (Paris: Editions du Seuil), 1206–1207.

Behler, Ernst, 1973 'Die Kunst der Reflexion: Das frühromantische Denken im Hinblick auf Nietzsche', *Untersuchungen zu Literatur als Geschichte: Festschrift für Benno von Wiese*, ed. Vincent J. Günther *et al.* (Berlin: E. Schmidt), 219–248.

1987 'Friedrich Schlegel's Theorie des Verstehens: Hermeneutik oder Dekonstruktion?' *Die Aktualität der Frühromantik* (Paderborn: Schöningh), 141–160.

1992 *Frühromantik* (Berlin: de Gruyter).

1993 *German Romantic Literary Theory* (Cambridge: Cambridge University Press).

Behler, Ernst, and Hörisch, Jochen, eds., 1987 *Die Aktualität der Frühromantik* (Paderborn: Schöningh).

Benary, Peter, 1967 'Die Technik der musikalischen Analyse dargestellt am ersten Lied aus Robert Schumanns "Dichterliebe"', *Versuche musikalischer Analysen: Sieben Beiträge*, ed. Peter Benary, Veröffentlichungen des Instituts für Neue Musik und Musikerziehung, Darmstadt 8 (Berlin: Merseburger), 21–29.

Benjamin, Walter, 1973 *Der Begriff der Kunstkritik in der deutschen Romantik*, ed. Hermann Schweppenhäuser (Frankfurt am Main: Suhrkamp).

1977 *The Origin of German Tragic Drama*, trans. John Osborne (London: Verso).

Berg, Alban, 1982 'The Musical Impotence of Hans Pfitzner's "New Aesthetic"' (written in 1920 about Schumann's *Träumerei*, Op. 15, No. 7), in Willi Reich, *The Life and Works of Alban Berg*, trans. Cornelius Cardew (New York: Da Capo).

Berman, Antoine, 1984 *L'Epreuve de l'Etranger* (Paris: Gallimard).

Biedermann, Hans, 1989 *Knaurs Lexikon der Symbole*, ed. Gerhard Riemann (Munich: Droemer Knaur).

Blanchot, Maurice, 1969 'L'Athenaeum', *L'Entretien Infini* (Paris: Editions Gallimard), 515–527. Also available as *The Infinite Conversation*, trans. Susan Hanson (Minneapolis: University of Minnesota Press, 1993).

1980/95 *L'Ecriture du désastre* (Paris: Editions Gallimard). Also available as *The Writing of the Disaster*, trans. Ann Smock (London: University of Nebraska Press, 1995).

Bloom, Harold, 1972 *The Visionary Company: A Reading in English Romantic Poetry*, 2nd rev. edn (Ithaca: Cornell University Press).

1973 *The Anxiety of Influence: A Theory of Poetry* (New York: Oxford University Press).

Blume, Friedrich, 1974 'Romantik', *Epochen der Musikgeschichte* (Kassel: Bärenreiter), 78–83.

Boetticher, Wolfgang, 1970 'Zur Zitatpraxis in R. Schumanns frühen Klavierwerken', *Speculum Musicae Artis: Festgabe für Heinrich Husmann*, ed. Heinz Becker and Reinhard Gerlach (Munich: Wilhelm Fink), 63–73.

Bohn, Volker, ed., 1987 *Romantik, Literatur und Philosophie: Internationale Beiträge zur Poetik* (Frankfurt am Main: Suhrkamp).

Bowie, Andrew, 1990 *Aesthetics and Subjectivity from Kant to Nietzsche* (Manchester: Manchester University Press).

Bowie, Malcolm, 1991 *Lacan*, Fontana Modern Masters, ed. Frank Kermode (London and Glasgow: Fontana).

Bracht, H. J., 1993 'Schumanns "Papillons" und die Ästhetik der Frühromantik', *Archiv für Musikwissenschaft*, 1, 71–84.

Brinkmann, Reinhold, 1997 *Schumann und Eichendorff: Studien zum 'Liederkreis' Opus 39*, Musik-Konzepte, no. 95, 1–89.

Broda, Martine, 1997 *l'amour du nom: essay sur le lyrisme et la lyrique amoureuse* (Paris: José Corti).

Brummack, Jürgen, ed., 1980 *Heinrich Heine: Epoche – Werk – Wirkung* (Munich: Beck).

Butor, Michel, 1967 'Musik, eine realistische Kunst', *MELOS Zeitschrift für neue Musik*, 2, 37–44.

Casey, Timothy J., ed., 1992 *Jean Paul: A Reader*, trans. Erika Casey (Baltimore: Johns Hopkins University Press).

Cone, Edward T., 1957 'Words into Music: The Composer's Approach to the Text', *Sound and Poetry*, ed. Northrop Frye (New York: Columbia University Press), 3–15.

1974 *The Composer's Voice* (Berkeley: University of California Press).

1992 'Poet's Love or Composer's Love?' *Music and Text: Critical Inquiries*, ed. Steven Paul Scher (Cambridge: Cambridge University Press, 1992), 177–192.

Conrad, Dieter, 1982 'Schumanns Liedkomposition – von Schubert her gesehen', *Musik-Konzepte Sonderband: Robert Schumann II*, ed. Heinz-Klaus Metzger and Rainer Riehn (Munich: Edition text + kritik), 129–169.

Cooper Martin, 1952 'The Songs', *Schumann: A Symposium,* ed. Gerald Abraham (Oxford: Oxford University Press).

Culler, Jonathan, 1975 *Structuralist Poetics: Structuralism, Linguistics and the Study of Literature* (London: Routledge).

Dällenbach, Lucien, ed., 1984 *Fragment und Totalität* (Frankfurt am Main: Suhrkamp).

Dahlhaus, Carl, 1969a 'Klassizität, Romantik, Modernität: Zur Philosophie der Musikgeschichte des 19. Jahrhundert', *Die Ausbreitung des Historismus über die Musik: Aufsätze und Diskussionen*, ed. Walter Wiora, Studien zur Musikgeschichte des 19. Jahrhunderts 14 (Regensburg: Bosse), 261–276.

1969b 'Geschichtliche und ästhetische Erfahrung', *Die Ausbreitung des Historismus über die Musik*, ed. Walter Wiora (Regensburg: Bosse), 243–247.

1973 'Das "Verstehen" von Musik und die Sprache der musikalischen Analyse', *Musik und Verstehen*, ed. Peter Faltin and Hans-Peter Reinecke (Cologne: Volk and Gerig), 37–47.

1978 *Die Idee der absoluten Musik* (Kassel: Bärenreiter).

1980 *Die Musik des 19. Jahrhunderts* (Wiesbaden: Akademische Verlagsgesellschaft Athenaion).

1988 *Klassische und Romantische Musikästhetik* (Laaber: Laaber Verlag).

1992 'Sprache und Tonsprache', *The Romantic Tradition: German Literature and Music in the Nineteenth Century*, ed. Gerald Chapple, Frederick Hall and Hans Schulte (Lanham: University of America Press).

Daverio, John, 1993 *Nineteenth-Century Music and the German Romantic Ideology* (New York: Schirmer).

1996 'The Song Cycle: Journeys through a Romantic Landscape', *German Lieder in the Nineteenth Century*, ed. Rufus Hallmark (New York: Schirmer), 279–312.

1997 *Robert Schumann: Herald of a 'New Poetic Age'* (New York: Oxford University Press).

2001 'Robert (Alexander) Schumann', *The New Grove Dictionary of Music and Musicians: Second Edition*, ed. Stanley Sadie, 29 vols. (London: Macmillan).

De Mul, Jos, 1999 *Romantic Desire in (Post)modern Art and Philosophy*, The Suny Series in Postmodern Culture, ed. Joseph Natoli (Albany: State University of New York).

2000 *The Tragedy of Finitude: Dilthey's Hermeneutics of Life* (New Haven: Yale University Press).

Deleuze, Gilles, and Guattari, Félix, 1980/88 *Mille Plateaux*, 2 vols. (Paris: Les Editions de Minuit), II: *Capitalisme et Schizophrénie*. Also available as *A Thousand Plateaus: Capitalism and Schizophrenia*, trans. and foreword by Brian Massumi (London: Athlone, 1988).

Deleuze, Gilles, and Parnet, Claire, 1977 *Dialogues* (Paris: Flammarion). Also available as *Dialogues*, trans. Hugh Tomlinson and Barbara Habberjam (London: Athlone, 1987).

Derrida, Jacques, 1967 *La voix et le phénomène: Introduction au problème du signe dans la phénoménologie de Husserl* (Paris: Presses Universitaires de France).

1968 'La Différance', *Tel Quel: Théorie d'ensemble (choix)* (Paris: Editions du Seuil), 43–68.

1972 *Marges de la philosophie* (Paris: Editions de Minuit).

1980 *La Carte postale de Socrate à Freud et au-delà* (Paris: Flammarion).

Dietel, Gerhard, 1989 *'Eine neue poetische Zeit': Musikanschauung und stilistische Tendenzen im Klavierwerk Robert Schumanns* (Kassel: Bärenreiter).

Dill, Heinz J., 1989 'Romantic Irony in the Works of Robert Schumann', *The Musical Quarterly*, 73:2, 172–195.

Draheim, Joachim, 1991 'Robert Schumann als Übersetzer', *Robert Schumann und die Dichter*, ed. Joseph A. Kruse (Düsseldorf: Droste), 41–48.

Dunsby, Jonathan, 1983 'The Multy-Piece in Brahms: Fantasien Op. 116', *Brahms: Biographical and Analytical Studies*, ed. Robert Pascall (Cambridge: Cambridge University Press), 167–189.

Dürr, Walter, 1984 *Das deutsche Sololied im 19. Jahrhundert: Untersuchungen zu Sprache und Musik* (Wilhelmshaven: Heinrichshofen).

Eagleton, Terry, 1983 *Literary Theory* (Minneapolis: University of Minnesota Press).

Erler, Hermann, 1887 *Robert Schumanns Leben aus seinen Briefen geschildert*, 2 vols. (Berlin: n.p.).

Estermann, Alfred, and Galley, Eberhard, eds., 1981 *Heinrich Heines Werk im Urteil seiner Zeitgenossen* (Hamburg: Hoffmann und Campe).

Feldmann, Fritz, 1952 'Zur Frage des "Liederjahres" bei Robert Schumann', *Archiv für Musikwissenschaft*, 9, 246–269.

Ferris, David, 2000 *Schumann's 'Eichendorff Liederkreis' and the Genre of the Romantic Cycle* (New York: Oxford University Press).

Finson, Jon W., 1994 'The Intentional Tourist: Romantic Irony in the Eichendorff Liederkreis of Robert Schumann', *Schumann and His World*, ed. R. Larry Todd (Princeton: Princeton University Press), 156–170.

Firchow, Peter, 1991 translator of the *Athenaeum* (see above), available as *Philosophical Fragments* (Minneapolis: University of Minnesota Press, 1991).

Floros, Constantin, 1977 'Literarische Ideen in der Musik des 19. Jahrhunderts', *Zur Musikgeschichte des 19. Jahrhunderts*, ed. Constantin Floros *et al.*, Hamburger Jahrbuch für Musikwissenschaft 2 (Hamburg: K. D. Wagner), 7–62.

1981 'Schumanns musikalische Poetik', *Musik-Konzepte Sonderband: Robert Schumann I*, ed. Heinz-Klaus Metzger and Rainer Riehn (Munich: Edition text + kritik), 90–104.

Foster, Peter, 2001 'Multi-piece', *The New Grove Dictionary of Music and Musicians: Second Edition*, ed. Stanley Sadie, 29 vols. (London: Macmillan).

Foucault, Michel, 1954 *Maladie mentale et personnalité* (Paris: Presses Universitaires de France); 2nd rev. edn retitled *Maladie mentale et psychologie* (Paris: Presses Universitaires de France, 1962).

1963 *Naissance de la clinique* (Paris: Presses Universitaires de France). Also available as *The Birth of the Clinic*, trans. Alan Sheridan (London: Travistock, 1973).

1970 *The Order of Things: An Archaeology of the Human Sciences*, trans. Alan Sheridan (London: Pantheon).

Frank, Manfred, 1972 *Das Problem 'Zeit' in der deutschen Romantik: Zeitbewußtsein und Bewußtsein von Zeitlichkeit in der frühromantischen Philosophie und in Tiecks Dichtung* (Munich: Winkler).

1985 *Das individuelle Allgemeine: Textstrukturierung und Textinterpretation nach Schleiermacher* (Frankfurt am Main: Suhrkamp).

1989 *Einführung in die frühromantische Ästhetik: Vorlesungen* (Frankfurt am Main: Suhrkamp).

1990 'Was ist ein literarischer Text und was heißt es, ihn zu verstehen?' *Das Sagbare und das Unsagbare: Studien zur deutsch-französischen Hermeneutik und Texttheorie*, new edn (Frankfurt am Main: Suhrkamp).

1990 'Das "wahre Subjekt" und sein Doppel: Jacques Lacans Hermeneutik', *Das Sagbare und das Unsagbare: Studien zur deutsch-französischen Hermeneutik und Texttheorie*, new edn (Frankfurt am Main: Suhrkamp), 334–361.

1994 'Philosophische Grundlagen der Frühromantik', *Athenäum: Jahrbuch für Romantik*, 4, 37–130.

1997a *'Unendliche Annäherung': Die Anfänge der philosophischen Frühromantik* (Frankfurt am Main: Suhrkamp).

1997b 'Wie reaktionär war eigentlich die Frühromantik? Elemente zur Aufstörung der Meinungsbildung', *Athenäum: Jahrbuch für Romantik*, 7, 141–166.

Frenzel, Elisabeth, 1992 *Motive der Weltliteratur: Ein Lexikon dichtungsgeschichtlicher Längsschnitte*, 4th rev. edn (Stuttgart: Körner).

Freud, Sigmund, (1969–1975) *Die Freud-Studienausgabe*, ed. Alexander Mitscherlich, Angela Richards and James Strachey, 10 vols. (Frankfurt am Main: Fischer Verlag).

'Trauer und Melancholie', SA 3 (1917).

'Das Unheimliche', SA 4 (1919).

'Das Unbehagen in der Kultur', SA 9 (1930).

Die Traumdeutung, SA 2 (1900).

Fuerst, Norbert, 1966 'The Age of Heine?' *The Victorian Age of German Literature* (London: Dobson), 75–100.

Futterknecht, Franz, 1985 *Heinrich Heine: Ein Versuch* (Tübingen: Narr).

Gadamer, Hans-Georg, 1987 'Frühromantik, Hermeneutik, Dekonstruktivismus', *Die Aktualität der Frühromantik*, ed. Ernst Behler and Jochen Hörisch (Paderborn: Schöningh), 251–260.

1990 *Gesammelte Werke*, ed. Hans-Georg Gadamer, 10 vols. (Tübingen: Mohr, 1960–95), I: *Wahrheit und Methode: Grundzüge einer philosophischen Hermeneutik*, ed. Hans-Georg Gadamer, 6th edn. Also available as *Truth and Method*, ed. John Cumming and Garrett Barden, trans. William Glen-Doepel (London: Sheed & Ward, 1981).

Galley, Eberhard, and Estermann, Alfred, eds., 1981 *Heinrich Heines Werk im Urteil seiner Zeitgenossen* (Hamburg: Hoffmann und Campe).

Garland, Henry and Mary, eds., 1986 *The Oxford Companion to German Literature*, 2nd edn (Oxford: Oxford University Press).

Gerstmeier, August, 1982 *Die Lieder Schumanns: Zur Musik des frühen 19. Jahrhunderts*, Münchner Veröffentlichungen zur Musikgeschichte 34 (Tutzing: Hans Schneider).

Habermas, Jürgen, 1985a *Die Neue Unübersichtlichkeit* (Frankfurt am Main: Suhrkamp).

1985b/87 *Der philosophische Diskurs der Moderne* (Frankfurt am Main: Suhrkamp, 1985). Also available as *The Philosophical Discourse of Modernity*, trans. Frederick Lawrence (Cambridge, Mass.: MIT University Press, 1987).

Haesler, Ludwig, 1982 'Sprachvertonung in Robert Schumanns Liederzyklus "Dichterliebe" (1840): Ein Beitrag zur Psychoanalyse der musikalischen Kreativität', *Psyche*, 36, 908–950.

1987 'Sprachvertonung in Robert Schumanns Dichterliebe: Zur Psychoanalyse von Persönlichkeit und Werk', *Schumanns Werke: Text und Interpretation: 16 Studien*, ed. Akio Mayeda and Klaus Wolfgang Niemöller (Mainz: Schott), 155–164.

Hallmark, Rufus, 1977 'The Sketches for *Dichterliebe*', *19th Century Music*, 1, 110–136.

1979 *The Genesis of Schumann's 'Dichterliebe': A Source Study*, Studies in Musicology 12 (Ann Arbor: UMI Research Press).

1987 'Schumanns Behandlung seiner Liedtexte: Vorläufiger Bericht zu einer neuen Ausgabe und zu einer Neubewertung von seinen Liedern', *Schumanns Werke: Text und Interpretation: 16 Studien*, ed. Akio Mayeda and Klaus Wolfgang Niemöller (Mainz: Schott), 29–42.

1996 'Robert Schumann: The Poet Sings', *German Lieder in the Nineteenth Century*, ed. Rufus Hallmark (New York: Schirmer), 75–118.

Hamburger, Käte, 1957 *Die Logik der Dichtung* (Stuttgart: Klett).

Hanslick, Eduard, 1991 *Vom Musikalisch Schönen* [Photographic reprint of the first edn of Leipzig, 1854] (Darmstadt: Wissenschaftliche Buchgesellschaft).

Hegel, Georg Wilhelm Friedrich, 1965 *Ästhetik*, ed. Friedrich Bassenge, 2 vols. (Frankfurt am Main: Europäische Verlagsanstalt). Also available as *Aesthetics*, trans. T. M. Knox, 2 vols. (Oxford: Oxford University Press, 1975).

Hoeckner, Berthold, 1997 'Schumann and Romantic Distance', *Journal of the American Musicological Society*, 50:1, 55–132.

2001 'Poet's Love and Composer's Love', *Music Theory Online. The Online Journal of the Society for Music Theory*, 7:5 (October).

Hoffmann, Ernst Theodor Amadeus, 1988 *Schriften zur Musik*, ed. Friedrich Schnapp (Berlin [East]: Aufbau Verlag).

Hofmann, Kurt, 1979 *Die Erstdrucke der Werke von Robert Schumann* (Tutzing: Hans Schneider).

Horton, Charles T., 1979 'A Structural Function of Dynamics in Schumann's "Ich grolle nicht"', *In Theory Only*, 8, 30–46.

Jackson, John E., 1998 *La Poésie et son Autre. Essai sur la modernité* (Paris: Editions José Corti).

Jacobs, Robert L., 1949 'Schumann and Jean Paul', *Music and Letters*, 30, 250–258.

Jakobson, Roman, 1987a 'Linguistics and Poetry', *Language in Literature*, ed. Krystina Pomorska and Stephen Rudy (Cambridge, Mass.: Harvard University Press), 62–94.

    1987b 'Subliminal Verbal Patterning in Poetry', *Language in Literature*, ed. Krystina Pomorska and Stephen Rudy (Cambridge, Mass.: Harvard University Press), 250–261.

    1987c 'What is Poetry?' *Language in Literature*, ed. Krystina Pomorska and Stephen Rudy (Cambridge, Mass.: Harvard University Press), 368–378.

Jankélévitch, Vladimir, 1983 *La Musique et l'ineffable* (Paris: Seuil).

Jankélévitch, Vladimir, and Berlowitz, Béatrice, 1978 *Quelque part dans l'inachevé* (Paris: Editions Gallimard).

Jansen, Gustav, 1904 *Robert Schumanns Briefe* (Leipzig: Breitkopf & Härtel).

Jokl, Johann, 1991 *Von der Unmöglichkeit romantischer Liebe: Heinrich Heines 'Buch der Lieder'* (Opladen: Westdeutscher Verlag).

Jost, Peter, 2000 'Komponieren mit Schumann: Henri Pousseurs Dichterliebesreigentraum', *Musiktheorie*, 15:2, 121–136.

Kaldewey, Helma, 1991 'Die Gedichtabschriften Robert und Clara Schumanns', *Robert Schumann und die Dichter*, ed. Joseph A. Kruse (Düsseldorf: Droste), 88–99.

Kapp, Reinhard, 1984 *Studien zum Spätwerk Robert Schumanns* (Tutzing: Hans Schneider).

    1987 'Tempo und Charakter in der Musik Schumanns', *Schumanns Werke: Text und Interpretation: 16 Studien*, ed. Akio Mayeda and Klaus Niemöller (Mainz: Schott), 193–222.

Kierkegaard, Søren, 1966 *The Concept of Irony with Constant Reference to Sokrates* (1841), trans. Lee Chapel (London: Collins).

Köhler, Hans Joachim, ed., 1986 *Robert Schumann: Dichterliebe nach Gedichten von Heinrich Heine: Op. 48 für Singstimme und Klavier* (Leipzig: Peters).

    1994 'Schumann, der Autodidakt: Zum genetischen Zusammenhang von variativem Prinzip und poetischer Idee', *Schumann Studien 3/4*, ed. Gerd Nauhaus (Cologne: Verlag Dr Gisela Schewe), 188–198.

Komar, Arthur, 1971 *Robert Schumann: Dichterliebe*, ed. Arthur Komar, Norton Critical Score (New York: Norton).

Koopmann, Helmut, 1975 'Heinrich Heine in Deutschland: Aspekte seiner Wirkung im 19. Jahrhundert', *Heinrich Heine*, ed. Helmut Koopmann, Wege der Forschung 289 (Darmstadt: Wissenschaftliche Buchgesellschaft).

Kramer, Lawrence, 1984 *Music and Poetry: The Nineteenth Century and After* (Berkeley and Los Angeles).

Kramer, Richard, 1994 *Distant Cycles* (Chicago: University of Chicago Press).

    1997 'The Hedgehog: Of Fragments Finished and Unfinished', *19th Century Music*, 21:2 (Fall), 134–148.

Kretzschmar, H., 1906 'Robert Schumann als Ästhetiker', *Jahrbuch der Musikbibliothek Peters*, 13, 49–73. Also in *Gesammelte Aufsätze*, II (Leipzig: Breitkopf & Härtel, 1911), 294–324.

Kristeva, Julia, 1969 *Séméiotiké: Recherches pour une sémanalyse* (Paris: Editions du Seuil).

    1974 *Des Chinoises* (Paris: Editions des femmes).

1979 'Le vréel', *Folle vérité: vérité et vraisemblance du texte psychotique*, ed. Julia Kristeva and Jean-Michel Ribette (Paris: Editions du Seuil), 11–35.

1987 *Soleil Noir: Dépression et Mélancholie* (Paris: Editions Gallimard). Also available as *Black Sun: Depression and Melancholia*, trans. Leon S. Roudiez (New York: Columbia University Press, 1989).

Kruse, Joseph A., ed., 1991 *Robert Schumann und die Dichter* (Düsseldorf: Droste).

Lacan, Jacques, 1966 'Le stade du miroir comme formateur de la fonction du Je' (1949), *Ecrits I* (Paris: Editions du Seuil), 89–97. Also available in *Ecrits: A Selection*, trans. Alan Sheridan (London: Travistock, 1977).

Lacoue-Labarthe, Philippe, 1997 *La poésie comme expérience* (Paris: Bourgois).

Lacoue-Labarthe, Philippe, and Nancy, Jean-Luc, eds., 1987 *L'Absolu littéraire: Théorie de la littérature du romantisme allemand* (Paris: Editions du Seuil). Also available as *The Literary Absolute: The Theory of Literature in German Romanticism* (Albany: State University of New York Press).

Laplanche, Jean, and Pontalis, J.-B., 1994 *Vocabulaire de la Psychanalyse*, 12th edn (Paris: Presses Universitaires de France). Also available as *The Language of Psychoanalysis*, with an Introduction by Daniel Lagache, trans. Donald Nicholson-Smith (London: Karnac Books and The Institut of Psychoanalysis, 1988).

Lenau, Nikolaus, 1993 *Gedichte*, ed. Hartmut Steinecke (Stuttgart: Reclam).

Lévinas, Emmanuel, 1982 *Ethique et Infini: Dialogues avec Philippe Nemo* (Paris: Fayard).

1992 *Totalité et Infini: Essai sur l'extériorité* (The Hague: Kluwer Academic).

Lippmann, E. A., 1964 'Theory and Practice in Schumann's Aesthetics', *Journal of the American Musicological Society*, 17, 310–345.

Lukács, Georg, 1975 *Kurze Skizze einer Geschichte der deutschen Literatur* (Neuwied: Luchterhand).

Lurker, Manfred *et al.*, eds., 1991 *Wörterbuch der Symbolik*, 5th rev. edn (Stuttgart: Kröner).

Lyotard, Jean-François, 1984 *The Postmodern Condition: A Report on Knowledge* (Minneapolis: University of Minnesota Press).

MacDonald, Hugh, 1988 'G-flat', *19th Century Music*, 13 (Spring), 221–237.

McCreless, Patrick, 1986 'Song Order in the Song Cycle: Schumann's *Liederkreis*, op. 39', *Music Analysis*, 5, 5–28.

McFarland, Thomas, 1981 *Romanticism and the Forms of Ruin: Wordsworth, Coleridge, and Modalities of Fragmentation* (Princeton: Princeton University Press).

McGann, Jerome J., 1985 *The Romantic Ideology: A Critical Investigation* (Chicago: University of Chicago Press).

Maintz, Marie Luise, 1995 *Franz Schubert in der Rezeption Robert Schumanns: Studien zur Ästhetik und Instrumentalmusik* (Kassel: Bärenreiter).

Marston, Nicholas, 1991 'Schumann's Monument to Beethoven', *19th Century Music*, 14 (Spring), 247–263.

1992 *Schumann: Fantasie: Op. 17*, Cambridge Music Handbooks (Cambridge: Cambridge University Press).

Mauser, Siegfried, 1997 '"Ich höre den Dichter sprechen, wenn ich ihn lese..." : Zu Wilhelm Killmayers Liederbuch Heine-Portrait', *Neue Zeitschrift für Musik*, 158:5 (Sept.–Oct.), 46–49.

Meissner, Bernhard, 1985 *Geschichtsrezeption als Schaffenskorrelat* (Bern: Francke).

Mooral, Christine, 1997 'Romantische Ironie in Robert Schumann's Nachtstücken, op. 23', *Archiv für Musikwissenschaft*, 54:1, 68–83.

Moore, Gerald, 1981 *Poet's Love: The Songs and Cycles of Schumann* (New York: Taplinger).

Nägli, Hans Georg, 1811 'Historisch-kritische Erörterungen und Notizen über die deutsche
    Gesangs-Cultur', *Allgemeine Musikalische Zeitung*, 13 (Leipzig: Breitkopf & Härtel), cols.
    629–642 and 645–652.
    1817 'Die Liederkunst', *Allgemeine Musikalische Zeitung*, 19 (Leipzig: Breitkopf & Härtel),
    col. 765.
Neumeyer, David, 1982 'Organic Structure and the Song Cycle: Another Look at
    Schumann's "Dichterliebe"', *Music Theory Spectrum*, 4, 92–105.
    1997 'Synthesis and Association, Structure, and Design in Multi-Movement Composi-
    tions', *Music Theory in Concept and Practice*, ed. James Baker, David Beach and Jonathan
    W. Bernard (Rochester: University of Rochester Press), 197–216.
Newcomb, Anthony, 1984 'Once More "Between Absolute and Program Music": Schu-
    mann's Second Symphony', *19th Century Music*, 7 (Spring), 133–250.
    1987 'Schumann and Late Eighteenth-Century Narrative Strategies', *19th Century Music*,
    11 (Fall), 164–174.
Nietzsche, Friedrich, 1980 'On Music and Words', trans. Walter Kaufmann as an appendix
    in Carl Dahlhaus, *Between Romanticism and Modernism*, trans. Mary Whittall (Berkeley:
    University of California Press), 103–119.
Novalis, 1953–57 *Werke: Briefe: Dokumente*, ed. Ewald Wasmuth, I–IV (Heidelberg:
    L. Schneider).
    1962 *Werke und Briefe*, ed. Alfred Kelletat (Munich: Winkler).
Nussbaum, Martha, 1990 *Love's Knowledge: Essays on Philosophy and Literature* (Oxford: Oxford
    University Press).
    2001 *Upheavals of Thought: The Intelligence of Emotions* (Cambridge: Cambridge University
    Press).
O'Brien, William Arctander, 1995 *Novalis: Signs of Revolution* (Durham, NC: Duke Univer-
    sity Press).
Peake, Luise Eitel, 1968 'The Song Cycle: A Preliminary Inquiry into the Beginning of
    the Romantic Song Cycle and the Nature of an Art Form' (unpublished doctoral
    dissertation, Columbia University).
Perraudin, Michael, 1989 *Heinrich Heine: Poetry in Context: A Study of the Buch der Lieder*
    (Oxford: Berg).
Perrey, Beate, 1999 'Rationalisierung von Sinnlichkeit in Heines Lyrischem Intermezzo',
    Aufklärung und Skepsis. Internationaler Heine-Kongreß 1997 zum 200. Geburtstag, ed. Joseph
    A. Kruse, Bernd Witte and Karin Füllner (Stuttgart and Weimar: Metzler), 846–857.
Plantinga, Leon B., 1966 'Schumann's View of "Romantic"', *The Musical Quarterly*, 52,
    221–232.
Pontalis, J.-B., ed., 1994 'L'inachèvement', *Nouvelle Revue de Psychanalyse*, 50 (Paris: Editions
    Gallimard).
    2000 'Une pensée qui serait rêvante', *Fenêtres* (Paris: Editions Gallimard).
Pousseur, Henri, 1982 'Schumann ist der Dichter: Fünfundzwanzig Momente einer Lektüre
    der *Dichterliebe*', trans. H. R. Zeller, *Musik-Konzepte Sonderband: Robert Schumann II*, ed.
    Heinz-Klaus Metzger and Rainer Riehn (Munich: Edition text + kritik), 3–128.
    1993 *Schumann, Le Poète: Vingt-cinq moments d'une lecture de 'Dichterliebe'* [with a postscript
    to the French edition] (Paris: Méridiens Klincksieck).
Prawer, Siegfried S., 1960 *Heine: Buch der Lieder*, Studies in German Literature 1 (London:
    Arnold).
Praz, Mario, 1951 *The Romantic Agony*, trans. Angus Davidson, 2nd edn (Oxford: Oxford
    University Press).
Rank, Otto, 1993 *Der Doppelgänger: Eine psychoanalytische Studie*, reprint of 1925 edn (Vienna:
    Turia & Kant).

Rathert, Wolfgang, 1998 'Ende, Abschied und Fragment: Zur Ästhetik und Geschichte einer musikalischen Problemstellung', *Abschied in der Gegenwart: Teleologie und Zuständlichkeit in der Musik* (Vienna: Universal), 211–235.

Reeves, Nigel, 1974 *Heinrich Heine: Poetry and Politics* (Oxford: Clarendon).

Ricoeur, Paul, 1965 *De l'interprétation: Essai sur Freud* (Paris: Editions du Seuil).

1979 'The Metaphorical Process as Cognition, Imagination, and Feeling', *On Metaphor*, ed. Sheldon Sacks (Chicago: University of Chicago Press), 141–157.

1989 *Zeit und Erzählung*, 3 vols. (Munich: Wilhelm Fink, 1988–91), II: *Zeit und literarische Erzählung*, trans. Rainer Rochlitz (1989). [French original: *Temps et écrit, tome II. La configuration dans le récit de fiction* (Paris: Editions du Seuil, 1984)].

1991 *Die lebendige Metapher* [with an extensive foreword prepared for the German edition by the author], trans. Rainer Rochlitz, 2nd edn (Munich: Wilhelm Fink). [French original: *La métaphore vive* (Paris: Editions du Seuil, 1975)].

Roesner, Linda, 1990–91 'Schumann's "Parallel" Forms', *19th Century Music*, 14, 265–278.

Rose, William, 1962 *The Early Love Poetry of Heinrich Heine: An Inquiry into Poetic Inspiration* (Oxford: Clarendon Press).

Rosen, Charles, 1988 *Sonata Forms*, rev. edn (New York: Norton).

1995 *The Romantic Generation* (Cambridge, Mass.: Harvard University Press).

Rosenberg, W., 1988 'Paradox, Doppelbödigkeit und Ironie in der *Dichterliebe*', *Dissonanz / Dissonance*, 15, 8–12.

Rothgeb, John, 1979 'A Structural Function of Dynamics in Schumann's "Ich grolle nicht"', *In Theory Only*, 5:2, 15–17.

Sammons, Jeffrey L., 1969 *Heinrich Heine: The Elusive Poet* (New Haven: Yale University Press).

Sams, Eric, 1980 'Robert (Alexander) Schumann' [list of works and bibliography], *The New Grove Dictionary of Music and Musicians*, ed. Stanley Sadie, 20 vols. (London: Macmillan), XVI, 854–870.

1993 *The Songs of Robert Schumann*, 3rd edn (London: Faber & Faber).

Sams, Eric, and Johnson, Graham, 2001 'The Romantic Lied', *The New Grove Dictionary of Music and Musicians: Second Edition*, ed. Stanley Sadie, 29 vols. (London: Macmillan).

Schenker, Heinrich, 1979 *Free Composition*, ed. and trans. Ernst Oster (New York: Longman).

Schering, Arnold, 1951 'Kritik des romantischen Musikbegriffs', *Vom musikalischen Kunstwerk*, 2nd edn (Leipzig: Köhler und Amelang), 42–79.

Schlegel, August Wilhelm, 1964 *Vorlesungen über schöne Kunst und Literatur: Kritische Schriften und Briefe*, ed. Edgar Lohner, 3 vols. (Stuttgart: Kohlhammer).

Schlegel, Friedrich, 1971 'Lessings Geist aus seinen Schriften', *Kritische Schriften*, ed. Wolfdietrich Rasch, 3rd edn (Munich: Hanser).

Schnapp, Friedrich, 1924 *Heinrich Heine und Robert Schumann* (Hamburg: Hoffmann und Campe).

Schneider, Anneliese, 1970 'Robert Schumann und Heinrich Heine: Eine historisch/ästhetische Untersuchung anhand der Vertonungen mit Berücksichtigung einiger Probleme der Liedanalyse' (unpublished doctoral dissertation, University of East Berlin).

Schneider, Hans, 1974 *Robert Schumann: Manuskripte, Briefe, Schumannia*, catalogue no. 188 (Tutzing: Hans Schneider).

Schneider, Michel, 1989 *La tombée du jour: Schumann* (Paris: Editions du Seuil).

2001 'Le piano qui parle', *Musiques de Nuit* (Paris: Editions Odile Jacob), 31–59.

2001 'Schubert et Schumann', *Musiques de Nuit* (Paris: Editions Odile Jacob), 195–208.

Schoenberg, Arnold, 1955/75 'Vorwort zu Die sechs Bagatellen von Anton Webern', *Anton Webern*, ed. Karl-Heinz Stockhausen and Herbert Eimert, *Die Reihe* (Vienna: Universal Edition, 1955), 15. Also available as 'Anton Webern: Foreword to his Six Bagatelles for

String Quartet, Op. 9', *Style and Idea*, ed. Leonard Stein, trans. Leo Black (London: Faber & Faber, 1975), 483–484.

1978 *Theory of Harmony*, trans. Roy Carter (London: Faber & Faber).

1989 *Structural Functions of Harmony* (London: Faber & Faber).

1992/75 'Das Verhältnis zum Text', *Stil und Gedanke*, ed. Ivan Vojtech (Frankfurt am Main: Fischer, 1992), 9–13. Also available as 'The Relationship to the Text', *Style and Idea*, ed. Leonard Stein, trans. Dika Newlin (London: Faber & Faber, 1975), 141–145.

Schoppe, Martin, 1991 'Schumanns Litterarischer Verein', *Robert Schumann und die Dichter*, ed. Joseph A. Kruse (Düsseldorf: Droste), 17–32.

Schubart, Christian Friedrich, 1806 'Charakteristik der Töne', *Ideen zu einer Ästhetik der Tonkunst*, ed. Ludwig Schubart (Vienna: n.p.), 377–382.

Schumann, Robert & Clara, 1994 *The Marriage Diaries of Robert & Clara Schumann*, ed. Gerd Nauhaus, trans. with a preface by Peter Ostwald (London: Robson).

Simpson, David, 1988 *The Origins of Modern Critical Thought: German Aesthetic and Literary Criticism from Lessing to Hegel* (Cambridge: Cambridge University Press).

Solie, Ruth A., 1980 'The Living Work: Organicism and Musical Analysis', *19th Century Music*, 4, 147–156.

Sørensen, Bengt Algot, 1963 *Symbol und Symbolismus in den ästhetischen Theorien des 18. Jahrhunderts und in der deutschen Romantik* (Copenhagen: Munksgaard).

1974 *Panorama oder Ansichten vom 19. Jahrhundert* (Frankfurt am Main: Suhrkamp).

Sørensen, Bengt Algot et al., eds., 1972 *Allegorie und Symbol: Texte zur Theorie des dichterischen Bildes im 18. und frühen 19. Jahrhundert* (Frankfurt am Main: Athenaeum).

Starobinski, Jean, 1961 *L'Œil vivant* (Paris: Gallimard).

Steblin, Rita, 1996, *A History of Key Characteristics in the Eighteenth and Early Nineteenth Centuries*, 2nd edn (Rochester: University of Rochester Press).

Sternberger, Dolf, 1974 *Panorama oder Ansichten vom 19. Jahrhundert* (Frankfurt am Main: Suhrkamp).

1976 *Heinrich Heine und die Abschaffung der Sünde*, 2nd edn (Frankfurt am Main: Suhrkamp).

Stricker, Rémy, 1984 *Robert Schumann: le Musicien et la Folie* (Paris: Gallimard).

Struck, Michael, 1984 *Die umstrittenen späten Instrumentalwerke Schumanns: Untersuchungen zur Entstehung, Struktur und Rezeption* (Hamburg: Verlag der Musikhandlung Wagner).

Suurpaa, Lauri, 1996 'Schumann, Heine, and Romantic Irony: Music and Poems in the First Five songs of Dichterliebe', *Integral*, 10, 93–123.

Sylvester, David, 2002 'Kandinsky', *About Modern Art: Critical Essays 1948–2000*, revised edn (London: Pimlico), 76–79.

Szondi, Peter, 1978 'Friedrich Schlegel und die romantische Ironie', *Schriften 2* (Frankfurt am Main: Suhrkamp).

Tadday, Ulrich, 1999 *Das schöne Unendliche: Ästhetik, Kritik, Geschichte der romantischen Musikanschauung* (Stuttgart and Weimar: Metzler).

Thalmann, Marianne, 1967 *Zeichensprache der Romantik* (Heidelberg: Lothar Stiehm).

Thibaut, A. F. J., 1907 *Über Reinheit der Tonkunst*, ed. R. Heuler (Paderborn: Schöningh).

Thym, Jürgen, 1992 'Text-Music Relations in Schumann's Eichendorff Song "Frühlingsfahrt"', *The Romantic Tradition: German Literature and Music in the Nineteenth Century*, ed. Gerald Chapple, Frederick Hall and Hans Schulte (Lanham: University of America Press), 333–360.

Turchin, Barbara, 1981 'Robert Schumann's Song Cycles in the Context of the Early Nineteenth-Century "Liederkreis"' (unpublished doctoral dissertation, Columbia University).

1981 'Schumann's Conversion to Vocal Music: A Reconsideration', *The Musical Quarterly*, 67, 392–404.

1985 'Schumann's Song Cycles: The Cycle within the Song', *19th Century Music*, 8 (Spring), 231–244.

Vaughan, William, 1988 *Romantic Art*, 2nd edn (London: Thames and Hudson).

1994 *German Romantic Painting*, 2nd edn (New Haven: Yale University Press).

Wackenroder, Wilhelm Heinrich, 1938 *Werke und Briefe* (Berlin: Verlag Lambert Schneider).

Walsh, Steven, 1971 *The Lieder of Robert Schumann* (London: Cassell).

Walz, Matthias, 1996 '*Frauenliebe und -leben* op. 42: Biedermeierdichtung, Zyklenkonstruktion und musikalische Lyrik', *Schumann-Studien*, 5, 97–118.

Windfuhr, Manfred, 1966 'Heine und der Petrarkismus: Zur Konzeption seiner Liebeslyrik', *Jahrbuch der Deutschen Schillergesellschaft*, 10, 266–285.

Wiora, Walter, 1965 'Die Musik im Weltbild der deutschen Romantik', *Beiträge zur Geschichte der Musikanschauung des 19. Jahrhunderts*, ed. Walter Salmen, Studien zur Musikgeschichte des 19. Jahrhunderts 1 (Regensburg: Bosse), 11–50.

Wolff, Viktor Ernst, 1914 *Robert Schumanns Lieder in ersten und späteren Fassungen* (Leipzig: H. S. Hermann).

INDEX

Printed in Great Britain by
Amazon.co.uk, Ltd.,
Marston Gate.